AN ARCHAEOLOGICAL GUIDE TO
CENTRAL AND SOUTHERN MEXICO

AN ARCHAEOLOGICAL GUIDE TO CENTRAL AND SOUTHERN MEXICO

By Joyce Kelly

Photographs by Jerry Kelly and the Author

Drawings, Maps, and Site Plans by the Author

University of Oklahoma Press : Norman

Also by Joyce Kelly

The Poetic Realism of Alan Flattmann (Jackson, Miss., 1980)
The Complete Visitor's Guide to Mesoamerican Ruins (Norman, 1982)
An Archaeological Guide to Mexico's Yucatán Peninsula (Norman, 1993)
An Archaeological Guide to Northern Central America: Belize, Guatemala, Honduras, and El Salvador (Norman, 1996)

Library of Congress Cataloging-in-Publication Data

Kelly, Joyce, 1933–
    An archaeological guide to central and southern Mexico / by Joyce Kelly ; photographs by Jerry Kelly and the author ; drawings, maps, and site plans by the author.
       p. cm.
    Includes bibliographical references and index.
    ISBN 0–8061–3344–9 (alk. paper) — ISBN 0–8061–3349–X (pbk. : alk. paper)
    1. Indians of Mexico—Antiquities—Guidebooks.   2. Indians of Mexico—Museums—Guidebooks.   3. Mexico—Antiquities—Guidebooks.   I. Kelly, Jerry.   II. Title.

F1219 .K436 2001
917.204'836—dc21

                                                            2001027136

This book is affectionately dedicated to the wonderful people of Mexico, and to the memory of their ancient ancestors who created the superb architecture and exquisite works of art that we see today at the archaeological sites. It is both the Mexicans of today and the monuments of their ancestors that keep us coming back to Mexico, a place we forever enjoy.

CONTENTS

ILLUSTRATIONS

ALPHABETICAL LIST OF SITES AND MUSEUMS WITH SECTION NUMBERS AND MAP NUMBERS

Acozac: (3) 3 and 3E

Amparo Museum: (3) 3 and 3F

Anahuacalli Museum: (3) 3 and 3B

Balancán Museum: (6) 6 and 6C

Bonampak: (7) 7 and 7A

Cacaxtla and Cacaxtla Museum: (3) 3 and 3F

Calixtlahuaca and Calixtlahuaca Museum: (3) 3 and 3A

Cañada de la Virgen: (2) 2 and 2A

Cantona: (5) 5 and 5B

Castillo de Teayo and Castillo de Teayo Museum: (5) 5, 5B, and 5B1

Cerro de las Minas: (4) 4

Chalcatzingo: (3) 3 and 3G

Chiapa de Corzo: (7) 7

Chinkultic: (7) 7

Cholula and Cholula Museum: (3) 3 and 3F

Ciudad Madero Museum: (5) 5 and 5A

Comalcalco and Comalcalco Museum: (6) 6 and 6B

Coatetelco and Coatetelco Museum: (3) 3 and 3G

Cuernavaca Museum: (3) 3 and 3G

Cuicuilco and Cuicuilco Museum: (3) 3B

Cuyuxquihui: (5) 5, 5B, and 5B1

Dainzú: (4) 4 and 4B

Ehécatl Temple: (3) 3B

El Azuzul Museum: (6) 6 and 6A

El Cerrito: (2) 2 and 2A

El Tajín and El Tajín Museum: (5) 5, 5B, and 5B1

Emiliano Zapata Museum: (6) 6 and 6C

Guadalajara Museum: (1) 1

Huamelulpan and Huamelulpan Museum: (4) 4

Huapacalco: (3) 3 and 3D

Huexotla: (3) 3 and 3E

Huitzo: (4) 4 and 4A

Ihuatzio: (1) 1 and 1B

Ixtlán del Río: (1) 1 and 1A

Izapa: (7) 7

Jalapa Museum: (5) 5 and 5B

Jonuta and Jonuta Museum: (6) 6 and 6C

La Herradura: (3) 3 and 3E

Lambityeco: (4) 4 and 4B

La Quemada: (1) 1

Las Higueras and Las Higuras Museum: (5) and 5B

La Venta and La Venta Site Museum: (6) 6 and 6A

La Venta Park Museum: (6) 6 and 6B

Los Melones: (3) 3 and 3E

Malinalco: (3) 3 and 3A

Mexico City Museum: (3) 3B

Mitla and Mitla Museum: (4) 4 and 4B

Monte Albán and Monte Albán Museum: (4) 4 and 4A

Morelia Museum: (1) 1

Museum of the West: (1) 1

Na Bolom Museum: (7) 7

Oaxaca Museum: (4) 4, 4A, and 4B

Palenque and Palenque Museum: (6) 6, 6C, 7, and 7A

Pátzcuaro Museum: (1) 1 and 1B

Pomoná and Pomoná Museum: (6) 6 and 6C

Potrero Nuevo Museum: (6) 6 and 6A

Puebla Museum: (3) 3 and 3F

Querétaro Museum: (2) 2 and 2A

Quiahuiztlán: (5) 5 and 5B

Ranas: (2) 2 and 2B

San José Mogote and San José Mogote Museum: (4) 4 and 4A

San Luis Potosí Museum: (1) 1

San Miguel de Allende Museum: (2) 2 and 2A

San Pedro de los Pinos: (3) 3 and 3B

Santa Cecilia and Santa Cecilia Museum: (3) 3B

State Museum of Michoacán: (1) 1

Suchilquitongo Museum: (4) 4 and 4A

Tamayo Museum: (4) 4, 4A, and 4B

Tamuín: (5) 5 and 5A

Tecoaque: (3) 3 and 3E

Templo Mayor and Templo Mayor Museum: (3) 3B

PREFACE

Every book is unique and presents its own particular problems to the writer, even when it is similar in style and format to earlier books on the same general subject by the same author. *An Archaeological Guide to Central and Southern Mexico* is the third part of a trilogy that updates my original book, *The Complete Visitor's Guide to Mesoamerican Ruins,* published by the University of Oklahoma Press in 1982. The first two parts of the trilogy are *An Archaeological Guide to Mexico's Yucatán Peninsula* (1993) and *An Archaeological Guide to Northern Central America: Belize, Guatemala, Honduras, and El Salvador* (1996), both also published by the University of Oklahoma Press.

Many problems were worked out in the first two parts, but this third part has taken longer to produce than the others, mainly because of the greater area covered. For example, the Yucatán volume covered an area of 53,833 square miles (139,907 square kilometers); the northern Central America work included an area almost double that, 102,310 square miles (264,962 square kilometers). This book covers 252,612 square miles (656,513 square kilometers), more than doubling the last.

More sites were covered in the Yucatán volume—91 as opposed to 38 for northern Central America and 70 for central and southern Mexico—but the Yucatán sites are fairly close together. I included more museums in Central America—25 as opposed to 8 for Yucatán. In this book I include 60 museums, which could have created another problem. It is easy to remember the major museums, but the smaller places tend to blur together in one's memory, especially when one is visiting many museums in a short time. To avoid this pitfall, I carried a micro tape recorder to make spoken notes on the various collections, their highlights, and the museums' schedules. Later I transcribed the notes, and they and our photographs (where photography was permitted), allowed me to recall and write about each one.

Following my usual procedure, I have included only sites and museums that I have personally visited. I should mention, however, that four museums that are indicated on the maps are not rated or covered in the text. Two of these are site museums (at La Quemada and Xochicalco) that had not yet opened when we were last there. The third is the site museum at Toniná. I wrote about it in my original work, then it improved, and then it closed. Reportedly, it was due to reopen and probably has by now.

The fourth museum is the one at Tapachula. It was supposed to be open when we arrived, but because of a staff meeting it was still closed. Time constraints did not allow us another attempt to see these museums, but no doubt when you are at these sites, the museums would be worth a visit. The Tapachula Museum is reported to have a nice collection, so I feel sure it would be worthwhile as well.

In the central and southern Mexico sections of *The Complete Visitor's Guide to Mesoamerican Ruins,* 41 sites and 24 museums were included. Since then, one of the sites has closed—the Archaeological Museum In Situ, in San Miguel de Allende, which I covered as a site in my original book. It may have since reopened, so you might want to check when you are in the area. One small site museum (Zempoala) has closed since my original work appeared.

All but one of the sites and all of the museums covered in that work were revisited in the preparation of this book, and 28 sites and 39 museums have been added. It took four trips of one month each (over a period of four years) to revisit sites and to see new ones.

As I warned readers of my last book, changes are to be expected. A good road deteriorates, a dirt road gets paved, a museum changes its visiting hours. But over the last decade, central and southern Mexico have changed dramatically for visitors. On the positive side, there are now more good hotels throughout the area, not just in large cities. Many new four-lane highways have been constructed, and many previously unpaved roads have been surfaced. Some archaeological sites now have road access, whereas earlier they could be reached only on foot. Several sites are now open to the public, where previously they were not, and others have been upgraded in the ratings because of improvements. A good deal of consolidation and restoration has been undertaken at some of the major sites, and many new site museums have opened—while some existing ones have been upgraded. On the negative side, some sites now close one or even two days a week, whereas at one time all the sites were open every day.

Overall, the changes have been for the better—by far.

What hasn't changed is the graciousness of the Mexican people and their helpfulness. Those are things you can count on.

ACKNOWLEDGMENTS

During the preparation of this work, a number of people kindly provided me with information, some of which would have been difficult to find elsewhere. To all of them I express my heartfelt thanks. My job was made easier because of their help. They are Victoria Bricker, Bonnie and Jim Bade, Barbara Edmonson, Elizabeth Boone, Donald Graff, and Donald Patterson.

This time a special group of people should also be thanked; they are the list members of AZTLAN, a news group on the Internet dedicated to pre-Columbian history. I posed a number of questions to them and got many of my questions answered. I am pleased to be a part of this group. My sincere thanks also to Jane Kepp for a superb job of editing this book and for her consideration while doing so.

I would also like to thank my husband, Jerry, for accompanying me to the sites, for taking most of the black-and-white photographs used in this volume and for printing all of them, and for offering loving encouragement while this work was in progress.

PART ONE

• • • •

INTRODUCTION

THE ARCHAEOLOGY OF CENTRAL AND SOUTHERN MEXICO

The story of the archaeology of central and southern Mexico is part of the broader story of the archaeology of Mesoamerica—and even that of the entire Western Hemisphere. The generally accepted theory begins with the migrations of people from eastern Asia across the Bering Strait at a time of glacial advance, when a land bridge formed. These migrations started perhaps as early as 40,000 years ago (although the earliest widely accepted date is 15,000 years ago) and continued in several waves.

The early immigrants were hunters who followed game across the land bridge. Once across, they followed the ice-free routes in present-day Alaska and Canada, heading south and eventually spreading throughout the Americas.

Recent data from Monte Verde in south-central Chile show that the site was occupied in 11,000 B.C. This date comes from multiple radiocarbon samples run between 1979 and 1994. The work at Monte Verde was carried out by Tom D. Dillehay of the University of Kentucky. There is also evidence that the southern tip of South America was occupied at least by 7000 B.C.

The early inhabitants of the New World were a mobile population. In addition to hunting, they gathered wild plants to supplement their food supply. In the coastal areas where some of the earliest settled villages formed, the sea provided bountiful food resources, although people consumed agricultural products as well. Some of the wild plants that were originally gathered were later cultivated and domesticated, and as time went on, these agricultural products became an increasingly important part of the diet. This shift gradually resulted in some groups' becoming semisedentary and, later, in the formation of settled inland villages. These changes proceeded at an extremely slow pace that varied in different regions.

Plants domesticated by the ancient Mesoamericans included maize (corn), beans, squash, chili peppers, and amaranth. Maize was the most important of these foodstuffs and remains so today in the diet of the native peoples.

The monumental work of Richard MacNeish and his colleagues in the 1960s, carried out in the Tehuacán Valley of central Mexico, has added greatly to our knowledge of the early stages of human progress in Mexico. MacNeish and others discovered that in the earliest period they recorded (pre-10,000 to 7000 B.C.), people lived in caves and seasonal outdoor camps in small groups. The people hunted some big game but relied more on hunting and trapping small game and gathering wild plants for their food supply. Chipped flint tools were in use.

Even at this early time, the Mesoamerican cultural tradition was distinct from traditions farther north, such as Clovis, although there were general similarities among them.

When the larger animals became extinct, people relied even more on small game and plant collecting. Some of the plants, including corn, were domesticated around 7600 to 5000 B.C.—the beginning of cultivation. The tool assemblage included mortars and pestles and other ground and pecked stone tools.

An important discovery for this period was evidence for a complex burial ceremonialism, implying strong shamanistic leadership.

Around 5000 B.C., agriculture began in earnest and accounted for 10 percent of the human diet. Sometime between 5000 and 3400, avocados, chili peppers, and other plants were domesticated, and agricultural products became an ever-increasing part of the food consumed. Between 2300 and 1500, a crude pottery was manufactured, and food production increased due to the use of hybrids.

Between 1500 and 900 B.C., the people became full-time agriculturists living in small villages. There is evidence of a complex religious life, shown by the existence of a figurine cult. This is the Early Preclassic period, when developments in other areas of

Mexico were taking place as well. At the Olmec site of San Lorenzo on the Gulf Coast plain, a staggering quantity of monumental sculpture was produced. In Oaxaca, San José Mogote became a major center, as did Tlapacoya and Tlatilco in the Valley of Mexico. Figurines found in the Tehuacán Valley from this period show Olmec influence, and Olmec traits are found at Tlapacoya.

During the later part of the Middle Preclassic and in the Late Preclassic period, ceremonial constructions appeared throughout Mesoamerica. Various cultural groups were developing at different rates. For instance, during the Middle Preclassic period (900 to 400 B.C.), there was abundant activity at La Venta, Chalcatzingo, Xochitécatl, Totimehuacán, San José Mogote, Monte Albán, and other sites.

The Late Preclassic period (400 B.C. to A.D. 250) also saw developments all over Mesoamerica. In central Mexico the important site of Cuicuilco was dominant in the Basin of Mexico in the early part of the period, later followed by Cholula and Teotihuacán. Monte Albán became the most important center in the Valley of Oaxaca.

In the Early Classic period (A.D. 250 to 600), the Mayas were approaching their intellectual and artistic peak. There were large populations, the economy flourished, and trade was widespread. There were also bloody wars among polities and shifts in power among the elites. Some of the great centers of the lowlands grew tremendously in area and volume of construction, and monumental sculpture was produced in enormous quantities.

Teotihuacán dominated central Mexico and conducted trade with most other parts of Mesoamerica, as far south as Copán in Honduras and east to the Gulf Coast to El Tajín. Monte Albán remained dominant in Oaxaca, and Teotihuacán had relations with that area as well.

Many of the Maya sites, including Palenque and Yaxchilán, continued to develop and reached a peak in the Late Classic period (A.D. 600 to 830). The same is true of El Tajín. Monte Albán continued in importance during this time and throughout the Terminal Classic period (830 to 1000).

Elsewhere during the Terminal Classic, Tula was becoming the principal center in central Mexico, and its dominance continued through most of the Early Postclassic period (A.D. 1000 to 1200).

By the Late Postclassic period (A.D. 1200 to 1520), many of the earlier centers had been abandoned, but others arose in a number of places. Zempoala on the Gulf Coast became an area center, as did Mitla in Oaxaca, and the Tarascan capital at Tzintzuntzan became an important center in west-central Mexico.

And last, late in this period, the Aztecs (Mexica) arrived in the Valley of Mexico and came to dominate much of Mesoamerica. Their supremacy ended only with the Spanish conquest.

CHRONOLOGICAL CHART

The sites included in the chronological chart are large and important ones where significant excavations and ceramic studies have been undertaken. The thick lines in the chart indicate the major period or periods at the site, the thinner lines indicate the time the site was occupied, and a dashed line shows the years when a site was abandoned for a time.

The information used to compile this chart came from various sources and reflects the view of several authorities. Others use slightly different beginning and ending dates for some of the periods and for the major period at some of the sites. Some archaeologists divide the chronology into more periods, especially for certain areas, but for simplicity's sake those periods have not been

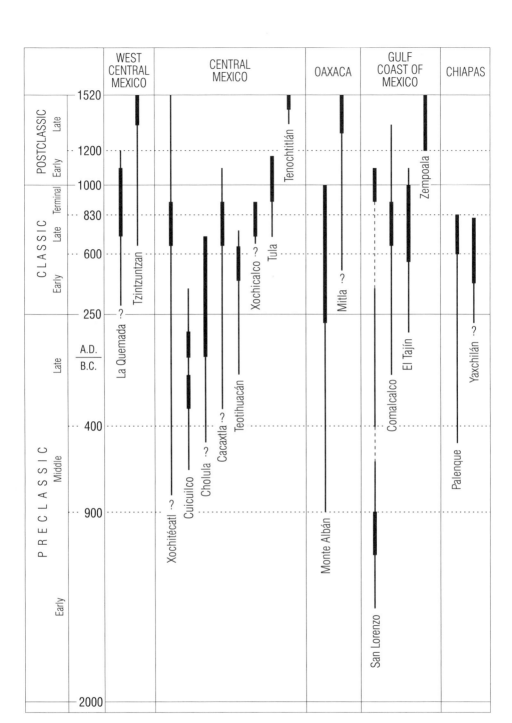

included in the chart shown here. Those periods are the Terminal Preclassic, or Protoclassic, period (A.D. 50 or 75 to 250), the Middle Classic period (475 or 550 to 650 or 680), and the Middle Postclassic period (1200 to 1400). In any case, the chart should give the reader a fair idea of what was happening in central and southern Mexico (at least at a few sites) during the times in question.

A Note on Dates Used in the Text

The hieroglyphic dates for inscribed Maya monuments given in the text have been converted to the Christian calendar using the Goodman-Martínez-Thompson (11.16.0.0.0) correlation.

GEOGRAPHIC DIVISIONS

Central and southern Mexico, as the term is used here, includes an area bordered on the north by the states of Tamaulipas, San Luis Potosí, Zacatecas, and Nayarit and on the southeast by the states of Tabasco and Chiapas. All this forms the northern part of Mesoamerica.

Since this book covers part of a single country, a general information section for all of Mexico is included. I recommend reading this while your trip is in the planning stages.

For ease of presenting travel information, it seemed logical to subdivide central and southern Mexico into seven geographic sections. General information about each section precedes the coverage of the sites and museums in that area and should be read first.

The general information for each section includes something about the geography and climate of the area, the best stopovers, the general condition of the roads, and the location(s) of the major airport(s). The points of reference from which distances and driving times are tabulated are also listed (driving times are given in hours and minutes—for example, 1:20), as are places where you can rent a vehicle and find a travel agency. For some sections, as it seemed appropriate, I have provided additional information such as special points of interest other than the archaeological sites and museums.

The accompanying map of Mexico delineates which part of the country is covered in the text. Another map shows an enlargement of the delineated area and the locations of the sites within it; a third map covers the same area but shows the museums. (It was impossible, unfortunately, to fit both sites and museums on a single map.) The last two maps also show the areas covered by the sectional maps that appear later in the book. These first three maps are named, not numbered, and are intended to give readers the general locations of the sites and museums.

The sectional maps, one for each of the seven geographic divisions, are numbered in coordination with the text for that section. For some areas, even more detailed maps are included. They bear the number of the section followed by a letter and sometimes by another number. For example, the northern Gulf Coast is covered in Section 5, and the map covering all of that region is Map 5. Map 5B is a detail of part of the area, and Map 5B1 is a detail of 5B. The area covered by the detail maps is indicated on the sectional maps, and together they show how actually to reach the sites and museums.

To aid readers in locating a particular site or museum, an alphabetical list of sites and museums is given at the front of this book, following the list of illustrations. After the site or museum name is a number (in parentheses) indicating the section where the site or museum is covered. This is followed by a number indicating on which sectional map the site or museum will be found, and sometimes by additional notations. For example, the entry "El Tajín: (5) 5, 5B, and 5B1" indicates that the text for El Tajín will be found in Section 5 and that the location of El Tajín is shown on maps 5, 5B, and 5B1. In general (but not always), the individual sites and museums within a section are covered from north to south or west to east.

My sincere hope is that these features will help readers find the information they want easily and quickly.

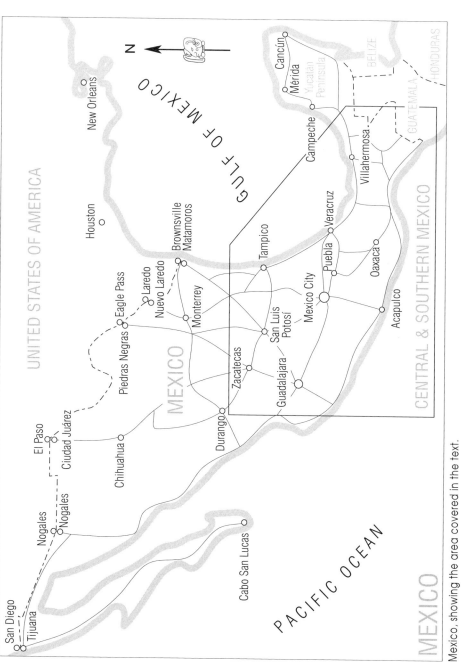

Mexico, showing the area covered in the text.

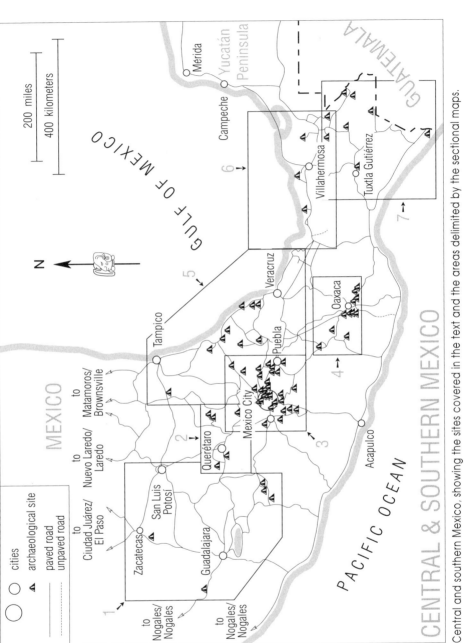

MEXICO

GULF OF MEXICO

N

PACIFIC OCEAN

CENTRAL & SOUTHERN MEXICO

Central and southern Mexico, showing the sites covered in the text and the areas delimited by the sectional maps.

GUATEMALA

Yucatán
Peninsula

Mérida
Campeche

6

Villahermosa

Tuxtla Gutiérrez

7

Tampico

5

Veracruz

Oaxaca

Puebla

4

Mexico City

3

Acapulco

Querétaro

2

San Luis
Potosí

Zacatecas

Guadalajara

1

to
Nogales/
Nogales

to
Nogales/
Nogales

to
Ciudad Juárez/
El Paso

to
Nuevo Laredo/
Laredo

to
Matamoros/
Brownsville

200 miles

400 kilometers

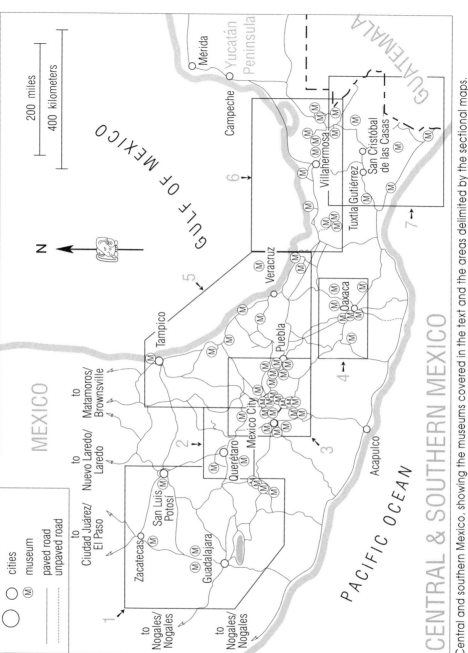

CENTRAL & SOUTHERN MEXICO

Central and southern Mexico, showing the museums covered in the text and the areas delimited by the sectional maps.

GENERAL ADVICE AND MISCELLANEOUS NOTES

Driving or Flying

Mexico can be reached by car from anywhere in North or Central America. Having your own vehicle will save travel time once you get there and will give you more flexibility in making travel plans. The country's highway system is constantly being improved, and driving allows you to enjoy Mexico's spectacular scenery.

There are flights to Mexico City from all over the world. From the United States and some Central American countries there are flights to other destinations in Mexico as well. Domestic flights within Mexico go to all parts of the country.

Flying in and renting a vehicle is a good way to get around if you prefer not to drive all the way. Car rental costs are at least what they are in the United States. Places where you can rent a vehicle are covered in the "General Information" for each section.

A standard vehicle is adequate to reach almost all of the sites included in this book. In a few cases a high-clearance vehicle or one with four-wheel drive will be needed. When this is the case, I mention it in the text for that site.

Buses travel all the main roads and most of the minor roads in Mexico as well. Where buses can get you to a site, or close to it, I say so in the text. To reach some sites you must have a private vehicle, and this is likewise mentioned.

Maps and Site Plans

The road maps included in this volume are intended to help readers reach the archaeological sites and museums covered in the text. They do not show *all* the roads and towns in the area. For this you will want to have one or more good road maps. The site plans are to help visitors get around the sites; buildings and monuments of interest are included, but not every building is shown.

The American Automobile Association (AAA) publishes a road map of Mexico, revised annually and available to members through AAA offices in the United States. At a scale of 1:3,800,000, it is generally adequate to get you to and around Mexico.

For a more detailed road map of southern Mexico (scale 1:1,000,000), try the one published by International Travel Maps called *Mexico South.* It can sometimes be found in map specialty stores in the United States, Canada, and the United Kingdom, or it can be ordered from the publisher at 345 West Broadway, Vancouver, B.C., V5Y 1P8, Canada.

Really good maps of Mexico, published there, come and go. In 1995, Guia Roji, a map company, published the first edition of *Mexico: Atlas de Carreteras 1995–1996.* The company has continued to update this map annually. It comes in booklet form at a scale of 1:1,000,000, and it has the advantage of showing the new toll roads that have opened in recent years—which generally take a while to appear on other maps. The booklet also includes maps of the major cities and tourist areas. You can find it in Mexico at some bookstores and at checkout counters in some large supermarkets, where other maps can also be found. Road maps and city maps are generally available from car rental agencies; the quality varies.

Guides—The Paper Kind

For your travels in Mexico you will want to have one or more guidebooks that offer more detailed general information than it is possible to give here, such as full hotel and restaurant listings, bus schedules, and points of interest other than the archaeological sites. *Mexico,* by John Noble and others, is published by Lonely Planet Publications (seventh edition, 2000). Like other Lonely Planet guidebooks, it has many clear city and town maps. It lists hotels and restaurants in all price ranges but concentrates its efforts on budget travelers. It includes detailed bus information.

The Rough Guide to Mexico, edited by John Fisher with contributions by Peter

Eltringham and others, had a 1999 edition and is often updated. It is published by Penguin Books (in various parts of the world) and is printed in the United States. Its thrust is toward budget travelers, as its name implies. It gives fairly detailed information on bus, train, and plane travel. Good city maps (though printed rather small) and area maps are included. A great deal of general information is covered in the text.

The American Automobile Association publishes a *Mexico Travel Book* annually, and it is available to members. Only AAA-rated hotels are listed. While all of these facilities are good to excellent, it excludes other, more modest but perfectly acceptable places.

Aimed almost exclusively at the budget traveler is *Let's Go Mexico* (Harvard Student Agencies, Inc., St. Martin's Press, New York), updated annually. It lists *only* budget accommodations and restaurants and has detailed bus information.

The Mexican government's National Institute of Anthropology and History (Instituto Nacional de Antropología e Historia, INAH—pronounced *EEN-ah*) has in the past published excellent small guides to the major archaeological sites, though they are becoming harder to find. More recently INAH began publishing even smaller ones called *mini-guias.* Sometimes a selection of *mini-guias* is available at a site. If you see one for a site you plan to visit, do not pass up the chance to buy it. Also look for them at museums and bookstores and at the Mexico City airport. For most sites, both Spanish and English versions are available.

Guides—The Human Kind

Guides (except for taxi drivers and driver guides in Mexico City) are not needed to reach any of the sites covered in the text, but in some cases you should have someone show you around a site. When this is the case, it is mentioned in the text for that site.

Language

Spanish is the official language in Mexico, but many Indian languages are spoken as well. In highly touristed areas, some English is spoken. If you do not speak some Spanish, I recommend carrying a small Spanish-English phrase book and dictionary. Berlitz's is the best known. If you are driving, you will want to know the Spanish for the parts of the car in case you need a mechanic.

Getting Lost and Unlost

While you should have no problems getting around on the highways, you may have problems getting to where you want to go within the cities, or getting out of the cities to the exit of your choice. This will be especially true when streets are blocked off for repair work (a frequent occurrence) and you have to change your preselected route. When this predicament arises—and it will—the solution is simple. Find a taxi. Tell the driver where you want to go and settle on a price. Pay the amount up front and ask the driver to lead the way. This can save a lot of time and a great deal of frustration. Drivers will not leave you stranded if you catch a red light and the taxi does not; they will wait for you to catch up. We have done this in various cities in Mexico (and Central America), and the drivers have always conscientiously led us to where we wanted to go.

Sometimes, such as in the case of metered taxis in Mexico City, a driver won't quote a price and will say you owe whatever the meter says at the end of the trip. Other times, after they have led you to where you wanted to go, they will simply say the cost is whatever you wish to give them. Play by their rules—you will still come out way ahead.

A Note on "Connections" and "Getting There"

The headings "Connections" and "Getting There" appear at the end of the coverage for each site. The driving times listed there are for *when the roads are in fair condition.* If a dirt road is very muddy, it will, of course, take longer. Road conditions (as far as it is possible to tell) are mentioned in the text for each site. But it should be noted that the conditions of roads, especially unpaved roads, are subject to change. Fortunately, few dirt roads to archaeological sites are encountered in this portion of Mexico.

A Note on Hotels

Although I make no attempt to give a comprehensive listing of hotels in this book, I do mention a few. These are generally smaller places in smaller towns where there is one "best" hotel—even though it may be only modest. Sometimes information about these places is hard to find. Information about hotels from modest to excellent in large urban areas is easily found in general guidebooks for Mexico. Only if there is a special reason—such as a good new facility that hasn't yet found its way into general guides, or a hotel that is in an especially convenient location—are hotels in urban or touristed areas listed.

Is It Dangerous?

One question we are often asked is, "Is it dangerous to travel in Mexico, especially in the remote areas?" I assume the questioner wants to know whether one is in any physical danger from the people. The answer is emphatically no. Maybe we have been inordinately lucky, but we have never felt the least bit threatened or even uncomfortable, and other frequent visitors report the same thing. In fact, the more remote the area, the nicer the people.

If news reports indicate that there is political or social unrest in an area you wish to visit, you could check with the Department of State in the United States to see if there is a travel advisory. Their World Wide Web address is http://travel.state.gov/index.html. Mexican consulates should also be able to provide current information on areas that should be avoided (if any). If you rent a car, your car rental agent will probably also have updated information.

Still, you should take normal precautions. Do not leave luggage or camera gear visible, even in a locked car. Keep the items out of sight in the trunk, and keep the trunk locked, especially in the more touristed areas.

When you drive around the country, you will come across occasional checkpoints where you must stop. These can be immigration and customs (*aduana*), federal police, or army. Have your passport (or other proof of citizenship) and your tourist cards (both driver's and passengers') ready for inspection. In some areas the checks may be for arms or drugs and you will be asked to get out of your vehicle so it can be searched. Again, present your official documentation and cooperate with a smile; these men are simply doing their job and it is nothing to be alarmed about—unless, of course, you have been foolish enough to bring arms or illegal drugs into the country. If you have, you are in serious trouble. There are more checkpoints (mostly army) in Chiapas than in most other areas.

A second question we often hear is, "What about snakes?" Yes, there are snakes, but we have encountered few, and never in a threatening situation. You will find insects to be a bigger problem. Nevertheless, it is advisable to look where you are stepping when you are walking along trails, especially in the more tropical areas.

What to Take

FOOTGEAR: Comfortable footgear is a must. Tennis shoes or the equivalent will suffice for most of the sites covered in this book. If boots are recommended for a particular site, it is mentioned in the text; otherwise, tennis shoes may be considered adequate.

CLOTHING: For visiting the ruins, the most comfortable clothing is lightweight but fairly sturdy cotton. Denim jeans or khaki work pants are fine. For the major cleared sites, women will find split skirts (culottes) more comfortable for climbing.

I recommend pants with belt loops whether or not you use a belt (see the section "Camera Gear" for why). Cotton or cotton-synthetic blends are best for shirts. Those that are 100-percent synthetic are hot as Hades and cling to you uncomfortably when you get wet, which is always in the more tropical areas. Long sleeves offer more protection from the sun, insects, and thorny bushes, whereas short sleeves are cooler. I use one or the other depending on the trip. For evenings in the highlands, you will want to have a sweater or light jacket.

You will find a few large handkerchiefs or bandanas useful to wipe the sweat from your brow in the lowland areas. Facial tissue just won't do.

Other items you should have are sunglasses (preferably glare free) and a sun hat (lightweight and with good ventilation), especially for the larger cleared sites.

MISCELLANEOUS GEAR: If you are traveling by car (yours or a rented one), by all means take or buy an ice chest. It will repay you a thousandfold. Inexpensive plastic-foam chests are available in cities and larger towns. Ice, water, and cold drinks whenever you want them can extend your endurance considerably. Unlike years ago, when I considered finding a good icehouse a major accomplishment, ice is now widely available—mainly in the form of *cubitos* (cubed or cut ice sold in plastic bags, just like at home). Block ice is also sold at ice houses, mainly in the warmer coastal areas.

Take a couple of terry-cloth towels. When dipped in the cold water in your ice chest and applied to your face and the back of your neck, they can be incredibly refreshing, especially when you return to your car after climbing around ruins.

To get rid of the bugs on your windshield, take along a pot cleaner, the sponge kind with a plastic mesh covering. The sponge holds enough water to make the job easier, and the plastic mesh will clean the glass without scratching it.

You will also want a plastic bottle for carrying drinking water with you in your vehicle. There are times when beer or *refrescos* (soft drinks) just won't do. Or you can buy bottled water in supermarkets and sometimes at the archaeological sites.

When you are walking to a site and will be away from your vehicle for more than an hour or so (especially in tropical areas such as El Tajín), you should have a canteen of water with you. When this is needed, it is mentioned in the text.

You should have insect repellent with you for all the sites, since even the cleared ones can have insects. Repellent is crucial for sites that are somewhat overgrown.

CAMERA GEAR: Since all photographers will have their own favorite equipment (preferably well tested), I make only general recommendations here. You will have a normal lens, of course, and a telephoto will sometimes be useful. Absolutely essential, however, is a wide-angle lens (the wider the better, short of a fish-eye), especially for sites that are not well cleared. Often it is impossible to back off far enough from a structure to get an overall shot with a normal lens. A wide-angle zoom lens (24 mm to 35 or 50 mm) is about ideal.

While we are at a site, we wear our cameras around our necks and attach them to our belt loops, which leaves our hands free for climbing. This way we don't have to

Top to bottom: Camera, screw that fits into camera bottom with attached metal ring; snap clip attached to leather loop, to be connected to belt or belt loop. Unless otherwise noted, black-and-white photographs are by Jerry Kelly.

Camera, screw and metal ring, and snap clip and leather loop, as they should be assembled.

worry about banging an expensive new lens against a stone. We attach metal rings to screws that fit into the bottom of the camera (the case may have to be removed). A machinist can make this for you. To our belt loops we attach a leather loop with a snap, to which is attached a spring-type clip. The clip can be hooked through the metal ring hanging from the camera. It is easy to engage and disengage (see illustrations). This arrangement is extremely helpful, especially if you are carrying more than one camera. Lens caps should be kept in place except while actually shooting.

Your gear will get dirty, and you should have lens-cleaning liquid, tissue, and a brush. Sunshades are a help, and a flash unit will be useful occasionally.

Bring your film from home. It is available in the cities and larger towns and at some sites, but it is more expensive, and generally the selection is limited.

Still photography for personal use is freely permitted at the archaeological sites and most museums, except sometimes in an area of a site that is in the process of being excavated. Some sites and most museums prohibit the use of flash equipment. Where this is the case, it is mentioned in the text. If in doubt, ask before using your flash. You will need fast film for all museums. If you can, dedicate a separate camera to this purpose. Video cameras are prohibited at some sites, whereas at others they are permitted if you pay an extra charge or get a special permit. Photography for commercial purposes also requires a special permit.

Entry Requirements

Citizens of the United States and Canada are not required to have passports to enter Mexico. They must, however, have proof of citizenship and a tourist card. A birth certificate or passport can be used as proof of citizenship. Naturalized citizens of the United States can use their naturalization papers, but naturalized citizens of Canada must have a passport. Tourist cards can be obtained at the border when you enter Mexico upon presentation of proof of citizenship. If you fly to Mexico, you can get a tourist card through your airline, with proper proof of citizenship.

Requirements vary for citizens of other countries; check with the nearest Mexican consulate for particulars. In general, however, a valid passport with a visa for Mexico will probably be required.

You should have your tourist card with you at all times, since officials at certain checkpoints will want to see it, as mentioned earlier.

If you are driving your own car into Mexico, the requirements are as follows. The driver who is importing the vehicle into Mexico must sign a declaration promising to return the vehicle to the United States and must pay a fee equivalent to about $17 in United States currency using an international credit card (Visa, Mastercard, or American Express) issued *in the name of the driver* by a United States or Canadian bank. Cash and checks are not acceptable, nor is a credit card in the name of a passenger. The purpose is to prevent cars from being illegally sold in Mexico. You must also present your driver's license, original car title, and the original current registration, along with two copies

Camera arrangement shown as used when attached to belt. Photograph by author.

of each, and copies of your proof of citizenship (for example, your passport).

A hologram will be affixed to the vehicle's windshield. Passengers may leave Mexico in a different vehicle, but the *driver* who imported the vehicle must leave in it.

If the vehicle is not registered in the name of the driver, or if it is in the name of a company, you must have a notarized letter from the owner giving you permission to bring the car into Mexico for a specified period of time. If the vehicle is not fully paid for, you must have a notarized letter from the lienholder to the same effect. You must, of course, also have a valid driver's license. You will be issued a vehicle permit at the border (as part of your tourist card) enabling you to bring your vehicle into Mexico, upon presentation of the above documents.

When you leave Mexico, you must return your tourist card and vehicle permit before exiting the country. Someone will scrape the hologram off your windshield and retain it, or will ask you to remove it and return it. You will then be given a *comprobante* (receipt). This is an *important* document; keep it and be ready to present it the next time you enter Mexico in your own vehicle. The *comprobante* is proof that you left Mexico legally on your previous visit. You are supposed to be in the government's computer, but sometimes you are not, especially if you enter the country at one spot and leave from another. Having your *comprobante* will save you time and money.

In July 1999 a new tourist tax went into effect. In 2000 the tax was equivalent to $19.50 in United States currency. It applies to all visitors who fly to Mexico or who drive in beyond the 15.5-mile (24.9-kilometer) checkpoints. Your tourist card is stamped, showing that the fee has been paid.

Since regulations tend to change, it would be best to check with your nearest Mexican consulate beforehand for current requirements.

Auto Insurance

If you are driving your own car to Mexico, you *must* buy auto insurance; your United States, Canadian, or Central American policy is not valid. If you are involved in an accident in Mexico and do not have valid auto insurance, you will find yourself in a great deal of trouble.

Sanborn's, one of the best-known agents, has several offices in cities in the United States that border Mexico. If you want your Sanborn's policy ahead of time, write to Sanborn's Mexican Insurance Service, Post Office Box 310, McAllen, Texas 78502. They will also give you excellent road logs for your trip. Other agents can be found near the border as well. The American Automobile Association also sells insurance for Mexico and can provide you with a map and tour guide of that country.

If you fly to Mexico and rent a car, you can get insurance through your rental agent.

Driving in Mexico

Mexico's highway system has grown over the years as new roads have been added and unpaved roads have been surfaced. In recent years, many new toll roads have been constructed. These are generally four lanes (sometimes more) with a good surface—mostly. When there is a choice of a toll road or a free road to the same destination, I recommend taking the toll road. It will save you time and wear and tear on your vehicle and nerves. You will also encounter less traffic, because trucks and buses don't generally use these roads. They are worth the tolls. These roads are called *autopistas* or *cuotas* (the word for toll), and occasionally *libramientos* (freeways, although they are not free). A little later you will hear about one downside to the toll roads. Many of the country's free roads are very good, though some segments are not as good as one might wish—generally the poorer sections are in low-lying areas.

You should drive carefully in Mexico, of course, as anywhere else. But in Mexico you should especially avoid night driving on the highways. The hazards include people walking along the edge of the road, animals crossing the road (or sleeping in the middle of it), and slow-moving vehicles without taillights. A more recent hazard presents itself when you are driving some of the newer toll roads where the speed limit is 110 kilometers per hour (68.4 miles per hour). Although these roads are generally excellent, sometimes there are a few potholes. If you are driving the speed limit and hit one, you could blow out a tire or damage your vehicle. To make matters worse, these toll roads are generally fenced off, meaning you won't find mechanics alongside them. In addition, you are often many miles from an exit to a free road where you can find help.

Hoy No Círcula
(Don't Drive Today)

In order to control pollution in the Mexico City metropolitan area, a program to reduce driving there was established in 1989; it is called *"Hoy no círcula."* This means that vehicles are prohibited from driving one day of the week in this area, depending on the last digit of the vehicle's license plate.

On Monday you may not drive if the license plate ends in 5 or 6; on Tuesday, if 7 or 8; on Wednesday, if 3 or 4; on Thursday, if 1 or 2; and on Friday, if 9 or 0. If your plate is all letters (no numbers), you may not drive on Friday. You will be fined if you drive on the wrong day.

When pollution rises above certain levels, a second "don't drive" day is initiated. Announcements of this are broadcast on radio and television, noting which digits are restricted on which days, over and above the normal restriction.

It is important to note that tourist vehicles, whether your own or rented, are included in the restriction. Even more important is that in addition to the Federal District, areas of the state of Mexico are also included. These are the areas that are considered part of the Mexico City metropolitan zone. Unfortunately, this is unknown to many people,

Mexicans and visitors alike. Included are Tuitítlán, to the north of the city, and Nezahualcoyotl and Ixtapaluca, to the east. Other parts of the state of Mexico are also included, but I never could learn exactly which.

You can call the Secretaría de Turismo (Ministry of Tourism) toll free from the United States at 1-800-482-9832 for specific information about a particular place.

Gas Stations and Car Repairs

There are adequate numbers of gasoline stations along Mexico's highways and in cities and towns, though they are not as abundant as they are in the United States. If you start looking for a station when your tank is half full, you should have no problems. The cost of gasoline in Mexico in the summer of 2000 was $2.08 per gallon in United States currency; the price is raised slightly every few months.

All gas stations in Mexico are operated by Pemex (Petróleos Mexicanos), the national oil company. Magna Sin (unleaded gasoline), Premium (a higher-octane unleaded), and diesel fuel are sold. The old Nova (leaded gasoline) has been phased out.

Sometimes stations or individual pumps run dry. This is signaled by putting the pump hose across the top of the pump.

There are mechanics even in the small towns, as well as along the roads (except for some of the toll roads, as noted earlier). Look for a sign saying *Taller Mecánico.* They can handle minor repairs on the spot with a minimum of equipment. If your problems are serious, of course, you will have to get to the nearest large town or city.

If you need a tire repaired, look for a sign saying *vulcanizadora* or *llantera,* or keep an eye out for a tire propped up near the road or hung from a pole. This indicates the same thing.

Mechanics and *vulcanizadoras* are often found near gas stations.

Climate and Travel in the Rainy Season

The tropical lowlands are warm to hot year-round; this includes both coastal areas of Mexico. The highlands are more moderate in temperature and can be chilly to cold at night, especially in the winter months. The rainy season in Mexico runs roughly from late May to October, with some regional variation; in some areas there is a slackening of precipitation in July and August. Generally it rains hard but for short periods in the afternoon or evening, and usually the rain does not interfere with travel plans. If you plan to travel on unpaved roads, however, you should check locally about their condition. Extremely wet weather can render some unpaved roads impassable.

Archaeological Sites and Artifacts

Fees are charged to enter most of the archaeological sites and museums, but they are always reasonable. A few sites and museums are free every day, and most are free on Sundays and holidays. The hours that the sites and museums are open are covered in the text. Schedules vary, however, and are subject to change; check locally if in doubt.

Laws prohibit the removal of pre-Columbian artifacts from Mexico. These items are considered part of the national patrimony, and the United States Customs Service cooperates in preventing the entry of such items into the United States.

Looting of the ancient sites has reached alarming proportions, and the Mexican government is enforcing its regulations more stringently than ever in order to halt this illegal traffic. An incredible amount of information is lost to the world of archaeology because of this illicit digging and thievery.

Museum Names and Schedules

In each museum section, the formal name of the museum is listed first, followed by its popular name in parentheses. The popular name denotes the city or site in which the museum is found.

The popular name is used in the table of contents, in the list of sites and museums by ratings, in the photograph captions, and in the alphabetical list of sites and museums.

It should be noted that throughout Mexico, *most* museums, though not all, are closed on Monday. Specific schedules are given in the text for each museum.

Some of the small community museums, run by villagers as a labor of love and pride, get few visitors and cannot afford to have a full-time guardian. This means, of course, that there is no set schedule. When visitors arrive, they will be noticed, and someone will come to open the museum.

Glossary

Many specialized words, foreign words, acronyms, and names of deities are used in the text. Those that occur frequently are explained in the glossary at the end of the book. Those used infrequently are explained in the text.

THE RATING SYSTEM

The rating system was devised to help readers see at a glance how worthwhile a visit to a particular site would be. The rating does not necessarily indicate the importance of a site in ancient times but reflects a combination of factors, of which relative importance is one. Other considerations are the degree of preservation or restoration and the ease of access compared with the visual rewards received.

Ratings

★ ★ ★ ★ A world-class site that should be seen by all visitors.

★ ★ ★ A site of major importance and a must for the enthusiast. Fairly to very interesting for others, depending on the site.

★ ★ Of some importance and moderately to very interesting for the enthusiast. Slightly to moderately interesting for others. (I recommend reading the text for these sites before deciding upon a visit. You will find some more appealing than others.)

★ Of interest only to the enthusiast. Others may ignore these.

No Stars Of minor importance—only for the avid enthusiast.

LIST OF SITES AND MUSEUMS BY RATINGS

Above All Ratings
Mexico City Museum

Four Stars ★ ★ ★ ★
Amparo Museum
Anahuacalli Museum
El Tajín
Jalapa Museum
La Venta Park Museum
Mitla
Monte Albán
Oaxaca Museum
Palenque
Teotihuacán

Tuxtla Gutiérrez Museum
Villahermosa Museum
Yaxchilán

Three Stars ★ ★ ★
Bonampak
Cacaxtla
Chalcatzingo
Cholula
Comalcalco
Comalcalco Museum
Cuernavaca Museum
Dainzú
Guadalajara Museum

Izapa
Malinalco
Morelia Museum
Monte Albán Museum
Palenque Museum
Pomoná Museum
Puebla Museum
Querétaro Museum
San José Mogote Museum
San Luis Potosí Museum
San Miguel de Allende Museum
Tamayo Museum
Templo Mayor
Templo Mayor Museum
Teotenango
Teotenango Museum
Teotihuacán Museum
Tepoztlán Museum
Toluca Museum
Toniná
Tula
Tula Museum
Veracruz Museum
Xochicalco
Xochitécatl
Yagul

Two Stars ★★
Acozac
Balancán Museum
Cacaxtla Museum
Calixtlahuaca
Calixtlahuaca Museum
Cañada de la Virgen
Castillo de Teayo
Castillo de Teayo Museum
Cerro de las Minas
Chiapa de Corzo
Chinkultic
Cholula Museum
Ciudad Madero Museum
Coatetelco
Coatetelco Museum
Cuicuilco
Cuyuxquihui
El Azuzul Museum
El Tajín Museum
Emiliano Zapata Museum
Huamelulpan
Huamelulpan Museum
Huapacalco
Ixtlán del Río

Jonuta Museum
Lambityeco
La Quemada
Las Higueras
Las Higueras Museum
La Venta
La Venta Site Museum
Mitla Museum
Museum of the West
Na Bolom Museum
Pomoná
Quiahuiztlán
Ranas
San José Mogote
Santa Cecilia
Santa Cecilia Museum
State Museum of Michoacán
Suchilquitongo Museum
Tamuín
Tecoaque
Tenayuca
Tenayuca Museum
Tenochtitlán Museum
Teopanzolco
Tepepulco
Tepozteco
Tingambato
Tizatlán
Tlatelolco
Tlatilco Museum
Tlaxcala Museum
Tonalá Plaza, Park, and Museum
Tres Zapotes Museum
Tuxteco Museum
Tzintzuntzan
Tzintzuntzan Museum
Xochitécatl Museum
Yohualichan
Zaachila
Zempoala

One Star ★
Cuicuilco Museum
Ehécatl Temple
El Cerrito
Huexotla
Huitzo
Ihuatzio
La Herradura
Los Melones
Potrero Nuevo Museum
Pátzcuaro Museum

San Pedro de los Pinos
Tlapacoya
Toluquilla
Totimehuacán
Yucuita

No Stars
Jonuta

Unrated
Cantona

PART TWO

• • • •

THE SITES AND MUSEUMS

GENERAL INFORMATION FOR MEXICO

Mexico has long been called "The Land of Contrasts." Perhaps this sounds like a cliche, but these four words, maybe better than any other four, truly describe the country. The terrain varies from arid deserts to tropical rain forests, from hot, humid tropical lowlands to cool, high mountain chains. Mexico has active volcanoes, high plateaus, broad meandering rivers, and steamy mangrove swamps.

The country is well known for its cacti, but it hosts a wide variety of orchids and bromeliads as well, not to mention colorful crotons, bougainvilleas, and jacarandas, among other tropical plants.

Mexico covers 761,600 square miles (1,972,392 square kilometers) and has more than 4,971 miles (8,000 kilometers) of coastline. It is bordered on the north by the United States, and its southern reaches share borders with Guatemala and Belize. The Gulf of Mexico and the Caribbean Sea form Mexico's eastern border, and the Pacific Ocean bounds the country on the west.

In 1990 Mexico had a population of more than 81 million people, of which its capital, Mexico City and its immediate suburbs, was home to 20 million. It is the most populated city in the world.

Mestizos (people of mixed ancestry, generally Spanish and Indian) form the largest segment of the population. Indians of various ethnicities and people of European descent (mostly Spanish) are the next largest segments.

The peso is Mexico's unit of currency, and it is subdivided into 100 *centavos* (cents). The lower-denomination peso bills are physically smaller than the higher denominations, and there are also 1, 2, 5, and 10 peso coins. The exchange rate between the peso and other currencies floats, so it is impossible to say what it will be at a given time. As a guide, it was 9.3 pesos to one United States dollar in 2001. Major newspapers carry Mexico's exchange rate in their financial sections.

United States dollars are the easiest foreign currency to exchange. Banks in Mexico change money only during certain hours, generally 10:30 A.M. to 12:30 P.M. Private money exchanges (*casas de cambio*) will change money whenever they are open (generally all day). You will find them in large cities and resort areas; any taxi driver can get you there. The *casas de cambio* are not only faster than the banks, but often they also give a better exchange rate. You will also find private exchanges in the United States at the main border crossings into Mexico. If you are driving to Mexico from Canada or the United States, you will be able to change some money before you enter Mexico; this is recommended. Wherever you change money, try to get some smaller-denomination bills.

Some banks and all *casas de cambio* will also exchange United States travelers checks. Again, the *casas de cambio* are to be preferred. Travelers checks from other countries are harder to change.

Large hotels will accept United States dollars in payment, but the exchange rate is not as favorable as that given by the banks or *casas de cambio*. Your best bet is to use an international credit card whenever possible to pay hotel and restaurant bills and for purchases. Major cards are accepted throughout Mexico except at markets and at most gas stations and toll stations. These two last, however, are great places to break a large-peso bill to get smaller change—which is always in short supply.

It is a good idea to have a supply of United States one-dollar bills with you when you enter Mexico. These can be used for tips for maids, porters, and so forth, at least until you get some Mexican currency in smaller denominations. Other currencies are harder for people to change into pesos.

For villagers who are helpful in showing you around a site or opening a museum for you, a few pesos discretely handed to them "por refrescos" (for soft drinks) will be appreciated. It would be better in these cases to use pesos rather than dollars.

SECTION 1

• • • •

WEST-CENTRAL MEXICO

Huastec sculpture from Colonia de las Flores, Tampico.
Postclassic period. On display in the San Luis Potosí Museum.

GENERAL INFORMATION FOR SECTION 1, WEST-CENTRAL MEXICO

Section 1 covers part of Mexico's high plateau, with elevations from around 5,000 feet (1,524 meters) to above 8,000 feet (2,438 meters). The plateau lies between two mountain chains, the Sierra Madre Oriental and the Sierra Madre Occidental, although there are mountains on the plateau as well. Surprisingly little real mountain driving (tight curves and steep grades) is encountered in getting around most of this part of Mexico.

The climate of Mexico's high plateau is pleasantly cool to slightly warm most of the time in most areas. It can be chilly in the winter months and in the morning and evening, even in the summer.

The roads in Section 1 are very good, with many miles of toll roads.

The best stopovers for visiting the sites and museums covered in the text are Zacatecas, Guadalajara, Uruapan, Pátzcuaro, and Morelia. Other places to stay in the area are San Luis Potosí, Aguascalientes, León, Guanajuato, Irapuato, and Zamora. All the cities and towns mentioned have hotels in various price ranges.

Points of reference for distances and driving times are the following: (1) in Zacatecas, the junction of Highways 49 and 54, on the west side of the city; (2) in Guadalajara, the junction of Highway 15 and the bypass that goes around the west side of the city; (3) in Uruapan, the market facing Highway 37; (4) in Pátzcuaro, the main entrance to town from Highway 14; and (5) in Morelia, the west entrance to town at Highway 15 and the bypass around the city.

There are international airports at Guadalajara and León, and domestic airports at Zacatecas, Aguascalientes, Uruapan, and Morelia. Car rentals are available at the international airports and at some of the other airports. Car rental agents can also be found in most of the cities mentioned.

Guadalajara is the largest city in Section 1 (and the second largest in the country). The artisans' markets in the city itself sell a wide variety of handicrafts, and the suburb of Tlaquepaque (now enveloped by the growing city) is noted for its production of ceramics. Other places to shop are the artisans' markets in Pátzcuaro, Tzintzuntzan, and Morelia. In addition to ceramics, items made of copper are also a good buy.

Travel agents can be found in Guadalajara and Morelia and in the other cities in this section.

For most other sections of this book, I drove and logged every (or almost every) road shown on the maps. In Section 1, I drove and logged only the roads going to the archaeological sites, and those distances and driving times are indicated on the maps. For approximate distances and driving times between other points, see maps such as the one of Mexico produced by AAA that shows this information in schematic form.

★ ★ ★
POTOSINO REGIONAL MUSEUM
(SAN LUIS POTOSÍ MUSEUM)

The collection of the San Luis Potosí Museum is housed in an attractive building that was originally part of a Franciscan convent constructed in 1592. The pre-Columbian collection is on the first floor, and a highly decorated eighteenth-century chapel is found upstairs. The museum was inaugurated on November 20, 1952.

The museum has an extensive collection of Huastec sculpture; one fine example

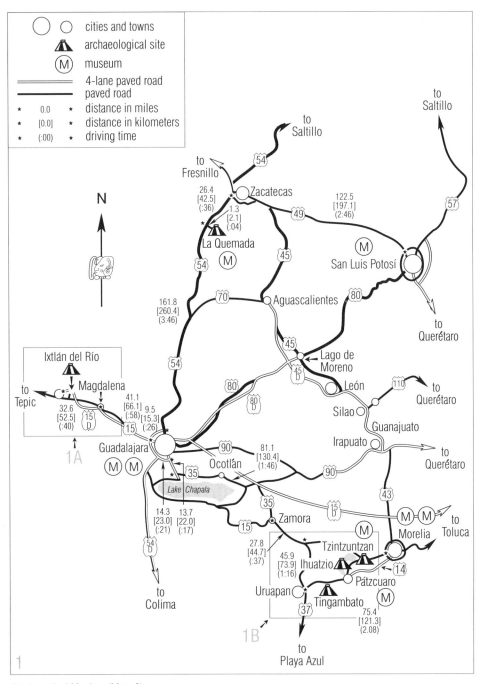

West-central Mexico (Map 1).

Bas-relief stone carving, probably Huastec. On display in the San Luis Potosí Museum.

is the well-preserved upper part of a female figure wearing a large headdress with a pointed top. It comes from Colonia de las Flores in Tampico. A large stone bas-relief carving is unlabeled but it is probably Huastec. The lack of labeling is one flaw in an otherwise fine museum.

Other areas of Mexico are also represented. There are smiling clay heads, a number of carved *hachas,* and a beautiful carved yoke from Veracruz, an elaborate ceramic urn from Oaxaca, a Teotihuacán-style stone mask, hollow ceramic human figures and dogs from western Mexico, and figurines from Jaina. One display case holds a variety of unusual clay smoking pipes. Ceramic pots and bowls from various parts of the republic are exhibited.

Although there are a few dark spots, lighting in the museum is generally good. Photography without flash is permitted.

The museum is located at Calle Galeana 450, near the center of the city. It is open Tuesday through Sunday from 10:00 A.M. to 5:00 P.M.; it is closed on Monday. Allow 45 minutes to see the collection. This will allow enough time to see the upstairs chapel as well. There are rest rooms at the museum but no food or drink.

★ ★
LA QUEMADA
(lah keh-MAH-dah)
CHICOMOZTOC
(chee-koh-MOHS-tohk)

Derivation:
La Quemada is Spanish for "The Burned One." The site was named after a nearby hacienda. *Chicomoztoc* means "Seven Caves" and is the name of a legendary place from which the Aztecs and other Nahua groups claim to have come.

Earlier Name:
Tuitlán.

Culture:
Chalchihuites or Malpaso.

Location:
East-central Zacatecas.

Map: 1 (p. 28)

The Site

The hilltop fortress of La Quemada is in a rather arid zone at an elevation of about 6,500 feet (1,981 meters). The northwest part of the hill is surrounded by a stone wall.

From the parking area, follow the trail uphill to the south part of the site, about an eight-minute climb. There are three areas of major importance for visitors at the site.

1. You come first to a large sunken plaza with an impressive building on the east side. This is called the Palace or the Hall of the Columns. It is composed of a large platform supporting a structure with 11 huge columns and a western stair facing the plaza. The entrance to the building is flanked by two more columns. The columns are made of slablike stones, as are the remaining walls of the building; the dimensions are truly impressive. A broad causeway begins near the sunken plaza and extends 1,300 feet (395

meters); it connects to other roads that cross the Malpaso Valley.

2. A short distance north of the Palace and on the same level is a small platform with a southern stair that leads to a ball court. It is one of only two ball courts known in the northern area of Mesoamerica and is by far the more impressive. At the north end of the ball court is an unusually steep, plain-sided pyramid called the Votive Pyramid, the lower portion of which, including a southern stair, has been restored. The top of the structure is missing; it is likely that an enclosure or temple made of perishable materials once crowned it.

West of the Votive Pyramid is a broad stairway that climbs to a higher level. At one time in La Quemada's history the stairway was covered by a rampart to impede access to the upper levels of the site for defensive purposes. The stairway was discovered and cleared only in recent years.

3. Now climb to the upper levels of the site, called the Citadel or Acropolis. A number of structures are found in this area; among them is a large courtyard surrounded on all four sides by platforms. Higher up you come to remains of interconnecting rooms.

Near the top of the hill is an open sunken courtyard with a stepped pyramid—locally called the Temple of Sacrifices—on the north side. The pyramid has an inset stairway on the south side, which faces a small rectangular altar. The other three sides of the courtyard have stairs leading to the lower level. Remains of high walls border the east and south sides of the courtyard and were parts of structures that must have been two stories high.

On a still higher level, northeast of the Temple of Sacrifices, is another structure with a steep south stair flanked by *alfardas*. This building is called La Terraza; it is

Front (west side) of the Palace, La Quemada. Early Postclassic period.

Southeast corner of the Votive Pyramid, La Quemada. Early Postclassic period.

Overall view of the fortified hilltop called the Citadel, La Quemada. The Votive Pyramid is on the far right. Early Postclassic period.

perched on a portion of the top of the hill. From atop La Terraza there are great views of the courtyard and its surrounding structures and of the Votive Pyramid and the Palace far below. Bring along a telephoto lens for good shots of the Palace from various places on the hill and a wide-angle lens for overall views of the upper courtyard.

In addition to the structures already described, there are others on the hill that are in a more ruinous condition. Roadways extending out from La Quemada and leading to smaller sites have been discovered; they cover a total length of more than 102 miles (164 kilometers).

La Quemada occupies the northen periphery of what we know today as Mesoamerica. Less technologically advanced peoples lived beyond its frontiers, and they are not considered to have been part of Mesoamerican civilizations.

La Quemada had its beginnings in the Early Classic period and continued developing in the Late Classic. The greatest concentration of occupation was from A.D. 900 to 1000, though the site remained active into later times. By 1350 to 1400, Mesoamerican culture had deserted the area, and La Quemada was depopulated. Archaeological evidence shows that at the end of its period of occupation, the site was burned.

La Quemada is generally listed as belonging to the Chalchihuites culture (or the neighboring Malpaso culture).

Recent History

La Quemada was visited by early Spanish explorers. A letter dated 1535 gives a description of the site and mentions that it was unoccupied. In 1650, Fray Antonio Tello described the site in a history of Nueva Galica (northwestern Mexico). He used the name Tuitlán for La Quemada.

In the 1830s, a map of the Malpaso Valley was made by the mining engineer C. de Berghes; it showed La Quemada and other sites. It was published in part in 1839, along with a description of the site by Carlos Nebel. Thirty years later, a map of La Quemada itself was published by Edmond Guillemín Tarayre.

View from the Citadel, La Quemada, looking southeast. The Votive Pyramid is on the left, a maze of rooms on a lower level of the Citadel is at the right of center, and the Palace is in the distance. The ball court is seen as a bordered rectangle between the Votive Pyramid and the Palace. Early Postclassic period.

Early-twentieth-century visitors who described the site were Leopoldo Batres, Eduardo Noguera, and Agustín García Vega, who also cleared much of the site.

La Quemada was excavated in the mid-twentieth century by Carlos Margain and Hugo Moedano and by Pedro Armillas. In 1955 the lower stairway of the Votive Pyramid was reconstructed by José Corona Núñez, and in 1963 additional work was carried out by Armillas, who directed a group from Southern Illinois University. More work was carried out in the late 1980s and early 1990s by Ben Nelson of Arizona State University, Charles Trumbold of Washington University in St. Louis, and Pedro Betts Jiménez of INAH.

Connections

1. Zacatecas to La Quemada: 27.7 miles [44.6 kilometers] by paved road (:40).

2. Guadalajara to La Quemada: 172.6 miles [277.8 kilometers] by paved road (4:16).

Getting There

1. From Zacatecas, head southwest on Highway 54 to the cutoff for La Quemada (marked with a sign), 24.6 miles [42.5 kilometers], and turn left. From there continue to the parking area for the site.

2. From Guadalajara, take the west bypass around the city from Highway 15 to Highway 54, 9.5 miles [15.3 kilometers], and turn left. Continue to the cutoff for La Quemada, 161.8 miles [260.4 kilometers]. Turn right at this junction and proceed to the site.

La Quemada is open daily from 10:00 A.M. to 5:00 P.M. Allow two hours for a visit. There is a restaurant on Highway 54 at the cutoff for La Quemada. Food and drink are not available at the site. Rest rooms are found in a service building at the site.

While you are at La Quemada, you should see the site museum as well.

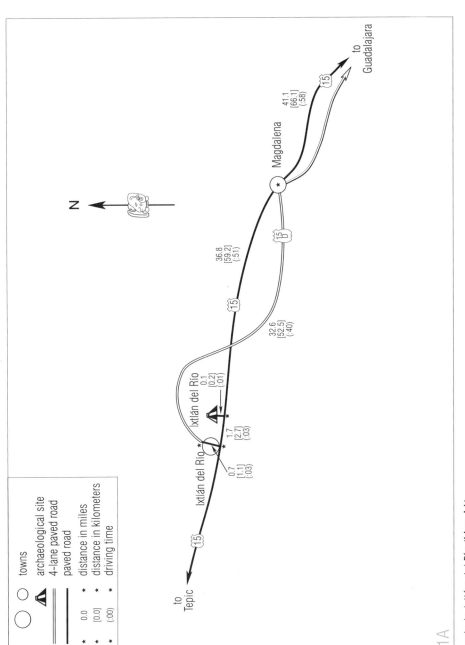

N

Legend:

○ ○ towns
▲ archaeological site
═ 4-lane paved road
━ paved road

0.0 * distance in miles
[0.0] * distance in kilometers
(:00) * driving time

to Tepic

Ixtlán del Río

15

0.7
[1.1]
(.03)

1.7
[2.7]
(.03)

Ixtlán del Río

Ixtlán del Río
0.1
[0.2]
(.01)

15

36.8
[59.2]
(.51)

32.6
[52.5]
(.40)

15
B

Magdalena

41.1
[66.1]
(.58)

15

to
Guadalajara

1A

Route to Ixtlán del Río (Map 1A).

★ ★
IXTLÁN DEL RÍO
(eesh-TLAHN dehl REE-oh)

Derivation:
  Ixtlán is Nahuatl for "Place of the Obsidian"; *del Río* is Spanish for "of the River."
Culture:
  See text.
Location:
  Southern Nayarit.
Maps: 1 (p. 28) and 1A (p. 34)

The Site

Ixtlán del Río, sometimes called simply Ixtlán, is one of the most interesting sites in western Mexico. You enter the site from the south and proceed from there (Group C) through Group B and on to Group A on the north. A nice touch is the labeling of some of the buildings with signs giving a brief description (in Spanish).

Structure C1, an L-shaped palace, has numerous square columns, remains of walls, and stairways that enter the building on the west and south sides, and an interior stairway as well.

Nearby, Structure C2, called the Central Altar, has been nicely reconstructed. It is rectangular, rising in two tiers, and it has stairways, bordered by *alfardas,* on all four sides. Also in Group C is a two-tiered platform called Structure C3; it is located near the west end of Structure C1.

In Group B, several structures have been reconstructed. These are mostly platforms with columns and stairways and an altar with a circular stone on top.

Group A is the most interesting at the site, and Structure A1 is the building for which the site is best known. This building has a circular plan, rises in two tiers, and has two projecting access stairways rising in two levels. The stairs are flanked by *alfar-das,* and vertical upper zones still remain on those on the second level. The wall that forms the upper level of the structure has cross-shaped perforations as decorations around the circumference. Enclosed within the wall are two rectangular platforms with a single stair. The stairs of these platforms face each other, and each has *alfardas* with vertical upper zones. The platforms are made of cut stone slabs, and the same material is used in the circular portion of the structure along with boulders and stone blocks. Structure A1 was dedicated to Ehécatl, the wind god.

Northeast of Structure A1 and connected to it by a cobblestone walkway is Structure A2, a rectangular building with an eastern stair. The building sits on a three-tiered platform, and the remains of lower walls and columns can still be seen. Of special interest here is a carved slab on the south face of the building near the west end. It is set at an angle between the second and third tiers of the platform. Another carved slab is reported from this structure, but I have never found it.

Another structure with rectangular columns, Structure A3, lies southeast of Structure A2. North of Structure A3, a rectangular altar with stairs on the north, east, and west sides occupies a plaza area faced by Structures A2 and A3.

During the Early Classic period—and perhaps as far back as the Preclassic—an unusual type of shaft tomb was constructed in the area of Ixtlán del Río and as far south as southern Colima; some tombs have been found on the outskirts of the site itself.

Ixtlán del Río was active from A.D. 500 until the Spanish conquest. Its greatest period was the Postclassic, and the buildings seen today date to this time. The site was built by West Mexicans who perhaps spoke a Uto-Aztecan language distantly related to Nahuatl.

Structure A1, Ixtlán del Río, viewed from the northeast. Postclassic period.

Recent History

From 1947 to 1949, José Corona Núñez explored Group A and restored Structure A1. In 1950, E. W. Gifford published a paper based on his collection of surface sherds. Eduardo Contreras worked in Group C from 1962 through 1968, and he reported on the reconstruction of some of the buildings in 1966. Group B was investigated by Raúl Arana in 1988 and 1989; he consolidated seven structures in two plazas.

The art of Ixtlán del Río is well known to collectors. Many large, hollow ceramic figures from the area are in private collections and probably came from looted tombs. Several types are represented; Gifford believed they dated to the phase called Early Ixtlán (Late Preclassic and Early Classic periods).

Connection

Guadalajara to Ixtlán del Río: 73.7 miles [118.6 kilometers] by paved road (1:38).

Getting There

The distance and driving time given under "Connection" were recorded before the section of Highway 15D between Guadalajara and Magdalena was completed. We used Highway 15 for that part of the trip. If you use Highway 15D for the whole trip, it will be somewhat shorter and certainly faster.

If you take Highway 15D, then upon reaching the outskirts of the town of Ixtlán del Río, leave the toll road, head south through the town 0.7 mile [1.1 kilometer], and turn left (east) onto Highway 15 for 1.7 miles [2.7 kilometers]. This brings you to the final cutoff for the site (marked with a sign). Turn left at the cutoff and proceed 0.1 mile [0.2 kilometer] to the parking area. You will cross a railroad track on the way.

If you take Highway 15 the whole way from Guadalajara, you will reach the cutoff for the site (on the right) before the town.

Ixtlán del Río is open daily from 9:00 A.M. to 4:00 P.M. Note, however, that when you cross the border from Jalisco to Nayarit, you will be changing time zones from Central Standard to Mountain Standard time. Allow 1.25 hours for a visit. There is no food or drink at the site. Rest rooms are available near the ticket office. Archaeological publications (in Spanish) are sold at the ticket office.

Buses pass the cutoff to the site.

★ ★ ★

GUADALAJARA REGIONAL MUSEUM (GUADALAJARA MUSEUM)

The late-seventeenth-century seminary of San José in the city of Guadalajara houses the collection of the Guadalajara Museum. The first floor contains the archaeological specimens; the upper story displays colonial and more modern items.

The archaeological displays are almost exclusively from the western Mexican states of Jalisco, Nayarit, and Colima. One of the most interesting is a stone carving of a headless male figure standing on a column. It comes from Teleacapan and dates to around A.D. 1300. Another stone carving represents the head of a serpent. An abundance of solid and hollow figurines, typical of western Mexico, is also included. Some of the most attractive are the warrior figures and musicians from Ixtlán del Río. Some geometric polychrome ceramics that date to the seventh century also come from Ixtlán del Río.

Colima is represented by ceramic vessels from various periods and by some of the figures of fat dogs that are typical of the area. Coral and turquoise jewelry, copper bells, and items of pressed gold all make attractive displays. One exhibit that caught my attention was a case containing large obsidian rings. They were perfectly circular and beautifully polished, and my guess is that they were ear flares. They are about the size of napkin holders.

Both the labeling and the lighting at the museum are fairly good. Photography without flash is permitted. No food or drink is available, but there are rest rooms.

The Guadalajara Museum is found on the corner of Avenida Hidalgo and Calle Liceo, in the center of town. It is diagonally across the street from the cathedral. It is open Tuesday through Sunday from 9:00 A.M. to 3:45 P.M. It is closed on Monday. Allow 45 minutes for a visit.

Headless stone figure standing on a column, from Teleacapan. Late Postclassic period. On display in the Guadalajara Museum.

★ ★
ARCHAEOLOGICAL MUSEUM OF WESTERN MEXICO
(MUSEUM OF THE WEST)

Though small, the Museum of the West in Guadalajara is a good two-star museum. It has archaeological remains from the states of Jalisco, Nayarit, and Colima. The collection includes small solid and large hollow ceramic figurines, spindle whorls and flat stamps, necklaces of obsidian and shell, and various types of ceramic vessels.

One unusual display contains ceramic pectorals in the form of conch shell trumpets from the Valley of Atema, Jalisco. One is painted with the emblem of Quetzalcóatl. A case holds small tripod vases with representations of the rain god Tlaloc on them. On the feet of the tripod are depictions of birds.

Of the many ceramic figures displayed, those depicting dancers with alligator-like snouts seemed most unusual to me. More commonly seen are acrobats doing back bends. A solid figurine in a case with others is in a reclining position reminiscent of the posture of a *chacmool*. A ceramic model of a house in red clay is said to have contained two seated figures inside.

Labeling in the museum generally reveals only the area where the items were found; rarely is a specific site mentioned. Lighting is good, but unfortunately photography is prohibited. The museum is open Tuesday through Sunday from 10:00 A.M. to 2:00 P.M. and from 4:00 P.M. to 7:00 P.M., except on Saturday, when it is open from noon to 2:00 P.M. and 4:00 P.M. to 7:00 P.M. It is closed on Monday. Allow 30 minutes to see the collection. There are no rest rooms, food, or drink at the museum.

The Museum of the West is on Calzada Independencia Sur a little south of Avenida Niños Heroes and somewhat northeast of the railroad station. Even taxis sometimes have trouble finding it. Nearby landmarks that are better known are the Casa de la Cultura and the Casa de Artesanías. The museum and both Casas are in Parque Agua Azul.

★ ★
TINGAMBATO
(teen-gahm-BAH-toh)

Derivation:
  Tarascan for "Hill of Temperate Climate."
Other Name:
  Tinganio.
Culture:
  See text.
Location:
  West-central Michoacán.
Maps: 1 (p. 28) and 1B (p. 39)

The Site

The cleared and consolidated part of Tingambato is composed of both civil and religious areas. As you enter the site from the north, you come to the civil area first. The remains of lower walls of habitations (which probably housed the elite) are found there. Remains of *talud-tablero* construction can be seen in one area of the rooms and in other parts of the site as well. The rooms surround a sunken courtyard with stairs on all four sides and, in the center, two low altars.

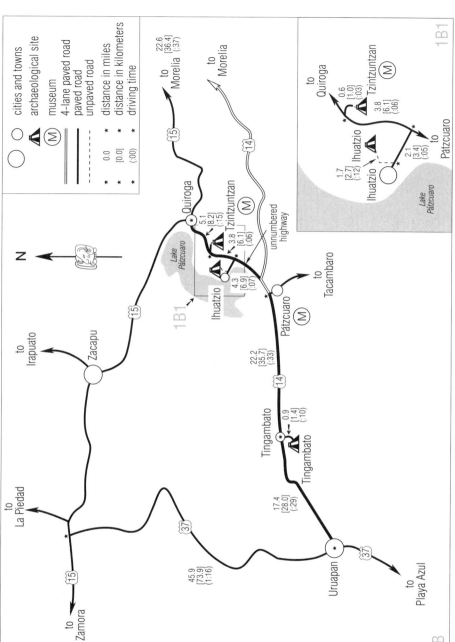

1B1

to Quiroga
0.6
[1.0]
(.03)

Tzintzuntzan Ⓜ

3.8
[6.1]
(.06)

to Páatzcuaro

1.7
[2.7]
(.12)

Ihuatzio

2.1
[3.4]
(.05)

Ihuatzio

Lake Pátzcuaro

1B1

N

Legend

	cities and towns
Ⓜ	archaeological site
Ⓜ	museum
═══	4-lane paved road
───	paved road
- - -	unpaved road

	distance in miles
	distance in kilometers
	driving time

0.0	∗
[0.0]	[∗]
(.00)	(∗)

to Irapuato

to La Piedad

to Zamora

⑮

Zacapu

⑮

⑮

⑯

45.9
[73.9]
(1:16)

17.4
[28.0]
(.29)

Uruapan

to Playa Azul

⑯

Tingambato

Tingambato
0.9
[1.4]
(.10)

⑭

22.2
[35.7]
(.33)

Pátzcuaro Ⓜ

to Tacambaro

⑭

to Morelia

unnumbered highway

Ihuatzio

1B1

Lake Pátzcuaro

4.3
[6.9]
(.07)

Ⓜ

3.8
[6.1]
(.06)

Tzintzuntzan

5.1
[8.2]
(.15)

Quiroga

⑮

22.6
[36.4]
(.37)

to Morelia

1B

Routes to Tingambato, Ihuatzio, and Tzintzuntzan (Map 1B)

Rooms surrounding a sunken patio, Tingambato. Classic period.

A short distance to the east is Tomb 1, sheltered by a protective roof. A few narrow steps lead down to the tomb entrance, which you can look into but which you may not enter. When the tomb was excavated, five large slabs, one of which had served as a lintel, were found blocking the entrance to the chamber. The chamber's roof was made of large staggered slabs that formed a sort of dome. Both primary and secondary burials were found in the tomb, including complete skeletons, 32 skulls, long bones scattered about, and numerous offerings—ceramics, stone artifacts, shells, even a shell bracelet inlaid with turquoise. The offerings, however, were not associated with a particular individual.

South of the habitational units and the tomb lies the sunken Plaza 1. The remainder of the site forms the religious area. Bordering the east side of the plaza is the East Structure, a six-tiered pyramid with the walls of the tiers sloping inward and a stairway bordered by *alfardas* on the west side, facing the plaza. The small, very low Altar 1 is found in the center of the plaza.

A large l-shaped sunken ball court occupies the area west of Plaza 1. It is approached by stairs on the north and south ends of the playing alley. When the ball court was excavated, one ball court marker with a tenon was found in the playing alley. It was carved with the design of a six-pointed star. The other marker was not found.

West of the ball court is the West Structure, a sizable mound that has not been studied. It seems to be about the size of the East Structure. It can be seen from the ball court but cannot be visited; it is fenced off from other parts of the site.

The East Structure, Tingambato. Classic period.

Habitational units (center) and the sheltered entrance to Tomb 1 (right), Tingambato. Classic period.

Tingambato had two major periods of development. From A.D. 450 to 600, the site was settled by agriculturists who also hunted and fished. From 600 to 900, influence from Teotihuacán is evident in the *talud-tablero* architecture. The ceramics discovered during excavation show affinities with other areas of western Mexico such as Jalisco, Colima, and other parts of Michoacán; none show resemblances to Teotihuacán ceramics.

The East Structure is in the style of the earlier phase of the site, and some substructure bases in the habitational area also date to this time. The Teotihuacán-style *talud-tablero* additions date to the later period, as do the ball court and Altar 1.

Around A.D. 900 Tingambato was burned, and there is no evidence of Postclassic architecture or ceramics.

Although the name for the site today is Tarascan, that group had nothing to do with Tingambato; they entered the area only centuries later.

Recent History

The first mention of Tingambato appeared in a Michoacán newspaper in 1842, when the discovery of some of the living quarters and a tomb was reported.

At the end of the nineteenth century, Nicolás León, founder of the Michoacán Regional Museum, undertook a short excavation at Tingambato related to his study of the physical anthropology of various places in Michoacán.

In 1933, when he was a young man, Salvador Próspero Román (later the municipal president of the town) was taken to the site with a group led by the director of a school. Próspero Román reported two hills (the East and West Structures) and said the director told the group that the structures were dedicated to the sun and moon.

Próspero Román remained devoted to the site and in the 1970s invited the archae-ologist Román Piña Chan to visit. In 1978 and 1979, Piña Chan and Kuniaki Oi excavated and consolidated the site during the Tinganio Project.

Connections

1. Uruapan to Tingambato: 18.3 miles [29.4 kilometers] by paved road (:39).

2. Pátzcuaro to Tingambato: 23.1 miles [37.1 kilometers] by paved road (:43).

Getting There

1. From Uruapan, take Highway 14 northeast to the town of Tingambato, 17.4 miles [28.0 kilometers], where you will see a pyramid sign. Turn right at the sign. The site is on the south end of town, but you can't go straight through. There is a market in the center of town, and the streets going through it are closed off. You have to make a jog to the left and then two jogs to the right to get around it. At that point you turn left and you will be back at the same street you came in on. Shortly ahead you will see a school on the right and a sign indicating a right turn. Follow this to the parking area. If you have trouble finding your way, anyone around will be able to give you directions. From the parking area you walk through a gate and follow the trail to the ticket office and on to the site.

2. From Pátzcuaro, follow Highway 14 west to the town of Tingambato and the sign, 22.2 miles [35.7 kilometers], and turn left. Then follow the directions already given.

Tingambato is open daily from 10:00 A.M. to 5:00 P.M. Allow one hour for a visit. There is no food or drink at the site, but rest rooms can be found near the parking area. Buses go to the town of Tingambato.

★
REGIONAL MUSEUM OF POPULAR ARTS (PÁTZCUARO MUSEUM)

You may well wonder how a popular arts museum found its way into an archaeological guide. The reason is that behind one of the rooms of this museum in Pátzcuaro you will find a few pre-Columbian remains. The structure housing the museum dates mostly to the eighteenth century, but the first Spanish construction in this location began in the sixteenth century. At that time a priest, Vasco de Quiroga, founded a college. Early in the eighteenth century, the Jesuits built the later part of the building. The museum has 11 *salas* (rooms) arranged around a patio, and you tour them counterclockwise.

The Spaniards called the people responsible for the pre-Columbian remains Tarascan, but the Tarascans referred to themselves as Purépecha. As you visit Sala 5, walk out the back of the room and you will be looking at a stone-faced, terraced mound that dates to the Late Postclassic period. It was dedicated to the god Curicaveri. Nearby, abutting the outside wall of the museum, is a cross wall with a low, narrow doorway. Its jambs and lintel are made of large stone blocks. Farther along the outside wall you will see another wall with some pecked dots in a couple of sizes. This wall was a part of

the sixteenth-century college, and the dots reportedly were made by students to keep tracks of the weeks. Above the terraced mound is found a *troje*, a typical Purépecha wooden house.

The museum is at the corner of Calles Alcantarillas and Enseñaza, a block east of the Plaza Vasco de Quiroga in the center of Pátzcuaro. It is open Tuesday through Saturday from 9:00 A.M. to 7:00 P.M. and on Sunday from 9:00 A.M. to 3:00 P.M. It is closed on Monday. Photography without flash is permitted. The pre-Columbian remains are outside and flash is not needed.

Allow a total of 30 minutes at the museum. This will give you time to see both the Tarascan mound and the collection of popular arts. The latter is quite impressive—the one-star rating refers only to the pre-Columbian remains. Included in the arts collection are, among other items, religious arts, textiles, ceramics, a typical kitchen with all manner of utensils, copper ware, carnival masks, and silver jewelry. Most of this part of the collection originated in the state of Michoacán.

★
IHUATZIO
(ee-WAHT-see-oh)

Derivation:
Tarascan (Purépecha) for "Place of the Coyotes."

Culture:
Tarascan.

Location:
West-central Michoacán.

Maps: 1 (p. 28), 1B, and 1B1 (p. 39)

The Site

Although Ihuatzio is a fairly large site, only one area is open to visitors. Two pyramidal structures of rectangular plan share a platform and face east onto a large open area called the Parade Ground. When you enter the east end of this area, the pyramids lie straight ahead. They are nearly identical and rise in tiers. The construction is the same slab and rubble core with cut stone facing seen at Tzintzuntzan, although few of the basalt facing stones have survived in place; some can be observed on the base of the east side of the northernmost structure.

Two massive stepped walls border the north and south sides of the Parade Ground. On the south wall you will see a stairway (near the pyramids), and by climbing it and looking south you can see the side of one of the site's three *yácatas* (a pyramid-like mound unique to the Tarascans) aligned in a north-south line. It appears as a green mound surrounded by neatly planted fields. You can get something of a frontal view of the *yácatas* from the road, shortly before you reach the entrance gate to the site.

Ihuatzio is reported to have had two periods of occupancy. The first, between A.D. 900 and 1200, was by Nahuatl-speaking farmers and fishermen. Between 1200 and

Two pyramidal structures, Ihuatzio. Postclassic period.

1530 Ihuatzio was dominated by the Tarascans, who also dominated the entire northern area of Michoacán.

Recent History

In 1931, Ignacio Marquina made a reconnaissance of Ihuatzio and produced a rough plan of the site. In 1937, Alfonso Caso carried out some explorations, and the engineer Aquiles Rivera Paz made a more complete plan. An interesting *chacmool* discovered at Ihuatzio is now on display in the Mexico City Museum.

Connections

1. Pátzcuaro to Ihuatzio: 6.4 miles [10.3 kilometers] by paved road (:12), then 1.7 miles [2.7 kilometers] by rock road (:12).

2. Morelia to Ihuatzio: 33.6 miles [54.1 kilometers] by paved road (1:03), then 1.7 miles [2.7 kilometers] by rock road (:12).

Getting There

1. From Pátzcuaro, take Highway 14 northeast to the cutoff for Quiroga and the unnumbered highway that goes there. Follow this highway to the cutoff for Ihuatzio (marked with signs for the town and ruins). Total distance from Pátzcuaro is 4.3 miles [6.9 kilometers]. Turn left and go 2.1 miles [3.4 kilometers] to another sign for the ruins. Turn right onto the rock road and continue to another sign and turn right again. Proceed to the gate for the site (on the left). You will pass through a steep and rough part of the road on this last stretch, but it can be driven in a standard vehicle.

2. From Morelia, take Highway 15 west to Quiroga, 22.6 miles [36.4 kilometers], and turn left. Head southwest on the unnumbered highway to the cutoff for Ihuatzio, 8.9 miles [15.1 kilometers], and turn right. Then follow the directions already given.

Ihuatzio is open daily from 10:00 A.M. to 3:00 P.M. Allow 45 minutes for a visit. There is no food or drink at the site. Rest rooms are found at the ticket office.

Buses go to the town of Ihuatzio but do not pass the ruins. If you decide to take a taxi from Pátzcuaro to Ihuatzio, you might ask the driver to wait for you.

★ ★
TZINTZUNTZAN
(tseen-TSOON-tsahn)

Derivation:
   Tarascan (Purépecha) for
   "Place of the Humming Birds."
Culture:
   Tarascan.
Location:
   West-central Michoacán.
Maps: 1 (p. 28), 1B, and 1B1
   (p. 39)

The Site

Tzintzuntzan is one of the largest and most important sites in Michoacán, and it was the capital of the Tarascans at the time of the Spanish conquest.

When you enter the site and follow the indicated path, you come first to a building called the Palace. This is a complex of rooms surrounding a patio. The lower walls of the rooms remain. From there, head west and then southwest to the *yácatas,* of which there are five aligned in a more or less north-south

Northernmost of the five *yácatas*, partly restored, Tzintzuntzan. Late Postclassic period.

row on top of a huge platform, 1,335 feet (407 meters) long and 600 feet (183 meters) wide.

The shape of the *yácatas* differs from the shapes of other pyramidal substructures found in Mesoamerica, but they served the same purpose, as bases for temples. The shape is generally described as that of the letter *T*, with a short stem and rounded bottom. The bodies of the *yácatas* rise in stepped levels to a height of over 40 feet (12.2 meters), and it is thought that the circular portions originally supported temples of perishable materials. Each *yácata* originally had a stair on the east side (on the rectangular portion of the base).

The platform east of the *yácatas* forms a wide, open area that was used for ritual activity. Near one of the *yácatas* (west side), trenches dug during excavation revealed earlier construction. The trenches have been left open so that visitors can see some of this.

The methods by which the *yácatas* were constructed can best be studied on the west side. They were built of rough stone slabs and rubble, without the aid of mortar, and then faced with large cut stones of basalt joined by mud mortar. Off the west edge of the platform you can see a walled enclosure built in colonial times.

After you leave the site, you can get some overall shots of it from the highway below.

Yácatas were a development of the Tarascans and have not been found in other parts of Mesoamerica. The Tarascans moved into the area around A.D. 1200, establishing their capital first at Pátzcuaro, then at Ihuatzio, and finally at Tzintzuntzan. From 900 to 1200, before the Tarascans took over, Nahuatl-speaking groups of farmers and fishermen occupied the area.

The culture of the Tarascans developed differently in most regards from the cultures of central and southern Mexico and the Maya area. The Tarascans were outstanding practitioners of the metallurgical arts, especially copper working. They were also noted as workers of obsidian and as fine potters. Excavation of graves in and around the *yácatas* has brought to light many of the Tarascans' lovely creations.

The Tarascans were one of the few cultural groups who successfully defended their frontiers against the Aztecs. When the Spaniards came in 1522, however, the Tarascans offered little resistance, even though their population reportedly was sizable. Certainly they knew of the Spaniards' defeat of the Aztecs, and perhaps that accounts for their lack of resistance.

Many puzzles remain in Tarascan archaeology, including an apparent linguistic relationship to South American languages and the Tarascans' production of pottery vessels with stirrup spouts of a kind also found in South America in earlier time periods.

Recent History

The earliest written references to the archaeological remains at Tzintzuntzan are found, as might be expected, in Spanish colonial documents of the sixteenth century.

Excavations (apparently disastrous) were attempted in 1852 by a priest, Ignacio Trespeña, and in 1902, Nicolás León described the monuments. Only in 1937 and 1938 did serious work begin at the site. It was conducted by Alfonso Caso with the help of Jorge Acosta, Daniel F. Rubín de la Borbolla, and Hugo Moedano. In the 1960s, further work was carried out by Román Piña Chan, and in the 1980s, more excavations were undertaken. All of the later excavations were sponsored by INAH.

Connections

1. Pátzcuaro to Tzintzuntzan: 8.7 miles [14.0 kilometers] by paved road (:16).

2. Morelia to Tzintzuntzan: 28.3 miles [45.6 kilometers] by paved road (:55).

Getting There

From Pátzcuaro, head northeast on Highway 14 to the cutoff for Quiroga and the unnumbered highway that goes there. Take this highway to the town of Tzintzuntzan and the cutoff for the site (on the right). Total distance from Pátzcuaro is 8.1 miles [13.0 kilometers]. The road to the archaeological zone takes you uphill to the parking area for the site. The very last part of this road is unpaved.

2. From Morelia, take Highway 15 heading west to Quiroga, 22.6 miles [36.4 kilometers], and turn left. Proceed southwest on the unnumbered highway to the cutoff for Tzintzuntzan, 5.1 miles [8.2 kilometers]. Turn left and go on to the site.

There is a parking area just outside the museum, and entry to the site is through the museum. The site is open daily from 10:00 A.M. to 3:00 P.M. Allow 1.5 hours for a visit. No food or drink is available at the site; rest rooms can be found next to the museum.

The rounded portions of the *yácatas* (the most interesting parts) are best lighted in the afternoon, making that the best time for a visit.

Buses go to the town of Tzintzuntzan, and from there you could walk to the site or maybe find a taxi. A visit to Tzintzuntzan can easily be combined with a visit to Ihuatzio.

★ ★
TZINTZUNTZAN MUSEUM

The Tzintzuntzan Museum, at the entrance to the site, has one fair-sized room. The collection includes a model of the site, some stone carvings with spirals and other motifs in bas-relief, and jewelry made of turquoise, obsidian, and metals. Ceramics are displayed in glass cases, and one Purépecha spouted vessel is especially fine. There is some labeling.

Another model depicts the basin of Lake Pátzcuaro with the archaeological sites marked. There are also displays of obsidian, stones, and cotton, and a chart indicating the

Tarascan (Purépecha) ceramic vessel. Late Postclassic period. On display in the Tzintzuntzan Museum.

principal fiestas. One diagram shows the various items that came from the state of Michoacán. Some of the Purépecha ceramics did not come from the site of Tzintzuntzan, but items in the other displays did.

The lighting in the museum is rather poor. Photography without flash is permitted for some of the items, but others may not be photographed. There are no signs indicating this, so it might be best to ask.

The Tzintzuntzan Museum is open daily from 9:00 A.M. to 6:00 P.M. Allow 15 minutes for a visit.

★ ★ ★
MICHOACÁN REGIONAL MUSEUM (MORELIA MUSEUM)

The Morelia Museum, inaugurated in the city of Morelia in 1886, is housed in an eighteenth-century palace originally built by Isidro Huarte. The collection is displayed on two floors surrounding a patio. The first floor contains the pre-Columbian materials, and the second displays items from the colonial period, the period of independence, and the times of Porfiro Díaz and Lázaro Cárdenas.

The corridor around the first-floor patio contains some interesting stone carvings, though unfortunately none is labeled. One of the best is a *chacmool*. It is almost identical to one displayed in the Mexico City Museum that came from Ihuatzio and dates to the Postclassic period.

One room of the museum is devoted to ecology and Preclassic archaeology; another pertains to Classic and Postclassic times. Some

Stylized stone carving of a coyote, Tarascan culture. Postclassic period. On display in the Morelia Museum.

of the highlights are carved stone coyotes done in a simplified geometric style similar to some from Tzintzuntzan and typical of Postclassic Tarascan sculpture; a large, square stone column with a smiling face at the top and starlike designs below; and carved stone seated figures.

A carved conch shell is beautifully worked. Another *chacmool,* similar to the one on the patio, is found inside the museum, along with figurines, other ceramics, a model of Tingambato, and a display of metallurgy.

The elegant stairway that leads to the second floor is flanked by murals painted by the Mexican artist Alfredo Alce.

The Morelia Museum is located at Calle Allende 305, at the corner of Calle Abasolo, in the center of town. It is open Tuesday through Saturday from 9:00 A.M. to 7:00 P.M., and on Sunday from 9:00 A.M. to 2:00 P.M. It is closed on Monday. Allow 45 minutes for a visit.

Lighting in the museum is fair, and photography without flash is permitted. A small shop sells publications. There are rest rooms in the museum, but food and drink are not available.

★ ★
STATE MUSEUM OF MICHOACÁN

The State Museum of Michoacán, also located in Morelia, is composed of rooms surrounding a patio. The first floor is devoted to archaeological finds, and the second floor contains materials from the conquest to modern times. When you enter the museum you go first to the left, into the room with the earliest remains; from there you proceed through the other rooms to increasingly later time periods.

Posters are displayed throughout the museum giving explanations of the archaeological objects, but there is little specific labeling. The collection includes ceramic pots, bowls, and figurines from various pre-Columbian time periods. Spindle whorls, stone tools, and photo displays make up other exhibits.

Some of the highlights are a Teotihuacán-style mask in black stone that is in mint condition, a decorated ladle censer, or *incensario,* a fine alabaster vase, and thin obsidian ear spools. A good deal of jewelry is included in the collection; the most outstanding piece is perhaps a necklace made of small skulls carved from amethyst. Some elaborate copper necklaces are also attractive. Other metal objects are small axes and tweezers. Ceramic smoking pipes and stone carvings are included but not numerous.

The upstairs rooms are devoted to ethnology and popular arts. An interesting map shows the route the Spaniards took through Michoacán during the conquest. Costumes are displayed, as are a flat-bottom dugout carved from a single log, guitars, and a loom, among other items.

The lighting in the museum is good for viewing. Photography is not permitted. The museum is located on the corner of Calles Guillermo Prieto and Santiago Tapia, near the center of town. It is open Monday through Friday from 9:00 A.M. to 2:00 P.M. and 4:00 P.M. to 8:00 P.M. On Saturday, Sunday, and holidays it closes at 7:00 P.M. Allow 25 minutes for a visit. There are no rest rooms, food, or drink at the museum.

SECTION 2

• • • •

CENTRAL MEXICO— AROUND QUERÉTARO

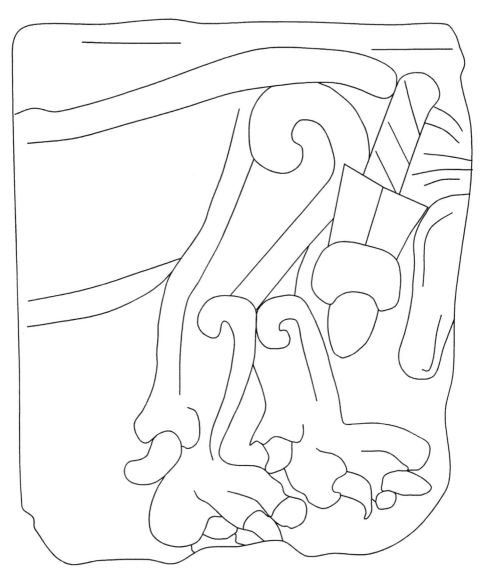

Stone bas-relief of the front part of a feline, from El Cerrito. Early Postclassic period. On display in the Querétaro Museum.

GENERAL INFORMATION FOR SECTION 2, CENTRAL MEXICO— AROUND QUERÉTARO

The area around Querétaro is part of Mexico's high plateau. For the most part it lies at an elevation of around 5,500 feet (1,676 meters) to 6,500 feet (1,981 meters); it is not quite as high as the part of the plateau around Mexico City, so it is a little warmer. See "General Information for Section 3" for more details.

Roads in Section 2 are very good, and there are many miles of toll roads. The only place where real mountain driving is encountered (among the places mentioned in this book) is from Highway 120 to the town of San Joaquín and on to the sites of Ranas and Toluquilla. These sites are in the Sierra Gorda of Querétaro, and they lie at an altitude of over 8,000 feet (2,438 meters).

The best stopovers are San Miguel de Allende, Querétaro, and Tequisquiapan. All have hotels in various price ranges. There is also a good hotel (Misión la Mansión) on Highway 57D, 7.3 miles [11.8 kilometers] northwest of San Juan del Río, and there are a couple of modest hotels in San Juan del Río itself.

There are no commercial airports in this section, although Querétaro has a small airport for private planes. The closest airports are in León to the west and Mexico City to the southeast. The León airport (international) is closer to this section than is the latter.

Cars can be rented through agencies in Querétaro and San Miguel, and there are travel agencies in both places.

San Miguel is a charming colonial town and, I must admit, one of my favorite places in Mexico. It offers lots to enjoy in addition to the nearby archaeological site and the museum in town. It features historic and beautiful buildings everywhere, a most unusual church (the Parroquia), a delightful main square (the Jardín), and untold numbers of shops, restaurants, and bars of various types. San Miguel is a good place to shop; look for items of brass and silver, Talavera pottery, and hand-blown glass, among other things.

There is a variety of charming hotels in San Miguel, some in the town and others on the outskirts. Some of the hotels in town have parking available, but others do not, and street parking is often difficult to find. Overnight street parking is not recommended. There are only a couple of commercial parking lots.

The streets in San Miguel are narrow, and many are steep. If you are driving a large vehicle, such as a van, you might want to stay at one of the hotels on the outskirts where there is ample parking, and taxi into town and back. Taxis are abundant in San Miguel. There is a taxi stand on the east side of the Jardín. Taxis are easy to flag down almost anywhere, and they can be requested by phone.

One of my favorite places is the Rancho Hotel El Atascadero. It has lovely gardens and grounds, a pool, friendly and helpful personnel, delightful rooms and suites (many with fireplaces), and a dining room that serves good food. The atmosphere is decidedly tranquil. El Atascadero is on a cobblestone road that goes under a large stone entrance arch. It is a right turn (north) off of Highway 111, the road that comes into San Miguel from Highway 57D, just where it meets the bypass that goes around the town. This is on the east edge of town, and high above it.

Several hotels with easy access can be found on the south end of town on Highway 51 as it approaches San Miguel from Celaya. Highway 51 becomes Calle Ancha de San Antonio as it nears San Miguel.

Querétaro, another historic city, is the largest in this section; it has all amenities.

Points of reference for distances and driving times are the following: (1) in San Miguel de Allende, the junction of Highway 111 and the bypass (east end); (2) in Querétaro, the junction of Highway 57D (as it goes *through* Querétaro) and Highway 45 (the free road to Celaya); and (3) in San Juan del Río, the junction of Highway 57D and Highway 120 (the southernmost entrance to San Juan del Río).

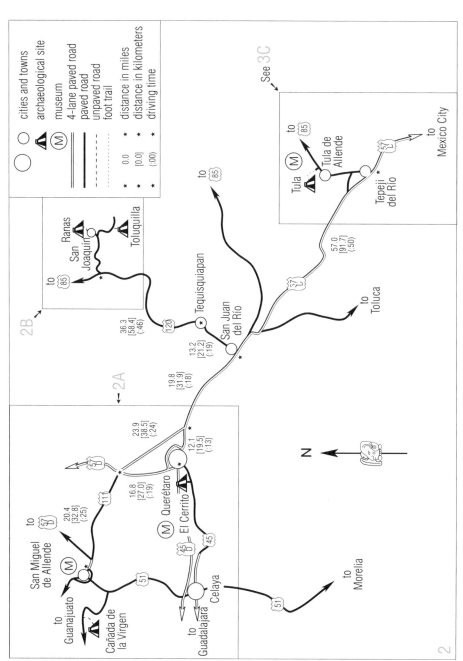

Legend:

○		cities and towns
○		archaeological site
▲		museum
Ⓜ		museum
═══		4-lane paved road
───		paved road
- - -		unpaved road
⋯⋯		foot trail
★	0.0	distance in miles
★	[0.0]	distance in kilometers
★	(:00)	driving time

2B →

San Ranas
San Joaquín ▲
Toluquilla ▲

to 85

2A ↓

to 85

Tequisquiapan ○

36.3
[58.4]
(:46)
120

13.2
[21.2]
(:19)

San Juan
del Río

19.8
[31.9]
(:18)

57

to Toluca

57.0
[91.7]
(:50)

See 3C

Tula Ⓜ ▲
Tula de Allende ○

to 85

Tepejí
del Río
57

to Mexico City

23.9
[38.5]
(:24)

57

San Miguel
de Allende Ⓜ

to 57

20.4
[32.8]
(:25)
111

16.8
[27.0]
(:19)

Querétaro Ⓜ
El Cerrito ▲

12.1
[19.5]
(:13)

to Guanajuato

Cañada de
la Virgen ▲

51

45

45

Celaya ○

to Guadalajara

51

to Morelia

N ←

2

Central Mexico, around Querétaro (Map 2).

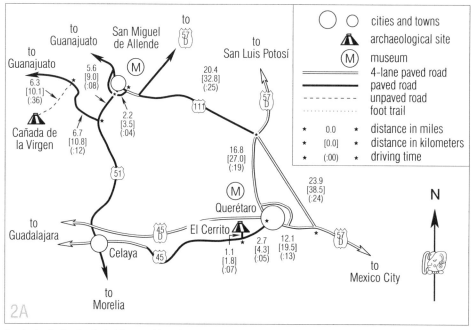

Route to Cañada de la Virgen (Map 2A).

★ ★ ★
HISTORICAL MUSEUM OF SAN MIGUEL DE ALLENDE
(SAN MIGUEL DE ALLENDE MUSEUM)

Inaugurated in February 1990, the San Miguel de Allende Museum has become a nice added attraction to a town that has always drawn visitors. The collection includes pieces from various parts of Mexico, and although it is not particularly large, many of the items are choice.

The first room displays mastodon bones and maps showing the migration of early people to Mesoamerica. Next, in the Preclassic section, cases with ceramics are displayed along with a Zapotec urn, a plain yoke, and items from western Mexico. Other items seem to show Olmec influence.

The two following rooms have Classic and Postclassic objects. One of the finest is a carved stone *palma* in pristine condition. A kneeling figure is depicted on its lower section, with volutes and what appears to be a tall headdress above. The *palma,* produced for ceremonial purposes, was made by artisans of the Late Classic Totonac culture of northern Veracruz. An *hacha* is found in the same case. Teotihuacán is represented by ceramics, obsidian artifacts, and a tiny fragment of a fresco (all Classic period).

The Postclassic displays include some handsome Tarascan (Purépecha) ceramics,

Carved stone *palma* from northern Veracruz, Totonac culture. Classic period. Displayed in the San Miguel de Allende Museum.

Another has a nice sculpture of a seated Mexica stone figure. There are vases and flat figurines and some well-preserved flat stamps. A map indicates the territory of the Mexica, and one case has ear flares of jade and ceramics produced by the Toltecs. Another map shows the territory of the Purépecha.

One room is devoted to the archaeology of the state of Guanajuato. Its exhibits include a nice selection of Chupícuaro figurines dating to the Late Preclassic period, an early mammiform ceramic vessel, and other Chupícuaro ceramics. From the Postclassic, a gourd-shaped pot from the area of Agua Blanca is displayed.

San Miguel de Allende is in the central part of the Laja River drainage, and sites in the immediate vicinity of the town are indicated on a map. A diagram shows the architectural style of the area, and objects found there are displayed. These include manos and metates, a hand stone, a ceramic ladle *incensario,* and items of obsidian and shell.

The following room has a small collection of items from the colonial period, and a separate room, off a side patio, is used for changing exhibits of contemporary art.

The San Miguel Museum is conveniently located in the center of town in the Casa Allende, off the southwest corner of the Jardín (main plaza). It is open Tuesday through Sunday from 10:00 A.M. to 4:00 P.M. Allow 30 minutes for a visit. Labeling and lighting are fairly good in the museum, and photography without flash is permitted. There are rest rooms off the side patio, and food and drink can be found at numerous nearby restaurants.

copper axes, and photographs of Calixtlahuaca, Tula, and the Templo Mayor of Tenochtitlán. One case houses Mexica objects including ceramics and a shell necklace.

★ ★
CAÑADA DE LA VIRGEN
(kah-NYAH-dah deh lah VEER-hehn)

Derivation:
Spanish for "Canyon of the Virgin."
Culture:
Central Río Laja (see text).
Location:
East-central Guanajuato.
Maps: 2 (p. 54) and 2A (p. 55)

The Site

When you walk to the main architectural assemblage (Complex A) at Cañada de la Virgen, you pass some small constructions along the way; these are parts of some of the seven complexes recorded at the site. These complexes of artificially raised platforms make up the major area of the site, and together they cover 0.03 square mile (0.08 square kilometer).

Complex A at Cañada de la Virgen consists of a stepped pyramid rising in six tiers that reaches the impressive height of 52.5 feet (16 meters). Three construction stages have been discovered. Atop the pyramid, remains of walls made of stone with a rubble fill were found. The interiors of the walls were stuccoed and painted, and this superstructure probably originally supported a thatch roof.

The pyramid defines the west side of a sunken plaza, and it has an eastern stair that faces the plaza. The other three sides of the plaza are bounded by lower constructions, some of which were residential. The structures on the north and east sides also have stairs facing the plaza. Remains on the south side were not as excavated or consolidated at the time of our visit, but it seems likely that that side had stairs facing the plaza as well.

On the east side, remains of rectangular pillars can be seen; they were parts of rooms. This side has access from an eastern stair on the outside of the complex, and this would have been the major access to the assemblage in the past.

When you walk around the north side of Complex A (on the outside), you will see an interesting construction system. The tiers of the pyramid slope inward—that is, they are in the form of a *talud,* but without a *tablero* above. This feature is found elsewhere. But the retaining wall of the *talud* that held the rubble-fill core was completely faced with small bricklike stones that were then stuccoed, and that is unusual for a pyramidal base in Mesoamerica.

Near the northeast corner of the pyramidal structure, on the level of the top of the first tier, you will see a doorway (when standing near the front of the pyramid). When you go through it toward the west, you will get a good view of a drain that runs along the north side of the pyramid from east to west. Apparently there were drains on the top of each tier of the structure.

Another interesting feature at Cañada de la Virgen is a broad causeway that heads east from Complex A. It extends 0.6 mile [0.95 kilometer] to the bottom of a small canyon. A preliminary survey showed that if there are constructions at the canyon end of the causeway, they would be below the silt in the floodplain.

Cañada de la Virgen was occupied from around A.D. 900 to 1150, after which it was totally abandoned. The site lies in the Valley of the Río Laja (Laja River), which runs from north to south through the east-central part of the state of Guanajuato. More than 80 sites have been recorded in the valley, and all but one have the same east-west orientation as Cañada de la Virgen.

Archaeologists have no precise name for the culture of the people who lived in the area a thousand years ago. They call it simply "the culture of the Río Laja," and it appears to have had its own traditions while demonstrating Toltec influence.

Front of the main pyramid, undergoing restoration, Cañada de la Virgen. Postclassic period. Note the doorway on the far right.

Recent History

Cañada de la Virgen has been known for some time; archaeologists have found evidence of four separate looting attempts at the site, all in the twentieth century.

Archaeological work at the site started in December 1995 and has been ongoing. It is directed by Luis Felipe Nieto, with Donald Patterson as field coordinator. They are affiliated with INAH, the University of Guanajuato, and California State University at Monterey Bay.

Funding for the project comes from local and state governments, with some contributions from the federal level.

Connection

San Miguel de Allende to Cañada de la Virgen: 14.5 miles [23.3 kilometers] by paved road (:24), then 6.3 miles [10.1 kilometers] by dirt road (:36).

Getting There

From Highway 111 at the entrance to San Miguel, take the bypass around the town to Highway 51. Turn left onto Highway 51 and go to the junction for the road that goes to the dam (marked with a sign). Turn right and go 6.7 miles [10.8 kilometers] to the junction with the dirt road that goes to Cañada de la Virgen (unmarked). Turn left onto the dirt road and follow it to the site.

When we took this road in the rainy season, it was very muddy and slippery and we needed four-wheel drive to negotiate it. It would be best to check ahead in San Miguel with Patterson at phone (415) 2-26-04, fax (415) 2-01-21, or email pmexc@gto1.telmex. net.mx. You could learn the condition of the road from him, or, if the site has not yet opened to the public, you could ask him to take you there. If the road is good and the site is open, ask what the visiting hours are. There were no specific hours at the time of our visit; we went in with Patterson, a long-time friend.

Allow 1.5 hours for a visit. There are no rest rooms, food, or drink at the site. Driving your own vehicle is the recommended way to reach Cañada de la Virgen, although you might be able to find someone in San Miguel with a pickup truck who would be willing to take you. Buses, of course, go to San Miguel de Allende.

★ ★ ★
REGIONAL MUSEUM OF QUERÉTARO (QUERÉTARO MUSEUM)

The Querétaro Museum's collection is housed on two floors of a structure begun in 1540; construction continued until 1727. The first room on the first floor of the museum deals mostly with political matters. The next section pertains to archaeology. Although the Querétaro Museum is a regional museum, it contains archaeological items from several areas of Mexico. After that are exhibits of the early Spanish occupation and the ethnography of the indigenous groups in the state of Querétaro. The upstairs has religious art and displays showing Querétaro's role in independence and the later history of the state and country.

The first room of the archaeological section begins with Mesoamerica. A map shows migration routes, and another shows the locations of various cultures. Artifacts displayed include a ladle *incensario,* figurines, and ceramic vessels. The Gulf Coast is represented by a nice Totonac smiling head, an Olmec stone mask about 5 inches (12.7 centimeters) tall, and jade necklaces—some pieces of which are carved. Zapotec and Mixtec items also form part of the collection.

Following this is a section devoted mostly to the archaeological sites in Querétaro. Maps showing the locations of sites, and plans of them are given for El Cerrito, Ranas, Toluquilla, and others. Models of a few are displayed, in addition to photographs and diagrams of some of the sites. Artifacts include copper axes, stone vessels, Chupícuaro figurines, and a case with stuccoed bas-reliefs from El Cerrito. A stone bas-relief depicting the front legs and clawed feet of a feline seems similar to the striding jaguars found on Pyramid B at Tula. Nearby, a merlon in the form of a cut shell from a structure at El Cerrito is exhibited. It is similar in size and style to the merlons found on the Coatepantli (Serpent Wall) at Tula, although the example from El Cerrito probably came from a building rather than a wall.

A lovely, thin alabaster vase, pipes, and very small eccentric flints are displayed. From outside Querétaro come a stucco glyph from Palenque, a Maya jade bas-relief and jade beads, a small Olmec bas-relief, and part of a yoke from the Gulf Coast. High up, on a long shelf, rests a selection of bas-relief decorations, some of which show Gulf Coast traits.

Querétaro was an important mining area in pre-Hispanic times, and an interesting cutaway model of a mining operation is displayed. Elsewhere, a map shows an area where pictographs are found, and a copy of one of the paintings is reproduced.

The Querétaro Museum is on Calle Corregidora in the city of Querétaro, next to the church of San Francisco and diagonally across from the Jardín Obregón (the main plaza) in the center of town. It was inaugurated on March 1, 1990. The museum is open Tuesday through Saturday from 10:00 A.M.

Merlon in the form of a cut shell from El Cerrito. Displayed in the Querétaro Museum.

to 5:00 P.M. and on Sunday from 9:00 A.M. to 4:00 P.M. It is closed on Monday. Allow 45 minutes for a visit.

Items in the collection are labeled in only a general way, with few specifics.

Lighting is fair and photography without flash is permitted. There are rest rooms at the museum but no food or drink; these are available at nearby restaurants.

★
EL CERRITO
(ehl sehr-REE-toh)

Derivation:
Spanish for "The Little Hill."
Other name:
El Pueblito, Spanish for "The Little Town."
Culture:
See text.
Location:
Far western Querétaro.
Maps: 2 (p. 54) and 2A (p. 55)

The Site

El Cerrito is a well-named site. The "hill" can be seen from great distances away, though it is actually a pyramid built over a small elevation. It rises 100 feet (30.5 meters) and measures 433 feet (132 meters) along each of the four sides of its base. Its size is indeed impressive, especially since it stands above relatively flat terrain in the southern part of the Valley of Querétaro.

The area around El Cerrito was occupied from about A.D. 1, when it was an important agricultural settlement. It was contemporary with Chupícuaro and other nearby early centers. El Cerrito itself was erected in two construction stages. The first was during the apogee of Teotihuacán (A.D. 400 to 650), when El Cerrito became a political center of importance in the valley and had interchange with the great metropolis. Ceramics at El Cerrito during this time followed a local tradition but imitated popular forms from Teotihuacán.

The second construction stage occurred later, between A.D. 650 and 1050, and partly overlapped the time when Tula dominated central Mexico. During this time the orientation of the buildings was changed and the main structure was added to. Most of the architecture produced at El Cerrito dates to this period. There is evidence of a disastrous fire at El Cerrito in the eleventh century, after which the site was abandoned.

When we saw El Cerrito, it was not officially open to the public; it was surrounded by a wire fence and had a locked gate. We could, however, get photographs through the wire and from a nearby road that we were given permission to enter.

Other pre-Hispanic remains have been reported around the pyramid, but they were not in evidence from our viewpoints. The original facing stones of the large pyramid have been mostly removed, and today visitors are looking at the core of the structure.

Recent History

At the end of the eighteenth century, a Franciscan friar, Juan Agustín Marfi, inspected El Cerrito and realized that the hill was not natural. He made drawings of some of the sculptures from the site, including a *chacmool* and a small Atlantean figure originally produced when Tula was influencing El Cerrito and other centers. Other connections with Tula have since been uncovered, including a merlon in the form of a cut shell (now in the Querétaro Museum).

In the mid-nineteenth century, a small fort was built atop the pyramid. It was later converted to a home by the landowner in the late nineteenth century, but its location proved inconvenient. This building is clearly visible today.

In 1985, archaeological work ensued at El Cerrito; a reconnaissance was conducted by Carlos Castañeda and students of the University of Veracruz. Later excavations

The main pyramid, El Cerrito. Late Classic period. A mid-nineteenth century fort was built atop the pyramid.

were directed by Ana María Crespo, and work was reportedly still in progress at the time of our visit. That was why El Cerrito was not open to the public.

Connections

1. Querétaro to El Cerrito: 3.8 miles [6.1 kilometers] by paved road (:12).

2. San Miguel de Allende to Querétaro: 37.2 miles [59.8 kilometers] by paved road (:44).

Getting There

1. From Querétaro, take Highway 45 (free road to Celaya) heading west to the cutoff for El Cerrito, 2.7 miles [4.3 kilometers] (:05). The cutoff is not marked for the site, but there is an elaborate entrance marked Nuevo Puebla and a business sign saying Cofia. Turn right and you will be looking straight at El Cerrito. Take this cobblestone road to the site. There is one zigzag along the way— just keep heading for the pyramid.

2. From San Miguel de Allende, head east on Highway 111 to the junction with Highway 57D. Turn right (do not get on the bypass around Querétaro) and proceed to Querétaro. Then follow the directions already given.

Since El Cerrito is not technically open, there are no specific visiting hours and no food or drink at the site, but you are only minutes from Querétaro. Allow 15 minutes to look at the pyramid and take a few photos. This is a good place to have a telephoto lens.

You can also reach El Cerrito by taxi from Querétaro, although not all drivers are exactly sure how best to get there. We followed a taxi there by a longer route but returned the way described. If you go by taxi, ask the driver to wait.

★ ★
RANAS
(RAH-nahs)

Derivation:
   Spanish for "Frogs."
Culture:
   Classic culture of the Sierra Gorda.
Location:
   East-central Querétaro.
Maps: 2 (p. 54) and 2B (p. 63)

The Site

Ranas, perched in the Sierra Gorda of Querétaro, lies at an altitude of over 8,000 feet (2,438 meters); it covers the tops of two adjacent hills and the slope of the higher hill. From the parking area for the site, a trail leads uphill to the low spot between the two hills. You will see stone retaining walls on the way up. The trail enters the site at the west end of Ball Court III. This ball court is part of the area called Ranas I. The rest of Ranas I occupies the hill on the right, while Ranas II and III are on the higher hill on the left. Ranas II is the most interesting part of the site; it contains more monumental architecture and can be seen from the parking area below.

When you tour Ranas II, you will climb to structures on increasingly higher levels of the hill. It is easy to find your way around. You start from Ball Court III and head west to one of the more impressive buildings, a stepped pyramid. The walls of the lower level slant inward; those of the second level are almost vertical. A stairway with *alfardas* is found on the east side. Higher up you will see stepped platforms with projecting stairways, some with rounded corners. These are habitational units. Even higher is an open area

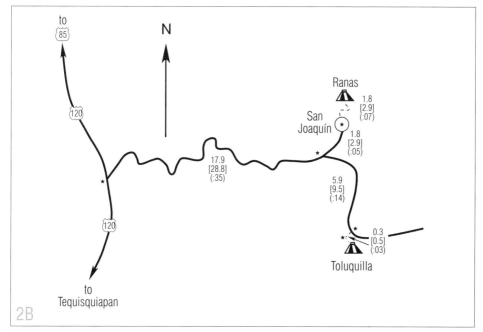

Routes to Ranas and Toluquilla (Map 2B).

called the Sunken Courtyard that is flanked by buildings. From the west side of the Sunken Courtyard, a stairway leads to the Main Temple, another stepped pyramid with an eastern stair flanked by *alfardas*. A few bottom stones are all that remain of the walls of the temple on top.

From there you head back downhill by a somewhat different path (toward the southeast) to see some of the structures of Ranas III. Actually, there is no clear demarcation between Ranas II and the adjacent Ranas III. Continue downward to where you started. As you approach the bottom of the hill, you will get a good view of Ball Court III, the north side of which has been restored. Walk through the ball court and up the other hill to see the rest of Ranas I.

Once you reach the top of Ranas I, the structures are more or less on one level. Interesting features here are two semicircular platforms, a stepped pyramid, Ball Court II (the north side of which has been restored), and remains of rectangular platforms.

To the northeast of this area lies another group of structures, including another ball court, but this area has not been consolidated and is not open to the public. The three ball courts at Ranas (and the two at Toluquilla) are of the open-ended type.

People of the Classic culture of the Sierra Gorda built Ranas, Toluquilla, and many other sites in the region. Occupied from around A.D. 450 to 1000, this area had contacts with or received influences from Teotihuacán and the Gulf Coast, mainly El Tajín. After the area was abandoned by its builders due to social unrest, it was taken over by the nomadic Chichimecs, principally the Pames and Jonaces. Mining was practiced in this region, primarily for cinnabar, calcite, and fluorite.

The architecture at Ranas (and Toluquilla) was constructed with a stone and clay core faced with hewn stone slabs. Only rarely was the exterior of a building coated with stucco. This style of architecture was also used at other sites in the Sierra Gorda.

The main temple, Ranas. Late Classic period.

Recent History

According to Ignacio Marquina, writing in a 1951 book, Ranas (and Toluquilla) were mentioned in a work published by Bartolomé Ballesteros and José María Reyes in 1881. This work was illustrated with plans and drawings by Pawell Primer. In 1930, Eduardo Noguera and Emilio Cuevas visited Ranas (and Toluquilla), photographed them, and collected data.

In 1978, an archaeological and mineralogical project in the Sierra Gorda began under the direction of the archaeologist Margarita Velasco Mireles. There were five field seasons, the last being in 1987–88. In 1981, 1984, and 1987, Ranas (and Toluquilla) were explored and partly restored. In 1996, excavations were still in operation at Toluquilla.

Connections

1. Tequisquiapan to Ranas: 56.0 miles [90.1 kilometers] by paved road (1:26), then 1.8 miles [2.9 kilometers] by good rock road (:07).

2. Querétaro to Tequisquiapan: 41.5 miles [72.6 kilometers] by paved road (:50).

3. Mexico City (Diana Circle) to Tequisquiapan: 111.4 miles [179.2 kilometers] by paved road (2:14).

Getting There

1. From Tequisquiapan, take Highway 120 north, east, and then north to the marked cutoff for San Joaquín, 36.3 miles [58.4 kilometers]. Turn right and go to and straight

through San Joaquín, 17.9 miles [28.8 kilometers]. There you pick up the rock road that goes to the parking area for Ranas; the way is well marked. Tequisquiapan is a delightful town, an old-time spa with hotels in various price ranges. It is the best stopover for visiting Ranas and Toluquilla.

2. From Querétaro, take Highway 57D southeast to San Juan del Río, then pick up Highway 120 (on the left) and follow it to Tequisquiapan.

3. From Mexico City, take Highway 57D northwest to San Juan del Río and Highway 120, 98.2 miles [158.0 kilometers]. Turn right and continue to Tequisquiapan.

Ranas is open daily from 9:00 A.M. to 4:00 P.M. There is no food or drink at the site, nor are there rest rooms. Allow 1.5 hours for the visit. Driving your own vehicle is the recommended way to reach Ranas (and Toluquilla), but a bus could probably get you to San Joaquín, and from there you could taxi to the site. If you do this, you should arrange for the driver to return for you later.

If you drive your own vehicle, be prepared for some serious mountain driving on the road from Highway 120 to San Joaquín. The surface of this road is good, but there are tight curves and steep grades. This should be no problem if you take it slowly.

★ TOLUQUILLA

(toh-loo-KEE-yah)

Derivation:
A hybrid Nahuatl-Spanish word meaning "Little Hunchback Hill." The site is named for the hill on which it lies.
Culture:
Classic culture of the Sierra Gorda.
Location:
East-central Querétaro.
Maps: 2 (p. 54) and 2B (p. 63)

The Site

Toluquilla stretches out along an artificially flattened hilltop (with a more or less north-south orientation) at an altitude of over 8,000 feet (2,438 meters). The only access is from the north. More than 50 structures have been recorded at Toluquilla, and the architectural style and construction methods were the same as those used at Ranas. See

"Ranas" for this information and for the ancient and recent history of the Classic culture of the Sierra Gorda.

As you enter the site, you pass through a few remains of a residential cluster. The trail then enters the north end of Ball Court I, the sides of which are stepped. Bordering the south end of Ball Court I is a stepped pyramid with a northern stairway, the second level of which has *alfardas*. Of the temple on top, only the bottom stones of the walls remain.

As you face the pyramid, Structure 13 is off to the right (west), just beyond the end of the west wall of Ball Court I. Structure 13 is noteworthy because it is the only building at Toluquilla where remnants of stucco facing have been found.

From there, just take the easy-to-follow trail to the south end of the site. Beyond the stepped pyramid you will find a plaza area with surrounding structures, one of which is a semicircular platform. From there a passageway leads through a cluster of buildings facing different directions; some of these were ceremonial, whereas others were residential.

Ball Court 1, looking south to a pyramidal structure, Toluquilla. Classic period.

You then enter a rather open area with a few remains of lower walls and many agave plants. Later you will see another group of residential structures, and finally Ball Court II. This ball court is similar to Ball Court I, and it also has a stepped pyramid at its south end.

The site continues toward the south and somewhat downhill, but this sector has not been fully investigated—nor is it open to the public.

Recent History

See "Ranas."

Connections

1. Tequisquiapan to Toluquilla: 60.1 miles [96.7 kilometers] by paved road (1:35), then 0.3 mile [0.5 kilometer] by rutted dirt road (:03).

2 and 3. Querétaro or Mexico City to Tequisquiapan: See "Ranas."

Getting There

1. From Tequisquiapan, take Highway 120 north, east, and then north to the cutoff for San Joaquín (marked), 36.3 miles [58.4 kilometers]. Turn right and go 17.9 miles [28.8 kilometers] to the cutoff for Toluquilla. This junction is marked with a pyramid sign, but the name of the site isn't shown. Turn right at the sign and go 5.9 miles [9.5 kilometers] to the final cutoff for Toluquilla (marked Toluquilla). Watch out for *topes* (speed bumps) on this stretch. Turn right onto the rough dirt road and go 0.3 mile [0.5 kilometer] to the parking area for Toluquilla.

From the parking area it is a rather long, steep climb to the site. Stone-paved walkways and steps give good footing, but the climb at this altitude can be tiring.

Toluquilla is open daily from 9:00 A.M. to 4:00 P.M. There is no food or drink at the site, nor are there rest rooms. Allow one hour to climb to the site, visit it, and return to your vehicle. Having your own vehicle is the recommended way to reach Toluquilla, but you could probably get a bus to San Joaquín and a taxi from there to the site. If you do this, ask the driver to wait for you or to return for you later.

If you are driving a standard vehicle, you may find the dirt road difficult to drive. If it looks too bad, you could park and walk the rest of the way.

SECTION 3

• • • •

CENTRAL MEXICO—
AROUND MEXICO CITY

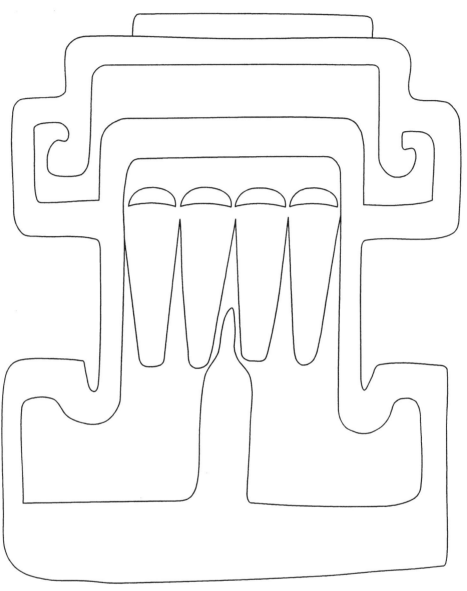

Merlon depicting a stylized image of Tlaloc, from Teotihuacán. Classic period. On display in the Mexico City Museum.

GENERAL INFORMATION FOR SECTION 3, CENTRAL MEXICO— AROUND MEXICO CITY

The area in and around Mexico City is the most densely populated region of the country. Besides the capital megacity, there are other sizable cities such as Toluca, Puebla, and the tourist destination of Cuernavaca. This region is part of Mexico's high plateau; the altitude is above 5,000 feet (1,524 meters) throughout, and most areas are above 7,000 feet (2,134 meters). More miles of four-lane highways (both toll and free) are found in this section than in other parts of the republic, and there are more miles of two-lane highways as well. Although there are mountains all over this region, little mountain driving is involved in getting around. The roads are good almost everywhere.

More archaeological sites and museums can be visited in this section than in any other area covered in this book. The best stopovers for visiting the sites and museums are, for the portion shown on Map 3A, Toluca; for Map 3B, Mexico City; for Map 3C, Tula; for Map 3D, Tulancingo; for Map 3E, Teotihuacán; for Map 3F, Puebla, the nearby Cholula, and Tlaxcala; and for Map 3G, Cuernavaca. Hotels that can be recommended are the Hotel Sharon, near the archaeological zone in Tula, the Hotel La Joya in Tulancingo, and the Archaeological Villa at Teotihuacán. The other cities mentioned have hotels in all price ranges.

The climate in the area covered by Section 3 is similar to that in the area covered by Section 1. See "General Information for Section 1" for more details. It is, of course, cooler at the higher altitudes.

The Benito Juárez International Airport, just to the east of Mexico City, is Mexico's hub. It is the airport where most foreign visitors arrive in the country. There are airports at Toluca and Puebla as well.

Car rentals are available at the airports mentioned and through agencies and major hotels in Mexico City, Toluca, Puebla, Tlaxcala, and Cuernavaca, all of which also have travel agencies.

The points of reference for distances and driving times are the following: (1) in Toluca, the Hidalgo statue at Calles Hidalgo and Isidoro Fabela in the eastern part of the city; (2) in Mexico City, the Diana Fountain on Paseo de la Reforma at the east end of Chapultepec Park (see note that follows); (3) in Tulancingo, the junction of Highway 130 and the west end of the bypass that goes around the north part of the city; (4) in Puebla, the *glorieta* at the junction of Avenida Atlixco and Calle Juárez; (5) in Tlaxcala, the junction of Highway 117 and the highway interchange; (6) in Cuernavaca, the *glorieta* on Highway 95 at the north end of the city.

Note: The reference point in Mexico City relates to the distances and driving times to sites outside of Map 3B. On Map 3B (Mexico City and its near environs), distances and driving times to the sites and museums are not shown, although a distance scale is. Reason? I found it quite impossible to navigate the city, record the information, and find the best route to the sites without getting on the wrong thoroughfare. Twenty years ago I was able to get to Tenayuca, Santa Cecilia, and Cuicuilco without help. No longer. The traffic and congestion have increased and complicated matters. The best possible advice I can give readers, and this is *strongly* recommended, is to hire a taxi or the driver of a private vehicle as a guide to get you there. Even a local driver will have to ask directions to reach Tenayuca, Santa Cecilia, and San Pedro de los Pinos and to get to the Tlatilco and Anahuacalli Museums. The routes to these places are not marked in any way.

Another problem is that if you try to drive to the area of Mexico City's main plaza, the Zócalo, to visit the sites nearby, you are faced with finding a place to park. Taxis and driver guides know how.

When we last visited the sites in downtown Mexico City, we hired a driver who took us to Tlatelolco and waited for us. He

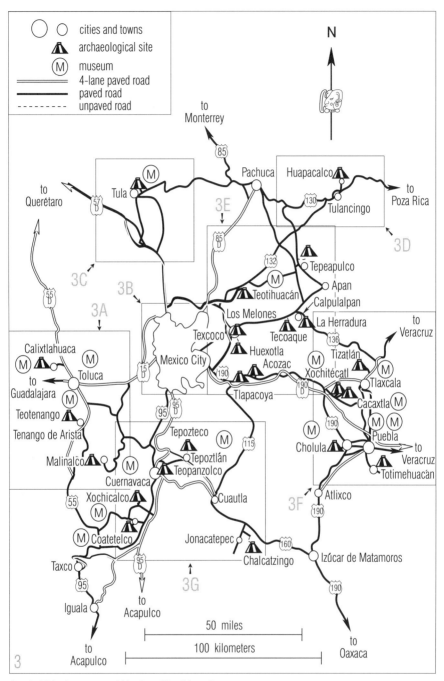

Central Mexico, around Mexico City (Map 3).

then took us to the area near the Templo Mayor, and we walked a block or so to the site while he again waited for us. He had suggested earlier that from there we could get the Metro (subway) from the Zócalo station to the Pino Suárez station, where the Ehécatl Temple is found. This was much easier than trying to drive there and find yet another parking place. This also gave us the opportunity to ride the Metro for the first time, something we would not have tried without having someone along who knew the routine. It was an interesting experience. The Metro is clean, fast (our ride took 45 seconds), and efficient, and in the corridors, glass cases display indigenous costumes and crafts. We saw what we considered to be throngs of people. Our driver insisted, however, that there were relatively few since it was a Saturday.

After visiting the Ehécatl Temple, we returned by Metro to the Zócalo station and walked to the driver's car. The upshot was that in a matter of a couple of hours, we were able to see three archaeological sites and the Templo Mayor Museum with no difficulty. In this instance, our method as explained in "Getting Lost and Unlost" in the "General Advice" section would not have worked well owing to parking problems.

Drivers (who also act as guides if you wish) can be found at the entrances to the large hotels in Mexico City. Most of them speak some English, and often their rates are posted. If they are not, settle on a price beforehand. An hourly rate is generally used if you want the driver to take you somewhere and wait for you. If you simply want to go to a single destination and do not plan to have the driver wait, then a taxi will suffice.

Because of air pollution problems, cars are prohibited from driving in Mexico City on one day of the week. The day you are not allowed to drive depends on the last number of the vehicle's license plate. Visitors with foreign plates are *not* exempt from this regulation.

Two sites that are not included in Section 3 are Copilco and Tlatilco (although the Tlatilco Museum is covered). At the Tlatilco Museum we were told that the site itself is covered over with modern housing. Copilco and its site museum were once open to the public, but now the buildings have been converted into an INAH office. Since both sites are often mentioned in the literature, I thought it best to alert readers that neither is currently open to the public. Some of the original burials from Tlatilco are displayed in the Mexico City Museum.

★ ★
CALIXTLAHUACA
(kah-leesh-tlah-WAH-kah)

Derivation:
  Nahuatl for "House on the Plain."
Original name:
  Probably Calixtlahuaca.
Culture:
  Matlatzinca (see text).
Location:
  Central state of Mexico.
Maps: 3 (p. 72) and 3A (p. 74)

The Site

Calixtlahuaca is a very good two-star site—perhaps two and a half stars would be a fairer rating.

Three separate sections of Calixtlahuaca are of interest to visitors, and all should be seen. Two of these are on different levels of an artificially terraced hill, and the other is at ground level at the base of the hill. I recommend seeing those on the hill first.

There is a parking area at the site, near the museum. From there, a short walk will get you to the Temple of Quetzalcóatl-Ehécatl

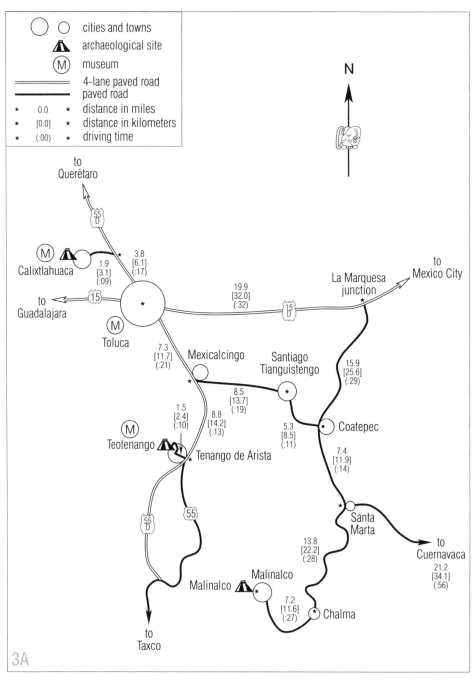

Routes to Calixtlahuaca, Teotenango, and Malinalco (Map 3A).

South side of the Temple of Quetzalcóatl (Structure 3), Calixtlahuaca. Late Postclassic period.

(Structure 3), the most interesting and most publicized building at the site.

This circular structure has a single stairway facing east onto a plaza. It was dedicated to Quetzalcóatl in his guise as the wind god, Ehécatl, and a life-size statue of this deity was found in the building.

Three earlier structures were found inside the latest one; all of them were circular and had a single eastern stairway. Some of the earlier remains, including crude stone serpent heads, can be seen from the outside as you circle the temple. These belong to the third construction. On the north side of the plaza a bas-relief carving has been erected.

From this area, climb up the hill to the next group. If someone offers to show you the way, accept the help; the trail is not terribly clear.

This upper level is made up of three partially restored structures around a small plaza. The most interesting is the Altar of the Skulls, in the shape of a T, with a circular extension at the top. The outside walls are covered with projecting stone skulls (poorly preserved) and knobs. For good overall shots

of the altar, climb one of the other structures. They are both rectangular platforms, each with a single stairway facing the plaza. From this vantage point you can also get good telephoto shots of the Calmecac (Structure 17) at ground level. During excavation of the larger platform in this upper-level group, items related to the god Tlaloc were uncovered, and for this reason the group of structures is called the Tlaloc cluster.

Now head back to your car, drive back along the entrance road, and take a hard left (more like a U-turn) at the first opportunity. A short distance away is the Calmecac, an architectural complex of many rooms and platforms. This complex is thought to have been a sort of seminary—hence its name, which means seminary in Nahuatl; it is also sometimes called the Seminario (Spanish for the same thing). One of the major features here is a large platform with a triple stairway facing a large plaza. Part of the Calmecac is constructed of adobe and part of stone.

Excavations at Calixtlahuaca have brought to light some interesting information that

The Temple of Quetzalcóatl (Structure 3), Calixtlahuaca, looking northwest. Late Postclassic period.

Altar of the Skulls (foreground) and two other structures in the Tlaloc cluster facing a plaza, Calixtla-huaca. Late Postclassic period.

has led archaeologists to recognize five periods of occupation. The earliest, during the Preclassic period, is represented by figurines and a few vertical walls constructed to support some terraces halfway up the hill. The second period of occupation dates to the third period of Teotihuacán (A.D. 300–600), when Calixtlahuaca was the home of people connected with the former site. The earliest building inside the Temple of Quetzalcóatl-Ehécatl dates to this time. The third period shows pronounced influence from Tula. During this time, the second building of the Temple of Quetzalcóatl-Ehécatl was constructed.

In the fourth period (A.D. 1200–1474), the Matlatzincas, a Nahua group related to, but enemies of, the Aztecs, became the predominant force in the area (although they had occupied it during the previous period), and the third building of the Temple of Quetzalcóatl-Ehécatl was undertaken. Excavation shows that this building was destroyed by earthquake in 1474. During the fifth period (1474–1510), Calixtlahuaca was conquered by the Aztecs, so it is referred to as the Azteca-Matlatzinca period. During this time, the final enlargement and some reconstruction were carried out on the Temple of Quetzalcóatl-Ehécatl. Also dating to this period are the Altar of the Skulls and the adjacent Structure 4. The Calmecac was built during the third and fourth periods and was burned in 1510 on the orders of Moctezuma II, to quell the rebellious Matlatzincas. The inhabitants then left the area but returned after the Spanish conquest, when they founded the new town near their ancient center.

Recent History

Excavations at Calixtlahuaca were undertaken by the Mexican government's Department of Monuments (now the National Institute of Anthropology and History [INAH]) in 1930, and continued for about eight years. Most of the work was done under the direction of the Mexican archaeologist José García Payón.

Connection

Toluca (Hidalgo statue at the junction of Calles Hidalgo and Isidro Fabela) to Calixtlahuaca: 5.7 miles [9.2 kilometers] by paved road (:26).

Getting There

From Toluca, take Highway 55D heading north for 3.8 miles [6.1 kilometers] and turn left at the marked junction. Follow the signs as you continue to the parking area. Part of this last stretch has a cobblestone surface.

Calixtlahuaca is open Tuesday through Sunday from 10:00 A.M. to 5:00 P.M. It is closed on Monday. There are restrooms at the site museum, but no food or drink is available in the immediate area.

A special point to keep in mind is that Calixtlahuaca is one of the highest sites in Mexico, with an altitude of over 9,000 feet (2,743 meters). This—plus the fact that the visit entails a little climbing—is likely to leave you a bit breathless.

Calixtlahuaca can also be reached by taxi or bus from Toluca. Allow 2.5 hours for a visit.

★ ★
CALIXTLAHUACA MUSEUM

The collection in the Calixtlahuaca Museum is not extensive, but some of the items are interesting, as is the building itself. The structure is built in a shape that repeats the circular configuration of the Temple of Quetzalcóatl-Ehécatl.

The one-room museum has at its center a low, walled area where a bas-relief carving is displayed. It gets natural light from above, which helps bring out the design. Although it is somewhat eroded, it appears that part of the motif depicts a shield and darts or spears.

Bas-relief carving in the Calixtlahuaca Museum. Late Postclassic period.

Other displays include the head and headdress of a three-dimensional human figure, a seated figure with hands on knees, glass cases containing ceramics, a second bas-relief slab that was previously on an upper level of the site, and the feet of a statue.

The museum is open Tuesday through Sunday from 10:00 A.M. to 5:00 P.M. It is closed on Monday. Allow 10 minutes for a visit. There are rest rooms at the museum, but no food or drink is available. Photography without flash is permitted.

★ ★ ★

MUSEUM OF ANTHROPOLOGY AND HISTORY OF THE STATE OF MEXICO
(TOLUCA MUSEUM)

The Toluca Museum was inaugurated on April 27, 1987. It is part of the city of Toluca's large Mexican Cultural Center, which also includes museums of modern art and popular arts, concert halls, and a library.

The collection includes displays covering early nomads, migrations to the New World, and early stone artifacts and ceramics.

One chart shows the development of Olmec civilization, and another, the characteristics of Mesoamerica. Figurines dating to 2000–1200 B.C. are included with the early materials, and there is a model of Tlapacoya. The displays are nicely done; some items are labeled specifically, but others are not.

Chacmool in the Calixtlahuaca section of the Toluca Museum. Postclassic period.

The Teotihuacán section has merlons and other carved stones, fragments of mural paintings, and a carved stone tail of a rattlesnake. A drawing of a composite stela, used for ball games and sometimes called a ball court marker, is shown. The stela is made of four parts: the top element is disc shaped, the element below is nearly spherical, the next is conical, and the bottom element is cylindrical. All sections are carved. Near the drawing is a conical section of another marker that came from Toluca.

In the Tula section, drawings, ceramics, and stone masks and figurines are displayed, as is a carved, coiled, and feathered serpent of stone. Some information on Teotenango from A.D. 900 to 1162 is given. Other displays include jewelry, other metal items, copies of *lienzos,* or native Mesoamerican manuscripts, and carved stones.

The Calixtlahuaca section shows Matlatzinca ceramics and gives information about the group. There is a seated stone figure and a *chacmool* with straight hair. Teotenango from A.D. 1162 to 1521 is represented with another exhibit.

Photographs, old drawings, and ceramics that relate to Malinalco form other displays.

In addition to the pre-Columbian section, there are displays devoted to the colonial period, independence, and modern history.

The Toluca Museum, and the cultural center of which it is a part, is about 5.0 miles (8.0 kilometers) west of the center of the city. It is a short distance off the *periférico* that loops around the city. Toluca is difficult to navigate on your own. I recommend taking a taxi and having the driver wait for you, since the cultural center is in a rather isolated area where you are unlikely to find a taxi.

The museum is open Tuesday through Sunday from 10:00 A.M. to 6:00 P.M. It is closed on Monday. The lighting is fairly decent, and photography without flash is permitted. Allow 30 minutes for a visit. There is no food or drink at the museum but rest rooms are available.

★ ★ ★
TEOTENANGO
(teh-oh-teh-NAHN-goh)

Derivation:
Nahuatl for "Within the Sacred Wall" or "In the Place of the Sacred Wall."
Culture:
Teotenaca and Matlatzinca.
Location:
West-central state of Mexico.
Maps: 3 (p. 72) and 3A (p. 74)

The Site

Teotenango, at an elevation of 8,859 feet (2,700 meters), occupies the eastern part of Cerro Tetépetl. The post-Hispanic settlement of Tenango de Arista lies at the base of the hill to the east. The site covers 0.8 square mile (2.0 square kilometers).

You enter the site from the north over a broad stairway. It climbs to the top of a huge platform that forms the base of the site. Parts of the top of the hill itself were terraced and filled in ancient times, and structures are found on various levels.

When you climb the stairway, look to the left to see two bas-relief carvings partway up. One depicts a seated jaguar with the date Two Rabbit, and the other records the date Nine House. When you reach the top of the stair, walk to the left (east) and enter Plaza A with the impressive Structure 1A on the east side. It is composed of four stepped tiers in front and an inclined wall at the rear. The three lower tiers are each formed of a *talud*

topped by a projecting cornice, recalling the architecture of the Citadel at Teotihuacán. Once a temple crowned the top, but it is now destroyed.

In the adjacent Plaza B, and on a higher level, is Structure 1B, another base for a temple. The three lower tiers of the structure are each composed of a *talud* topped by a vertical wall, this time similar to constructions at Xochicalco. Structure 1B encloses part of an earlier structure, the top of which is formed of plain walls that are visible today.

On the north side of Structure 1B is the small Structure 2B, built during a later occupation at the site. The south side of Plaza B is bounded by Structure 3B, a three-tiered platform that probably supported habitations rather than a temple.

From there you head northwest past other remains to Teotenango's large ball court. When this l-shaped court was excavated, a steam bath was discovered near the east end; this was originally covered when the ball court was built but has been left uncovered since excavation. The court itself is 174 feet (53 meters) long. At one time, stone rings were fitted into the side walls of the ball court.

Northwest of the west end of the ball court are the remains of low walls that were once habitations. Again to the northwest is Structure 2D (Base of the Serpent), which rises in two tiers. Embedded in the front (east) base of the building, near its northeast corner, is a large stone carved in the form of a serpent's head. From there, head east and exit the site.

Structure 1A (center), facing Plaza A, Teotenango. Postclassic period.

Ball court, Teotenango. Early Postclassic period.

Excavations at Teotenango have revealed five stages of occupation and development. From A.D. 600 to 750, modest agricultural settlements existed in the valley next to Cerro Tetépetl. Their inhabitants made ceramics related to those found near the end of Teotihuacán, as well as local wares.

From A.D. 750 to 900, the population was concentrated in what we now know as the ceremonial center of Teotenango. During this time a stone carving of two glyphs with numbers was produced, and constructions with well-cut stones were built. The ceramics, some with geometric designs, were well executed. Parts of the hill were filled during this same time.

Between A.D. 900 and 1200, the Teotenacas who founded Teotenango began expanding to other parts of the Valley of Toluca and to the Basin of Mexico. At Teotenango they also constructed various architectural groups that show influence from Teotihuacán and Xochicalco. The ball court was built during this period. Some of the structures covered earlier ones, and architecture and bas-relief carving flourished. Some of the reliefs also show influence from Xochicalco. Teotenango's stela (now in the site museum) is one of the gems from this period.

A group of Matlatzincas arrived in the next period, A.D. 1200 to 1476; they brought a militaristic organization to Teotenango and other customs that modified the existing culture. They burned part of the ceremonial center, which then became used for the dwellings and cemeteries of the Matlatzincas. They built other structures in nearby areas and from them administered the site. The new military governors constructed a defensive wall around part of the base of Cerro Tetépetl and built other fortifications as well. It is the wall that gives the site its name. The architecture changed little from the previous period, because the local masons who did the work continued their own tradition. This period marked the maximum expansion of the Matlatzinca communities.

In 1476, the Matlatzincas of Teotenango were conquered by the Aztecs (Mexicas) of Axayácatl, the lord of Tenochtitlán, and tribute was imposed. The Aztecs remained in power until the Spanish conquest, and in 1582 the post-Hispanic town (Tenango de Arista) was founded.

Recent History

Although known since the time of the Spanish conquest, Teotenango began to be excavated and consolidated only in 1971; the work of the Teotenango Project continued through 1975 under the direction of Román Piña Chan. All of the consolidation seen at the site was undertaken during this project.

Connection

Toluca to Teotenango: 17.6 miles [28.3 kilometers] by paved road (:44).

Getting There

Leave Toluca heading south on Highway 55D to Tenango de Arista, 16.1 miles [25.9 kilometers]. Turn right and go straight ahead until you come face to face with a church (where you must turn). Turn right and follow the road as it climbs the hill and curves to the left. You will come to the site museum first, and shortly thereafter, the parking area for the site.

Teotenango is open Tuesday through Sunday from 9:00 A.M. to 5:00 P.M. It is closed on Monday. Allow 1.5 hours for a visit. There are rest rooms at the museum, and snacks and cold drinks are sold at a stand nearby. Afternoon hours are best for photography, though the light is fair most of the day.

★ ★ ★
ARCHAEOLOGICAL MUSEUM OF THE STATE OF MEXICO DR. ROMAN PIÑA CHAN (TEOTENANGO MUSEUM)

From its formal name you can tell that this is more than an average site museum; it is also larger than most others.

The museum's collection contains a nice selection of stone carvings, both three dimensional and bas-relief, from various parts of the state of Mexico. Especially impressive are a couple of serpent heads, one of which comes from the Templo Mayor at Tenochtitlán, a bas-relief panel of a seated jaguar shown in profile, and a carved stone head with mother-of-pearl inlays for the eyes and teeth. There is also a very nice stela from Teotenango, carved with two Teotihuacán yearsigns and two dates on each face; it is in almost pristine condition.

Early ceramics from Tlatilco and Tlapacoya are displayed, as are later Matlatzinca wares. Large photos show the reconstruction of the Palace of the Quetzal Butterfly at Teotihuacán. Others show the progress of the work conducted at Teotenango from 1971 to 1975. Three carved slabs are placed below photos of Calixtlahuaca, so perhaps they came from that site. There is little specific labeling. Also interesting is a carving of Xiuhcóatl, the fire serpent, that dates to the Late Postclassic period.

The Teotenango Museum, at the entrance to the site, opened on April 27, 1988. Lighting is fair inside, and photography without flash is permitted. Allow 30 minutes for a visit. The museum is open Tuesday through Sunday from 9:00 A.M. to 5:00 P.M. It is closed on Monday. Snacks and cold drinks are sold at a stand outside the museum, and there are rest rooms inside the museum.

Buses from the town of Tenango go to the museum and site.

Teotenango stela carved with date glyphs and yearsigns (the geometric figures at the top and in the middle). Early Postclassic period. On display in the Teotenango Museum.

★ ★ ★
MALINALCO
(mah-leen-AHL-koh)

Derivation:
Nahuatl, from *malinalli,* meaning "grass" or a certain weed used for cordage.

Culture:
Aztec (see text).

Location:
South-central state of Mexico.

Maps: 3 (p. 72) and 3A (p. 74)

The Site

Malinalco is one of the most unusual sites in Mexico. Some of its temples are carved into living rock. The only other place in Mexico where something similar is known is Texco-tzingo, where rock-cut baths and canals are found at the summer palace of Nezahual-cóyotl, king of Texcoco. The Texcotzingo features date perhaps a bit earlier than those at Malinalco but are not nearly so impressive.

The archaeological zone is 400 feet (122 meters) above the level of the town of Malinalco. On the way up, keep an eye out to the left of the path to see the remains of a structure partly hidden by trees. It is a stepped pyramidal base with an inset stairway. Resume your climb to the main part of the archaeological zone.

The most interesting building at Malinalco is Temple I, also known as the Temple of the Eagle and Jaguar Knights. This circular building, with all its sculptural decorations, its pyramidal base, and its stairway with *alfardas* is a single unit carved into the

Temple of the Eagle and Jaguar Knights (Temple I), Malinalco. Late Postclassic period.

Jaguar sculpture east of the stairs of the Temple of the Eagle and Jaguar Knights, Malinalco. Late Postclassic period.

mountainside. It is really quite a fantastic achievement and is best thought of as sculptured architecture.

There are remains of a sculptured jaguar to the right of the Temple I stairway, and a few remains of one to the left. Little is left of the carving in the center of the stairway.

At the top of the stair, a low platform fronts the doorway of the temple. Flanking the doorway are three-dimensional sculptures of a serpent's head with an Eagle Knight seated on top (east or right side) and, on the left (west), a drum covered with a jaguar skin surmounted by the remains of a Jaguar Knight.

On the exterior wall of the temple, next to the doorway, are bas-relief representations of the open mouth of the serpent; its tongue protrudes from the doorway and lies on the platform, stretched out like a mat. Each half of the serpent relief can be seen as a serpent's head in profile, while together they depict a frontal view. Some authorities believe this mouth-doorway represents Tepeyolotl, the earth monster.

The interior chamber of Temple I is almost 19 feet (5.8 meters) in diameter and contains a semicircular bench. Three sculptures adorn the bench: a stretched-out jaguar skin in the center and eagle skins on either side. Another outstretched eagle skin is found in the center of the floor of the shrine. Behind this is a circular hole, perhaps a receptacle for offerings. Originally, the whole building (including the sculptures) was covered with a thin layer of stucco that was then painted.

A modern conical thatched roof tops the temple; it is probably like the original roof. A channel at the back of the roof was carved into the living rock to carry off rainwater. Visitors are no longer allowed inside the shrine, but you can see the sculptures there from outside a wire fence. They are nicely illuminated from the inside.

Structure or Temple II, a two-tiered truncated pyramid with a western stair, lies a few feet southeast of Temple I. Climb Temple II for overall shots of Temple I; a wide-angle lens is useful here.

West of Temple II is Temple V, a circular structure with an eastern stair built of stone and mortar and set upon a small platform.

From there, walk northwest between Temples I and II to Temple III. Temple III is composed of two chambers, one circular and one rectangular; each has a rectangular altar of dressed stone surrounding a cistlike

Jaguar-skin sculpture on the bench in the interior of the Temple of the Eagle and Jaguar Knights, Malinalco. Late Postclassic period.

Front (west side) of Temple II, Malinalco. Late Postclassic period.

depression. You first enter the rectangular room through openings formed by the remnants of two pillars and lower masonry walls.

When this chamber was excavated, remains of a mural painting were found on the western wall, but almost nothing can be seen of it today. The mural depicted three warriors in full regalia, carrying shields and lances, and according to José García Payón it represented the souls of warriors transformed into a stellar god in the guise of Mixcóatl.

From the rectangular room there is a single entrance to the large circular chamber of Temple III; the whole is formed of thick masonry walls.

Temple IV lies to the north of Temple III and is partially carved into living rock. This huge single room has a bench running around three of its sides, upon which are found two altars. In the center of the room are some stone bases that originally supported wooden posts that held up the roof. Archaeological evidence indicates that the roof was of solid rubble made in two sections and resting on beams.

Farther north is Temple VI, carved from living stone. This temple is incomplete—the Spanish conquest apparently brought work on it to a halt. During excavation, a large number of stone chisels were found in the debris.

Malinalco was occupied by the Matlatzincas, a branch of the Nahua, who were conquered by the Aztecs during the reign of Axayácatl (around 1469, according to native and early Spanish documents). Matlatzinca ceramics have verified their presence at the site. It was the Aztecs, however, who carved and constructed the temples. The work began in 1476 or 1501, depending on your choice of authority, and was carried out under the Aztec rulers Ahuizotl (who followed Axayácatl) and Moctezuma the younger.

Temple I was closely associated with the elite military orders of the Eagle and Jaguar Knights, organizations described in early Spanish colonial documents as being composed of warriors of noble birth. The whole site may have been reserved for their rituals.

Although Temple I is circular, it is not connected with the cult of Quetzalcóatl, as are many other circular edifices in Mesoamerica.

Two beautifully carved wooden drums were found at Malinalco. Both bear representations of eagles, and one also depicts jaguars with headdresses, symbolizing the warrior knights. They further verify Malinalco as an important center of the Eagle and Jaguar Knights.

Recent History

Malinalco was conquered in 1521 by Andrés de Tapia, who led a detachment sent by Cortés. Some of the buildings were burned and destroyed. Two decades later the Augustinians used stones from the site to construct their church in the town below. There is little to be said about the site for the period from then until INAH began research and reconstruction in 1936. Most of what we know of the site is due to the efforts of José García Payón, who undertook work there in the 1940s and 1950s.

Connections

1. Toluca to Malinalco: 49.5 miles [79.0 kilometers] by paved road (2:00).

2. Cuernavaca to Malinalco: 42.2 miles [67.9 kilometers] by paved road (1:51).

Getting There

1. From Toluca, head south on Highway 55D to Mexicalcingo, 7.3 miles [11.7 kilometers], and turn left (east). Proceed east to Santiago Tianguistengo, then south and east to Coatepec, 13.8 miles [22.2 kilometers]. Turn right and follow the road south to Santa Marta and Chalma; curve north to the town of Malinalco, 28.4 miles [45.7 kilometers].

2. From Cuernavaca, take Highway 95 north to a junction that is the cutoff for Huitzilac, 4.9 miles [7.7 kilometers], and turn left. Continue to Santa Marta, 16.4 miles [26.4 kilometers], and turn left again. Follow the road south through Chalma and curve north to the town of Malinalco, 21.0 miles [33.8 kilometers].

As you approach the town, the road forks; take the left branch into town and go to the plaza, where there is an information booth. There you can get a map of the town and directions to the parking area. This lies at the base of the hill on which the site is located.

From the parking area it takes about 5 minutes to climb to the ticket office, where there are rest rooms. From there it takes an additional 25 minutes to reach the site. It will take about 20 minutes coming down. Malinalco is open Tuesday through Sunday from

10:00 A.M. to 4:30 P.M. It is closed on Monday. Allow two hours from the time you start your climb until you return. Cold drinks are sold at the site, and there are a number of restaurants in town.

Malinalco can also be reached by bus.

★ ★

SANTA CECILIA

(SAHN-tah seh-SEEL-ee-ah)

Derivation:
    Spanish for "Saint Cecilia."
Culture:
    Chichimec, Aztec.
Location:
    State of Mexico, just north of Mexico City.
Map: 3B (p. 90)

The Site

Santa Cecilia is a gem, the only place where a fully restored Aztec temple tops its pyramidal base. It serves to give a good idea of what other Aztec-period architecture must have looked like originally.

The main pyramid and temple are abutted by a lower pyramidal base, whose temple is not restored. A low platform is found in front. The whole sits on the rear of a large flat area (presumably a plaza) that has been restored with cobblestones. The main pyramidal base rises in four tiers, and almost its whole width in front is occupied by a stairway and flanking *alfardas* with vertical upper zones. A plain pillar, or stela, stands in the center at the top of the stair, and banded, drum-shaped sculptures are found on either side. The temple itself is composed of a single chamber with one doorway. Within it is a headless figure of the *chacmool* type.

Two sides of the plaza are now flanked with trees and well-kept grassy areas, giving a nice parklike atmosphere and forming a pleasant setting for the temple.

Santa Cecilia is of Late Postclassic date and is typical of Aztec construction. It was once a district of the Chichimec capital at Tenayuca.

Restored one-room Aztec period temple fronted by a long low platform, Santa Cecilia. Photograph by author.

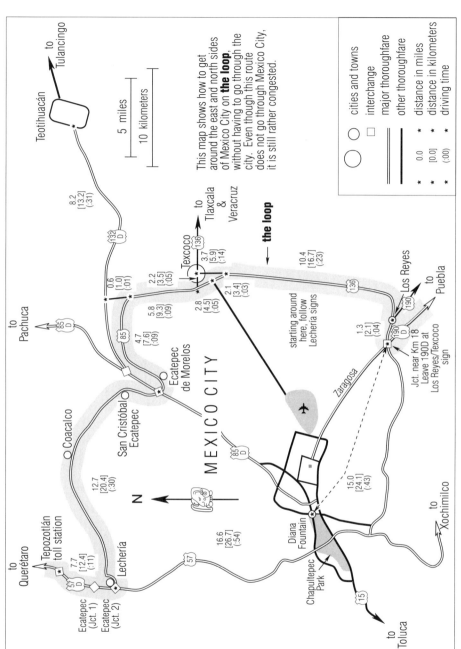

This map shows how to get around the east and north sides of Mexico City on **the loop**, without having to go through the city. Even though this route does not go through Mexico City, it is still rather congested.

to Tulancingo

Teotihuacán

5 miles
10 kilometers

8.2
[13.2]
(.31)

132
D

to Pachuca

0.6
[1.0]
(.01)

85
D

2.2
[3.5]
(.05)

Texcoco

to Tlaxcala & Veracruz

3.7
[5.9]
(.14)

136

the loop

4.7
[7.6]
(.09)

85

5.8
[9.3]
(.09)

2.8
[4.5]
(.05)

2.1
[3.4]
(.03)

starting around here, follow Lechería signs

10.4
[16.7]
(.23)

136

Los Reyes

to Puebla

190
D

190

Jct. near Km 18
Leave 190D at Los Reyes/Texcoco sign

1.3
[2.1]
(.04)

Ecatepec de Morelos

San Cristóbal Ecatepec

Coacalco

Zaragosa

85
D

MEXICO CITY

N

15.0
[24.1]
(.43)

to Xochimilco

12.7
[20.4]
(.30)

Tepozotlán toll station

to Querétaro

7.7
[12.4]
(.11)

57
D

Ecatepec (Jct. 1)

Ecatepec (Jct. 2)

Lechería

57

16.6
[26.7]
(.54)

Diana Fountain

Chapultepec Park

15

to Toluca

Legend:

- ○ ○ cities and towns
- □ interchange
- major thoroughfare
- other thoroughfare
- ★ 0.0 distance in miles
- ★ [0.0] distance in kilometers
- ★ (.00) driving time

Loop road around the east and north sides of Mexico City.

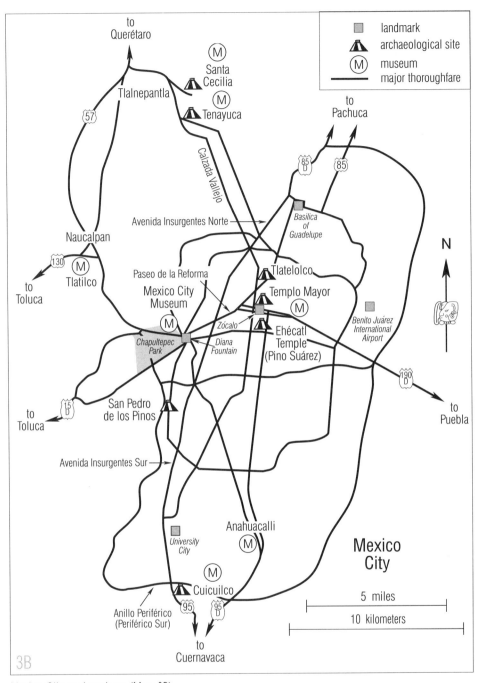

Mexico City and environs (Map 3B).

Recent History

Santa Cecilia was restored in 1961 (the same year the site museum was established) by María del Pilar and Eduardo Pareyón in a project sponsored by INAH.

Getting There

From the central part of Mexico City, take Calzada Vallejo heading northwest to Tenayuca and on to Santa Cecilia. If you are driving your own vehicle, you will probably have to ask directions several times, because the way is not marked. For this reason I recommend taking a taxi.

Santa Cecilia is open Tuesday through Sunday from 10:00 A.M. to 4:30 P.M. It is closed on Monday. There is no food or drink at the site, and no rest rooms. The entrance to the site is through the museum. Allow one hour for a visit.

A visit to Santa Cecilia can easily be combined with a visit to Tenayuca. The two make a pleasant half-day trip from Mexico City.

★ ★
SANTA CECILIA MUSEUM

The Santa Cecilia Museum occupies a late-nineteenth-century L-shaped building that surrounds two sides of a patio-garden. Two rooms of the building and the patio house the pre-Columbian collection, and three others represent a typical Mexican living room, dining room, and kitchen, all fully furnished.

On the outside wall of the museum are displayed some carved stone skulls. Inside, there are stone sculptures including a stand-ing figure and a headless *chacmool*. An elaborately decorated ceramic *incensario* is found nearby. The lush patio is adorned with more stone sculpture, including an attractive feathered serpent and a serpent head.

Some of the items displayed were excavated at Santa Cecilia, and others—which come from the collection of the Mexico City Museum—were found at various other locations.

Headless *chacmool* in the Santa Cecilia Museum. Late Postclassic period.

Lighting outside is, of course, excellent; inside it is fair to poor. Photography without flash is permitted. There is minimal labeling. There are no rest rooms, food, or drink.

The museum is open Tuesday through Sunday from 10:00 A.M. to 4:30 P.M. It is closed on Monday. Allow 15 minutes for a visit.

★ ★
TENAYUCA
(teh-nah-YOO-kah)

Derivation:
  Nahuatl for "Fortified Place."
Original Name:
  Tenayuca.
Culture:
  Chichimec (see text).
Location:
  State of Mexico, just north of Mexico City.
Map: 3B (p. 90)

The Site

Tenayuca is a very fine two-star site—perhaps two and a half stars would be a fairer rating.

The site includes a large double pyramid rising in four tiers, which has been partially restored, and a few small structures around it. The whole is enclosed by a low modern wall. You enter the site on the east side, at the back of the pyramid. From there, circle the base counterclockwise. Along the north side you will see one of the long rows of serpents for which Tenayuca is famous. They surround three sides of the base of the pyramid and have carved stone heads. The rather fat S-shaped bodies are made up of small stones and mortar and were originally plastered and painted. While hardly graceful, they are plentiful. In addition to those at the base, more serpent heads project from the slope of the pyramid.

The most interesting sculptures at the site, however, are two coiled serpents found at ground level on the north and south sides of the pyramid. As with the other serpents,

only the heads are carved, but these have a crested decoration on top identifying the sculptures as representing Xiuhcóatl, the fire serpent. They are accompanied by low platforms.

When you circle around to the front of the pyramid, you will want to climb the steps, some of which are made of carved stone blocks. At the top of the steps you get a good view of the inner stairway of an earlier structure. A wide-angle lens is good here.

To the right (south) of the outer stairway at ground level is a projecting platform with some interesting sculpture. There are bas-relief depictions of crossed bones and three-dimensional projecting skulls. Several tunnels were cut into the pyramid during excavation, and you can see a serpent's head on an earlier building inside one of them.

Historical tradition speaks of the founding of Tenayuca by Xolotl, a Chichimec lord, in A.D. 1224, although ceramics from a somewhat earlier period have been found there. Tenayuca was perhaps the principal center in the Valley of Mexico between the fall of Tula and the rise of Tenochtitlán, but it never reached the size of the latter, by which it was conquered. Tenayuca's double pyramid served as a model for the larger Templo Mayor at Tenochtitlán.

There were at least six major construction phases at Tenayuca and a couple more that produced minor alterations. The original double pyramid was covered over and enlarged on five occasions, probably beginning in A.D. 1299 and continuing at 52-year intervals until the last building was erected in 1507. Aztec influence becomes evident upon the third reconstruction, in 1351. The

The large double pyramid, Tenayuca. Late Postclassic period.

Row of serpents as seen from above, Tenayuca. Late Postclassic period. Photograph by author.

Coiled fire serpent (Xiuhcóatl), Tenayuca. Late Postclassic period.

following three stages were purely Aztec. This is made clear by the sloping, rather than vertical, walls on the tiers that make up the body of the pyramid. Nothing remains today of the temples that once topped the pyramid.

Vertical upper zones on the *alfardas* flanking the stairway belong to the two latest reconstructions and are visible on the inner stairway of the fifth stage.

Tenayuca was a living town at the time of the Spanish conquest, and fighting occurred there in 1520. The conquistador Bernal Díaz del Castillo appropriately referred to it as "Town of the Serpents."

Recent History

Tenayuca was apparently forgotten for many years. It was generally believed that the mound seen there was of natural origin. This was disproved during excavation by Mexican archaeologists starting in 1925. Among those working at the site were Alfonso Caso, Eduardo Noguera, Ignacio Marquina, and José Reygadas Vertiz. Later studies were undertaken by Jorge Acosta. A great deal of restoration has been done, and this is one of the best places to see typical Aztec architecture.

Getting There

From the central part of Mexico City, take Calzada Vallejo heading northwest to Tenayuca. If you are driving your own vehicle, you will probably have to ask directions several times, because the way is not marked. For this reason I recommend taking a taxi.

Tenayuca is open Tuesday through Sunday from 10:00 A.M. to 5:00 P.M. It is closed on Monday. Allow 1.5 hours for a visit. There are rest rooms at the site museum but no food or drink at the site. The entrance to the site is through the museum.

A visit to Tenayuca can easily be combined with a visit to Santa Cecilia. The two make a pleasant half-day trip from Mexico City.

★ ★
TENAYUCA XOLOTL
ARCHAEOLOGICAL MUSEUM
(TENAYUCA MUSEUM)

The Tenayuca Museum, inaugurated in December 1984, is a very good two-star enterprise and a fine site museum with a nice layout. The collection includes many stone carvings and ceramics. Some attractive illustrative paintings decorate the walls and also provide informative text. None of the items is individually labeled, but apparently all are from Tenayuca. A scale model of the double pyramid forms another display. Another painting depicts the way Tenayuca looked in its various stages. A large ceramic *incensario* shows an elaborately attired figure and bears some remnants of paint.

Some of the more interesting of the stone carvings are a headless *chacmool*, a bas-relief panel showing part of an eagle holding a serpent, a shield with darts behind it, standing human figures, and a serpent's head.

Lighting in the museum is fair, and photography without flash is permitted. There are rest rooms at the museum but no food or drink. The museum is open Tuesday through Sunday from 10:00 A.M. to 5:00 P.M. It is closed on Monday. Allow 30 minutes for a visit.

Carved serpent's head in the Tenayuca Museum. Late Postclassic period.

★ ★
MUSEUM OF TLATILCO CULTURE
(TLATILCO MUSEUM)

The Tlatilco museum just outside Mexico City exhibits items from the early site of the same name. The site itself is now covered by modern housing.

Tlatilco was first settled around 1200 B.C. on the west edge of a lake, later known as Lake Texcoco. The site was discovered only in 1936 while brick makers were digging for clay. Archaeologists uncovered 340 burials at Tlatilco, which are believed to be only a fraction of those that existed. The skeletons were all found in an extended position, and they were accompanied by sumptuous offerings of large hollow and small solid figurines and elaborate ceramic bowls and pots. Some of the female figurines carry children or dogs, and some of the figurines and pots show Olmec influence.

An unusual hollow head wearing a kind of skullcap, painted red and bearing a zigzag design, was recovered from the burials. The original is in the Mexico City Museum, but a copy is displayed in the Tlatilco Museum.

Much of the collection is made up of early figurines, but it also includes ceramic jars, bowls, and bottles; some of the bottles with stirrup spouts are particularly attractive. Other displays include obsidian lance heads and necklaces. There are photo displays of some of Tlatilco's burials and an exhibit of mammoth bones and tusks. Some of Tlatilco's burials are on display in the Mexico City Museum.

The Tlatilco Museum is in the Naucalpan section in the state of Mexico (northwest of the Federal District) in Colonia San Luis Tlatilco. It is located at Avenida Gustavo Boz 200, on the corner of Calle Oeste. It sits diagonally across the street from the Hotel Plaza Naucalpan.

Tlatelolco, showing pre-Columbian structures from the Late Postclassic period, a colonial church, and modern office and apartment buildings. Photograph by author.

There are no rest rooms, food, or drink at the museum. The skylight dome in the center of the museum admits good ambient light. Photography without flash is permitted. There is little labeling. The museum is open Monday through Friday from 9:00 A.M. to 6:00 P.M. and on Saturday and Sunday from 10:00 A.M. to 5:00 P.M. Allow 15 minutes for a visit.

★ ★

TLATELOLCO
(tlah-teh-LOHL-koh)
(PLAZA OF THE THREE CULTURES)

Derivation:
 Nahuatl for "Artificial Mound of Sand."
Original Name:
 Tlatelolco.
Culture:
 Aztec.
Location:
 North-central Mexico City.
Map: 3B (p. 90)

The Site

Tlatelolco, the rival sister-city of Tenochtitlán, the Aztec capital, is one of the places where you can see the three major periods of Mexico's long history at a glance: the pre-Hispanic temple bases, a colonial church (built in 1610) and convent, and modern office and apartment buildings. For this reason it is also called the Plaza of the Three Cultures.

There are raised walkways threading among the ancient buildings, and from them you get good views of the various temple bases and a burial containing two skeletons, covered with glass. Just follow the indicated path.

One of the largest structures is the double pyramid opposite the church. It is of typical Aztec design, having double *alfardas* with vertical upper zones. It now tilts at an odd angle, apparently due to settling of the soil.

Other pyramids and platforms, some circular, lie adjacent to the walkways. The most interesting is the Templo Calendárico, which has individual carved panels depicting dates. They form a frieze around the top of the lower tier of the temple on three sides and total 39 in all. Unfortunately, only the panels on one side are easy to see and photograph from the walkway. A telephoto lens is useful here for detail shots of the panels.

From two higher sections of the walkways you get good overall views of the site. Here you will want a wide-angle lens.

Note: Although there are no signs saying so, you are not allowed to leave the walkways and traverse the grassy areas. It is tempting to do so for a closer look at some of the structures, but guards will promptly ask you to return to the walkways.

Tlatelolco was probably founded in the fourteenth century—although there is some evidence for occupancy of the area a century or more before that—by a branch of the Aztecs, sometime before another branch founded Tenochtitlán in 1325. The two rival centers grew and prospered but remained independent until 1473, when Axayácatl, the lord of Tenochtitlán, conquered Tlatelolco. He then installed his own governors.

The city that the Spanish conquistadors entered in 1519 was actually the double metropolis of Tenochtitlán-Tlatelolco, which occupied an area of 20 square miles [51.8 square kilometers] and had a population estimated at 200,000.

Tlatelolco long held a reputation as a great mercantile center even before its subjugation by Axayácatl. It still had the largest market in Mexico at the time of the Spanish conquest. The Spaniards were amazed at its size, variety of merchandise, and orderliness. Bernal Díaz del Castillo wrote a lengthy description of it in his *The Discovery and Conquest of New Spain.* He ended by saying that "one would not have been able to see and inquire about it all in two days." It is estimated that between 20,000 and 25,000 people attended the daily market at Tlatelolco and that twice that many assembled for the special market held every fifth day.

This was also the site of the last battle of the Spanish conquest in central Mexico. It took place on August 13, 1521, when Tlatelolco fell to Hernán Cortés. A marble plaque near the church records the date and further informs viewers that "it was neither triumph nor defeat, but the painful birth of the Mestizo people that is the Mexico of today."

Recent History

Although numerous artifacts were uncovered at Tlatelolco many years ago, and ceramic reports were published during the 1940s and 1950s, it was only with the inauguration of a large urban renewal project in the 1960s that the site was restored to its present condition. The archaeological project was directed by Ricardo de Robina and Mario Pani. More recently, additional work has been carried out by INAH.

Getting There

Tlatelolco is on the corner of Avenida Lázaro Cárdenas and Calle Ricardo Flores Magón, a few blocks north of the Zócalo in Mexico City. Because finding a parking place nearby is difficult, I recommend taking a taxi there.

Tlatelolco is open Tuesday through Sunday from 9:00 A.M. to 6:00 P.M. It is closed on Monday. Allow one hour for a visit. Afternoon hours are the best for photography, since the main structure faces west. There are no rest rooms, food, or drink at the site.

★ ★ ★
TEMPLO MAYOR
(TEHM-ploh mah-YOHR)
(TENOCHTITLÁN)
(teh-nohch-tee-TLAN)

Derivation:
　　Templo Mayor is Spanish for "Great Temple." Tenochtitlán is Nahuatl for "Place of the Fruit of the Cactus."

Culture:
　　Aztec (also Mexica and Tenocha).

Location:
　　Central Mexico City.

Maps:　3B (p. 90)

The Site

Tenochtitlán, the capital city of the ancient Aztecs, founded in A.D. 1325 (or 1345, according to some sources), underlies modern Mexico City. The Templo Mayor, actually a twin temple facing west, was the most important structure in the Aztec city. The temple on the south (the right, as you face it) was dedicated to Huitzilopochtli, the god of war, and that on the left, to Tlaloc, god of rain. The double temple rose perhaps 200 feet (61 meters) in its final form and was approached by a dual stairway. It had reached this size by the time of the Spanish conquest in 1519; below it lay six earlier stages, many of which can be seen when you tour the site. You can get an overall

Composite serpent with a carved head, Templo Mayor. Late Postclassic period.

view of the front of the structure from Calle Argentina at any time, but some of the sculptures are covered when the site is closed.

The entrance to the site is at the southwest corner of the temple, and from there you follow the modern walkways around the site. You come first to the remains of walls of different stages, some with projecting serpent heads. Then you see a complete serpent with a carved stone head and an undulating body made of small stones that were plastered and painted. Nearby are more carved serpent heads. Next is a copy of a circular bas-relief carving of Coyolxauhqui, the moon goddess. The original, in the site museum, measures 10.7 feet (3.25 meters) in diameter. Coyolxauhqui was the sister of Huitzilopochtli; he killed and dismembered her when she and his 400 brothers plotted to kill their mother, Coatlicue, for having become pregnant with Huitzilopochtli when she placed a ball of feathers under her garment.

You now walk east toward the Stage II remains of the Temple of Huitzilopochtli, passing the stairs of later stages of the temple. Leaning against the Stage III stairs are stone statues, exact replicas of those found here when this area was excavated; they may represent some of Huitzilopochtli's brothers. The originals are believed to date to A.D. 1431. Nearby you will see a brick drain, part of an early-twentieth-century sewer line.

Soon the walkway turns north and passes the front of the Stage II Temple of Huitzilopochtli, where a sacrificial stone can be seen. Still farther along you pass the Temple of Tlaloc with a polychromed *chacmool* dated to Stage II (A.D. 1390). Some remnants of painted decoration are found on the walls at the entrance to the temple.

North of the Templo Mayor lies a patio with three shrines. The walkway turns west near the center shrine, a *tzompantli* with more than 240 stuccoed stone skulls on the

Replicas of four (of the original eight) satues found during excavation, Templo Mayor. Late Postclassic period.

walls of three sides of the platform. On the remaining west side is a stairway.

The walkway jogs around a couple of times more and comes to the House of the Eagle Warriors. Remains of carved and painted benches depicting richly attired warriors are its prominent features. Follow the walkway south to the North Red Temple, with a circular altar on the east side and circular stone rings in its walls. The temple retains some painted decoration. From there, the walkway leads to the site museum.

Recent History

Spaniards razed the Templo Mayor in 1521, during the conquest, and some of its stones were used in postconquest structures. Mexico City gradually grew above the ruins of Tenochtitlán.

In 1790, the statue of Coatlicue and the Sun Stone (Aztec Calendar Stone) were discovered, and the Tizoc Stone the following year. All these monuments are in the Mexico City Museum. When the sewer built in 1900 cut through all layers of the Templo Mayor, Leopoldo Batres discovered part of the stairway of the platform of the last stage of the temple's construction, not realizing that it was part of the Templo Mayor. In 1901, more stairs, a large serpent head, and a sculpture of a jaguar were uncovered near the Templo Mayor. Most of these finds were accidental.

In 1913 and 1914, Manuel Gamio excavated the southwest corner of the Templo Mayor and found serpent heads belonging to the Huitzilopochtli stairway. For the first time, apparently, this was recognized as part of the Templo Mayor. Opposite this corner, in 1933, the architect Emilio Cuevas found part of a

Stairways from two of the construction phases, Templo Mayor. Late Postclassic period.

ramp from the last stage of construction. Additional excavations were conducted in 1948 by Hugo Moedano and Elma Estrada and in 1964 by Eduardo Matos Moctezuma. Reinforcement work in and around the cathedral in 1975 turned up remains of other buildings. A couple of years later, plans were developing to excavate the Templo Mayor, and early documentation about it was carefully studied.

In February 1978, electric company workers digging at the corner of Calles Argentina and Guatemala discovered the monumental carving of Coyolxauhqui and reported it to authorities. This find spurred the Templo Mayor Project, by far the most extensive excavation in the area. It began a month after the discovery of the carving and continued through November 1982 under the direction of Matos Moctezuma. The impressive results are what visitors see today.

Many offerings were deposited in various stages of the Templo Mayor. The more important pieces are displayed in the site museum, and some are described in that section that follows.

A number of date glyphs were also found, which helped in dating the various stages of construction.

Getting There

The Templo Mayor is located at the corner of Calles Argentina and Guatemala, diagonally across from the rear of the Metropolitan Cathedral. It can be reached by taxi (recommended), by bus, or by the Metro (exit at the Zócalo station about a block away).

The site is open Tuesday through Sunday from 9:00 A.M. to 5:00 P.M. It is closed on Monday. Photography without flash is permitted. There is an extra charge to bring a camera into the site. Guided tours are available at the entrance. Allow 45 minutes for a visit. Rest rooms are found in the site museum, and restaurants are nearby.

★ ★ ★
TEMPLO MAYOR MUSEUM

The Templo Mayor Museum, inaugurated in 1987, was specially constructed to house the items uncovered during the Templo Mayor Project. In the entrance hall of the museum there is a scale model of the ceremonial center of Tenochtitlán and a *tzompantli.* Most of the stucco-covered stone skulls were found on the south side of the Templo Mayor, and it was decided to exhibit them this way. Beyond the entrance hall are several rooms on different levels devoted to various topics. One wing of the museum is devoted to Huitzilopochtli and the other to Tlaloc, reflecting the orientation of the Templo Mayor.

Some of the outstanding displays are a headless *chacmool,* a huge stone eagle found under a house a block away, a skull with shell incrustations and flint knives in the nose and mouth, and a clay figure of an Aztec warrior. Many other interesting items are found in the collection.

Since Tenochtitlán received tribute from all over Mesoamerica, it is not surprising that foreign articles were found in addition to those of local manufacture. Included are an Olmec mask dating to 800 B.C., obviously an heirloom, a Teotihuacán mask, an alabaster mask and a delicate alabaster duck head from Puebla, small stone statuettes from the Mixtec area and gold items from the same region, a stone mask from the Mezcala area, figurines from Guerrero, and numerous other pieces from Teotihuacán. The prize of the collection is the now well-known large stone carving of Coyolxauhqui discovered in 1978. It is in nearly pristine condition.

Signs posted give information about the history of the Aztecs, and labeling is generally fair. Lighting in the museum is rather poor in many areas. Photography without flash is permitted.

The museum is open Tuesday through Sunday from 9:00 A.M. to 5:00 P.M. Allow 45 minutes for a visit. There are rest rooms in the museum, and food and drink can be found nearby.

★
EHÉCATL TEMPLE
(eh-HEH-kahtl)
(PINO SUÁREZ)

Derivation:
  Nahuatl name for the wind god.
Culture:
  Aztec.
Location:
  Central Mexico City.
Map: 3B (p. 90)

The Site

The charming small shrine at the Pino Suárez Metro (subway) station was dedicated to Ehécatl; it was discovered in 1967. The structure was found remarkably well preserved and was restored.

The nucleus of the structure was made of earth and stones, which were held in place by stone slabs that were then stuccoed. The circular upper body of the temple rests on a circular platform. Stairs on the east side are bordered

The Ehécatl Temple at the Pino Suárez Metro station. Late Postclassic period.

by *alfardas* with vertical upper zones. The upper body of the structure is divided into three zones; the upper and lower are plain, but the middle zone is formed of upper and lower rectangular moldings bordering a central section decorated with circular volcanic stones.

During excavation, a statue of Ehécatl-Ozomatli was uncovered under the front steps of the structure. It is in the form of a monkey wearing the bird-beak mask of Ehécatl.

At the time the temple was constructed it would have been at the south end of the island that supported Tenochtitlán. The construction took place in the Late Postclassic period, shortly before the arrival of the Spaniards. The temple was part of a ceremonial center now called Pino Suárez.

Recent History

In 1966, work on the Metro began near the Zócalo, and during its construction many significant Aztec remains were uncovered, not the least of which was the Ehécatl Temple.

Getting There

The Ehécatl Temple is located at the junction of Calles Pino Suárez and Izazaga. It is somewhat below present-day street level, but the area above it was left open so it can be viewed from above—as well as head on, if you take the stairs down into the Metro station. The temple can be reached by street (taxi or bus), and of course on the Metro. Since it is in the heart of downtown Mexico City, going there in your own vehicle is not recommended; parking nearby will be difficult at best. The temple can be seen at any time from street level. Allow 15 minutes for a visit. There are restaurants nearby.

Above All Ratings
THE NATIONAL MUSEUM OF ANTHROPOLOGY (MEXICO CITY MUSEUM)

The Mexico City Museum is probably the finest of its type in the world, and it so far surpasses any other museum in this guide that I decided it would be unfair to apply the rating system to it. If this museum got four stars, then the excellent regional museums throughout Mexico would have to receive lower ratings, which would not give a fair idea of their worth.

The Mexico City Museum is indeed in a class by itself. Even the visitor who does not particularly care for museums or is not especially interested in ancient or modern cultures cannot fail to be impressed by this one. For the enthusiast, it is like a visit to heaven. The only problem is that there is so much to see that you are torn between lingering over each exhibit and hurrying on to the next fascinating section.

For the most casual tourist, a good half day is needed for a visit. The enthusiast could spend months here. I suggest a once-over-lightly (a full day with a lunch break) on your first visit to get an idea of the layout, then several return trips to absorb properly what is presented. This way you can pay special attention to the sections that interest you most.

There are several guidebooks for the museum in English, ranging widely in price. They are available at the museum bookstore, as are other publications in Spanish, English, French, German, and Japanese. If you prefer a personal guided tour, check at the desk where you buy your ticket. Tours in various languages begin frequently.

Wheelchairs are provided for those who need them, and the gentle slope of the ramps was designed with this in mind. Elevators are also available.

Before entering the museum, you will want to stop for a look at the 200-ton sculpture near the entrance. It is popularly called Tlaloc, the rain god, but most authorities believe it is

more likely Chalchiuhtlicue, his female counterpart, the water goddess. Earlier, the sculpture was thought to date to Aztec times; now it is believed to date to the period of Teotihuacán.

Esther Pasztory, in her 1997 book *Teotihuacan,* called the figure simply the Goddess and believed she was possibly the major deity at Teotihuacán, at least from A.D. 200 to 750. Though the sculpture is unfinished, Pasztory further wrote that it represented the same deity as the one on the colossal statue found near the Pyramid of the Sun at Teotihuacán (and now on display inside the Mexico City Museum) and on a similar fragment.

The statue was carved near the village of Coatlinchán, about 17 miles (27 kilometers) east of the center of Mexico City, where its sculptors left it attached to bedrock. It is assumed that they lacked the engineering skills to remove and transport it. In 1964, the same year the museum was inaugurated, it was cut loose and moved to its present location on special flatbed trucks.

The main entrance to the museum is at ground level. That level houses the archaeological exhibits in rooms surrounding a patio. It also contains an area for temporary exhibits, an auditorium, a bookstore, and a checkroom. Pedro Ramírez Vásquez was the principal architect for the complex building.

The patio itself is outstanding. A 40-foot-high column designed by the Mexican artist José Chávez Morado supports a cantilevered, umbrella-like roof that protects part of the patio. The column is sheathed in sculptured copper with depictions of pre-Columbian motifs. Around the column is a shower of water—a sort of raining fountain. The roof covers an area of 70,000 square feet (6,500 square meters); it is the largest of its type in the world and weighs 2,000 tons (1.8 million kilograms). Part of the patio is occupied by a reed-garnished reflecting pool

Stucco mask panel from Placeres, Campeche. Early Classic period. Displayed in the Mexico City Museum.

whose focal point is a huge stylized conch shell symbolizing the wind.

The second floor is occupied by the ethnographical section and the library. A basement level houses a restaurant that can be reached by stairways from the left side of the patio (as you enter the museum).

The dais of the orientation theater is located at the entrance to the museum on the first level, but you go down some stairs to the theater proper. There is a small charge for the 20-minute film (in Spanish), which presents the history of humankind in Mesoamerica in chronological order beginning with the arrival of people in the Valley of Mexico thousands of years ago.

The museum was designed with a particular visiting sequence in mind for best and most rapid comprehension. When you enter, you go to the right, and from there you circulate counterclockwise through the other rooms. The rooms have direct access from the patio as well as connections to each other.

To begin your tour of the ethnographical section, return to the first room, take the stairway up, and again circulate in a counterclockwise direction.

Since it would take a huge volume to describe the multitude of exhibits in the museum, I give only a few of the highlights here. The museum is so well laid out that if you follow the path indicated, you will miss nothing and will do little or no backtracking. Some of the rooms have adjacent outdoor exhibits, and two rooms have basement sections. Make sure to see them all.

Some of the highlights of the museum's collection are a few of the actual burials from Tlatilco with offerings included, the enormous statue of Chalchiuhtlicue found near the Pyramid of the Moon at Teotihuacán, a funerary mask of stone covered with a mosaic of turquoise and red shell from the same site, a stucco mask panel from Placeres, Campeche, and three stelae, in pristine condition, from Xochicalco. That site is also represented by a ball court marker depicting a stylized macaw head.

The Mexica or Aztec section contains some powerful stone carvings, most of which are large; some of the best are the statue of Coatlicue, the Sun Stone (or Aztec Calendar Stone), and the Stone of Tizoc with scenes from the life of Tizoc carved along its edge. One of the gems in the Oaxaca section is the jade mask of the bat god from Monte Albán. The Huastec "Adolescent" with tattooed body is a justly famous piece of stone sculpture.

Veracruz is represented by a nice collection of carved *hachas, palmas,* and yokes and

Stela from Xochicalco. Classic period. Displayed in the Mexico City Museum.

the bottom fragment of the important Stela C from Tres Zapotes. Colossal Head 2 from San Lorenzo and a jade figurine from Cerro de las Mesas also come from Veracruz and represent Olmec culture. Some white and green jade figurines, found as a group, come from La Venta and are also Olmec.

The Maya section is very strong, with numerous lintels and stelae from Yaxchilán, some in mint condition. Some Calakmul stelae form other displays. Western Mexico is represented by typical hollow ceramic figures of people and dogs, and the Tarascan region, by geometric stone coyotes and a *chacmool* from Ihuatzio.

All the exhibits are well labeled in Spanish and, in some rooms, in English as well. The lighting is good and in some cases quite dramatic. Photography without flash is permitted; there is a small extra charge to bring a camera into the museum. Fast film is recommended and tripods are prohibited.

The museum, on the east side of Chapultepec Park and to the west of downtown Mexico City, can be easily reached by private car, taxi, bus, or Metro (subway) from anywhere in Mexico City.

The museum is open Tuesday through Saturday from 9:00 A.M. to 7:00 P.M. and on Sunday from 10:00 A.M. to 4:00 P.M. It is closed on Monday.

Rest rooms are conveniently situated in various locations on all levels.

★
SAN PEDRO DE LOS PINOS
(sahn PEH-droh deh lohs PEE-nohs)

Derivation:
  Spanish for "Saint Peter of the Pines."
Culture:
  Aztec.
Location:
  Central Mexico City.
Map: 3B (p. 90)

The Site

San Pedro de los Pinos covers an area approximately 328 feet (100 meters) on each side and reaches a maximum height of 23 feet (7 meters), though building remains are found on different levels. No special sequence for visiting is recommended, as it is easy to get around and to see from one area to another. The lower remains of walls have been restored, and these define passageways

Low walls, pillars, and platforms at San Pedro de los Pinos. Late Postclassic period.

and chambers. Sunken patios, the remains of stucco floors, and rectangular pillars can be seen from paved pathways and clipped lawns. An especially interesting part is a high interior wall with large stones at the corner.

The architecture is made of adobe, stone, *tepetate*—a fine-grained earth of volcanic origin—and stucco. It is believed that the site was dedicated to the god Mixcóatl, and offerings to this deity have been found there. San Pedro de los Pinos is an Aztec site with typical Aztec architecture and ceramics.

Recent History

San Pedro de los Pinos was built shortly before the Spanish conquest as a suburb of Tenochtitlán. It was greatly destroyed during the conquest, after which it became simply an overgrown mound. The mound was thought to be a natural elevation until 1915, when Señor Fernández del Castillo discovered that it was an artificial construction. In 1920, exploration and study of the site were undertaken by Eduardo Noguera, who reported his findings in 1945.

Getting There

San Pedro de los Pinos is adjacent to the east side of the Periférico Sur—in fact, part of the site is under an elevated section of the *periférico*. The entrance to the site is on Calle Pirámide (a street that runs only two blocks between Calle 20 and Calle 24). The site is about 1.7 miles [2.7 kilometers] south of the south edge of Chapultepec Park as the *zopilote* flies.

Taking a taxi is the recommended way to reach the site, and it would be best to ask the driver to wait for you. You might want to have the location written down to instruct the driver. This is not a usual destination and not all drivers are familiar with it.

Note that the schedule here is unusual for a site in Mexico. It is open Monday through Friday from 9:00 A.M. to 3:00 P.M. It is closed on Saturday and Sunday. Allow 15 minutes for a visit. There are no rest rooms, food, or drink at the site.

★ ★ ★ ★
ANAHUACALLI MUSEUM

This one is a real sleeper, and it was a big surprise for me: I did not expect to find a new four-star museum in Mexico. Although it was inaugurated in Mexico City on September 18, 1964, I only saw it 32 years later, and during that time I never talked to anyone who *had* seen it. Although I had been aware of its existence for some time, I did not realize from what I had read how extensive the collection was. I actually visited it as an afterthought.

The structure that houses the collection is remarkable. Designed by Diego Rivera to house his extensive pre-Columbian art collection, it is made of dark lava rock in a severely geometric style with incorporated pre-Columbian motifs. On the inside, the ceilings are done in lava rock mosaics with pre-Columbian themes, and the narrow windows on the first floor are made of Mexican onyx. That, unfortunately, makes for reduced light levels. The other two floors are somewhat better illuminated. Labeling in the museum is rather minimal.

The first floor contains a huge selection of Preclassic figurines, some Olmec-style ceramic vessels, some stone figures from later periods, and stone heads and skulls high up on shelves. In another area there are more stone carvings from various places, as well as bas-reliefs. Greenstone carvings, Teotihuacán-style stuccoed and painted pots, Teotihuacán stone masks, numerous small dancing figures, and an Olmec jade figurine form other displays. Stone statues of Huehuetéotl outnumber those exhibited at the Mexico City Museum.

On the second floor, west-coast ceramic figures are prevalent, but some greenstone Mezcala carvings are also exhibited. Also on this floor are some of Rivera's drawings for murals and some smaller drawings.

Aztec stone carvings, skulls, and serpent heads are displayed on the third floor, as are a Totonac yoke and *palmas* from Veracruz. Also from that area are ceramics and stone figurines and heads. Zapotec culture is represented mostly by ceramic figurines, and items from the Mixtec culture are also included.

The Anahuacalli Museum is located in the southern part of Mexico City in the Coyacán section on Calle de Museo 150. It is open Tuesday through Sunday from 10:00 A.M. to 6:00 P.M. It is closed on Monday. Allow one hour for a visit.

Photography is not allowed inside the museum, but you may photograph the structure from the outside. A nearby building houses a bookstore and rest rooms. No food or drink is available.

★ ★
CUICUILCO
(kwee-KWEEL-koh)

Derivation:
Nahuatl for "Place of Singing and Dancing."
Culture:
See text.
Location:
Southern part of Mexico City.
Map: 3B (p. 90)

The Site

The "pyramid" of Cuicuilco is actually a stepped, truncated cone approached by ramps on the east and west sides. It is of interest to visitors primarily because of its massiveness and age, rather than for any strong aesthetic appeal.

The structure is 472 feet (144 meters) in diameter at its base, and it rises to 66 feet (20 meters). Encased in the visible pyramid are two earlier constructions of a similar circular plan. The core of the structure is composed of compressed earth surrounded by large stones, and later additions were of mud and rocks. Both lava blocks and river boulders were used as the final facing for the pyramid and its ramps.

Cuicuilco's heyday dates to the late Middle Preclassic and Late Preclassic periods, and it has the earliest monumental and ceremonial architecture found in the Valley of Mexico. This fact alone makes a visit worthwhile.

When you leave the parking area, head east toward the pyramid. A recommended tour would be to take the trail to the north and walk around the base of the pyramid. After you return to the west side, climb the ramp to the top. When you follow the trail to the north you get good overall views of the pyramid and its main western ramp. From a distance the pyramid seems unusually squat, but its impressive dimensions become more apparent as you approach. You are actually walking on top of a lava flow that covered the base of the structure. As you circle the base, you can clearly see the four terraces that make up the pyramid.

Halfway around the base you come to the eastern ramp, which is not as well preserved as its western counterpart. When you reach the south side of the pyramid you can most easily appreciate the depth of the

The "pyramid," Cuicuilco, showing the main western ramp. Late Preclassic period

---

lava (25 to 30 feet [7.6 to 9.1 meters]) that covers the base; it has been cut back from the pyramid, leaving a sort of trench.

When you get back to the west side of the pyramid you will see a small construction protected by a modern roof. It is composed of large slabs driven deeply into the ground and tilted inward. On the inner surface of the slabs are remains of red paint applied in spiral-like designs.

Head now to the western ramp and climb it to the top of the pyramid, where you will see a horseshoe-shaped altar covered by river boulders. Beneath this latest altar are two earlier ones that were covered over when the pyramid was enlarged.

The area around Cuicuilco was occupied by simple farmers perhaps as early as 900 B.C., a time when other villages appeared around the lake in the Valley of Mexico. Its monumental constructions, however, date from 600 to 200 B.C., when Cuicuilco was the major center in the valley.

During the following period (200 B.C. to A.D. 300), various outside influences were felt in the valley, and Cuicuilco's importance diminished. By A.D. 150 the emerging Teotihuacán had eclipsed Cuicuilco. At this time the site was abandoned, or at least the structures were no longer maintained and enlarged. The stone veneer became weakened by rains, allowing the sides to slump.

The death knell rang around A.D. 300 or 400 with the eruption of Xictli, a nearby volcano. Its lava flow covered the base of Cuicuilco's pyramid and formed what is known today as the Pedregal, a volcanic desert on the southern extremity of Mexico City. This same eruption also engulfed the earlier site of Copilco—a Preclassic cemetery 2 miles (3.2 kilometers) north of Cuicuilco. Unfortunately, Copilco is no longer open to visitors.

The principal deity at Cuicuilco was Xiutecuhtli (or Huehuetéotl), the old fire god. Depictions of him in clay were found during excavations at the site. He is represented as an old man seated with a bowed head; upon his head and shoulders he supports a brazier for burning incense. He was thought to control volcanoes and was worshiped continuously into Aztec times; it is their name for him that is used today.

Although Cuicuilco's pyramid is circular, there is no particular evidence that it was dedicated to Quetzalcóatl, as were later circular structures in Mesoamerica.

Recent History

In 1922, Byron Cummings, of the University of Arizona, and Manuel Gamio, director of anthropology for the Mexican government, visited a hill in the Pedregal. They felt that there were indications that the hill might not be natural and decided to excavate. What they uncovered was the Preclassic pyramid. Work was carried out under the direction of Cummings as a cooperative venture between the Mexican government and the University of Arizona, and later with the aid of the National Geographic Society, during the years 1922–25. In 1955 further investigation was undertaken by the University of California, and in the 1990s additional work was conducted by INAH.

Getting There

From central Mexico City, head south on Avenida Insurgentes Sur (Highway 95) to the south part of the city until you cross the Anillo Periférico (Peripheral Ring), where there is a major cloverleaf interchange. Continue south on Insurgentes Sur a bit farther and look to the left for an industrial chimney labeled "Inbursa" (a defunct paper company). Make a U-turn just past the chimney, return north on Insurgentes Sur a short distance, and turn right onto the entrance road for Cuicuilco. Soon you will see the parking area for the site. From there follow the foot trail to the pyramid.

Cuicuilco is open daily from 9:00 A.M. to 5:00 P.M. Allow one hour for a visit. The most interesting side of the pyramid is the west, so an afternoon visit is best for photography. No food or drink is available. There are rest rooms at the museum.

The site can also be reached by taxi from anywhere in Mexico City, and this is the recommended way to get there. You might ask the driver to wait for you.

★
CUICUILCO MUSEUM

The Cuicuilco Museum is nicely laid out. The original museum, below ground under part of the lava that covered the site, was inaugurated in 1949. Later the above-ground museum was built.

Although the collection is not extensive, photo displays, charts, and ceramics are exhibited. A nice selection of early figurines forms one of the more impressive displays.

Lighting in the museum is rather poor, and labeling is sparse. Photography without flash is permitted. There are rest rooms at the museum, but no food or drink is available.

The museum is open daily from 9:00 A.M. to 5:00 P.M. Allow 10 minutes for a visit.

TULA
(TOO-lah)

Derivation:
  Nahuatl for "Place of Reeds." It also implies "Metropolis" or "Capital City."
Original Name:
  Tollán or Tulan (variants of Tula).
Culture:
  Toltec.
Location:
  South-central Hidalgo.
Maps: 3 (p. 72) and 3C (p. 112)

The Site

You enter Tula from the north, on a path that leaves from the service building that houses the museum. As you enter the site, you come first to Ball Court 1. This large I-shaped court is sunk below ground level. Several stairs give access to the playing alley. The sides of the playing area are flanked by platforms joining vertical walls, which originally supported rings.

One carved panel was found in situ when the ball court was excavated. It depicts the lower part of a ball player and is found just around the corner from the central playing section, on the southwest, at ground level.

South of Ball Court 1 lies the Coatepantli, or Serpent Wall, and the Pyramid of Tlahuizcalpantecuhtli. The freestanding Serpent Wall originally extended along the entire north side of the pyramid, but it was thrown down when Tula was destroyed. Fortunately, some parts fell in such a way that they could be accurately restored. The wall is composed of five sections with identical carvings on either side. On top are openwork, stylized, connecting shells; below is a solid bas-relief in three parts; and below this is a plain section reaching to ground level.

The center section of the bas-relief is the most interesting, complex, and, frankly, gory. It depicts a human skull in the open mouth of a serpent, which presumably devoured the human. Bones are intertwined with the undulating body of the serpent. The sections above and below feature carved meanders. There are some remains of paint on the three central sections, and each section is separated from the others by a simple molding. The wall reaches more than 7 feet (2.1 meters) to the top of the bas-relief section. The open-work shells on top—found on only one part of the wall today—added perhaps another 2 feet (0.6 meter) to the height.

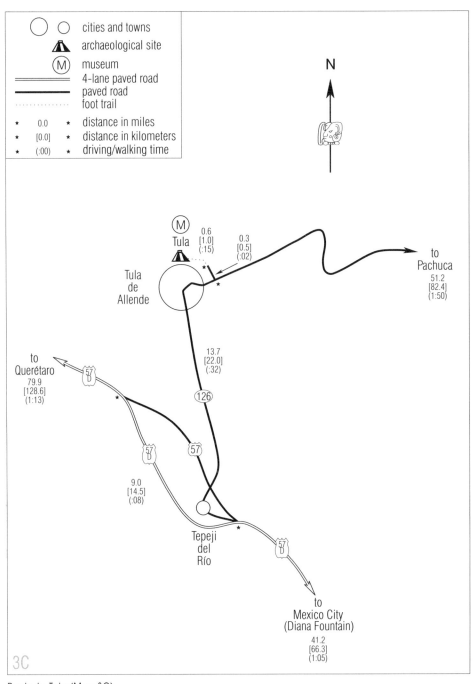

Legend:

○ ○ cities and towns
🔺 archaeological site
Ⓜ museum
═══ 4-lane paved road
▬▬ paved road
·········· foot trail
★ 0.0 ★ distance in miles
★ [0.0] ★ distance in kilometers
★ (:00) ★ driving/walking time

N

Ⓜ
Tula 🔺
Tula
de
Allende

0.6
[1.0]
(:15)

0.3
[0.5]
(:02)

to
Pachuca
51.2
[82.4]
(1:50)

13.7
[22.0]
(:32)

126

to
Querétaro
79.9
[128.6]
(1:13)

57
D

57
D

57

9.0
[14.5]
(:08)

Tepeji
del
Río

57
D

to
Mexico City
(Diana Fountain)
41.2
[66.3]
(1:05)

3C

Route to Tula (Map 3C).

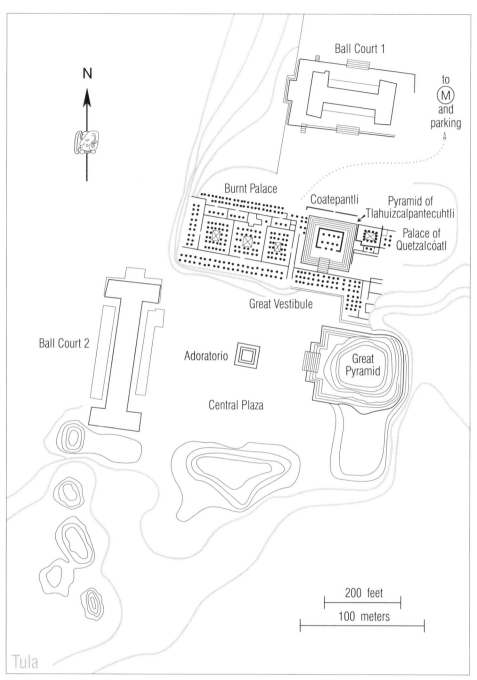

N

Ball Court 1

to (M) and parking

Burnt Palace

Coatepantli

Pyramid of Tlahuizcalpantecuhtli

Palace of Quetzalcóatl

Great Vestibule

Ball Court 2

Adoratorio

Great Pyramid

Central Plaza

200 feet

100 meters

Tula

Modified after Heyden and Gendrop, 1975.

Bas-relief carving of an eagle eating a human heart, on the Pyramid of Tlahuizcalpantecuhtli, Tula. Early Postclassic period.

The wall measures more than 130 feet (39.6 meters) long and is separated from the rear face of the pyramid by a sort of alley, 15 or 20 feet (4.6 or 6.1 meters) wide.

To the east of the Serpent Wall is the Palace of Quetzalcóatl, a complex of several structures erected against the east side of the Pyramid of Tlahuizcalpantecuhtli. This addition, fortunately, preserved the bas-relief panels on this side of the pyramid. They depict, at the top, a procession of jaguars in a row. On the row below it is a series of eagles in profile, eating bleeding hearts; this motif is occasionally interrupted by a frontal depiction of Tlahuizcalpantecuhtli, portrayed as a human emerging from the mouth of an animal.

The Pyramid of Tlahuizcalpantecuhtli and the sculptures that surmount it form the most interesting part of the site. The Great Atlantean statues for which Tula is famous are found on top, along with the remains of serpent columns and carved pillars. All originally supported the roof of the temple. Three of the Atlantes are original; the fourth is a copy, replacing one that was moved to the Mexico City Museum.

The Atlantes are truly some of the masterpieces of Toltec sculpture. The statues are each nearly 15 feet (4.6 meters) tall and were carved in four sections that were then tenoned together. Some remnants of paint still adhere to their surfaces. The Atlantes depict Toltec warriors who represent Quetzalcóatl in his manifestation as the planet Venus as the morning star. In this guise, the deity is called Tlahuizcalpantecuhtli; hence the name of the pyramid. It is sometimes called—more prosaically—Building B or the Pyramid of Quetzalcóatl.

The warrior figures are shown in full regalia, with elaborate headdresses, butterfly-shaped breastplates, ornamented aprons,

Atlantean figures and carved pillars atop the Pyramid of Tlahuizcalpantecuhtli, Tula. Early Postclassic period. Photograph by author.

and decorative sandals. Each holds an atlatl in his right hand and darts in his left. The eyes and mouths may originally have had inlays. At the waist in the rear are large discs, each with a human face in the center; below are bare behinds.

The pyramid on which the statues stand rises in four tiers that originally were covered with panels of bas-reliefs. Some of these remain on the north side, in addition to those on the east side.

In the twelfth century, when Tula was destroyed, a great trench was dug into the north face of the Pyramid of Tlahuizcalpantecuhtli, and the Atlantes, serpent columns, and pillars were thrown in. When the pyramid was excavated, the statues and other carvings were discovered in and around it. They were eventually reassembled and placed on top of the pyramid in what were assumed to be their original positions.

The Burnt Palace lies west of the Pyramid of Tlahuizcalpantecuhtli. This palace is a complex of structures mainly made up of three rooms in an east-west line. All are worth a look, but the most interesting is the central room. In it are two remnants of polychromed bas-relief sculptured benches, both protected by modern roofs. The best preserved is the one in the northeast corner. It shows a procession of richly attired individuals in the lower section; above them is a cornice depicting an undulating serpent. Much of the original color remains.

A *chacmool* (my absolute favorite) was found in the same room in front of an altar on the east side. The original has been moved

Front (west side) of the Great Pyramid (Building C), Tula. Early Postclassic period.

to the Tula Museum, and a copy has been placed at the site. The copy is a good one and very photogenic. Despite its name, it is not believed that the Burnt Palace was residential; it was likely used for administration and gatherings.

Throughout the chambers of the Burnt Palace and the Great Vestibule (which fronts the Burnt Palace and the Pyramid of Tlahuizcalpantecuhtli) are numerous pillars that originally supported beam, pole, and mortar roofs. The pillars are all restorations; the originals were dismantled in ancient times, though impressions of their placement remained.

The Burnt Palace, the Pyramid of Tlahuizcalpantecuhtli, and the Great Vestibule border the north side of the Central Plaza, and the Great Pyramid (Building C) borders the east side. On the way there, in a section of the Great Vestibule, you pass another polychromed bas-relief bench showing a procession of figures. These are similar to those in the Burnt Palace, and likewise are sheltered by a roof.

The Great Pyramid is the largest structure at Tula. It was found in a ruinous state but was similar in design to the restored Pyramid of Tlahuizcalpantecuhtli. Much of the stone facing of the Great Pyramid was removed in pre-Columbian times, and the lower part of its stairway and the lower tiers on the west side, facing the plaza, were all that could be restored.

You can climb the Great Pyramid by a foot trail on the north side. From the top you can get good overall and telephoto shots of the Pyramid of Tlahuizcalpantecuhtli.

Now descend the Great Pyramid by its western stairway and head across the Central Plaza. On the way, stop for a look at the small platform (adoratorio) in the center of the plaza. This was perhaps an altar; it had stairs on all four sides. Continue west to Ball Court 2, which bounds the plaza on the west side. Like Ball Court 1, Ball Court 2 is I-shaped.

The area around Tula was first occupied in the Middle Preclassic period. From roughly 800 to 600 B.C., small agricultural settlements developed in places near rivers and arroyos. Ceramics during this period were decorated with iconographic elements characteristic of Olmec culture. For the Late Preclassic period, evidence of social stratification has been detected, and ceramics show connections with the Basin of Mexico, Guanajuato, and Michoacán.

In the early centuries A.D., Tula and other parts of the area were controlled by Teotihuacán, and the sites around Tula show similarities to Teotihuacán in architecture—including habitations, ceremonial structures, and administrative complexes—and in ceramics, shell, and other materials. This domination continued until the fall of Teotihuacán in the seventh century.

From A.D. 700 to 800, the area called Tula Chico, 0.9 mile (1.5 kilometers) northeast of the Central Plaza, developed rapidly. It was a religious, political, and administrative center, and it was partly destroyed, sacked, and abandoned around 900.

The major structures around the Central Plaza, in the part of the site that visitors see, were built between A.D. 900 and 1100. Tula reached its apogee during that time and had an estimated population of around 60,000; it covered an area of 5.8 square miles (15 square kilometers). At this time Tula was the largest city in central Mexico. Tula collapsed in the late twelfth century, and there is evidence that it was burned in a great fire.

Recent History

The first modern report on Tula was that of Antonio García Cubas, a Mexican who presented his findings to the Mexican Society of Geography and Statistics in 1873. The French traveler Désiré Charnay visited the site, carried out limited excavations, and published his results in 1885.

For many years scholars sought to determine the location of the legendary Tollán or Tula, a question made more complex by the existence of many Tulas in Mexico. Some thought the ancient Toltec capital was Teotihuacán, an idea that has resurfaced recently.

The Mexican historian Wigberto Jiménez Moreno diligently studied the old sources and came to the conclusion that Tollán was the Tula in the state of Hidalgo. Excavations were carried out beginning in 1940, primarily by Jorge Acosta. This work, plus information presented at a round-table conference of the Mexican Society of Anthropology in 1941, corroborated Jiménez Moreno's conclusion.

Archaeological work by INAH at Tula continued off and on during the 1950s and 1960s and has run almost continuously from the 1970s to the present.

Connections

1. Mexico City to Tula: 55.2 miles [88.8 kilometers] by paved road (1:39).

2. Querétaro to Tula: 102.9 miles [165.6 kilometers] by paved road (1:56).

Getting There

1. From Mexico City, take Highway 57D north to a cutoff for Tepeji del Río, 41.2 miles [66.3 kilometers], and turn right. Go through Tepeji and pick up Highway 126 to Tula. As you enter the town, the road curves around to the east. Just keep going until you come to a copy of an Atlantean figure (on your left) in the median of a double boulevard. Turn left onto the boulevard and go 0.8 mile [1.3 kilometers], then turn left to the entrance to the site. Go on to the parking lot in front of the service building.

2. From Querétaro, take Highway 57D east and then southeast to the cutoff for Tepeji, 89.9 miles [143.1 kilometers]. When you go this way you will see a couple of signs for cutoffs for Tula before the one mentioned here. This cutoff is recommended, because you stay on the toll road longer and have fewer miles of two-lane highway to drive. Turn left at the Tepeji del Río junction, then follow the directions already given.

Tula is open daily from 9:30 A.M. to 4:30 P.M. Allow three hours for a visit. The service building that houses the museum also has a restaurant, rest rooms, and a shop.

Buses go to the town of Tula.

If you want to stay in the town of Tula, try the rather nice Hotel Sharon, across the boulevard from the copy of the Atlantean figure where you turn to get to the site entrance. The hotel has a restaurant.

★ ★ ★
JORGE ACOSTA MUSEUM
(TULA MUSEUM)

This very nice site museum is named for Jorge Acosta, the Mexican archaeologist who did extensive work at Tula beginning in 1940. The museum was inaugurated on November 16, 1982, and is an improvement over the old museum.

The displays include a *chacmool,* the legs and feet of two large Atlantean figures, a smaller whole Atlantean figure, and bas-relief carved panels. A stela depicting a warrior in frontal view, with the face of Tlaloc in his feathered headdress, is carved in bas-relief.

Jewelry and ceramics are displayed in cases, and a chronological chart shows the various time periods at the site. Plans and photographs of the structures form other displays. A large ceramic *incensario* with a depiction of Tlaloc is especially fine.

Lighting in the museum is fair, and photography without flash is permitted. Video cameras are not allowed. All the items in the collection come from the site, and labeling is very general. There are rest rooms and a restaurant in the complex that houses the museum.

The museum is open daily from 9:30 A.M. to 4:30 P.M. Allow 30 minutes for a visit.

Stela from Tula depicting a warrior. Early Postclassic period. On display in the Tula Museum.

★ ★
HUAPACALCO
(wah-pah-KAHL-koh)

Derivation:
From the Nahuatl "Huapacalli," meaning "House of Beams."
Culture:
Toltec (see text).
Location:
Southeastern Hidalgo.
Maps: 3 (p. 72) and 3D (p. 120)

The Site

Huapacalco, set in front of sheer cliffs, enjoys a picturesque location. Because the main structure faces west and the cliffs form the background, afternoon hours are the best for photography.

Visitors approach from the west through the caretaker's yard and get a front view of the main pyramid as they walk to the site. The lower tier of the stepped pyramid has been restored and exhibits *talud-tablero* architecture; the upper tiers have been partly consolidated. When you approach the structure you will pass a free-standing stone in front. At one time a circular altar was in place in front of that. The front (west) side of the pyramid has a stairway in the middle, bordered by *alfardas*.

Some fragments of plaster floors can be seen near the pyramid and elsewhere around the site. Other architectural remains include a stairway near the rear (south side) of the pyramid that leads to a higher level. To the north of the pyramid, next to the first level, is a low rectangular enclosure and what appears to be a sunken patio, also with stairs.

When you leave the site and follow the trail back you will see an unrestored earthen mound that was also part of the site.

Huapacalco, situated as it was on a major "Teotihuacán corridor," shows influence from various regions. The ceramics found at the site (and nearby) are related to those at Teotihuacán, Monte Albán, and El Tajín. Some of Huapacalco's structures resemble those at Teotihuacán, and articulated figurines and ceramic heads in Teotihuacán style

The main structure at Huapacalco. Classic period.

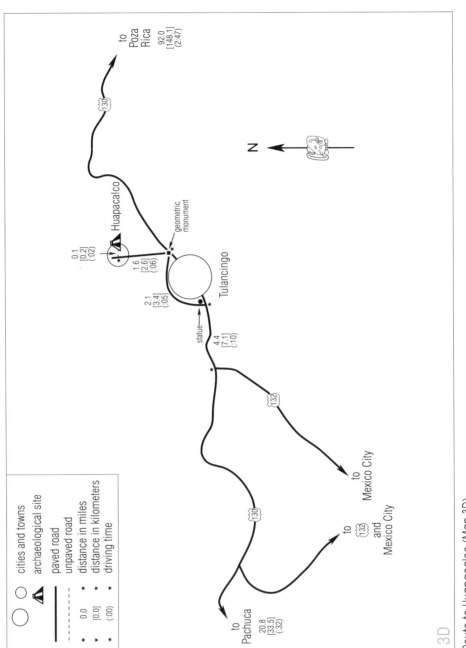

3D

Route to Huapacalco (Map 3D).

have been found there. A beautiful carved greenstone yoke and a fragment of another found at the site reflect the Totonac culture of Veracruz. In later periods, ceramics were similar to those at Tula and the Gulf Coast, and to Aztec styles.

Recent History

In the 1950s, César Lizardi Ramos and Florencia Müller excavated at Huapacalco, and later in the decade both issued reports of their findings.

Connection

Tulancingo to Huapacalco: 3.7 miles [6.0 kilometers] by paved road (:11), then 0.1 mile [0.2 kilometer] by dirt road (:02).

Getting There

From the statue at the west end of Tulancingo, take the bypass that goes around the north side of the city to the geometric monument at the east end, where the bypass rejoins Highway 130, 2.1 miles [3.4 kilometers]. Turn left at the monument and go 1.6 miles [2.6 kilometers] to the turnoff (on the right). I recommend you check the distance on your odometer, because there is no sign or other indication that this is the access and that you are in the town of Huapacalco. From there you can drive up the hill on the dirt road for 0.1 mile [0.2 kilometer] to the parking area for the site and walk in from there.

There seems to be no set schedule for when the site is officially open, but probably it would be during reasonable daylight hours. Allow 20 minutes for a visit. There are no rest rooms, food, or drink at the site. If you are without your own vehicle, you can easily taxi from Tulancingo to the site, although drivers may have to get directions from their dispatchers. Have the driver wait while you visit the site.

★ ★ ★ ★
TEOTIHUACÁN
(teh-oh-tee-wah-KAHN)

Derivation:
    Nahuatl for "Place of Deification" or "Place of the Gods."
Culture:
    Teotihuacán (see text).
Location:
    Northeast state of Mexico.
Maps: 3 (p. 72) and 3E (p. 122)

The Site

Teotihuacán is one of the largest, most visited, and easily accessible sites in Mexico. Even the most casual visitors generally see the pyramids. A great deal of excavation and restoration has taken place since the 1960s, and a cobblestone loop road encircles the site. Parking lots are strategically placed, which makes getting around a simple matter if you have a car. You can do it on foot, but it will take more time.

There are several possible itineraries. The following one is an efficient way to spend your time.

When you enter the archaeological zone, take the loop road heading north to Puerta 3. Puerta means "door" in Spanish, but in this case it refers to a parking lot. Puerta 3 is near the Pyramid of the Moon. See the pyramid, its plaza, and the adjacent structures. Proceed on foot to the Palace of the Quetzal Butterfly, the entrance to which is found at the southwest corner of the Plaza of the Moon. Then head south on the Avenue of the Dead to the

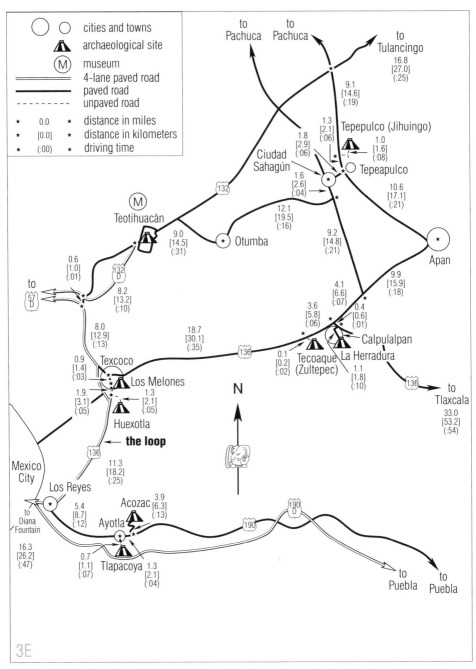

Area east of Mexico City (Map 3E).

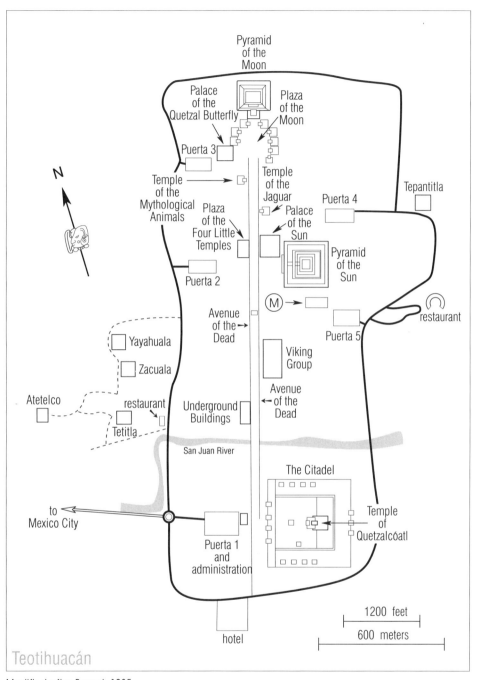

Pyramid
of the
Moon

Palace
of the
Quetzal Butterfly

Plaza
of the
Moon

Puerta 3

N

Temple
of the
Mythological
Animals

Temple
of the
Jaguar

Tepantitla

Puerta 4

Plaza
of the
Four Little
Temples

Palace
of the
Sun

Puerta 2

Pyramid
of the
Sun

(M)

restaurant

Avenue
of the
Dead

Puerta 5

Yayahuala

Viking
Group

Zacuala

Atetelco

restaurant

Avenue
of the
Dead

Tetitla

Underground
Buildings

San Juan River

The Citadel

to
Mexico City

Temple
of
Quetzalcóatl

Puerta 1
and
administration

1200 feet

600 meters

hotel

Teotihuacán

Modified after Bernal, 1985.

Temple of the Mythological Animals, which lies to the right (west) of the avenue. Continue south to the Temple of the Jaguar, on the left (east) side of the avenue. Again head south along the avenue to the Plaza of the Four Little Temples on the right (west), and then farther south to the Plaza of the Pyramid of the Sun and to the pyramid itself to the left (east) of the avenue. While you are in this area, it is convenient to visit the nearby site museum.

Then walk back to your car and follow the road east and south (clockwise) to Puerta 4. Walk east to Tepantitla and return to your car.

It is now time for a lunch break, and you have several choices. La Gruta Restaurant, housed in a cave, is off the east side of the loop road (the junction is marked with a sign). There is a restaurant in the Villas Arqueológicas Hotel on the south side of the south part of the loop road. And Las Pirámides Restaurant is on the west side of the west part of the loop, just after you cross the bridge over the San Juan River. Soft drinks and food are available at some of the parking lots, as are rest rooms.

After lunch, proceed to Puerta 1. Then walk across the Avenue of the Dead and see the Citadel and the Temple of Quetzalcóatl. Walk north along the avenue to the Underground Buildings on the left (west), then farther north to the Viking Group on the right (east) side of the avenue, and return to your car.

If you have some energy left, you might want to see some of the outlying groups. If so, head north on the loop road until you cross the bridge over the San Juan River. Shortly after this, a dirt cutoff joins the paved road on the left (west). The junction isn't marked, but a landmark is Las Pirámides Restaurant. Take this and then another marked cutoff to the right (north). This takes you to Tetitla, and later at a left fork, to Atetelco. After you visit Atetelco, return to the fork and go left. This will take you by Zacuala and Yayahuala; then the road continues back to the loop. From there, go right (south) to the main entrance of the site when you are ready to leave.

The main ceremonial structures at Teotihuacán lie along the Avenue of the Dead,

which runs in a north-south line for about 1.3 miles [2.1 kilometers]. If you are doing the whole tour on foot, begin at one end of the Avenue of the Dead and proceed to the other end. This will take you past everything covered here except Tepantitla and the four outlying groups.

Teotihuacán was occupied from around 150 B.C. and experienced fantastic growth. By the years from A.D. 1 to 150, it had an estimated population of 30,000. It was during this time that the Pyramids of the Sun and Moon were constructed. Certainly this was an outstanding achievement for any period, but especially so for such an early time. The early builders are unknown; they are referred to simply as Teotihuacanos. By 150, Cuicuilco, the earlier dominant center of the Valley of Mexico, had been eclipsed by the young giant, Teotihuacán. The city's growth continued until it reached a population peak of around 85,000 (some say as many as 200,000) sometime during between 450 and 600, making it the sixth largest city in the contemporaneous world. It covered an area of around 13 square miles (33.7 square kilometers).

During this time and even a bit earlier, Teotihuacán exerted a great deal of influence throughout Mesoamerica. Maya sites showing this influence in sculpture, ceramics, worked stone, or architecture are Becan in Campeche, Tikal in the Petén of Guatemala, Kaminaljuyú in the Guatemala highlands, Altun Ha in Belize, and Copán in Honduras—although the exact nature of a Teotihuacán presence in these areas is still being debated. Closer to home, Teotihuacán influenced the centers of Cholula, Monte Albán, and El Tajín.

After A.D. 650, the population declined somewhat, and the city was destroyed perhaps around 750. Who was responsible for the destruction is unknown, although several theories have been proposed. After this the bulk of the population departed; only some 2,000 to 5,000 people remained. Teotihuacán was never entirely unoccupied, nor was it completely forgotten.

The Aztecs revered it as a holy city and also believed it was a burial place. It is their names for the site and some of the structures that are used today. The great Moctezuma is said to have made pilgrimages there.

Interior courtyard of the Palace of the Quetzal Butterfly, with carved and obsidian-inlaid piers, Teotihuacán. Note merlon decorations on the roof. Late Preclassic or Early Classic period.

Let us begin our own pilgrimage at the Pyramid of the Moon. This structure and its plaza form the northern extremity of the Avenue of the Dead. Restoration in the 1960s converted the grass-covered mound that I first saw in 1957 into an intriguing architectural complex. The base of the pyramid rises in four sloped tiers, though only the lower three have been restored. A projection of three tiers lies on the southern side, and this is fronted by a five-tiered pyramidal platform of *talud-tablero* design. A stairway in three sections (the fourth, or top, one has not been restored) gives access to the southern side. It is a steep climb, but you should try to get at least as high as the top of the first platform. From there you get a comprehensive view of the Plaza of the Moon and of adjacent structures in the same style as the tiered platform abutting the front of the Pyramid of the Moon.

The remains of the lower portion of a structure containing 10 altars, and beyond it a low platform with stairways on all four sides, are found in the central area of the Plaza of the Moon. To the south of the platform is a crude and eroded piece of three-dimensional sculpture. It has been proposed that the plaza was used for ceremonial activities.

Go now to the Palace of the Quetzal Butterfly, a magnificent structure discovered in 1962 when this section of Teotihuacán was being extensively excavated. Access is up a broad stair to a columned hall. At the top of the stair on the right is a huge serpent head with some remnants of paint. Remains of

The Pyramid of the Sun (end of the Late Preclassic period), at left of center, as seen from the Pyramid of the Moon, Teotihuacán. The Plaza of the Moon and its surrounding structures are seen in the foreground. The Avenue of the Dead is at right center.

mural painting are found in the hall. A doorway at the northwest corner of the hall leads to an open courtyard surrounded by bas-relief carved pillars. The bas-reliefs depict mythological creatures and water symbols, and some obsidian discs are still in place on the pillars. The carvings were originally polychromed. Painted decorations in an inset panel rest above the pillars, and the whole is topped by merlons in the design of the Teotihuacán yearsign. More mural paintings are found on the lower walls of the structure.

Two other areas of interest are part of this structural complex. Return to the hall where you entered and head through the doorway at the southwest corner. A narrow stairway and alley lead to a series of rooms around a courtyard. This is the Jaguar's Palace, so named for painted jaguars found on the lower walls. On one side of the courtyard is a stairway with remains of carved

snake rattles at the bottoms of the *alfardas*. Another group of rooms—with more murals—surrounding a large courtyard connects to the first group. Access is from a passage in the northwest corner of the first group.

The other area of interest in this complex is the substructure of the Feathered Shells. This building was constructed between A.D. 100 and 200 and was later filled in to form a platform that supported the Palace of the Quetzal Butterfly. Access is by a modern tunnel in the northwest corner of the large courtyard. Polychromed bas-reliefs of feathered shells give the structure its name. They are accompanied by four-petaled flowers. Murals are also found on the platform that supports the temple.

Proceed now to the Temple of the Mythological Animals. The murals that give the temple its name are part of an older building, and access is by a modern door in the back

The Pyramid of the Sun, Teotihuacán, viewed from the west. End of the Late Preclassic period.

of the structure. This structure may not be open to the public.

Continue to the Temple of the Jaguar. An interesting mural painting of a jaguar can be seen behind a modern protective fence, sheltered by a roof, but you can take pictures of it over the fence from an adjacent stairway.

We now go to the major monument at the site, the Pyramid of the Sun. To reach it, you pass through the plaza that fronts it and some palace-type structures.

The Pyramid of the Sun is not only the largest structure at Teotihuacán, but it also has the most interesting history—and mythology. The Aztecs gave it its name; we do not know what it was called by the Teotihuacanos who built it. Some early native sources say that the pyramids were built by giants; others say they were erected by the gods before humans existed. The Pyramid of the Sun, including the original temple that topped it, is 243 feet (74.1 meters) high, and its square base measures 740 feet (225.6 meters) on each side.

The Pyramid of the Sun was the first major structure to be excavated at Teotihuacán, and in 1905 methods were still primitive. The work was carried out by the Mexican archaeologist Leopoldo Batres, who—the story goes—having done his homework, expected to find earlier pyramids beneath the existing one. He peeled off the badly ruined outer surfaces of three faces and found to his dismay (at least I assume he was dismayed) that there were no earlier structures beneath it. By this time tons of stone had been removed.

Rocks were used to re-cover the pyramid, but large projecting stones that originally were used to anchor stone slabs and the stucco finish may still be seen. They were once part of the core of the pyramid and were never meant to be visible.

For this reason, the Pyramid of the Sun as seen today is not what it looked like originally; the reconstruction presents "various defects." Batres was criticized for his methods by fellow Mexican archaeologists.

It is true that deep inside the core of the pyramid there is a very small earlier platform that was built atop a natural grotto, but the enormous mass that we see today was built in one great effort. Its interior was mostly adobe, the same material used for construction of the Great Pyramid of Cholula. A projecting platform at the west side of the base of the pyramid was added somewhat later.

A stairway in several sections gives access to the top of the pyramid. Whether or not to climb it I leave up to you, but as always,

Temple of Quetzalcóatl, south portion of the main (west) face, Teotihuacán. End of the Late Preclassic period.

the higher you go, the better the view of the other structures.

Tepantitla is not part of the ceremonial center of Teotihuacán but one of the site's suburban residential areas. A house there has been restored, but the reason for a visit is to see the remains of mural paintings that adorn the walls.

Motifs include depictions of Tlaloc (the rain god), and many small figures are shown singing, dancing, catching butterflies, and cutting flowers. These cheerful people are cavorting in "Tlalocan," Tlaloc's earthly paradise, a place of fertility and abundance. This is probably one of the "happiest" murals in pre-Hispanic art.

After you take a lunch break, drive to Puerta 1 at the south end of the Avenue of the Dead and walk across it to reach the Citadel. This is a large quadrangular complex bordered on all four sides by a broad raised area that supports pyramidal bases. The raised area encloses a lower courtyard. A stairway gives access on the western side to the top of the raised area, and another descends to the courtyard below.

In the center of the courtyard is a small rectangular platform, and behind this is a four-tiered structure that was built to cover the front of an earlier tiered structure. The earlier structure is the Temple of Quetzalcóatl, and it is the gem of this complex. (Although the structure has had this name for a long time, a better name is the Temple of the Feathered Serpent. It is used by archaeologists working at the site, since there is nothing to indicate a connection with Quetzalcóatl, who was a deity of a later culture. Nevertheless, I have used the old name because it will be more familiar to readers.)

The rear of the structure abutting the Temple of Quetzalcóatl has been cut away from the front of the latter, forming a passage through which you can walk. The face of the Temple of Quetzalcóatl is covered with magnificent sculptures—both three-dimensional and bas-relief—found on four tiers (it is assumed that there were six or seven tiers

Detail of sculptural decoration on the west face of the Temple of Quetzalcóatl, Teotihuacán. It possibly represents Tlaloc, a corn god, or another deity. End of the Late Preclassic period.

originally). Huge projecting serpent heads with feathered collars alternate with stylized geometrical sculptures that may represent Tlaloc or a corn deity. In between, in bas-relief, are undulating serpent bodies with rattles on their tails. The remaining space is filled with seashells—all Caribbean varieties—and the whole was originally painted. Some paint remains, but the inlays of obsidian that decorated the eyes of the sculptures are little in evidence today. A stairway divides the facade, and more serpent heads are found on the flanking *alfardas*.

The whole is truly spectacular, but it must have been even more so when it was first built. Evidence indicates that originally all four sides of the structure were covered with such sculptures. Those on the north, east, and south faces were removed when the

new tiered structure was added at the front. Some remnants of extra sculptured decorations lie on the ground north of the passageway. On the north side of the newer addition are remains of painted stucco.

Leave the Citadel and walk north on the Avenue of the Dead to reach the Underground Buildings. This complex was excavated in 1917 and was restored and reconstructed in such a way that you can see some earlier buildings beneath the later structures that covered them. Modern beams support the upper buildings, and a metal stairway gives access to the earlier ones below. Some remains of painted decorations are still visible.

The next area to visit is the Viking Group, named for the foundation that provided the funds for its exploration. An unusual feature was discovered here—the use of two layers

Patio with a miniature temple used as an altar, Atetelco, Teotihuacán. Classic period.

of sheet mica to cover the floor of one of the rooms. They were found below a floor of ground lava rock, a more commonly used material.

The remaining four groups are mostly residential. The most interesting are Tetitla and Atetelco, where remains of mural paintings are found. At Atetelco some interesting architecture can be observed, including a patio with a central altar in the form of a miniature tiered platform in *talud-tablero* style, with a small temple on top.

Recent History

Teotihuacán's large pyramids had been well covered with vegetation for centuries by the time of the Spanish conquest. Nevertheless, their existence was known, and they were mentioned in several early chronicles.

The first organized excavations were undertaken by Carlos de Sigüenza y Góngora, a literary figure, around 1675 and concentrated on the Pyramid of the Moon, into which he opened a tunnel. Little is known of this work. Sculpture from the site was described as early as 1687.

In 1760, Ypólito Guerrero, an Indian who claimed Moctezuma as an ancestor, was the owner of the pyramids, and he was given permission to excavate. The results of this work have not come to light.

Ramón Almaraz, a geologist, mapped the zone of Teotihuacán in 1864 and undertook some limited excavations. His report appeared a year later. He also said that most of the "dilapidation which is noted" was caused by people who were excavating the mounds in the hope of finding treasure. Looting is obviously not just a recent problem.

In 1885, Désiré Charnay reported on his excavations at Teotihuacán and a host of other sites. He hired 35 workers, who dug trenches, and he discovered burials containing figurines, masks, obsidian knives, and other artifacts.

Shortly afterward, Leopoldo Batres began excavating around the Pyramid of the Sun. This was some years before he began his assault on the pyramid itself.

Various others, scholars and visitors, commented on Teotihuacán. Some large-scale excavations were undertaken by Manuel Gamio in 1917. Work on a smaller scale by Eduardo Noguera, Pedro Armillas, Sigvald Linné, Laurette Séjourne, Jorge Acosta, and many others followed through the 1950s.

In 1962, more large-scale excavations were begun with the "Teotihuacán Project," under the direction of Ignacio Bernal for INAH. These continued for two years. During this massive effort the Pyramid of the Moon, its plaza, and adjacent structures were restored. One of the most interesting discoveries was the Palace of the Quetzal Butterfly, which likewise was restored. William T. Sanders, of Pennsylvania State University, conducted an intensive study of the ecology and rural settlement patterns of the valley, and René Millon began a detailed mapping project. The Cultural Unit, which once housed the site museum, was also built during the Teotihuacán Project, as was the loop road that encircles the site.

In the early 1970s, Jorge Acosta discovered the grotto under the Pyramid of the Sun. Other studies were conducted in the 1980s, and INAH's Teotihuacán Archaeological Project was still under way in the 1990s.

Connections

1. Mexico City (Diana Fountain) to Teotihuacán (via Los Reyes): 46.2 miles [74.3 kilometers] by paved road (1:54).

2. Mexico City (Diana Fountain) to Teotihuacán (via Highway 85D): see "Getting There."

Getting There

1. From Mexico City, head east and exit the city on Calzada Ignacio Zaragosa. Continue to the junction with Highway 190D, but do not join it; go on to Los Reyes. There you pick up Highway 136 and head north toward Texcoco. Take the bypass to the west of Texcoco and continue to a junction with a two-lane road (you go straight as the four-lane road curves to the left). After 0.6 mile [1.0 kilometer] this connects with Highway 132D. Turn right on this highway and proceed to the entrance gate for Teotihuacán.

2. A shorter route, going out Avenida Insurgentes Norte (Highway 85D), *may* be somewhat faster—if you don't get lost or caught in snarled traffic. This route goes through heavily congested parts of Mexico City. If you choose this connection, stay on 85D until the interchange with Highway 132D and take it (heading east) to the entry gate at Teotihuacán. I have not done this in recent years, so I cannot give the exact driving time; it would be about 14 or 15 miles [22.5 or 24.1 kilometers] shorter.

The site can be reached by bus (they leave frequently), taxi, or conducted tour from Mexico City. Teotihuacán is open daily from 8:00 A.M. to 5:00 P.M. The enthusiast should really allow at least a full day to see the site properly—a day and a half would be better. Now that a hotel is operating, staying there the night before you visit Teotihuacán gives you an early start.

If you are carrying a plan of the site, then a guide is unnecessary; however, if you prefer having one, you can bring one along from Mexico City or hire one at the site.

There is an extra charge to bring a car into the archaeological zone. The parking lots inside are free, but you may wish to tip the attendants who help you park.

From October to June a light-and-sound pageant is presented in the evening (except on Monday) at 7:00 P.M. in English and at 8:15 P.M. in Spanish. The performance lasts 45 minutes.

★ ★ ★
TEOTIHUACÁN MUSEUM

The Teotihuacán Museum, inaugurated in 1994, is the third museum to be built at the site. It is located just south of the Pyramid of the Sun, just about where the first museum was situated. The second museum was in a building on the opposite side of the Avenue of the Dead from the Citadel, near the south end of the ceremonial center in a building now used for administration.

Several topics are covered by the museum displays: flora, fauna, and resources, early stages of Teotihuacán, social and economic organization, technologies, and religion. There are informative general signs in Spanish and English, but the individual items are not labeled.

Some of the outstanding displays are numerous bas-relief and three-dimensional stone carvings, stone masks, fragments of mural paintings, beautiful cylindrical tripod pots with stuccoed and painted surfaces, articulated and solid figurines, and exhibits of obsidian and bone working. The space in one large room is completely taken up by an enormous scale model of the site—the largest model of a site that I have ever seen. A walkway crosses the room a few feet above the model, and from it you can see the various parts of the model in detail.

In one area, a sculpture of Huehuetéotl is eerily lighted from below, and in another, sculptures of Quetzalcóatl and Tlaloc from the Temple of Quetzalcóatl can be viewed close up.

The last room of the museum is devoted to Teotihuacán's relations with other areas. In it, materials from Puebla, the Gulf Coast, Oaxaca, and the Maya area are displayed.

The exhibits are attractively lighted although not always sufficiently. Photography without flash is permitted. In grassy areas outside the museum, some stone carvings are exhibited.

The museum is open daily from 8:00 A.M. to 5:00 P.M. Allow 30 minutes for a visit. There are no rest rooms, food, or drink at the museum, but these are available in nearby areas.

Stone mask in typical Teotihuacán style, Teotihuacán. Classic period. On display in the Teotihuacán Museum.

★ ★
TEPEPULCO
(teh-peh-POOL-koh)
(TEPEAPULCO)
(teh-peh-ah-POOL-koh)

Derivation:
 Nahuatl for "Place of a Very
 Large Town."
Other Name:
 Jihuingo.
Culture:
 Primarily Teotihuacán, also
 Toltec and Aztec.
Location:
 Southwestern Hidalgo.
Maps: 3 (p. 72) and 3E (p. 122)

The Site

The principal structure at Tepepulco, called the Pyramid of the Tecolote (Owl), is a three-tiered building with a stairway, bordered by *alfardas,* on the northwest side. The tiered section is in typical Teotihuacán *talud-tablero* style. Abutting it at the rear is a simple, single sloped tier. Remains of plaster can still be found on some of the surfaces of both parts, and plaster flooring is found in the plaza that the pyramid faces. Platforms on four sides surround the plaza, and a wide causeway extends away to the northwest in line with the pyramid.

In addition to the architecture, numerous pecked cross petroglyphs, related to those at Teotihuacán, have been found in the hills nearby.

A study of projectile points and ceramics indicates that the site was occupied from around 100 B.C. to A.D. 150, during which time the culture was that of Teotihuacán.

Except for two short interruptions, one in the Late Preclassic and another in the Early Postclassic, Tepepulco was occupied until the time of the Spanish conquest. During part of its history there was a Toltec settlement in what is now the town of Tepeapulco, 0.8 mile [1.3 kilometers] south of the archaeological site.

Ceramic evidence shows that in the Late Postclassic period, the area around the Tecolote pyramid was reoccupied, but this did not substantially affect the pyramid itself. New structures, probably habitational, were built near the pyramid during this time. The pyramidal base may have been used to support an Aztec-period temple that no longer exists. The settlement during this late period seems to have been marginal.

Recent History

Tepepulco is mentioned in early Spanish documents from shortly after the conquest. The second version of the name, Tepeapulco, is that found on modern maps and in some of the literature. Wigberto Jiménez Moreno, however, stated that Tepepulco was the correct version, and for this reason I have used Tepepulco as the name of the archaeological site and Tepeapulco as the name of the nearby town. The name Jihuingo is that of a nearby extinct volcano.

Although the site was known and had received some study earlier, the first archaeological field season there was undertaken in 1980 under the direction of Eduardo Matos Moctezuma, who, with others, published a report the following year. In 1984 a report on the *talud-tablero* architecture at the site was issued by Victor Rivera Grijalba.

Connections

1. Tulancingo to Tepepulco: 25.9 miles [41.7 kilometers] by paved road (:44), then 1.0 mile [1.6 kilometers] by dirt and rock road (:08).

Teotihuacán-style stepped pyramid, Tepepulco. Early Classic period.

2. Teotihuacán to Tepepulco: 25.8 miles [41.6 kilometers] by paved road (1:03), then 1.0 mile [1.6 kilometers] by dirt and rock road (:08).

Getting There

1. From Tulancingo, head west on Highway 130 for 4.4 miles [7.1 kilometers] to the junction with Highway 132 (on the left). Then head southwest on Highway 132 for 12.4 miles [20.0 kilometers] to the cutoff for Tepepulco (town) and turn left. Go 9.1 miles [14.6 kilometers] to the dirt cutoff for Tepepulco (marked with a sign saying Jihuingo) and turn left. After 0.6 mile [1.0 kilometer] you come to a junction where you must turn left or right. Take the branch to the left and follow it to the parking area for Tepepulco. This last part is rough rock, but you can make it in a standard vehicle if you drive very slowly and don't mind hitting bottom occasionally. Obviously, a high-clearance vehicle would be better.

2. From Teotihuacán, head northeast on Highway 132 until the junction for Otumba and turn right. Go to and through Otumba. Continue another 12.1 miles [19.5 kilometers] to a junction for Ciudad Sahagún and turn left. Go 1.6 miles [2.6 kilometers] to Ciudad Sahagún and turn right. Continue 1.8 miles [2.9 kilometers] to another road near the town of Tepeapulco and turn left. From there it is 1.3 miles [2.1 kilometers] to the dirt road marked for Jihuingo. Turn right and follow the directions already given.

A guardian is at the site, and generally when that is the case there are set hours to visit, but I was unable to learn what the schedule was. Allow 20 minutes for a visit. Tepepulco is a popular place on Sunday, when Mexican families come to have a picnic and play soccer. There are no rest rooms, food, or drink at the site.

Buses probably pass the junction with the dirt road, but if you do not have your own vehicle it would be better to try for a taxi in Tepeapulco. If you do, ask the taxi driver to wait for you while you visit.

★ ★
TECOAQUE
(teh-KWAH-keh)

Derivation:
 Nahuatl for "Place of the Stone
 Serpent."
Culture:
 Texcocan.
Other Name:
 Zultepec.
Location:
 Western Tlaxcala.
Maps: 3 (p. 72) and 3E (p. 122)

The Site

The Late Postclassic site of Tecoaque was
built in a frontier area between the Aztec
empire and the independent state of Tlaxcala. It was an outpost subject to Texcoco.

The most interesting building at the site
is a circular stepped structure with an eastern stairway, apparently dedicated to Ehécatl.
Parts of the three tiers and the stairway have
been restored. In front of this are the remains
of the lower walls and columns of another
building. All of this rests on a great platform.

A short but wide stairway leads down to a
plaza that contains an altar. Residential units
are found nearby, generally around sunken
patios. They are believed to have housed the
priests.

Recent History

Excavation and consolidation undertaken at
Tecoaque in 1992 greatly changed the look of
the site from earlier times. In May 1994,
during additional excavation, 14 human skulls
were discovered on the east side of the platform that supports the circular building, at the
stairway that descends to the plaza. All the
skulls had large holes cut into the temples, and
it is believed that a rod was inserted through
the holes in order to display the skulls in a
form of *tzompantli.* Twelve of the skulls
lacked mandibles. Studies determined that the
two skulls with mandibles belonged to an indigenous group, and the other twelve belonged
to Spaniards. In addition to the skulls, ceramic
specimens, fragments of horse bones, and
parts of a sword and lance were uncovered.

The discovery of the skulls was reported
in 1993 by Enrique Martínez Vargas, an

Circular structure dedicated to Ehécatl, Tecoaque. Late Postclassic period.

archaeologist and investigator for the Tlaxcala Regional Center of INAH. He and Ana María Jarquin, also of INAH, conducted the work at Tecoaque. Martínez Vargas reported Tecoaque under the name Zultepec.

Connections

1. Tlaxcala to Tecoaque: 44.2 miles [71.1 kilometers] by paved road (1:12), then 0.1 mile [0.2 kilometer] by dirt road (:02).

2. Mexico City to Tecoaque (via Los Reyes): 49.1 miles [79.0 kilometers] by paved road (1:55), then 0.1 mile [0.2 kilometer] by dirt road (:02).

Getting There

1. From Tlaxcala, take Highway 117 northeast to the junction with Highway 136, 7.2 miles [11.6 kilometers]. Turn left onto Highway 136 and go 33.4 miles [53.8 kilometers] to Calpulalpan (at the junction with the highway to Pachuca). Continue on Highway 136 for another 3.6 miles [5.8 kilometers] to the cutoff for the dirt road to Tecoaque and turn left. If you look carefully, you can see the circular structure from the highway.

2. From Mexico City, take Highway 190 east to Los Reyes; do not get on Highway 190D, the toll road to Puebla. In Los Reyes, turn left onto Highway 136 and continue to Texcoco, where Highway 136 turns to the right. From this turn it is 18.7 miles [30.1 kilometers] to the dirt cutoff for Tecoaque (on the right).

I am not sure of the hours, but I believe the site is open, because it is closed to visitors when excavations are in progress, as had been the case at the time of our previous visit. Allow 45 minutes to see Tecoaque. There are no rest rooms, food, or drink at the site.

Buses pass the site and could probably drop you off, but it might be difficult to get a return bus.

★
LA HERRADURA
(lah ehr-rah-DOO-rah)

Derivation:
  Spanish for "The Horseshoe."
Culture:
  Teotihuacán.
Location:
  Northwestern Tlaxcala.
Maps: 3 (p. 72) and 3E (p. 122)

The Site

La Herradura is actually a part of ancient Calpulalpan, and it lies within the modern town of that name. Remains include the low walls of platforms and rooms—made of stone with some remnants of stucco finish—and square pillars. You can see typical Teotihuacán-style *talud-tablero* construction on some of the platforms, which are approached by stairs bordered by *alfardas.* In one area, four of the platforms face a common patio.

La Herradura, as part of Calpulalpan, was occupied from around A.D. 300 to 650, and possibly as late as 750. It is considered to have been an urban center under the political and religious domination of Teotihuacán. Its settlement pattern, areal extent, and population are unknown. It was probably a conquered, dependent city-state that, along with others, contributed labor resources for major building projects at Teotihuacán.

Recent History

In 1934 and 1935, Sigvald Linné studied Calpulalpan and its ceramics; he published his findings in 1942.

Plaza surrounded by platforms with steps, La Herradura. Classic period.

Connections

1. Tlaxcala to La Herradura: 34.1 miles [54.9 kilometers] by paved road (1:04).

2. Mexico City to La Herradura (via Los Reyes): 53.8 miles [86.6 kilometers] by paved road (2:11).

Getting There

1. From Tlaxcala, take Highway 117 northeast to the junction with Highway 136. Turn left onto Highway 136 and go 33.0 miles [53.2 kilometers] to the junction in Calpulalpan marked "centro." From this junction to La Herradura it is 1.1 miles [1.8 kilometers]. Turn left at the "centro" sign onto Calle Zaragoza and continue a short distance to a dead end. Turn left at the dead end and continue to a triangular *glorieta*. Take the first cutoff to the right (Calle Nezahualcóyotl) and go a short distance to Avenida División del Norte, which comes in at an angle on the left. Take this and continue to La Herradura, found in a fenced island in a cul-de-sac.

2. From Mexico City, take Highway 190 east to Los Reyes; do not get on Highway 190D, the toll road to Puebla. In Los Reyes, turn left onto Highway 136 and continue to Texcoco, where the highway turns to the right (east). From this turn go 23.9 miles [35.9 kilometers] to Calpulalpan and the sign for "centro." Turn right onto Calle Zaragoza and follow the directions already given.

I do not know the schedule for La Herradura. The site was supposed to be open when we visited at 10:30 A.M. on a Sunday, but it wasn't. We saw and photographed it through the fence and locked gate. Allow 15 minutes for a visit. There are no rest rooms, food, or drink at the site. Buses go to Calpulalpan.

★
LOS MELONES
(lohs meh-LOH-nehs)
(CERRITO LOS MELONES)

Derivation:
  Spanish for "The Melons."
Culture:
  Acolhua.
Location:
  Eastern state of Mexico.
Maps: 3 (p. 72) and 3E (p. 122)

The Site

Los Melones is actually part of the larger site of ancient Texcoco, the city of Nezahualcóyotl—a ruler also revered as a philosopher, poet, author of a legal code, and military leader. Texcoco became the most famous cultural center in the Valley of Mexico during Nezahualcóyotl's reign, which began in A.D. 1418, although it had been important from 1371 onward.

Ancient Texcoco lies under the modern town of the same name, but Los Melones is the only part of the early city that has been carefully studied. Texcoco was greatly destroyed during the Spanish conquest, so the glory of the city as described by Don Fernando de Alva Itxlilxóchitl, the lord of Texcoco and a native eyewitness, is not in evidence today.

As you enter the site you see a number of interesting stone carvings—two ball court rings and part of another, and a coiled feathered serpent. From here, follow the path counterclockwise around the site.

Today at Los Melones you see two large mounds and remnants of other, smaller buildings. As you circle the base of the west mound, the use of adobe is evident; it belongs to the first construction stage. This adobe building and others at the site were covered with stucco. In the upper or later construction stage, stone was used abundantly, although both stages date to the Late Postclassic period. Part-

way around the site you come to the low remains of stone walls surrounding some fairly well preserved stucco floors on two levels.

Remains of more stucco floors and low walls are found atop the east mound, as is a drain. Traces of passageways and chambers are found on different levels.

On your way back to the entrance you pass along the north side of an impressive stone retaining wall and other remains of mostly ruined architecture. Most interesting in this area is a rather small, steep, stepped pyramidal structure topped by what appears to be an urn.

Some of the buildings at Los Melones are believed to have been used for religious rites, whereas others were residential. Los Melones is not believed to have been near the main ceremonial-center precincts of ancient Texcoco.

Recent History

Los Melones, as part of Texcoco, was never lost to memory—it was written about in the early years after the Spanish conquest. Archaeological reports of the site appeared only in the 1970s. They are a monograph on the Texcoco regional survey carried out by Jeffery R. Parsons and others under the auspices of the University of Michigan Museum of Anthropology and another by Eduardo Noguera that covers the architecture of Los Melones.

Connection

Mexico City (Diana Fountain) to Los Melones (via Los Reyes): 29.5 miles [47.5 kilometers] by paved road (1:17).

Getting There

From Mexico City, head east on Highway 190 to Los Reyes, 16.3 miles [26.2 kilometers].

Ball court ring at Los Melones. Late Postclassic period.

There you turn left onto Highway 136 and go 13.2 miles [21.2 kilometers] to Texcoco. (Do not take the bypass that goes around the west side of Texcoco). At this point you will be at Calle Abasolo. Turn right onto Abasolo and go half a block to the first gate on the right. This is the entrance to Los Melones; the address is Calle Abasolo 100. You can park on the street nearby.

Los Melones is reportedly open daily from 9:00 A.M. to noon and 3:00 P.M. to 5:00 P.M. Allow 30 minutes for a visit. There are no rest rooms, food, or drink at the site, but there are restaurants in Texcoco. Buses go to Texcoco.

★
HUEXOTLA
(weh-SHOH-tlah)

Derivation:
  Nahuatl for "Place of the
  Willows."
Original Name:
  Huexotla.
Culture:
  Acolhua.
Location:
  Eastern state of Mexico.
Maps: 3 (p. 72) and 3E (p. 122)

The Site

The ruins of ancient Huexotla are nestled among the more modern structures of the town of the same name. The most impressive feature is a wall some 21 feet (6.4 meters) high that borders a part of the site. It rises in several layers and is topped by wedge-shaped constructions with spaces in between. The wall was built of volcanic stone, and cone-shaped pieces of this material were embedded in some of its upper sections; they appear circular to the eye. The wall was reportedly built in A.D. 1409. In profile view it tapers toward the top. Its design is attractive and its mass impressive.

This is the only known wall of its type in the Basin of Mexico, although one early chronicle mentions a great wall that surrounded the Palace of Nezahualcoyótl at Texcoco. This is no longer in existence, however. The wall at Huexotla had a defensive function in addition to its use in partially defining the site. Behind the wall are some modern residences and a church, the foundation of which is the remains of a pyramid.

Massive wall partly enclosing Huexotla. Late Postclassic period.

Bas-relief carving of a figure seated in front of a glyph and the numeral five, Huexotla. Late Post-classic period.

After viewing the wall, follow it south to the first cross street (Calle San Francisco) and turn left. Go the equivalent of two long blocks past an area of houses (on the right) to a chain link fence with a gate (on the right). This is the entrance to two of Huexotla's structures, which are aligned east-west. The structure on the east is called the Community; it has two tiers with a ramp on the west side. The top of the building is paved, and the low remains of walls of rooms can be seen on top. This seems to have been a palace. To the left of the ramp (as you face it), a couple of carved stones have been placed atop the wall that forms the lower tier. One depicts a seated figure in front of a glyph and the numeral five.

The building to the west is called La Estancia, and a trail on the east side leads to the top. On the west side, at the base, a broad stairway has been consolidated. Both of these structures cover earlier buildings, and when you climb the trail to the top of La Estancia you will see a portion of a corner of its earlier structure.

Four other buildings are known at Huexotla, but to reach them you will have to ask in the town and perhaps have someone take you to them.

Recent History

During the late part of the Late Postclassic period, Huexotla was one of 13 dependent city-states that formed the nucleus of the kingdom of Acolhuacán. Texcoco was the capital of the kingdom, and its king was the supreme ruler. He appointed the rulers of the city-states and was assisted by them in his duties. According to William T. Sanders, who studied settlement patterns in central Mexico, "each of these states consisted of a central urban town and a constellation of rural villages." After the Spanish conquest, the city-states became pueblos. The Spaniards, in general, preserved the basic settlement pattern and built churches in each of the pueblos.

The ruins of Huexotla were mentioned in 1770 by the archbishop of Mexico City, Francisco Antonio de Lorenzana, and the site was investigated by Leopoldo Batres, who issued a report in 1904. In 1980 the Community and La Estancia were cleared and consolidated; this work was reported by C. L. Díaz and María Teresa García. In 1987 García issued a monograph on Huexotla.

Connection

Mexico City (Diana Fountain) to Huexotla: 27.6 miles [44.4 kilometers] by paved road (1:12), then 1.3 miles [2.1 kilometers] by poor dirt road (:14).

Getting There

From Mexico City, head east on Highway 190 to Los Reyes, 16.3 miles [26.2 kilometers]. There you turn left onto Highway 136 and go 11.3 miles [18.2 kilometers] to the cutoff for Huexotla, then turn right onto Calle Huautla (a dirt road). Landmarks at this junction are a stoplight, a bus stop, and an apartment complex on the north side of Calle Huautla. There is a pyramid sign as well, but it is hard to spot.

As you drive the dirt road, follow it as it turns to the right, until you come to the wall (on the left). The wall, of course, can be visited at any time. The gate to the two buildings described is open Tuesday through Sunday from 10:00 A.M. to 5:00 P.M. It is closed on Monday. Allow 40 minutes to see the wall and structures. There is no food or drink at the site, nor any rest rooms. Huexotla can be reached by bus from Mexico City.

★
TLAPACOYA
(tlah-pah-KOH-yah)

Derivation:
    Originally Tlapacoyan, Nahuatl for "Place Where They Wash."
Culture:
    See text.
Location:
    Eastern state of Mexico.
Maps: 3 (p. 72) and 3E (p. 122)

The Site

Tlapacoya is located in the southeast corner of the Basin of Mexico, near the town of Ayotla. It is considered a transitional site between Cuicuilco and Teotihuacán, although it overlapped both in time. It may have inherited the earlier site's function of serving as a religious center. The architecture at Tlapacoya indicates experimentation and is believed to have served as an inspiration for the builders of Teotihuacán.

Though modest in size, the main structure at Tlapacoya is complex. It rises in several tiers and has multiple stairways facing in different directions. There is no evidence of a permanent temple on top. Although Tlapacoya has been nicely reconstructed, and the area around it is kept cleared and planted with flowers, it is difficult to get a good descriptive photograph of the building. The front of the structure is just a few feet away from the edge of the hill on which it is built, so you cannot back off very far. A wide-angle lens will help but will not entirely solve the problem. Morning light is best. Two vertical openings

Tlapacoya pyramid. Middle Preclassic period.

are found on top of the structure; these are entrances to the remains of excavated tombs.

The area around Tlapacoya has apparently been occupied by humans for many thousands of years. Finds of some hearths, animal bones, and stone artifacts have been dated to 19,000 B.C. (although not all authorities agree with this early date). At one time Tlapacoya was an island or peninsula, depending on the fluctuations of Lake Chalco, which surrounded it. The lake was drained or dried up many years ago.

By 5000 B.C., sedentary groups were occupying Tlapacoya. Around 3000, a volcanic eruption rendered the area uninhabitable for some 500 years; then it was reoccupied. The first securely dated permanent settlement at the site began around 1300 B.C. Olmec traits show up in the record around 1200 and drop out around 950. During Olmec II times (1150–400 B.C.), Tlapacoya was a large village.

Some ceramics discovered in three burials at Tlapacoya demonstrate a transition to Classic forms. The building at Tlapacoya shows evidence of three phases of construction, dating from around 400 to 200 B.C., although the site continued to be active for some time thereafter. The earliest structure known at Tlapacoya, a circular adobe platform, was built around 400 B.C., and a sophisticated stone platform around 200.

Recent History

The major excavation and restoration at Tlapacoya were undertaken by the Mexican archaeologists Beatriz Barba de Piña Chan and her husband, Román Piña Chan. They published the results of their work in 1956 in Mexico. Later, some stratigraphic work was carried out at the site by the Americans Paul Tolstoy and Louise Paradis, the results of which were published in 1970. Results of this work were a new classification of phase names for the Basin of Mexico—which replaced an earlier system of overlapping subphases—and the discovery of a previously unknown Early Preclassic phase.

Beginning in 1965, INAH sponsored excavations at Cerro de Tlapacoya, which resulted in some of the early dates for the site. This work continued for several years and included many scholars.

Connection

Mexico City (Diana Fountain) to Tlapacoya: 21.7 miles [34.9 kilometers] by paved road

(:54), then 0.7 mile [1.1 kilometers] by paved and dirt road (:07).

Getting There

From Mexico City, head east on Highway 190 to Los Reyes, 16.3 miles [26.2 kilometers], and the junction of Highway 190 (marked Puebla Libre) and Highway 136 (to Texcoco). Take Highway 190 (to the right) and proceed to Ayotla and the cutoff for Tlapacoya. Landmarks at the junction are a stoplight, a fire station, and a pedestrian overpass. Turn right at the junction and proceed to the site. You may have to ask directions along this last part, because the way is not marked.

I do not know the hours when the site is open and could find no one to ask. Allow 25 minutes for a visit. There are no rest rooms, food, or drink at the site. The town of Ayotla can be reached by bus from Mexico City, and from there you could walk to the site, or you could taxi all the way there from the capital.

ACOZAC
(ah-koh-SAHK)

Derivation:
    Nahuatl for "Place of Yellow Water."
Culture:
    Acolhua.
Location:
    Eastern state of Mexico.
Maps: 3 (p. 72) and 3E (p. 122)

The Site

Acozac, resting near the top of a hill, has several structures of interest and many unconsolidated mounds. The south end of the restored section is defined by Structure 43, a rather ruined stepped pyramid exhibiting two construction stages. This is the major structure at the site, and it has a restored stairway of a few steps, bordered by *alfardas,* jutting from the east side. A large open space to the southwest of Structure 43 is believed to have been a market. It is speculated that it was used for religious ceremonies and trade or exchange. Nearby, to the north, three stepped platforms (Structures 46, 47, and 48) used as altars have been restored. All have east-facing stairways, and that of the southernmost and largest platform (Structure 46) is bordered by *alfardas* with vertical upper zones.

Farther north is Structure 49, a unit with different levels containing a number of rooms partly surrounded by a wall. Entry to this unit is from the west, and the floor plan is rather complex. It was used as an elite residence and administrative center and is actually a complex of buildings. Just north of it are the remains of very low walls—easy to miss—that formed a *tzompantli* (Structure 50).

Next to this, again to the north, is the most interesting building at Acozac—Structure 51, a stepped circular structure dedicated to Ehécatl, with a stepped eastern stairway. The stairs on the two upper tiers are bordered by *alfardas* with vertical upper zones. As you walk around the south side of the circular part of the building, you can observe two construction stages.

In the grassy area east of the buildings described are a couple of small pits or cists in the ground; watch that you don't accidentally step into one. West of the buildings you can see one of the unrestored mounds, which is the remains of a ball court.

In a couple of places the caretaker showed us stones in the walls that bore fragments of painted designs and, in one case, a bas-relief carving of a stylized flower; you will never find these without his help.

Pyramid of Ehécatl, Acozac. Late Postclassic period.

Recent History

The first archaeological work at Acozac was the exploration of the ball court in 1963 by H. B. Nicholson and David C. Grove, who reported the site under the name Ixtapaluca Viejo.

Between then and 1973, construction activity in the area destroyed a good part of Structure 49. INAH denounced this act. To mitigate the damage, Eduardo Contreras explored the site in 1973 and reconstructed the part visitors see today. He reported his findings in 1976.

Juergan Brueggemann excavated some test pits at the site and issued reports in 1976 and 1987.

Connection

Mexico City (Diana Fountain) to Acozac: 26.9 miles [43.3 kilometers] by paved road (1:16).

Getting There

From Mexico City, head east on Highway 190 to Los Reyes. Do not get onto the toll road, Highway 190D, shortly before Los Reyes. From Los Reyes, continue on Highway 190, the old road to Puebla, for 6.7 miles [10.8 kilometers] to a stoplight, where you will see a sign indicating a left turn for the Acozac Golf Club. When you follow this road uphill you will come to a gate with a guard. He will ask you where you are going and how long you will be, and he will allow you through after you tell him. From the gate, continue uphill to the clubhouse and follow the road as it turns left and shortly reaches a small *glorieta.*

So far this has been quite straightforward. From the *glorieta,* however, it's a different story. Roads, seemingly unmarked, meander all over the hill among new, very nice residences, and it is easy to lose your way—we did. When we finally got back to the *glorieta* (not having found the site), I noticed faint arrows painted on the roadway and a sign, likewise painted, saying "pirámides." We decided to try following the arrows—they were present at all the crucial turns—and we easily reached the site. With luck, maybe the arrows will have been repainted and will be easier to spot by the time you arrive.

At any rate, when you first reach the *glorieta,* go around it counterclockwise about three-quarters of the way—essentially making a left turn—and start looking for the arrows. (Legally you should go around *glorietas* counterclockwise, but since there is virtually no traffic here, you could go clockwise, in which case take the first road to the left. This would be going around about one-quarter of the way.)

Acozac is open daily from 9:00 A.M. to 5:00 P.M. Allow 35 minutes for a visit. There are no rest rooms, food, or drink at the site. Driving your own vehicle is the recommended way to reach Acozac, but you could taxi there from Mexico City.

★ ★
TIZATLÁN
(tee-saht-LAHN)

Derivation:
Nahuatl for "Place of White
Stone."
Culture:
Tlaxcalan.
Location:
Central Tlaxcala.
Maps: 3 (p. 72) and 3F (p. 122)

The Site

When you arrive at the parking area for this site, you will be facing the sixteenth-century open chapel of Tizatlán, and you will see a large stone statue on a pedestal outside of it. Presumably the statue was found at the site. It is worth looking at before or after you visit the ruins, which are reached by a path to the right (west).

The main reason to visit Tizatlán, however, is to see two pre-Columbian painted altars. They sit on a platform, and each measures approximately 6 feet (1.9 meters) by nearly 4 feet (1.2 meters) and is a bit over a foot high (0.3 meters). The paintings were done in true fresco technique on the smooth, unpolished lime surface that covered the sides of the altars. The colors used were yellow, red, blue, and black. The style is called Cholula-Puebla and is similar to that seen in the *Codex Borgia,* a famous Aztec manuscript.

Depicted in the paintings are the Nahua deities Tezcatlipoca (Smoking Mirror) and Tlahuizcalpantecuhtli (lord of the house of dawn—the planet Venus as morning star). Other motifs represent the fire serpent, Xiuhcóatl, skulls, hearts, and hands. There is a border of the stepped fret design on the lower part of each altar. One of the clearest paintings is on the side of one altar, where the design is broken into rectangular elements, each with its own motif.

Alfonso Caso believed that in accordance with the mythological concepts of the Nahua, the altars represented the west, both the region of the land and the death of the sun.

The altars are covered with glass cases, but you can get photos through them. Also found on the platform near the altars are the lower sections of large columns and pillars. All of this is shaded by a modern roof, and blue plastic curtains hang down from the roof for additional protection in certain areas.

A stairway on the south side of the platform leads to lower levels. From the lowest level, head to the right (west) for a look at other architectural remains. More stairs (going to other platforms) and low walls (some with *talud-tablero* construction) can be seen.

The open chapel contains some interesting sixteenth-century murals, one of which depicts the baptism of Xicoténcatl, the king of Tizatlán at the time of the Spanish conquest. At that time there was a Tlaxcalteca confederation, made up of four "dominions" of Tlaxcala; Tizatlán was the third dominion. After the conquest, the chapel was built on top of the platform of a pre-Columbian structure that had been the principal part of the Palace of Xicoténcatl.

Although the architectural remains at Tizatlán are Late Postclassic, ceramics dating to an earlier time have been found at the site.

Recent History

According to a local story (of which I have been unable to learn the date), some years ago one of the villagers had a dream in which King Xicoténcatl appeared to him and told him of treasure buried in the mound near the churchyard. He and his friends began digging and located a wall. Further secret probes at night ensued, and more of a temple was uncovered—but not the treasure they were hoping for. The Mexican government got wind of this and stopped the illicit excavation in time to preserve the remains.

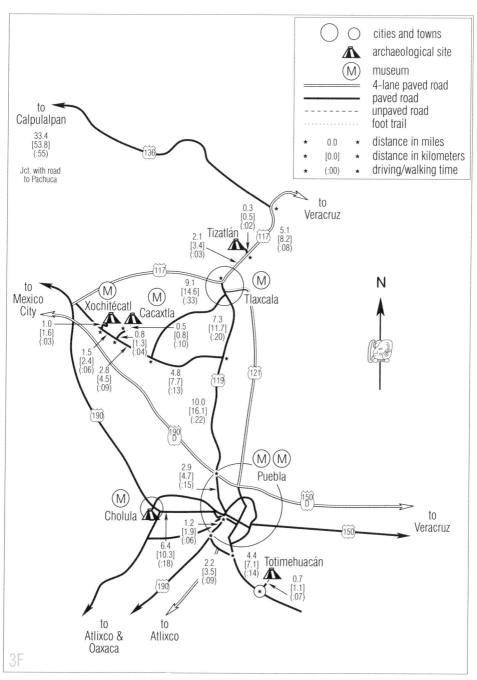

Area around Puebla and Tlaxcala (Map 3F).

Remains of columns and glass-encased, painted altar, Tizatlán. Late Post-classic period.

Tizatlán was studied by Alfonso Caso, who published his findings in 1927 in Mexico.

Connections

1. Tlaxcala to Tizatlán: 2.4 miles [3.9 kilometers] by paved road (:05).

2. Puebla to Tlaxcala: 20.2 miles [32.5 kilometers] by paved road (:57).

Getting There

1. From the Tlaxcala interchange (on the north side of the city), take Highway 117 northeast to the cutoff for Tizatlán. *Note:* This highway has four lanes, and when you approach the cutoff from Tlaxcala, you have to it pass up (there is no junction from that side of the highway). Make a U-turn at the next chance and return to it. After the U-turn, keep an eye out for the yellow tile dome of San Esteban church; you can see it on a hill on the right (north side of the highway). You can spot it near where the highway goes under a pedestrian overpass. The cutoff is between kilometers 26 (closest to Tlaxcala) and 27. I calculate that the cutoff is at kilometer 26.6. It goes uphill at a severe angle to the road (almost a U-turn to the right) from the north lane of the highway.

The cutoff for Tizatlán is 2.1 miles [3.4 kilometers] (:03) northeast of the Tlaxcala interchange. From there to the parking area for Tizatlán it is 0.3 mile [0.5 kilometer] (:03) steeply uphill.

2. From Puebla, take Highway 119 north to the Tlaxcala interchange, 20.2 miles [32.5 kilometers] (:57), then follow the directions already given.

Allow 25 minutes to visit the ruins and another 15 minutes if you want to visit the open chapel. Both are open Tuesday through Sunday from 10:00 A.M. to 5:00 P.M.; both are closed on Monday. The San Esteban church is open only on Sunday for mass at 10:00 A.M. Photography without flash is permitted at all three locations.

There is no food or drink at the site, but a nearby grocery has cold drinks and packaged snacks.

From Tlaxcala you can taxi to the site, and buses stop at the cutoff to it; you would have to walk up from there. Buses run between Puebla and Tlaxcala.

★ ★
TLAXCALA REGIONAL MUSEUM
(TLAXCALA MUSEUM)

The Tlaxcala Museum is at the Ex-Convent of Nuestra Señora de la Asunción (Franciscan), up a pathway from the Plaza Xicoténcatl in the central part of the city of Tlaxcala. The convent was founded in the sixteenth century, and the museum opened in 1986.

As you enter, you will see a *chacmool* along the edge of the patio. There are a few other carved stone figures around the patio as well, but most are unlabeled. I asked where the *chacmool* came from and was told by the guard (with some hesitation) that it was from Cacaxtla, but I was never able to verify this.

In one long room, to the left off the patio, there are other exhibits. They include obsidian and bone artifacts, ceramics, skulls, figurines, and printed information (in Spanish) about a few of the sites in the state of Tlaxcala. Photos of some of the structures and of the murals at Cacaxtla are shown.

The most interesting item is a very elaborate and well-preserved stone *hacha* showing a profile, seemingly of a monkey. It is unlabeled.

The museum is open Monday through Saturday from 10:00 A.M. to 4:30 P.M. It is closed on Sunday. Photography is not permitted. Lighting on the inside is sufficient for viewing. Allow 15 minutes for a visit.

★ ★ ★
XOCHITÉCATL
(soh-chee-TEH-kahtl)

Derivation:
   Nahuatl for "Place of the Flower Lineage."
Original name:
   Probably Xochitécatl at the time of the Spanish conquest.
Culture:
   Various (see text).
Location:
   Southwestern Tlaxcala.
Maps: 3 (p. 72) and 3F (p. 147)

The Site

Xochitécatl, open to the public since 1994, is a welcome addition to the sites that may be visited in Mexico. It is situated in beautiful surroundings, is well cleared, and has some impressive architecture.

From the parking area, steps lead up to the site museum, and from there you follow the path and steps to the left to tour the site clockwise. You come first to the Pyramid of the Spiral, which lies on the western edge of the Great Plaza. The pyramid is actually a truncated cone, rising in tiers, and it is believed to have been an astronomical observatory. It was built in the Middle Preclassic period. Though it has been excavated, no stairway has been found; a modern metal stair gives access to the top today. It is worthy of note that circular structures were rare in the highlands of Mexico during the Preclassic period.

Next, head to the Foundation of the Volcanoes, near the center of the plaza. It is a low platform, and two construction phases can be seen around its base. This structure dates to the end of the Classic period. When

Pyramid of the Spiral, Xochitécatl. Middle Preclassic period.

Front (west face) of the Pyramid of the Flowers, Xochitécatl. The pyramid was begun in the Middle Preclassic period.

it was excavated, archaeologists found a burial containing offerings of shell necklaces, jars, and figurines, all exhibiting Teotihuacán influence.

To the south of this structure is the Pyramid of the Serpent, a platform with an east-west orientation and a stair on the north side, facing the plaza. This building was constructed during the Middle Preclassic period. During excavation, a large sculpture of a serpent was found there, as were sculptures of a standing human and a jaguar.

You then go to the most impressive building at Xochitécatl, the Pyramid of the Flowers—the fourth largest pre-Columbian structure in Mexico, visible from neighboring Cacaxtla. The Pyramid of the Flowers shows a construction sequence beginning in the Middle Preclassic period and continuing to colonial times. Thirty infant burials and one adult burial were found during its excavation.

The pyramid faces west (away from Cacaxtla), rises in tiers, and has a stairway on the west side, facing the plaza. In front of the stairway, and in alignment with it, are two monolithic ritual basins, one above ground and one sunk into the ground. To the right of the stairway is an altar made of stone

Columns and lintel, once part of a temple atop the Pyramid of the Flowers, Xochitécatl. The Pyramid of the Spiral is in the background.

blocks. You can see a couple of the construction stages at each side of the stairway, showing the different construction methods used.

Atop the structure are some plain stone columns. Two are standing and are spanned by a plain stone lintel; the others are mostly lying on the ground. These are the remains of a temple that once topped the pyramid. From the top, there is a good view of Cacaxtla.

A nice touch at the site is the inclusion of discrete signs (in Spanish, Nahuatl, and English) that give information about the site and its buildings.

Xochitécatl was probably dedicated to Xochitl, the goddess of flowers and fertility. It was mentioned under the name Xochitécatl by the sixteenth-century chronicler Diego Muñoz Carmago.

During Xochitécatl's long history, it felt various influences. Middle Preclassic female figurines uncovered there are similar to figurines of the same date found in other parts of the Mexican highlands. Classic period ceramics show influence from the Gulf Coast, Oaxaca, Cholula, and Teotihuacán. It was also during this time that the Olmeca-Xicalanca arrived and Xochitécatl formed a cultural unity with nearby Cacaxtla. The Olmeca-Xicalanca were later overthrown by the Chichimecs of the central highlands.

Recent History

After Muñoz Carmago's mention of Xochitécatl, little was said about the site until 1883, when it was briefly mentioned in a study by Hubert Bancroft. In 1969, Bodo Spranz of the

East façade of the Pyramid of the Flowers, Xochitécatl, as seen from Cacaxtla.

University of Freiberg, Germany, carried out the first excavations at parts of the site. Work continued the following year as well.

In 1993, INAH undertook investigations and excavated four structures. This work, under the direction of Mari Carmen Serra Puche and coordinated by Ludwig Beutlspacher, continued through the first half of 1994. During that time the site was also cleared and consolidated.

Connections

1. Tlaxcala to Xochitécatl: 17.4 miles [27.9 kilometers] by paved road (:51).

2. Puebla to Xochitécatl: 23.0 miles [37.0 kilometers] by paved road (1:08).

Getting There

1. From Tlaxcala, take Highway 119 heading south to the cutoff marked for Cacaxtla and Nativitas, 7.3 miles [11.7 kilometers] (:20), and turn right. From the junction, go west on an unnumbered road for 9.1 miles [14.6 kilometers] (:28) to the final cutoff for Xochitécatl (marked with a sign). (This is 1.5 miles [2.4 kilometers] *past* the final cutoff for Cacaxtla.) Turn right and follow the road as it curves steeply up to the parking area for the site, 1.0 mile [1.6 kilometers] (:03).

Once you leave Highway 119 and get on the unnumbered road, you will drive through several small towns with lots of *topes*. Expect to drive slowly.

There is a second possible route from Tlaxcala to Xochitécatl that heads southwest. It is shorter but the road is poor, although driving time is the same. The route via Highway 119 is recommended.

2. From Puebla, head north on Highway 119 to the junction described above, 12.9 miles [20.8 kilometers] (:37), and turn left. Then follow the directions already given.

Xochitécatl is open from 10:00 A.M. to 5:00 P.M., Tuesday through Sunday. It is closed on Monday. When you buy your ticket for Xochitécatl, keep it. It will get you into Cacaxtla as well if you go on the same day. Visiting both sites from Tlaxcala or Puebla makes an interesting one-day trip.

Allow one hour to visit the site. Spanish-speaking guides are available from Thursday through Sunday and on holidays. Xochitécatl can be reached on tours from Tlaxcala or Puebla. There are rest rooms at the site museum.

Food and drink are sold by vendors in the parking area. One woman with a small stall was there when we visited. She made, sold, and served blue corn quesadillas stuffed with fresh squash flowers and *salsa verde*, hot off the *comal*, that were delicious. Her stall was immaculate and she had a cheerful and delightful personality. This made a most enjoyable lunch stop. Other stalls sell booklets (one is a guide for Xochitécatl and Cacaxtla and another covers points in interest in the state of Tlaxcala) and souvenirs, many made of onyx.

★ ★

XOCHITÉCATL MUSEUM

The Xochitécatl Museum has both indoor and outdoor sections. About a dozen stone carvings rest on low platforms outside; they are unlabeled but all come from the site. Both human and animal forms are represented.

On the inside, the displays are mostly ceramics from various periods in the site's history. There are rather large, flat figurines with some portions painted red, censer ladles, and bowls as well as other items. Some of the Classic period ceramics show styles of Teotihuacán and the Gulf Coast of Mexico. One especially interesting display is a greenstone head.

Photography is not permitted at either museum section. Allow 15 minutes for a visit. The museum is open from 10:00 A.M. to 5:00 P.M., Tuesday through Sunday. It is closed on Monday. There are rest rooms at the museum.

★ ★ ★

CACAXTLA
(kah-KAHSH-tlah)

Derivation:
 Originally "Cacaxtlan," Nahuatl for "Place of Pack Frames" (boxes for carrying goods).
Culture:
 Olmeca-Xicalanca (see text).
Location:
 Southern Tlaxcala.
Maps: 3 (p. 72) and 3F (p. 147)

The Site

Cacaxtla has attracted a great deal of attention since the discovery of murals there in 1975. It is clearly an exceptional site. Although known since the sixteenth century, its importance became evident only with the discovery of the murals. The original buildings were made of adobe (the material also used at Cholula). Later, they were partly demolished and filled to form a platform upon which new adobe buildings were constructed. This process was repeated several times, and the whole is called the Great Foundation or Great Basement.

The outside of the Great Foundation is surfaced with stones, and you can see the various layers of construction as you approach it. When you walk from the parking area, you will soon pass the Cacaxtla Museum and later a restaurant with a large basalt sculpture in front. The figure, from the neighboring site of Xochitécatl, depicts a

Overall view of Cacaxtla. Late Classic period.

monkey-jaguar-serpent. You then continue to a group called Los Cerritos ("the little hills"), where one of two mounds has been partly consolidated. The foot path passes between the two mounds. The consolidated structure is on the right; it rises in tiers and has a western stair. There are remains of a temple on top.

You now go east to the Great Foundation. This huge platform was built almost entirely by hand, although there may be a small natural rise within it. The platform is covered by an enormous protective steel roof, 459 feet (140 meters) long and 230 feet (70 meters) wide. It is considered to be the second largest roof in the world; only that at the archaeological zone of Xian, China, is larger. The roof at Cacaxtla was installed in 1986.

When you reach the Great Foundation, a modern wooden stairway gives access to the top. Walkways and other stairs lead around the site, which should be toured in a clockwise direction. You are not allowed to leave the walkways. Discrete signs label some of the structures.

Cacaxtla flourished between A.D. 650 and 900, and at least eight construction phases are known. You will see the various stages as you tour the site.

You come first to the Building of the Columns, one of the earlier constructions at the site. There you will see the bases of two cylindrical columns, the only ones of this type known so far at Cacaxtla.

Next you come to the Palace, a complex of rooms (used mainly as elite habitations) around patios where remains of sacrificed children were found. Part of this complex is the Patio of the Altars, in which several burials were discovered. The Palace belongs to the last stage of Cacaxtla's occupation.

At the southeast corner of the Great Foundation is the Stairway Room; you can look down into it, but you may not leave the walkway to enter it. Vestiges of murals on either side of the stairway date to A.D. 600—the earliest discovered so far at Cacaxtla.

To the north is Building F, with two porticoes. It is another of Cacaxtla's early structures, built between A.D. 600 and 650.

The next feature of interest is the Temple of Venus, so named because of Venus symbols painted on two pillars. One pillar also depicts a male human with a scorpion tail, and the other, a human female. Both figures are painted blue. Here, too, you can look down into the structure, but you may not enter it. These murals were discovered in 1986.

Another fairly recent discovery is the Red Temple, where the two walls abutting the stairway are painted with murals, the main background color of which is red. The east mural depicts an old merchant whose backpack leans against a lance. The backpack bears a sea turtle shell and quetzal plumes. Another part of the scene shows maize plants sprouting ears of maize in the form of human profiles. The surrounding border shows a cascade, birds, and a blue toad. The west wall (which must be viewed earlier on your tour, while you are at Building F) displays a similar border and maize plants, and a toad wearing a jaguar skin.

Nearby, on the other side of the walkway, you can look down into La Celosía, a building with a wall in a latticework pattern. Next is Building E, with the remains of *talud-tablero* construction and a bas-relief on a pillar showing the lower part of a richly attired figure made of stuccoed clay. The patterned skirt and sandals are similar to features found in the Maya area. From this vantage point you get a good view of the Pyramid of the Flowers to the west at Xochitécatl.

You now come to the Battle Mural, the most impressive—and goriest—one at Cacaxtla. It measures 72 feet (22 meters) long and almost 6 feet (1.8 meters) high, and two-thirds of it are intact. It is divided into two parts by a central stair that ascends Building B. Forty-eight human figures have been recorded in this mural, 17 of them mostly undamaged; they are jaguar warriors and bird soldiers, depicted in savage battle. The jaguar warriors are shown attacking the bird soldiers with spears, obsidian knives, and atlatls, and the spilled blood and entrails of the latter are everywhere. A long bench has been installed in front of the mural for visitors who wish to sit and study this gruesome scene.

Stone carving of a monkey-jaguar-serpent, located near the path to Cacaxtla. The monument is said to come from Xochitécatl.

The Battle Mural was painted between A.D. 650 and 700 in a lowland Maya style, although the glyphs that are included are non-Maya and hint at a blend of other Mesoamerican influences. The images, however, are so authentically Maya that the art historian Beatriz de la Fuente believes the people who painted them were actually Mayas. The nearest Maya at the time lived 500 miles (805 kilometers) away.

You now head to Building A, on a slightly higher level. The murals there are on an interior medial wall and on the adjacent jambs next to a central doorway. The north mural shows a figure in a jaguar skin holding a bundle of lances that drip a blue liquid, possibly blood turned into water. The figure stands on a catlike reptile. After the mural was painted, a carved clay relief of a seated figure was placed on top of the right end of it. The figure in the north jamb mural also wears a jaguar skin. He holds a snake in his left hand and a jar bearing the face of Tlaloc in his right arm. Water flows from the jar, and a plant sprouts from the figure's abdomen.

The south mural, the first painting discovered at Cacaxtla, depicts a figure painted black and dressed in a bird costume. He holds a serpent ceremonial bar and stands on a bearded feathered serpent. The figure in the south jamb mural is also painted black; he is dancing and holds a conch shell from which another figure emerges. The archaeologist Michael D. Coe believes the emerging figure is the Maya god "N." On the rear wall of Building A, centered on an axis with the doorway in the medial wall, is a fragmented and poorly preserved mural. It shows the legs of three figures, but from where you view it they are impossible to make out. All of the murals in Building A date to between A.D. 700 and 800.

Before the murals were painted at Cacaxtla, the adobe walls were prepared with a coating of stucco. The paint for the murals was made from pigments such as hematite, carbon, and yellow ochre, bound together with the juice of the nopal cactus. The murals are the most extensive and best preserved in Mesoamerica. Their fine state of preservation is due in part to the fact that they were deliberately and carefully buried in ancient times. A layer of fine sand was placed between the murals and the rough fill.

You now continue to the Sunken Patio, one of the few of Cacaxtla's existing buildings that date to its latest stages of occupation. The lower walls and stairways leading down to the patio are still standing, and an altar and two cist burials are found in the patio itself. One cist formerly held human remains, and the other, offerings.

From there, follow the walkway to the end. Below you will see two rooms. The one on the right is Las Conejeras ("the rabbit warrens"), an arbitrary name given to it because of some small enclosures on the floor. The room to the left has vertical panels in the wall and is called the Passage of the Vertical Panels. From this vantage point you get a comprehensive view of the site when you look to the south.

Although some areas around Cacaxtla were occupied as early as 1200 to 800 B.C. (nearby Xochitécatl dates back to the Middle Preclassic period), Cacaxtla itself was occupied somewhat later, around 300 B.C. Eight radiocarbon dates from the site gave readings ranging from A.D. 194 ± 103 years to A.D. 792 ± 83 years, with most clustering in the Late Classic period. Ceramics uncovered at Cacaxtla date from A.D. 450 to 1100. After that the site was abandoned.

The ethnic identity of the ancient Cacaxtlans is still uncertain, but many scholars believe them to have been Olmeca-Xicalanca (not to be confused with the Preclassic Olmec). The Olmeca-Xicalanca were a little-known group that had origins in the Maya region of the Gulf Coast and were made up of three ethnic strains, Nahua, Mixtec, and Chochopopoloca. Archaeologists place them in the general area around A.D. 650, but there are differences of opinion regarding exactly when they arrived and how long they stayed at Cacaxtla itself.

A number of scholars have studied Cacaxtla's paintings, and INAH's Carolyn Baus de Czitrom specialized in the writing and calendrics the paintings included. She identified resemblances between these glyphs and those from several other Mesoamerican regions, including the Gulf Coast, Teotihuacán, Tula, and the Zapotec, Mixtec, and Mexica areas. She saw the greatest number of similarities with Xochicalco.

Recent History

In 1975, looters tunneled into the mound now known as the Great Foundation searching for treasure. One morning their tunnel reached the wall with the painting of the bird man in Building A. The would-be looters realized it would be impossible to remove the mural intact and reported it to local authorities. Soon afterward, INAH learned of the discovery and archaeologists went to investigate.

The principal excavations were conducted by Diana López and Daniel Molina, who discovered that little remained of the latest structures. Much of those late remains, therefore, was stripped away, and the better-preserved earlier structures were studied and consolidated. The work continued for 15 years. Sonia Lombardo studied the paintings in connection with this project. Mexico's federal government provided major funding for it, and the Tlaxcala state government provided the remainder. Many archaeologists, students, art historians, geologists, and others participated.

Connections

1. Tlaxcala to Cacaxtla: 15.7 miles [25.2 kilometers] by paved road (:46), then 0.5 mile [0.8 kilometer] by foot trail (:10).

2. Puebla to Cacaxtla: 21.3 miles [34.3 kilometers] by paved road (1:03), then 0.5 mile [0.8 kilometer] by foot trail (:10).

Getting There

1. From Tlaxcala, take Highway 119 heading south to the cutoff marked for Cacaxtla and Nativitas, 7.3 miles [11.7 kilometers] (:20). From the junction head west on an unnumbered road. You will go through several small towns and over lots of *topes*; expect to drive slowly. Go 7.6 miles [12.2 kilometers] (:22) to the final cutoff for Cacaxtla, marked with a sign, and turn right. Follow the road steeply uphill for 0.8 mile [1.3 kilometers] (:04) to the parking area for the site. Then follow the wide foot path to it, 0.5 mile [0.8 kilometer] (:10).

2. From Puebla, take Highway 119 north to the junction described above, 12.9 miles [20.8 kilometers] (:37), and turn left. Then follow the directions already given.

Photography without flash is permitted at Cacaxtla. A wide-angle lens is useful for photographing some of the murals and for overall shots of the site, but you will still want to have a normal lens for other areas. The site is open Tuesday through Sunday from 10:00 A.M. to 4:30 P.M. It is closed on Monday. Bilingual guides are available Thursday through Sunday. Allow two hours to visit Cacaxtla.

There are rest rooms next to the museum and at the base of the Great Foundation, where cold drinks are sold as well. Food can be found only at the restaurant, which is very good; the management is accommodating. There is a good overall view of Cacaxtla from there. Try their blue corn quesadillas (dough of blue corn, flattened, stuffed, folded, and cooked). They come with three different fillings—squash flowers, *chicharrones* (fried pork rind), and cheese. The kind with the squash flowers is my favorite. There is a bookstore near the museum, but it is open only on certain days.

You can visit Cacaxtla and Xochitécatl in a single day from Tlaxcala or Puebla. When you buy your ticket for the first site, keep it; you can use it to get into the other site at no extra charge if you do so on the same day.

You can also get to Cacaxtla on tours from Tlaxcala or Puebla.

★ ★
CACAXTLA MUSEUM

The Cacaxtla Museum is relatively small, and the collection it houses is not extensive, but some very interesting pieces are displayed. One highlight is a stone carving of the upper torso and head of a figure who has a Mexican yearsign in his headdress. Another is part of an almost life-size clay figure wearing an elaborate collar; the arms and lower legs are missing, but the rest is mostly intact. A slab-like stone carving appears to represent a monkey, and a spherical stone seems to show a stylized jaguar. A clay *incensario* depicts a figure in ritual garb wearing an elaborate headdress and accompanied by subsidiary figures.

Stone carving of the upper part of a figure with a Mexican yearsign on his headdress, from Cacaxtla. On display in the Cacaxtla Museum.

Also included in the collection are a map showing archaeological sites in the area and a site plan and model of Cacaxtla. There is very little labeling. Attractive modern weavings, recreating some of the figures in Cacaxtla's murals, add a colorful note.

The museum is open from 10:00 A.M. to 4:30 P.M., Tuesday through Sunday. It is closed on Monday. Allow 20 minutes for a visit. Photography without flash is permitted. Rest rooms can be found next to the museum and at a restaurant a little farther along the path to Cacaxtla.

★ ★ ★
CHOLULA
(choh-LOO-lah)

Derivation:
  Nahuatl for "Place of Refuge (Sanctuary)."
Original Name:
  Cholula.
Culture:
  See text.
Location:
  North-central Puebla.
Maps: 3 (p. 72) and 3F (p. 147)

The Site

The Great Pyramid at Cholula is the largest one in volume on the American continents, though today it might be taken for a natural hill with a church on top. Entrance to the archaeological zone is through a tunnel (excavated by archaeologists) on the northeast side of the base of the pyramid. This connects with other tunnels, and you exit at the south end of the east side of the base of the pyramid. From there you turn right and circle part of the base of the pyramid going clockwise, following the indicated path. Restored structures are found along two sides of the base of the pyramid.

First you come to architectural remains in the Southeast Plaza, where different construction stages can be discerned. Next is the Patio of the Altars, one of the most interesting parts of Cholula. The patio is surrounded on three sides by typical Cholula-style architecture. There is a curved lower element—peculiar to the site—with fret designs supporting a *tablero*. Wide stairs also

Patio of the Altars, showing the north stairway, Cholula. Classic period. The Great Pyramid rises behind the stairway and supports a colonial church.

View of the east side of the Patio of the Altars, Cholula. Classic period. Altar 1 and its stela and two crude, three-dimensional sculptures are at center.

flank the patio. Two of the four altars that give the patio its name are accompanied by stelae that have bas-relief designs in the style of El Tajín. These are found on the east side of the patio and at the foot of the north stairway. The altar on the east has carved edges.

Another altar—a plain stone atop a small platform—is found in the northeast corner of the patio. Nearby on the patio floor are two pieces of three-dimensional sculpture. One is a rather crude head, the other seemingly part of an animal. Continue around the patio to the west altar, a large slab with carved edges depicting a serpent.

You now leave the Patio of the Altars and go west to the Southwest Plaza. Remains of construction from various periods are found there. It is a fascinating but, I must admit, rather confusing assemblage.

Continue now to the north for a look at the west face of the pyramid. There you will find the Stone Building, composed of three sloped tiers with a *tablero* atop each one and a broad central stairway. The tiers are faced with large, well-cut stone blocks. The inset panels of the *tablero* are decorated with a braid motif. This structure formed part of a platform projecting from the body of the pyramid. It is one of the best-constructed buildings at the site, and its severe crispness makes it seem almost over-restored.

All of Cholula's other buildings were constructed of an adobe nucleus faced with small stones and then stuccoed. This method allowed rapid deterioration once maintenance was discontinued.

There is an interesting tradition about the adobe bricks used in constructing the

Altar 1 and its stela, Cholula. Classic period.

Detail of the north side of the Patio of the Altars, Cholula, showing the curved element typical of Cholula architecture. Classic period.

The Stone Building projecting from the west side of the Great Pyramid, Cholula. Classic period.

pyramid. It is said that they were made at Amecameca, over 30 miles (48.3 kilometers) away as the *zopilote* flies. The bricks were reportedly transported by 20,000 prisoners who stood in line and passed them along. To do so, they would have had to stand about 8 feet (2.4 meters) apart—a figure that seems not unreasonable.

Facing the stairway of the Stone Building is a plain stela with a rectangular perforation of unknown significance. Continue to the north and then exit the site.

Across the street from the entrance to the site, and east of the site museum, more architectural constructions can be seen. There is a broad stairway (restored) abutting an unrestored mound, and nearby, another stairway and the lower wall of a structure.

Several miles of tunnels were dug into the pyramid in the 1930s, revealing several earlier pyramids within. Many paintings were discovered when the tunnels were excavated, and at one time visitors could see them. We saw none in the tunnels while walking through the base of the pyramid when we

entered the site, but we did see a number of locked gates leading to branch tunnels. If you are interested in seeing some of the paintings, you might ask at the ticket booth or talk to one of the many guides at the entrance.

Ceramic evidence indicates that the area around Cholula was occupied from the Middle Preclassic period (ca. 500 B.C.) to the Spanish conquest, and up until today. The pyramid, however, and the earlier structures it encloses were erected from around A.D. 1 until the eighth century. At that time (according to some authorities), the site was abandoned for unknown reasons. The city of Cholula that the Spaniards found in 1519 was located more to the northeast.

From its beginning, Cholula has been a place of pilgrimage and therefore shows influences from various areas. There are indications of connections with Monte Albán in the Middle Preclassic period. In the Early Classic (starting around A.D. 200 to 300) Cholula was an urban city-state under the domination of Teotihuacán. According to native histories, around 700 to 800 the city was conquered by the Olmeca-Xicalanca, who in turn were expelled by the Toltecs in 1168. Evidence of these various influences is found in the ceramics from the site. The Late Postclassic wares show a fusion of the earlier traditions, resulting in the famous Cholula polychrome.

Recent History

The Mexican government's Department of Pre-Hispanic Monuments (now INAH) initiated archaeological investigations at Cholula in 1930, under the supervision of Ignacio Marquina. During this work the tunnels were dug. The findings were reported in Mexico in 1939.

In 1966, Project Cholula began, with the aim of further exploring and restoring some of the structures. In 1967, Marquina was again put in charge; he was assisted by several other Mexican archaeologists and a group of architecture and engineering students from the University of Puebla. Work continued until 1970 and resulted in the restoration seen today. This work is a remarkable achievement when you consider that in some places 30 feet (9.1 meters) of debris—accumulated as a result of erosion—had to be removed. Both mechanized equipment and hand labor were used.

In the 1980s and into the 1990s, the Puebla Regional Center of INAH undertook additional excavation in neighborhoods a few blocks away from the Great Pyramid.

Connection

Puebla (junction of Avenida Juárez and Bulevar Atlixco) to Cholula: 6.4 miles [10.3 kilometers] by paved road (:18).

Getting There

From Puebla, head northeast on Avenida Juárez for a block, then bear to the left onto Calle Tezhuitlán Sur. Follow this street as it curves around to the right through an attractive residential section. Then turn left onto the Via Ripida Cholula. Later, as you enter the town of Cholula and cross a railroad track, bear to the left onto Calle 12 Oriente and go two blocks. Turn left onto Calle 6 Norte and go five blocks, at which point the Great Pyramid will be clearly visible. There is a parking area behind the museum.

Cholula is open from 10:00 A.M. to 5:00 P.M. daily. Allow two hours for a visit. Rest rooms are found at the site shortly after you exit the tunnel near the Southeast Plaza. There is no food or drink at the site, but restaurants are found nearby.

If you are interested in having a guide at Cholula, they can be found at the entrance to the site. Some are bilingual. You can also reach Cholula by taxi or bus from Puebla or take a guided tour from there.

Afternoon hours are best for photographing the Stone Building; the Patio of the Altars gets good light most of the day.

★ ★
CHOLULA MUSEUM

The Cholula Museum, inaugurated in the early 1970s and composed of three rooms, sits across the road from the entrance to the site. A cutaway model of the Great Pyramid and the surrounding structures occupies a sunken area in the center of the first room. It shows the earlier constructions beneath the pyramid. The walls around the room are lined with cases displaying ceramics from Cholula from various time periods labeled with the approximate dates.

The second room also has cases of ceramics along the walls, and more in cases in the middle of the floor. The collection includes some nice Late Postclassic painted plates.

A small third room exhibits copies of paintings found when excavation tunnels

Cutaway model of the Great Pyramid, Cholula, showing the crowning colonial church, an earlier pyramid, and the Stone Building at the bottom. Displayed in the Cholula Museum.

were dug into the Great Pyramid. The earliest mural dates to the second century A.D.

The museum is open Tuesday through Sunday from 10:00 A.M. to 5:00 P.M. It is closed on Monday. Lighting in the first room is only ambient; cases in the second room are lighted. Photography without flash is permitted. There is no food or drink, nor are there rest rooms. Allow 10 minutes for a visit.

★ ★ ★
PUEBLA REGIONAL MUSEUM
(PUEBLA MUSEUM)

The Puebla Museum houses an interesting collection of artifacts and some that are really spectacular. Unfortunately, many of the items are unlabeled, and some others are only vaguely labeled.

The first exhibit deals with Teotihuacán and the sites it influenced. There is a stone carving of Huehuetéotl, the god of fire, and other stone carvings, and a ceramic cylindrical tripod vessel in Teotihuacán style that is handsomely decorated. Another ceramic vessel depicts a seated monkey.

Then comes a chart showing migration paths. Early ceramics, corn, and projectile points are also displayed. There are models of the early sites of Purrón and Totimehuacán. The most impressive display for me is a large jadeite statue with Olmec characteristics that dates to the Middle Preclassic period and comes from the region of Acatlán in the southeastern part of the state of Puebla. The statue is 1.6 feet (0.5 meter) high and is in pristine condition; there are incised glyphs on the figure's skirt.

Other stone carvings include a yoke, a stela (in two pieces), and an impressive ball court marker. One case holds alabaster masks, the largest of which is in Teotihuacán style.

Farther along are displays that date to the Postclassic period and the colonial period (both religious and nonreligious items). The last section deals with popular arts, contemporary arts, and costumes.

The museum is open Tuesday through Sunday from 10:00 A.M. to 5:00 P.M. It is closed on Monday. Allow one hour for a visit. A bookstore next to the ticket office is not always open during museum hours. There is no food or drink at the museum, but there are rest rooms.

Photography without flash is permitted. Tripods are prohibited. Lighting is rather poor for photography, except in some of the display cases.

The museum is located in the northeast part of the city of Puebla, near the forts of Loreto and Guadalupe and the planetarium. It is not easy to find. I suggest going there in a taxi, although not all taxi drivers know where it is. Use the forts and the planetarium as landmarks.

Large jadeite figure with Olmec characteristics from the Acatlán region of Puebla. Middle Preclassic period. On display in the Puebla Museum.

★ ★ ★ ★
AMPARO MUSEUM

The Amparo Museum in the city of Puebla is an excellent state-of-the-art private museum. It is named in memory of the wife of Manuel Espinosa Yglesias, who created the Amparo Foundation in 1979. The museum is housed in two attractive buildings of the seventeenth and eighteenth centuries that were restored and adapted for this purpose. From the inside, you are unaware that you are moving through two buildings. Rooms and corridors surround a patio, and the museum has two floors. It opened in February 1991.

If you wish, you can rent headphones that can be plugged into monitors that have an interactive compact disc. You can then get additional information about the individual pieces by pressing the control buttons of your choice. A pamphlet explains how. There are nine monitors throughout the museum, and you can hear the audio in one of five languages: Spanish, English, French, Japanese, and German. The lighting in the museum is good, but photography is not permitted. The objects are well displayed and the labeling is fairly good.

On the walls of a room off the large entrance hall there are fine reproductions of petroglyphs from various places around the world. Nearby is a portrait of Amparo Rugarcía de Espinosa, for whom the museum is named, painted by Diego Rivera in 1952. Along the walls of the next corridor, a huge chronological chart is exhibited; it covers the time period between 2500 B.C. and A.D. 1500 and includes various parts of the world. Soon after that you come to a small side patio with an attractive modern bas-relief dedicated to maize, above which is a symbol of Tlaloc spewing water. The symbolism indicates the importance of water and the land in food production in the lives of Mesoamericans. You now come to the beginning of the most interesting parts of the museum.

The first three numbered rooms of the museum deal with techniques of art production, trends in art, and functions of art. Labeling in this section covers the techniques, styles, and uses of the items displayed, though no dates are given. In Room 1, three cases display ceramics showing how modeling, incising, and gouging were used. Two others deal with polychrome decoration and negative painting. One case exhibits outstanding ceramics from Teotihuacán and from the Toltec period; another case displays work in shell, bone, and metal. One exceptional piece is a carved conch-shell trumpet. Work in stone, gold, and silver is shown in two other cases.

Room 2 exhibits work from various parts of Mexico, grouped by area, and the displays show the art of the different cultures that inhabited those areas.

The displays in Room 3 include the various uses of art: ritual-festive, sumptuary, symbolic, commemorative, calendrical, and use by the cult of the dead. The calendrical exhibit includes an all-glyphic Maya stela and another Maya stela or panel with a standing figure and glyphs. Exhibits of ceremonial, festive, hierarchical, and domestic use are also included.

You now go upstairs to Rooms 4 through 8. Rooms 4 through 7 deal with the art of the Preclassic, Protoclassic, Classic, and Postclassic periods, respectively. Room 8 is a special room with some of the most outstanding objects in the collection. Highlights on the second floor are a large and exceptional collection of Mezcala stone figures from the Protoclassic period; a Classic period stone yoke from El Tajín carved with skulls and scrolls; a Maya relief with remains of paint from Chico Zapote, Chiapas, dating to around A.D. 900; and a Classic Maya openwork relief carved in limestone.

The museum also has a section where you can see furniture and objects used in a Puebla home in the nineteenth century. There are also earlier objects in this section, including religious paintings and statues.

Nineteenth- and twentieth-century paintings by Eugenio Landesio, Diego Rivera, and Dr. Atl (Gerardo Murillo) provide a colorful ending touch to the collection.

The Amparo Museum is at Calle Sur 2, number 708, at the corner of Avenida 9 Oriente in central Puebla. It is open on Monday and from Wednesday through Sunday from 10:00 A.M. to 6:00 P.M. It is closed on Tuesday; entry is free on Monday. Allow one hour to visit the museum.

The museum has a cafeteria and rest rooms as well as a bookstore where a catalog illustrating some of the collection is available.

★
TOTIMEHUACÁN
(toh-tee-meh-wah-KAHN)

Derivation:
A corruption of the Nahuatl Totomehuacán (Totomihuacán), meaning "Place of the Bird-Keeper."

Culture:
Texoloc del Valle and Tezoquipan del Valle.

Location:
North-central Puebla.

Maps: 3 (p. 72) and 3F (p. 147)

The Site

The pyramids of Totimehuacán are located in the northern part of the town of the same name. Several pyramids, mostly rather small, have been mapped at the site; the northernmost one is the feature of interest for visitors. This huge, late Middle Preclassic pyramidal structure rises in levels. It measures 492 feet (150 meters) long from east to west, 328 feet (100 meters) wide, and, at its highest point, 79 feet (24 meters) high; it was one of the largest constructions in central Mexico for its time period. There are no fine architectural details or superb sculptures, but the sheer mass of the structure—for such an early time—is indeed impressive.

The structure faces west, and the lower level is the most westerly; behind it rises a higher pyramid. As seen today—best viewed from the north, where you get a profile view—the grass-covered mound seems to have two levels. Excavations, however, showed that there were originally three.

A hole at the top of the high pyramid, covered with rods, shows where one burial was found. A large stone basin or sarcophagus was also found inside the structure, as were other burials. In another part of the site, heads and torsos of clay figurines were uncovered. A number of trenches were cut into the main structure, revealing walls of natural stone built without mortar.

Totimehuacán was one of the first ceremonial centers in the Puebla-Tlaxcala valley. From the front of the pyramid there are great views of the twin volcanoes Iztaccíhuatl and Popocatépetl.

Totimehuacán's pyramids date to 600 to 200 B.C., and the north pyramid is the only Preclassic pyramid known with interior rooms and tunnels; their function here is unknown.

Enormous Middle Preclassic pyramid, Totimehuacán.

Recent History

The name Totimehuacán has been used for the town from at least the early seventeenth century, and the site takes its name from the town.

Before 1963, a little work had been conducted at the site, but not all the structures had been investigated, and nothing had been published. In 1963, the Mexican-German Project in Puebla and Tlaxcala began. Its purpose was to locate sites in the area and to conduct limited excavations in some of them to get an overall idea of the region's archaeology. Later, Totimehuacán was selected for more thorough excavation, which began in October 1964 and continued for five months. During this work all the structures at the site were mapped.

Though all the structures date to the late Middle Preclassic period, a Postclassic surface deposit of destroyed ceramic vessels was found on one of the smaller structures.

A preliminary report on this work was issued by Bodo Spranz in 1966. Funding for the project came from the German Research Community.

Connection

Puebla to Totimehuacán: 8.1 miles [13.0 kilometers] by paved road (:31), then 0.4 miles [0.6 kilometer] by poor rock road (:05).

Getting There

From Puebla (at the junction of Avenida Juárez and Highway 190 to Atlixco), head southeast for 1.2 miles [1.9 kilometers] and turn left into the interior circuit (a road that bypasses central Puebla). Go 2.2 miles [3.5 kilometers] and join the road that goes to the town of Totimehuacán and Africam (a zoological park). Go 4.4 miles [7.1 kilometers] to the town of Totimehuacán and turn left at the first street past the church (on the left). From there it is 0.7 mile [1.1 kilometers] straight ahead to the pyramid (on the right). The first 0.3 mile [0.5 kilometer] is a paved street, but the last 0.4 mile [0.6 kilometer] is a rough rock road. Watch out for *topes* on the paved part. You can drive the rock road in a standard vehicle, but you will have to take it very slowly. A high-clearance vehicle would be better.

Allow 15 minutes to see the pyramid and a few more if you want to climb it. There are no facilities of any kind at the pyramid, and no specific open hours. Cold drinks are sold in town, which can be reached by taxi or bus from Puebla.

★ ★
TEPOZTECO
(teh-pohs-TEH-koh)

Derivation:
  Nahuatl for "Place of the Ax."
Culture:
  Tlahuica or Tepozteca (see text).
Location:
  Northern Morelos, on the edge of Tepoztlán.
Maps: 3 (p. 72) and 3G (p. 169)

The Site

The feature of interest at Tepozteco is a Late Postclassic shrine perched on a pinnacle some 1,969 feet (600 meters) above the town of Tepoztlán. Only you can decide whether you think it is worth the climb, but let me say that if you attempt it, it will seem like twice the recorded 1,969 feet. This one is definitely not recommended for anyone with heart or respiratory problems.

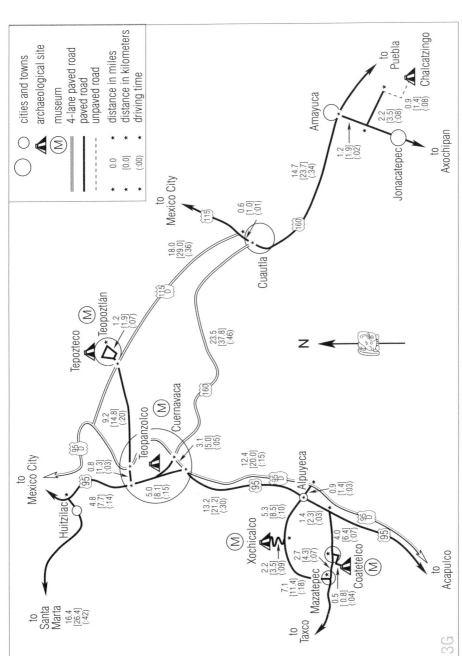

Area around Cuernavaca (Map 3G).

Back view of the Temple of Tepozteco and the pinnacle on which it is perched. Late Postclassic period.

And in all honesty, I have to say that this is the one site I did not revisit in preparing this book (although I did revisit Tepoztlán). Nevertheless, the information provided here should still be reasonably valid.

The climb takes about 1.5 hours, but it is exhausting. The footing is generally good, however, and the trail goes through some lovely scenery along the way.

The Temple of Tepozteco rest on a pyramidal base and is composed of two chambers, with a stairway giving access on the western side. Although there is no longer a roof, the massive walls of the temple rise over 6 feet (1.8 meters). The inner chamber—with a bench running around three sides—is the more interesting of the two, because it contains remains of sculptured decorations. The jambs that formed the doorway to the inner chamber are also carved. The inner chamber originally contained an idol of Tezpoztécatl, the god of pulque (an indigenous intoxicat-

ing beverage still imbibed in Mexico), to whom the shrine was dedicated. He is described as a sort of patron saint of Tepoztlán.

During the early colonial period, Fray Domingo de la Asunción sought to destroy this idol in an effort to convert the local inhabitants to Catholicism. Many legends have sprung from his act. One says he cast the idol over the cliff, but it landed intact, whereupon it was demolished by hand and the fragments were used in the foundation of a church in a neighboring town.

The Tlahuicas or Tepoztecas, both Nahua groups related to the Aztecs, are generally credited with having built Tepozteco. They were later conquered by the Aztecs. A carving with a glyph for the Aztec king Ahuítzotl was found in the debris of the temple, and he is known to have reigned from 1486 to 1502. The temple shows many Aztec architectural characteristics, and ceramics found there also confirm this late date. There is evidence,

Detail of carved stones that form the bench in the back of the inner chamber of the Temple of Tepozteco. Late Post-classic period.

however, that the site was occupied from the Preclassic period to the time of the Spanish conquest, and it is still occupied today.

The shrine of Tepozteco was a place of pilgrimage in pre-Hispanic times and, with the town of Tepoztlán below, was a living entity at the time of the Spanish conquest. From the pinnacle, views of the town below and the countryside are superb.

Recent History

Knowledge of Tepozteco was never lost, but the first archaeological report of the site was one dated 1895 by the Mexican architect Francisco Rodríguez, who also undertook some consolidation. He made a plan of the temple and sketches of the reliefs, and he discovered that the terrain at the top of the pinnacle had been leveled to accommodate the temple. There has been no systematic excavation at Tepozteco, but the German archaeologist Eduard Seler studied the reliefs.

Connection

Cuernavaca to Tepoztlán: 11.2 miles [18.0 kilometers] by paved road (:30), then 1.5 hours uphill on foot to Tepozteco.

Getting There

From Cuernavaca (at the junction of Highway 95 and the unnumbered road to Tepoztlán), head east to and into Tepoztlán. At the base of the pinnacle, where you start your climb, there is a park. It is at the north end of Avenida del Tepozteco. You could park there or in the yard mentioned under Tepoztlán Museum.

There is no food at the site, but at one time the caretaker sold soft drinks kept cool in pine needles. I could not help wondering who carried them all the way up. More recently I have heard that unchilled lemonade is available. Both food and drink can be had in Tepoztlán.

This is one trip for which you will want to strip your camera gear down to bare essentials. A normal lens will get you by. Allow 3.5 hours to climb to the temple, look around, and return to the town. Tepozteco is open daily from 10:00 A.M. to 5:00 P.M. (some sources say 4:30 P.M.). Keep this in mind so that you don't start the climb too late in the day.

Tepoztlán can be reached by bus from Cuernavaca.

★ ★ ★
COLLECTION CARLOS PELLICER ARCHAEOLOGICAL MUSEUM (TEPOZTLÁN MUSEUM)

On November 26, 1988, the attractive new Tepoztlán Museum was inaugurated in the town of that name; it is a much finer facility than its predecessor, which opened in July 1965. It houses the collection of Carlos Pellicer Cámara, a Tabascan poet who also donated part of his collection to the Villa-hermosa Museum.

A chart at the entrance shows the locations of the various cases and the state or culture from which the artifacts in them came. Otherwise, there is very little labeling. Items from all parts of Mexico are included,

Olmec greenstone head. Preclassic period. Displayed in the Tepoztlán Museum.

and the following are some of the highlights of the collection. There is a fine Olmec vase with an incised profile, some impressive Olmec greenstone heads, carved Maya vases and polychrome plates, and a bone carved with what appear to be Maya glyphs.

Veracruz is represented with figurines and typical smiling Totonac clay heads, carved *hachas* and other stones, and part of a yoke. There are clay figurines from western Mexico and a nice though somewhat eroded Maya stone bas-relief. Other displays include pieces from Teotihuacán and Oaxaca.

Mexica culture is well represented, with some fine stone carvings. One depicts a female wearing a *quechquémitl*, and another depicts an eagle resting on a drum that is also carved on the underside. A mirror allows you to view that part. Outside the museum, two carved ball court markers (one mostly eroded) and a couple of stone heads are displayed.

Lighting inside is above average, at least around the perimeter of the museum; displays along the inside wall are only fairly lighted. Photography without flash is permitted.

The museum is located in the center of Tepoztlán, on the east side of the square that abuts the plaza on the east. As you enter the town you will see museum signs pointing the way. The museum is open Tuesday through Sunday from 10:00 A.M. to 6:00 P.M. It is closed on Monday. Allow 30 minutes for a visit. A few publications are sold at the museum. Food and drink are available in town.

Across the street from the museum, a short distance away along a diagonal street, you can park in someone's yard. Parking signs point out the way. Finding street parking in this area is difficult.

If you are in Tepoztlán to see Tepozteco, don't miss seeing the museum as well.

★ ★
TEOPANZOLCO
(teh-oh-pahn-SOHL-koh)

Derivation:
Nahuatl for "In an Old (or Abandoned) Temple."
Culture:
Tlahuica (see text).
Location:
Northwestern Morelos.
Maps: 3 (p. 72) and 3G (p. 169)

The Site

Teopanzolco is a relatively small site made up of several structures, the most impressive of which is a double pyramid that faces west onto a plaza. The pyramid was built over an earlier one of similar design.

The inner pyramid has a double stairway broken by projections on the *alfardas.* The lower walls of two temples are found on top. The outer pyramid has a similar double stairway on the west side, but without the projections. A wide-angle lens is useful here for photos of the inner stairway.

Across the plaza are several small, low platforms, a couple of which are circular. In back (east) of the double pyramid is another structure, which appears to have been built in more than one construction stage, and to the north of the pyramid is a platform.

Teopanzolco was originally built by the Tlahuicas, according to most sources. This Nahua group was later conquered by the Aztecs. The Tlahuicas were still living in the area and paying tribute to the Aztecs at the time of the Spanish conquest.

According to Ignacio Marquina, the double pyramid at Teopanzolco, as well as the ceramics recovered during excavation, was contemporaneous with similar structures in central Mexico, such as those of Tenayuca, Santa Cecilia, and the Templo Mayor of Tenochtitlán. In other words, the Teopanzolco pyramid dates to the Late Postclassic period.

Recent History

The story goes that Teopanzolco was discovered in 1910, during the Mexican Revolution, when an artillery emplacement on a

Double pyramid, northwest corner, Teopanzolco. Postclassic period.

---

mound shook loose some dirt and revealed stone construction below. What was below was the double pyramid.

In 1921, Manuel Gamio and José Reggadas Vértiz explored Teopanzolco, and in 1956–57, Eduardo Noguera and Román Piña Chan reported on its stratigraphy.

Connection and Getting There

The site is in the city of Cuernavaca, near the railway station and northeast of the center of town. There is no regular parking area for the site, which is in a residential area, but on-street parking near the site is easy to find. Pyramid signs mark part of the way to the site, which can also be reached by taxi.

Teopanzolco is open daily from 10:00 A.M. to 4:30 P.M. Soft drinks and snacks are sold in the service building at the entrance to the site, and there are rest rooms there as well. Allow 45 minutes for a visit. Afternoon hours are the best, since the front of the double pyramid is well lighted then.

★ ★ ★

REGIONAL MUSEUM OF CUAUHNÁHUAC (PALACE OF CORTÉS) (CUERNAVACA MUSEUM)

Cuauhnáhuac means "in the middle of the grove" in ancient Nahuatl; the name was Hispanicized to Cuernavaca in the sixteenth century. The Cuernavaca Museum is housed in the Palace of Cortés, built by the conqueror Hernán Cortés in 1530 on top of ancient Tlahuica remains. It is said to have been his favorite residence in Mexico, and from it he supervised the vast domains that were granted him by the Spanish Crown. The palace served as the administrative center of the area until the late 1960s, when it was converted into an art museum. Later it became a museum of archaeology and history.

The Cuernavaca Museum is actually a very good three-star museum; three and a half stars would be a more accurate rating. It houses a fine collection of pre-Columbian, colonial, and later artifacts. It also contains murals by Diego Rivera.

On a lawn in front of the museum lie some boulders carved in bas-relief. One depicts the shield of Xipe Totec, with darts or arrows and accompanying date glyphs; another shows an eagle; and the third is hard to make out.

The museum has two stories, with the pre-Columbian section on the first floor. The first room displays a map of the world showing possible migration routes to Mexico. Next is a room devoted to the prehistory of Mesoamerica, where stone artifacts and remains of extinct mammals are exhibited.

The next three rooms of the museum are, to me, the most interesting—the Preclassic room, the Classic room, and the Xochicalco room, also relating to the Classic period. The Preclassic room displays ceramics from the Nexpa region, rubbings of some of the boulder carvings at Chalcatzingo, and artifacts excavated there. Also displayed is a nice collection of Preclassic figurines and a case showing a burial found near the caves of Cacahuamilpa.

There are several notable objects in the Classic room. One is a square stone, carved in bas-relief, showing figures and glyphs that depict an event at Coatlán, although the stone comes from Xochicalco. A stone bas-relief ball court ring is another interesting display. Both items are in mint condition. Also exhibited are ceramics showing Teotihuacán influence and a clay relief depicting Tlahuizcalpantecuhtli, or Quetzalcóatl in his manifestation as the planet Venus as morning star.

Bas-relief panel from Xochicalco with three date glyphs in three styles. Classic period. Displayed in the Cuernavaca Museum.

You next walk through an outdoor area where you will see the remains of the Tlahuica structure on which the palace was built, and then on to the Xochicalco room. One of the most interesting items there is a rectangular stone carved in bas-relief with three calendrical glyphs in three different styles—Maya, Zapotec, and Nahua. A nearby stone carving depicts a seated Xochiquetzal wearing a *quechquémitl.*

The next rooms cover the Postclassic period and feature pictographs and petroglyphs, a stone carving depicting the Aztec New Fire ceremony, enlargements of part of a sixteenth-century codex depicting the migrations of Nahua tribes, items representing Tlahuica culture (including a number of stone carvings), a facsimile of a tribute list, and Aztec and Tlahuica ceramics.

The second floor covers the period from the Spanish conquest to the early twentieth century. Diego Rivera's murals depicting the history of Cuernavaca are found in this section. Exhibits in several rooms include conquest period suits of armor, equipment used by early Spanish colonists, altar pieces and other religious art from the seventeenth through the nineteenth century, and colonial period furniture. There are paintings, drawings, and photographs depicting life in Mexico through hundreds of years, and a section devoted to the Mexican Revolution.

The Cuernavaca Museum was formally inaugurated on February 1, 1974, after two and a half years of study and work to develop the Palace of Cortés for this purpose. Archaeological and historical investigations were part of the project. The work was coordinated by Jorge Angulo Villaseñor, the first director of the museum.

The museum is located on the east side of the main plaza in the center of Cuernavaca. It is open Tuesday through Sunday from 10:00 A.M. to 5:00 P.M. It is closed on Monday. Photography without flash is permitted. The lighting, both ambient and artificial, is fairly good, as is the labeling, with some signs in English. Bilingual guides are available at the entrance. There are rest rooms. Food and drink are available at nearby restaurants. Allow 1.5 hours for a visit.

It is difficult to find a parking place near the museum, and driving around the congested center of Cuernavaca is difficult as well. I recommend taking a taxi to the museum.

★ ★ ★
XOCHICALCO
(soh-chee-KAHL-koh)

Derivation:
Nahuatl for "Place of the House of Flowers."
Culture:
See text.
Location:
Western Morelos.
Maps: 3 (p. 72) and 3G (p. 169)

The Site

Xochicalco is one of the most interesting, important, and thoroughly delightful sites in central Mexico. It is located on an artificially terraced and partially leveled hill, Cerro Xochicalco, overlooking a beautiful green countryside and some small lakes, although the area can become barren in the dry season.

The appearance of Xochicalco has changed dramatically in recent years with the inception of a huge archaeological project. When you drive up to the site, you will see reconstructed buildings on top, in light gray stone, rather than mounds covered with green vegetation. Access to the site (on foot) has also changed.

From the parking area, follow the trail west and uphill. The first important structure you come to is the consolidated North Ball Court, where a couple of stone rings are found at ground level in the playing alley. Walk around the north side of the north structure and follow the trail west and south toward the Observatory. Along the way you will pass near a steam bath. The entrance to the Observatory is through a cavelike opening in the side of the hill, approached by a stairway. Two other openings into the hill are found nearby; all three were deliberately cut.

Inside the tunnel that leads to the Observatory are remains of a broad stairway and, farther along to the east, a vertical hole (rather like a chimney) leading to the outside. This is believed to have served for astronomical

North Ball Court, Xochicalco, Late Classic period.

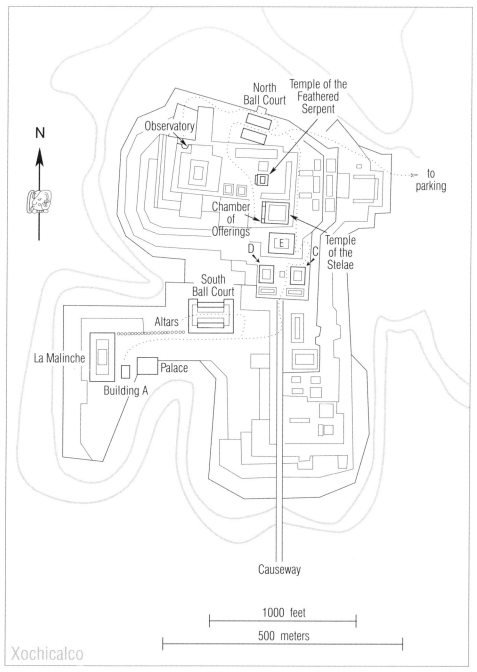

North
Ball Court

Temple of the
Feathered
Serpent

Observatory

to
parking

N

Chamber
of
Offerings

E

D

C

Temple
of the
Stelae

South
Ball Court

Altars

La Malinche

Palace

Building A

Causeway

1000 feet

500 meters

Xochicalco

Modified after Marquina, 1951.

Temple of the Feathered Serpent, northwest corner, Xochicalco. Late Classic period.

Detail of the lower face of the Temple of the Feathered Serpent, Xochicalco, showing a seated Maya-like figure. Late Classic period.

observations. The upper part of the shaft is lined with boulders. There are also remains of stucco floors in the tunnel. Generally a guard is posted there to lead you around inside with a flashlight, but it is a good idea to have a light of your own as well.

Now return to the North Ball Court and take the trail uphill to the Ceremonial Plaza, the upper part of the site.

The Temple of the Feathered Serpent, found on this level, is the real gem of the site. With lower walls intact, it rises on a pyramidal base with a western stair. Its fame lies in the multitude of carvings on its outer surfaces. At one time it was believed that there were no earlier constructions beneath it, but it is now known that there were two previous constructions. The interior of the structure was excavated, and now when you climb the stairway, you can look down into the structure. On one lower wall you can see two painted rows of small red circles. Also on the interior are masonry pillars and a low platform.

On the outside of the structure, on the lower, sloped face, are carved depictions of the feathered serpent, Quetzalcóatl, stylized

Detail of the lower face of the Temple of the Feathered Serpent, Xochicalco, showing a feathered serpent. Late Classic period.

shells—a symbol of this deity—and seated figures in Maya-like style. They are accompanied by glyphs and dates in the bar-and-dot system used by the Mayas and Zapotecs. Also found are glyphs and dates in the system used by the Mixtec and Nahua groups—dots without bars. One theory holds that these calendrical glyphs in two styles represent some adjustment in the calendar. The reliefs average some 3 inches (7.6 centimeters) deep, and the whole was originally painted.

The panel above the sloped face has additional carved remains, and the projecting cornice is formed of stylized seashells. The lower parts of the *alfardas* flanking the stairs have a design representing the scales of the serpent, and the remains of the temple walls and the jambs feature more carvings of sandaled figures, glyphs, birds, animals, and warriors with shields and darts. This temple and others at the site are thought to have had flat roofs originally. A wide-angle lens is good here, because you cannot step back very far from the reliefs. In the Ceremonial Plaza near the Temple of the Feathered Serpent is a pile of carved stones that originally adorned the temple.

From the Temple of the Feathered Serpent, head south to the Temple of the Stelae. When it was excavated in 1961, three beautifully carved though broken stelae were found beneath the flooring. They are now in the Mexico City Museum.

Now return to the North Ball Court and follow the path east and then south to the east side of Building E. From there a path leads downhill to the Main Plaza, with Buildings C and D on the east and west sides, respectively, and a low platform that supports the somewhat eroded Stela of the Two Glyphs.

Buildings C and D are virtually identical and are composed of a sloped lower wall with a vertical wall above it and the sloped walls and pillars of the temple on top. Each structure has a broad stairway facing the plaza.

Building E borders the plaza on the north; it is the largest structure at Xochicalco and can best be appreciated from the Main Plaza.

From there, follow the trail south (and downhill), then west to the South Ball Court. Xochicalco's impressive South Ball Court is over 200 feet (61 meters) long and is l-shaped, as is the North Ball Court. The walls flanking the playing area are sloped and meet vertical walls with stone rings. It is sometimes compared to the main ball court at Tula.

West of the South Ball Court you come to 21 low altars running in an east-west line; 20 of them are circular and 1 is rectangular. South of this is an architectural complex

The Temple of the Three Stelae (at top of stairway) and the Chamber of Offerings (at right of base of stairway), Xochicalco. Late Classic period.

Building D (right), northeast corner, and a low platform that supports the Stela of the Two Glyphs, Xochicalco. Late Classic period.

called the Palace. There you see the lower walls of many interconnecting rooms and patios. This is one of the most complex and elaborate habitation units at the site, and it included a sweat bath. This complex was no doubt used by elites.

A bit farther west is Building A—a small structure that may have been an altar.

There are some remains of lower walls and a stucco floor. Again to the west is the large pyramidal mound called La Malinche; although it has been partly excavated, no restoration has so far been attempted.

In addition to the ceremonial structures occupying the main portion of Cerro Xochicalco, there is an extensive complex of buildings on the neighboring hill (Cerro de Bodega), to which Cerro Xochicalco was connected by an ancient causeway. The structures on Cerro de Bodega were probably ceremonial but may also have acted as a fort, considering that the area is walled.

The area around Xochicalco was first occupied in the Middle Preclassic period, when a couple of small agricultural settlements existed. In the Late Preclassic and Early Classic the population increased, and more settlements were occupied.

Xochicalco's apogee came in the Late Classic, from A.D. 650 to 900, and during that time most of the site's monumental architecture was constructed. It is estimated that Xochicalco had a population of 10,000 to 20,000 in its heyday.

Around A.D. 900, the urban nucleus was destroyed and became practically uninhabited. Between 1250 and 1420, a nucleated population was again at the site, and then it was conquered by the Aztecs (Mexicas).

Xochicalco was influenced by various other cultural groups during its history. There may have been influence from the Maya area as early as A.D. 300, but certainly there was some by the eighth century. Other influences proceeded from Teotihuacán, the Zapotec and Mixtec areas of Oaxaca and Puebla, and the Gulf Coast. It is possible that Mixtec speakers settled at Xochicalco in Late Classic times.

And Xochicalco exerted its own influence upon Mesoamerica for years. This is evident in the sculptural style of the Toltecs and even, in a few instances, in sculpture from as late as the Aztec period. Xochicalco is sometimes thought of as a connecting link between Classic Teotihuacán and Postclassic Tula, with which it was partly contemporaneous.

Recent History

The ruins of Xochicalco were first explored by Antonio Alzate y Ramírez in 1777 and 1784; his description of them was published in 1791. His illustrations were also published by Alexander von Humboldt in 1810. Other explorers followed in the nineteenth century, including Guillermo Dupaix (accompanied by the artist Luciano Castañeda), Carlos

Nebel, and Jean Frédéric Waldeck. Even the ill-fated Maximilian visited the site while he was emperor of Mexico.

In 1910, Leopoldo Batres restored the Temple of the Feathered Serpent. Eduard Seler made some study of the sculpture in the early twentieth century, and in 1928, Marshall Saville compiled an annotated bibliography of works on the site.

Major work at Xochicalco, including excavation and restoration, was conducted from the 1940s to the 1960s by Mexican and American archaeologists. Of primary importance were the ceramic studies by Eduardo Noguera, published in 1947, and the discovery of three stelae by César A. Sáenz in 1961, as well as his later work at the site.

Other scholars conducting studies at Xochicalco were Pedro Armillas, William T. Sanders, Jaime Litvak King, Kenneth G. Hirth, and Ann Cyphers Guillén. In the 1980s, Norberto González Crespo and Silvia Garza Tarazona spent two seasons excavating in the area of the south access to the site. In 1991, a major excavation and restoration project began under the direction of González Crespo. It continued for several years, with 350 people taking part, and it almost completely changed the look of the site. During this work the site museum was also constructed.

Connection

Cuernavaca to Xochicalco: 25.8 miles [41.5 kilometers] by paved road (:52).

Getting There

From the northern *glorieta* in Cuernavaca, head south on Highway 95 to the south end of town, 5.0 miles [8.1 kilometers]. There you pick up Highway 95D. Continue south to the Alpuyeca cutoff, 12.4 miles [20.0 kilometers], and turn right (northwest) to Alpuyeca, 0.9 miles [1.4 kilometers]. Continue northwest to the cutoff for Xochicalco (marked with a sign), 5.3 miles [8.5 kilometers]. Turn right and proceed to the site slowly—there are lots of *topes* on this last stretch.

You can also reach Xochicalco by taking Highway 95 to Alpuyeca, but the road goes through many small towns with lots of *topes*.

For this reason Highway 95D (the toll road) is recommended.

When you reach the top of the hill, turn right and drive to the site museum and around to its east side. There you can use the museum's parking lot. Buy your ticket to the site at the museum and drive to the site's parking area. (The site museum was not yet open at the time of our last visit, so it is not covered here. It is reported to be excellent, however, with several large rooms displaying pieces recovered during recent excavations.

Surely it would be well worth a visit.) From the parking area it takes seven minutes to climb to the North Ball Court.

Xochicalco is open daily from 10:00 A.M. to 4:30 P.M., except for the Observatory, which is open from 11:00 A.M. to 2:00 P.M. Allow three hours to visit the whole site. Snacks and cold drinks are sold near the ticket office, where rest rooms are available. There is an extra charge to bring a video camera into the site. Bring plenty of film; Xochicalco is very photogenic. Carry a canteen of water.

★ ★
COATETELCO
(kwah-teh-TEHL-koh)

Derivation:
  Nahuatl for "Place of the
  Serpents on the Mounds of
  Stone."
Culture:
  Tlahuica.
Location:
  West-central Morelos.
Maps: 3 (p. 72) and 3G (p. 169)

The Site

From the parking area at the site, you enter the Ceremonial Plaza, surrounded by structures on all four sides. This is the most important part of the site, although other remains are also found in the modern town. The Principal Temple lies on the east side of the plaza. The wall of the base of the structure is sloped, and it once rose in three tiers; only the lower tier has been restored. Access to the top is by a wide stairway, bordered by *alfardas,* on the west side. When the building was excavated, a stone carving believed to represent Cuauhtlitzin, a female deity, was discovered.

To the left (north) is a smaller and lower platform, also with western stairs. The north side of the plaza is bordered by a greatly ruined and unrestored platform.

On the west, four smaller platforms abut the east side of the ball court. In one (the most northerly), a statue of Xipe Totec was recovered. Next to that platform is a circular one, almost certainly dedicated to Ehécatl. Burials accompanied by grave goods were found in some of these platforms. On the south side of the plaza is a platform with a double stairway.

The attractive ball court is I-shaped with enclosed ends. Its walls rise in two tiers, the lower tier being sloped and the upper vertical. This is one of the smallest ball courts known in Mesoamerica and one of the few surviving from the Late Post-classic period.

Although Coatetelco was apparently occupied from the time of Teotihuacán's influence (A.D. 450 to 600), all the remains seen there today date to the Late Postclassic. In all, four construction stages are evident in the architecture.

Recent History

Coatetelco has long been known as an archaeological site. A sixteenth-century chapel (near the existing eighteenth-century church) was built on top of pre-Hispanic remains.

The first serious excavations started centuries later. Raúl Arana Álvarez excavated Coatetelco in the 1970s and also

Ball court at Coatetelco. Late Postclassic period.

directed the reconstruction of the buildings. Some minor excavations have been undertaken since then.

Connection

Cuernavaca to Coatetelco (via Highway 95D): 24.2 miles [39.0 kilometers] by paved road (:47).

Getting There

From the *glorieta* at the north end of Cuernavaca, head south through the city. Near the south end get on Highway 95D and continue south to the exit for Alpuyeca (marked with a sign). Turn right and go to Highway 95, then left to the cutoff for Coatetelco. After

4.0 miles [6.4 kilometers] turn left (this is in the town of Coatetelco) and go uphill a short distance to a cross. Then turn right until you come alongside the church. Turn left and continue uphill to the gate for the site (on the left). There is a right-left jog in the road on this last part. There is a parking area inside the gate near the site museum.

You can also reach Coatetelco by taking old Highway 95 all the way from Cuernavaca, but it goes through a few villages with lots of *topes*. It will take you 12 minutes longer than using Highway 95D.

Coatetelco is open Tuesday through Sunday from 10:00 A.M. to 5:00 P.M. It is closed on Monday. Allow 30 minutes for a visit. There are rest rooms at the site museum; no food or drink is available.

★ ★
COATETELCO MUSEUM

The stone carving of Cuauhtlitzin discovered in the Principal Temple at Coatetelco stands on a brick platform outside the entrance to the Coatetelco Museum. The carving is well preserved, and a nearby sign gives information (in Spanish) about this deity.

The first room of the museum contains stone carvings, including one depicting Xipe Totec and a bas-relief recording the date One Death. Yet another shows a human head inside the jaws of a serpent. One display case contains Tlahuica ceramics while another

Stone carving of the female deity Cuauh-tlitzin, from Coatetelco. Late Postclassic period. Displayed in front of the Coatetelco Museum.

houses Aztec wares. There is a chronological chart showing influences on Coatetelco from Xochicalco and other sites. A model of Coatetelco is also found in the first room.

Another Xipe Totec, this one decapitated, is found in the second room. The rest of the displays include objects from the colonial period and later times. Armor and a wooden plow are displayed.

All the pre-Columbian objects in the collection come from Coatetelco. The museum opened in the 1970s to house the finds. The light in the museum is fairly good, and signs inside provide pertinent information. Photography without flash is permitted. The museum is open the same days and hours as the site. Allow 10 minutes to see the collection.

★ ★ ★

CHALCATZINGO

(chahl-kaht-SEEN-goh)

Derivation:
   Nahuatl, possibly meaning
   "Revered Place of Sacred
   Water," according to David C.
   Grove.
Culture:
   Central Mexican but showing
   Olmec influence.
Location:
   Far eastern Morelos.
Maps: 3 (p. 72) and 3G (p. 169)

The Site

Chalcatzingo, situated in lovely surroundings, is an intriguing site archaeologically and a most interesting one to visit. It is known for its abundance of early bas-relief carvings on stelae, altars, and boulders in a style related to Olmec art. When you buy your ticket, ask whether there is someone who can show you around. Often there are shepherds in the area, and with one of them along, you will not miss anything. If no one is available, the guardian will point up the hill to the major monument. Although there is no definite trail, once you climb partway you will see the thatch shelter protecting the monument and will be able to find your way. The climb to the monument takes about 20 minutes and is a bit tiring. After that the tour is easier, as it is mostly downhill.

   The major boulder carvings at the site are on different levels of Cerro Chalcatzingo, an igneous intrusion that stands out above the valley floor. There are other intrusions nearby, and they all can be seen from a great distance away.

   When you arrive at the shelter you will see Monument 1 (El Rey), a large bas-relief carved on a boulder. It depicts a richly attired personage seated on a throne inside a cave that represents the mouth of a supernatural earth-monster. The figure wears a tall headdress and holds a bar with a horizontal S symbol; this symbol appears on the throne as well. Large scrolls issue from the cave, probably representing mist or wind. The scene also includes stylized rain clouds, large raindrops, and sprouting maize plants. You will need a wide-angle lens and a flash unit to adequately photograph this monument and the other sheltered monuments as well.

   Nearby are other, smaller bas-reliefs. The two clearest are Monument 14, depicting a stylized animal, a rain cloud, and large raindrops, and Monument 6, which shows a squash plant. They are to the left and behind you when you are looking at El Rey, and they, too, are protected by a thatch shelter.

Monument 1, showing a throned personage inside a cave, Chalcatzingo. Middle Preclassic period.

Detail of Monument 2, showing the head of a seated figure, Chalcatzingo. Middle Preclassic period.

Descend partway down the hill, turn right, and continue ahead for a while to a stone stairway that lies at the base of Monument 2. Climb it and turn to the right to reach the monument. Unfortunately, this monument, with its four figures, can be seen only piecemeal, and you must lie on the boulder below it even to see it that way. According to David Grove in his 1984 book *Chalcatzingo,* "sometime after the scene had been carved across the north face of a large boulder, the stone was severely undercut by erosion, causing it to tilt forward until it rested against another rock below it on the hillside." In more recent times, portions of the lower boulder were removed, making the carving more accessible.

The figure on the far right is seated and faces left toward two others who are walking toward him. The figure on the far left is walking the other way; he carries what appears to be the stalk of a large plant. The other two standing figures (in the middle) carry paddle-shaped staffs. Grove believes the carving depicts an agricultural ritual.

Nearby, a carving of a feline is sheltered by a roof and rests in an enclosure. A horizontal S motif adorns the top of the scene, and a raindrop is found between it and the feline. The carving was discovered in the early 1990s.

You next come to Monument 3, a bas-relief of another feline in a recumbent pose, seemingly licking the base of a cactuslike branching object. Monument 4 is nearby, and it depicts two human figures being pounced upon by two felines with unsheathed claws. Both animals are shown with attributes that indicate they are supernaturals. Monument 4 is related to the next, Monument 5, which shows a human figure either emerging from the mouth of a saurian monster or being devoured by it. The human figure is very much like those on Monument 4. Three S motifs are also part of the scene. Some archaeologists think the monster represents the feathered serpent; others do not.

On a lower slope of the hill, in an enclosed and sheltered area, you will come to the fragmented Monument 13. It shows a human with a cleft head seated within the mouth of an earth-monster face, a theme similar to that on Monument 1. The figure on Monument 13, however, has supernatural attributes, whereas the one on Monument 1 is probably a portrait carving.

From there you return to the area where tickets are sold and continue north and then east. This will get you to another enclosed, sheltered area, this one housing Monument 27, a stela with a depiction of a walking figure wearing an animal skin (or perhaps with a deer over his shoulder). The stela was found in situ in front of a two-stage, stone-faced platform. The monument was deliberately mutilated in ancient times (as were others at

Monument 5, depicting a feathered serpent with a figure emerging from its mouth, Chalcatzingo. Middle Preclassic period.

Chalcatzingo and elsewhere); it is difficult to discern the design.

To the north of Monument 27 is a circular altar, Monument 25, approached by a wide trail. The altar is plain on top but is carved with pendant ovals around its upper circumference. From there, head northwest to an even lower terrace, where you will see Monument 22, a tabletop altar (significant because it is the only tabletop altar found outside the Gulf Coast Olmec region), and three smaller fragmented or eroded monuments within another enclosure. Monument 22 is sheltered, and the design on its face is hard to make out, but it is carved with the eyes and undulating eyebrows of a supernatural earth-monster.

You now head southwest to Monument 21 (La Reina), a stela lying on its back on top of a modern platform. The figure on the stela represents a standing female with her hands pressed against a sort of carved column. She wears a skirt, a trailing head scarf, and bands on her upper arms. Her one exposed breast confirms her sex as female, making this the earliest known depiction of a female on monumental art in Mesoamerica.

From there, head south to the ticket office. On the way, stop for a look at the low remains of a structure that may be part of a ball court, and beyond it, a large platform mound with a pyramidal construction on the west end. The lower steps on the west side have been consolidated. (You passed the east end of the platform earlier on your way to Monument 27.)

Evidence for the earliest occupation known at Chalcatzingo comes from a charcoal sample that gave a radiocarbon date of 1660 B.C. ± 90 years. The charcoal was collected from a deep excavation into the large platform mound and was found in a level with small quantities of early ceramics. Grove, who conducted the excavation, warned that this single early date must be viewed with caution, saying that "a date from a single radiocarbon assay cannot be considered definitive."

From the Amate phase (1500 to 1100 B.C.) there is more evidence for occupation of the site, though it probably housed no more than 60 people. Ceramics from this phase are like those found at other Early Preclassic sites in Morelos and like those at Tlatilco in the Basin of Mexico. Inside the platform mound was found an Amate phase structure—an earthen platform faced with stone cobbles that originally stood more than 6.6 feet (2 meters) high. It was enlarged at least once later in this phase, and its height was nearly doubled. Later phases saw additional enlargements of the structure; the last occurred in 600 B.C.

Another, smaller Amate phase structure was also found to the northeast. The presence of monumental architecture at such an early date at Chalcatzingo is surprising, because such structures are yet to be found at larger sites in richer areas.

During the Barranca phase (1100 to 700 B.C.), the hillsides at Chalcatzingo were terraced, an enterprise that required a great deal of human labor. The purpose was to minimize the loss of rainwater through runoff. To prevent erosion, artificial embankments (still in use today) were included in the terrace constructions. The terraces were used for farming and habitation. Grove believes the population at this time to have been between 130 and 325 people.

The basic culture at Chalcatzingo was central Mexican during these two early phases. Although ceramic traits from the Olmec heartland on the Gulf Coast had arrived at Chalcatzingo over a period of several hundred years, during the Cantera phase (700 to 500 B.C.) these influences reached an apex, and this was the same time that Chalcatzingo reached its apogee.

By this time the site had become a major regional center, perhaps the most important one in central Mexico. Chalcatzingo was a redistribution center for valuable resources such as obsidian, greenstone, and shells. It was also during the Cantera phase that most, if not all, of Chalcatzingo's bas-reliefs were carved. With its monumental architecture and elaborate carvings, the site was unique in central Mexico at that time. A population estimate, based on potsherds collected from the ground surface, indicated that 433 to 1,081 people lived at Chalcatzingo during the Cantera phase. Another estimate, using housing units as a measurement, yielded a much lower figure—140.

Chalcatzingo declined and was abandoned shortly after 500 B.C., although it was occasionally reoccupied later. Around 300 B.C., a few families briefly lived on some of the terraces, and around A.D. 400 there was a substantial reoccupation of the site, with evident influence from Teotihuacán. At this time the pyramid was built on the western end of the large platform mound. The presumed ball court and a couple of other, minor buildings were also constructed, but Chalcatzingo was by then a relatively small and inconsequential settlement.

A good deal of painted rock art (mostly stick figures painted red) was produced in the Late Classic period; many of the paintings are found in shallow caves near the site. The stairway below Monument 2 was constructed around A.D. 1200, and an area slightly north of Chalcatzingo was occupied until around 1350.

Recent History

Although people living in the area were aware of some of the carvings at Chalcatzingo, they believed them to be unimportant. On a night in 1932, a storm brought torrential rains and high winds, flooding the lower fields and felling trees on the hillside. In the morning, the villagers went to check on the damage to their crops and were called to by some children cutting firewood from the felled trees. They climbed to where the children were and saw the carving now called El Rey. Earth had been washed from the hillside during the downpour, exposing the carving. It was thought to be important, and word of it spread beyond the village.

The news soon came to the attention of the archaeologist Eulalia Guzmán in Mexico City, and shortly afterward she went to see it. She was shown not only El Rey but also some of the other monuments, and she recognized that two mounds at the site were ancient pyramids. She issued a report in 1934 and was the first to bring serious attention to the site.

Although the site was then recognized as important, it was not until 1953 that archaeological investigations were undertaken by Román Piña Chan. He excavated test pits on the terraced hillsides and recovered figurines and ceramics, from which he dated the earliest occupation to around 1000 B.C. and the demise of the site to around 200 B.C. His conclusions were based on the central Mexican chronological sequence as it was understood at that time. It has since been revised. He believed the bas-relief carvings dated to between 600 and 400 B.C.

Additional excavations were carried out by Grove from 1972 to 1974. During the first season, Jorge Angulo was co-director; Raul Arana held that position for the following two seasons. Major funding for the project came from the National Science Foundation, and other contributors were the National Geographic Society, INAH, and the Research Board of the University of Illinois, the institution with which Grove is affiliated. Excavations are still periodically carried out by Grove and doctoral students from the University of Illinois.

Grove studied the carvings as well, as did other scholars including Carmen Cook de Leonard, Carlo Gay, and Peter D. Joralemon.

Connections

1. Cuernavaca to Chalcatzingo: 41.6 miles [66.9 kilometers] by paved road (1:30), then 0.9 mile [1.4 kilometers] by cobblestone and dirt roads (:08).

2. Puebla to Chalcatzingo: 57.5 miles [92.4 kilometers] by paved road (1:25), then 0.9 mile [1.4 kilometers] by cobblestone and dirt roads (:08).

Getting There

1. From Cuernavaca (at the junction of Highways 95D and 160), take 160 southeast to Cuautla, 23.5 miles [37.8 kilometers], and turn right. Go to the south end of town and bear left (this junction is not marked). Continue on Highway 160 to the outskirts of Amayuca, 14.7 miles [23.7 kilometers], then turn right at the sign for Axochiapan and go 1.2 miles [1.9 kilometers]. There you will then see the welcome arch for Jonacatepec, but you might miss the small sign for Chalcatzingo just before it. You turn left at the sign (don't go under the arch). Drive to and through the town of Chalcatzingo, 2.2 miles [3.5 kilometers], to the end of the paved road. Then turn right at a small sign onto a cobblestone street. After the street enters a gate, it continues as a rough dirt road to the parking area for the site, near the ticket office. A standard vehicle is adequate to go as far as the end of the cobblestone street, but a high-clearance vehicle is needed for the last 0.3 mile [0.5 kilometer]. If your vehicle is low slung, you could park it just past the gate near the caretaker's house and walk in from there. If you are without a vehicle, you could get a bus to the town of Chalcatzingo and from there either walk or take a taxi to the site. If you want the taxi to return for you, make advance arrangements.

2. From Puebla, take the unnumbered toll road heading southwest to a junction near Atlixco, 15.0 miles [24.1 kilometers] (:18). This connects with Highway 190 heading south to Izúcar de Matamoros, 13.7 miles [22.0 kilometers] (:20). On the outskirts of Izúcar de Matamoros, turn right at the junction with Highway 160 and go to the cutoff on the outskirts of Amayuca, 25.4 miles [40.9 kilometers] (:37), then follow the final directions for Connection 1.

Chalcatzingo is open from 10:00 A.M. to 4:30 P.M. daily. No food is available at the site, but cool (not cold) soft drinks are sold. There are pole-sided rest rooms.

COLOR PLATES

Structure A1, from the northeast, Ixtlán del Río. Postclassic period.

The East Structure, from the west, Tingambato. Early Classic period.

Temple 1, the Temple of the Eagle and Jaguar Knights, Malinalco. Late Postclassic period.

Restored Aztec temple at Santa Cecilia. Late Postclassic period.

Replicas of some of the carved figures found leaning against the Stage III stairs on the Huitzilopochtli side of the Templo Mayor. Late Postclassic period.

The sculptured columns and atlantean columns atop stepped Building B (the Pyramid of Tlahuizcalpantecuhtli), Tula, Early Postclassic period.

Sculpture of Quetzalcóatl on the Temple of Quetzalcóatl, Teotihuacán. Late Preclassic period.

Pyramid of the Spiral, view from the northeast, Xochitécatl. Middle Preclassic period.

The Stone Building projecting from the west side of the Great Pyramid, Cholula, Classic period.

Relief carving of Quetzalcóatl and seated Maya-like figures on the Temple of the Feathered Serpent, Xochicalco. Late Classic–Early Postclassic period.

Monument 1, showing a throned personage inside a cave, Chalcatzingo. Middle Preclassic period.

The Great Plaza and structures in and around it, looking north. Monte Albán. Mound J, in the foreground, dates to the Late Preclassic period; other build-

Bas-relief carving of a ball player found in Group B, Dainzú. Middle Preclassic period.

The facade of Tomb 30, with three-dimensional heads and bas-relief stepped frets, Yagul. Postclassic period.

Stepped fret designs decorating the interior facade of one of the rooms of the north patio, Mitla. Late Postclassic period.

Front (east side) of the Pyramid of the Niches, El Tajín. Late Classic period.

The Building of the Grecas (left) and the Main Structure (right), Yohualichan, view from the northeast. Early Classic period.

Miniature temples serving as shrines for tombs, Quiahuiztlán. Postclassic period.

Two nearly identical Olmec sculptures at El Azuzul Museum. Early Preclassic period.

The Palace (left and center) and Temple V (right), Comalcalco. Late Classic period.

Aerial view of Palenque.

Stela 3, depicting Chaan Muan II and a kneeling captive, Bonampak, A.D. 785.

The facade of the Palace of the East, on the right, Tepic, Late Classic period

SECTION 4

• • • •
OAXACA

Monument 3 from San José Mogote. In place at the site. Middle Preclassic period.

GENERAL INFORMATION FOR SECTION 4, OAXACA

The state of Oaxaca is mountainous almost throughout, and the capital, Oaxaca City, lies in a high valley at an altitude of 5,084 feet (1,550 meters). The climate in Oaxaca is delightful, with warm days and cool mornings and evenings. It can get chilly in the evening during the rainy season.

For many years Highway 190 was the major connecting link between Mexico City (and Puebla) and Oaxaca. It is quite mountainous as it goes through southern Puebla and all of Oaxaca, but it once had a good surface the whole way. Unfortunately, it has deteriorated in parts, although it is being repaired. The good news is that in the early 1990s a new toll road opened—Highway 135D, connecting Oaxaca to Highway 150D, the toll road from Mexico City through Puebla to Veracruz. This is shorter, faster, and more pleasant to drive. It should be noted, however, that Highway 135D is four lanes only from Oaxaca City to Huitzo; after that it is two lanes to the junction with Highway 150D. Nevertheless, there is little traffic and the road is well engineered, so even though it goes through spectacular mountain terrain, it doesn't seem like "mountain driving" as does Highway 190 or Highway 131, another older route that goes through Tehuacán.

Oaxaca City is the best stopover in the part of the state covered by Map 4, but Huajuapan de León is a good stopover if you are driving Highway 190 or if you plan to visit Cerro de las Minas. The best hotel there is the Casa Blanca on the east edge of town. Oaxaca City has a variety of hotels in various price ranges.

Two restaurants worth checking out in Oaxaca City are El Asador Vasco and La Casita. El Asador Vasco is upstairs across from the southwest corner of the Zócalo (the central square), and its balcony overlooks it. La Casita is on Calle Hidalgo, the street that bounds the north side of the Zócalo, a couple of doors down from the northwest corner of the Zócalo. In the rainy season it serves *chapulines* (grasshoppers). These small red grasshoppers, fried with garlic, are tasty with a squeeze of lime and even better wrapped in a warm corn tortilla with a spread of guacamole. Other Oaxaca specialties are tamales wrapped in banana leaves and *mole negro* (black mole), generally chicken in a dark sauce.

The points of reference for distances and driving times are the following: (1) in Oaxaca City, the junction of Highway 190 (Calzada Niños Héroes de Chapultepec) and Calle Juárez, which heads south to the main part of town; and (2) in Huajuapan de León, the junction of Highway 190 and Calle José María Iglesias, the street that goes north (uphill) to Cerro de las Minas.

The domestic airport at Oaxaca (south of the city) is the principal one in the central area of the state. Two international airports are found along the Pacific coast of Oaxaca, one at Puerto Escondido and the other at Huatulco. Both have connecting flights to Oaxaca City, and there are several flights a day between Oaxaca City and Mexico City.

Car rentals can be found at the Oaxaca airport and at agencies in town. Travel agencies can be found in Oaxaca City as well.

Oaxaca City and nearby towns offer good shopping, owing to the abundance of handcrafted items produced in the region. Look for black pottery from San Bartolo Coyotepec and handwoven rugs from Teotitlán del Valle, or visit these towns to see how the items are made. In the city, semiprecious cut stones and jewelry made from them are offered, as are leather goods, indigenous clothing, and other textiles.

Oaxaca City and its environs are universally loved by visitors. I have never heard of anyone who didn't come home with glowing reports. I concur.

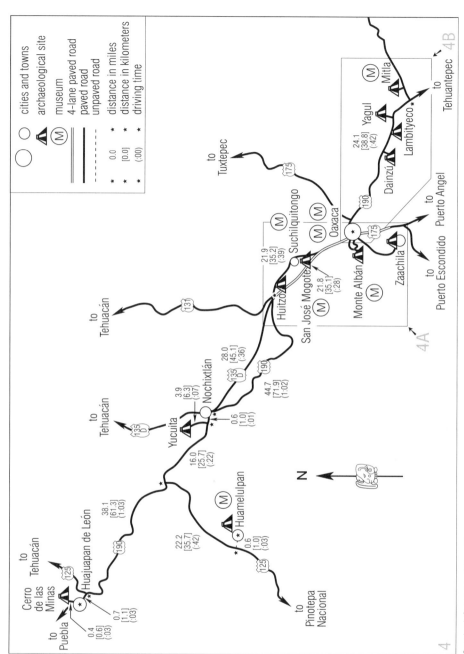

Central Oaxaca (Map 4).

★ ★
CERRO DE LAS MINAS
(SEHR-roh deh lahs MEE-nahs)

Derivation:
    Spanish for "Hill of the Mines."
Culture:
    Ñuu Yata (or Ñuu Sa Na'a) and
    Ñuiñe (see text).
Location:
    Northwestern Oaxaca.
Map: 4 (p. 194)

The Site

Cerro de las Minas is better than the average two-star site; two and a half stars would better reflect its worth. It lies in an area called the Mixteca Baja (Low Mixteca), a region of western Oaxaca and adjacent parts of Puebla and Guerrero. The adjacent Mixteca Alta (High Mixteca) is higher, wetter, and cooler; it lies to the east of the Mixteca Baja and west of the Valley of Oaxaca.

Cerro de las Minas, a hilltop site on the northern outskirts of Huajuapan de León, lies at an altitude of 5,512 feet (1,680 meters), about 300 feet (91 meters) above the town. Fortunately, you can drive up part of the hill to the parking area for the site; from there you climb the rest of the way on foot. The long axis of the artificially terraced hilltop is oriented northwest-southeast, and the site is made up of three large mounds separated by open spaces.

The first structure you reach (visible from the parking area) is H1A, on the southern part of the hill. It was found in a poor state of preservation and was extensively reconstructed. In ancient times it had been remodeled on several occasions. A nonresidential structure, possibly a temple, originally crowned its top, which was approached by a stairway bordered by *alfardas.*

You climb a little higher to Area M (and the adjacent Area L), which lie to the southwest of Mound 1 (unexcavated). There you will see a platform with residential remains on top. The walls of the platform are retaining walls, and it, too, was often remodeled in ancient times. From there take the easily followed trails uphill to other interesting parts of the site.

Near the middle of the top of the hill is an elite residential section (Area C), and on a slightly higher rise to the northeast (approached by stairways) is a patio surrounded by more residences (Area K). In this upper area you can see remains of *talud-tablero* construction in *bloque y laja* (block and slab) style. This style incorporated large stone blocks interspersed with thin slabs. Tomb 5 lies adjacent to this upper patio. When excavated, it produced an elaborate urn, vases, and human bones.

As you continue toward the northwest you come to Mound 2 (partly restored on the northwest side), an open plaza, and beyond it, Mound 3 (unexcavated).

Mound 2, a great platform rising in terraces, has a broad, inset stairway, bordered by *alfardas,* that ascends from plaza level to its top. Like some other structures at the site, Mound 2 was remodeled numerous times. From the front of Mound 3 you get a good view of Mound 2. The flat area between Mounds 2 and 3 seems not to have been residential; it is thought that it might have been used as a market.

Southwest of Mound 2 lies a ball court, although it is impossible to identify it as such visually. It has been studied but not totally explored or exposed.

The southwest side of the hill was used for habitations in ancient times. Today part of the area is covered with modern housing.

Cerro de las Minas had two major periods of occupation. It was founded by the Ñuu Yata around 400 B.C. and remained inhabited by that group until around A.D. 250. Ñuu Yata means "ancient people" in the Mixtec spoken in the Mixteca Baja; Ñuu Sa Na'a has the same meaning in the Mixtec used in the Mixteca Alta. This early period

Elite residential Area C, Cerro de las Minas. Classic period.

of occupation is called Ñudée, and the most extensive construction at the site occured during it.

The period from A.D. 250 to 350 is not well defined at Cerro de las Minas, but it was a time of cultural transformation. There is some evidence of the destruction of the site.

From around A.D. 350 to 800, Cerro de las Minas reached a second apogee when the Ñuiñe culture flourished in the Mixteca Baja. This was a different culture from that of the original inhabitants of the area, and influence from Teotihuacán is evident in the ceramics of the period. The Ñuiñe also had contacts with the Zapotecs. It is uncertain whether the Ñuu Yata were biological ancestors of the Ñuiñe, but it is probable that both groups spoke an old form of Mixtec, perhaps indicating that both groups could be considered Mixtec. The population of Cerro de las Minas at the Ñuiñe peak was around 2,000

to 3,000. Although more construction took place in the earlier phase, most of the remains exposed at Cerro de las Minas and seen there today date to the time of the Ñuine. Cerro de las Minas was abandoned around A.D. 800.

Recent History

Although Cerro de las Minas was undoubtedly known as an archaeological site for some time, there is a scarcity of documentation from the nineteenth and early twentieth centuries.

In the 1960s, John Paddock obtained some urns and other ceramics from Cerro de la Minas that had distinctive characteristics in a regional style not previously identified. He called the style Ñuiñe and published a resume of it in 1965. In 1968 he excavated a tomb on the north side of Cerro de las Minas and collected four carved stones and several ceramic vessels, further confirming the existence of the style.

In the following years, INAH personnel conducted work at the site, excavating more tombs and exploring residential areas that were in danger of destruction by new housing development in the area. The most extensive work at Cerro de las Minas began in 1987 and continued to 1993, carried out by the Oaxaca Regional Center of INAH. The project was directed by Marcus Winter, who published a guide for the site in 1996.

Connections

1. Huajuapan de León to Cerro de las Minas: 0.4 miles [0.6 kilometers] by paved street (:03).

2. Oaxaca City to Huajuapan de León: 121.4 miles [195.2 kilometers] by paved road (3:09).

Getting There

1. From Highway 190 in Huahuapan de Leon, go up the hill on Calle José María Iglesia to the parking area for the site.

2. From Oaxaca City, take Highway 190 northwest to Huajuapan de León. Alternatively, you could take Highway 135D as far as Nochixtlán and then Highway 190 to Huajuapan de León. Then follow the directions already given.

Cerro de las Minas did not have a ticket office at the time of our visit, so presumably it was open daily in the daytime. That could change, however. Allow 1.5 hours for a visit. There is no food or drink at the site, nor are there rest rooms, but all of these are available in the town. If you are without a private vehicle you could reach Huajuapan de León by bus and take a taxi to the site (or walk there).

You get good views of Huajuapan de León from the top of Cerro de las Minas. A bypass that goes north of Huajuapan de León and Cerro de las Minas connects Highway 190 (on the west) to Highway 175 (on the east). From it you get good views of Cerro de las Minas from below.

★ ★

HUAMELULPAN
(wah-meh-LOOL-pahn)
(SAN MARTÍN HUAMELULPAN)

Derivation:
  Nahuatl for "Place of Many
  Fallow Fields."
Culture:
  Mixtec (see text).
Location:
  West-central Oaxaca.
Maps: 4 (p. 194)

The Site

The archaeological site of Huamelulpan, located on a hill above the town of San Martín Huamelulpan, is composed of five groups of structures extending for a distance of about 0.5 mile [0.8 kilometer]. Its most interesting areas are the Church Group, uphill and to the east of the Catholic church on the plaza; Building C, north of the town plaza; and the open courtyard of the church itself, where some carvings from the site have been installed.

One of the principal structures of the Church Group has been partly restored and is composed of a broad stairway, bordered by *alfardas,* ascending a pyramidal base. Centered in the stairway, a doorway and narrow stairway lead downward to a dead end. To the right of the main stairway (as you face

One of the main structures in the Church Group, Huamelulpan. Early Classic period.

it), and just to the left of the *alfarda,* is another opening into the base of the structure. Again to the right is a niche that contains a crude carving of a skull.

On a slightly lower level there is a huge stairway, also partly restored, that faces a plaza. A low rectangular platform (surrounded by a low stone border) is placed in the plaza. On a still lower level, a large l-shaped ball court has been partly excavated and restored.

Now head to Building C. The southeast corner of the structure is made of massive stones adorned with bas-relief carvings. A naturalistic carving of a lizard is found on the south face of the corner, and two date glyphs below it. On the east face are four more glyphs in typical Monte Albán II style. This does not mean, however, that Huamelulpan was a Zapotec site like Monte Albán.

Continue now to the church on the plaza, to the right of which is an arch that gives access to an open courtyard. Four pre-Hispanic carvings are embedded in the face of the post-Hispanic arch—two on each side, a little above eye level. On the right are a naturalistic human head and, above it, a more abstract piece that could be a stylized head. On the left are another naturalistic

human head and, above, a more grotesque head, perhaps representing an animal.

You now enter the courtyard next to the church, go to the far end, and turn left. You will be facing the exterior side wall of the church, where a large pre-Hispanic carving depicting a stylized jaguar is embedded. It stands upright in an almost human pose; the head is three dimensional while the body is in low relief. We were told that this interesting carving had been in the church wall for about 60 years.

From archaeological work at the site, we know that Huamelulpan was occupied for 1,000 years, from 400 B.C. to A.D. 600. This span is broken into three periods: Huamelulpan I (400 to 100 B.C.), Huamelulpan II (100 B.C. to A.D. 200), and Huamelulpan III (A.D. 200 to 600).

During Huamelulpan I, the site was founded, probably as a small hamlet, the extent of which is unknown. During the second period, the site reached its peak. It is considered to have been the most important site in the Mixteca Alta at that time and for the later part of the preceding period, and it maintained relations with the other major sites in the Mixteca Alta. It also had ties to

Partly restored ball court, Huamelulpan. Late Preclassic period.

the Valley of Oaxaca, demonstrated by the use of common calendrical glyphs, urns of similar form, and gray ceramics.

Huamelulpan remained important during Period III, but eventually it was abandoned.

Recent History

During his explorations in the 1930s, Alfonso Caso discovered Huamelulpan. Only in the 1950s and early 1960s, however, were excavations undertaken, by Caso and Lorenzo Gamio. Reports were written, but they remain unpublished manuscripts in the archives of INAH.

In 1974, Marcus Winter, of the Oaxaca Regional Center of INAH, carried out five months of work at the site, assisted by Margarita Gaxiola and Adriana Alanís. Gaxiola published a report on the site in 1984.

In 1994, new excavations and consolidation were begun.

Connections

1. Oaxaca City to Huamelulpan (via Highway 135D): 88 miles [141.9 kilometers] by paved road (2:05), then 0.6 mile [1.0 kilometer] by dirt road (:03).

2. Oaxaca City to Huamelulpan (via Highway 190): 104.8 miles [168.7 kilometers] by paved road (2:45) , then 0.6 mile [1.0 kilometer] by dirt road (:03).

Getting There

1. From Oaxaca City, take Highway 135D (toll road) to Nochixtlán, 49.4 miles [79.5 kilometers]. (The toll road is four lanes as far

as Huitzo; from there to Nochixtlán it is two lanes.) Get off the toll road and join Highway 190 heading west; continue to the junction with Highway 125 (marked with a sign), 16.6 miles [26.7 kilometers]. Turn left and go 22.2 miles [35.7 kilometers] to the cutoff to the town of San Martín Huamelulpan (marked with a sign). Turn left and follow the dirt road to the town plaza, near which you can park.

2. Take Highway 190 northwest from Oaxaca City to the junction with Highway 125, 82.6 miles [132.9 kilometers]. Turn left and follow the directions already given.

When you arrive, the guardian will offer to show you around. This is a good idea. He will also open the museum for you. Huamelulpan is open Wednesday through Sunday from 10:00 A.M. to 5:00 P.M. It is closed on Monday and Tuesday. Allow one hour for a visit. There are no rest rooms, food, or drink at the site. From the town plaza it is a 10-minute climb to the Church Group.

★ ★
IHITALULU COMMUNITY MUSEUM (HUAMELULPAN MUSEUM)

The Huamelulpan Museum is located in the municipal building of the town of San Martín Huamelulpan, facing the plaza, and is marked with a sign. Although small, it contains some interesting items. The archaeological section was inaugurated in 1978, and in 1989 an exhibit of traditional medicine was opened.

Huamelulpan's fame (at least in the literature) rests on a cigar-shaped statue that reportedly was rolled down to the town from the hill above it some time ago. The statue—which has been widely published—is about 3 feet (0.91 meters) tall, and before the museum was opened, it stood outside the entrance of the municipal building. It is now inside. Alfonso Caso and Ignacio Bernal believed the figure was in Olmecoid style and dated to the period Monte Albán I (900–300 B.C.). Charles R. Wicke, writing in 1971, thought, on the basis of its style, that it could be considerably older. Joyce Marcus, writing with Kent Flannery in 1983, held a still different opinion. She saw nothing iconographically Olmec about the statue and believed it was carved between 400 B.C. and A.D. 200.

Another interesting piece is a rectangular slab with the hieroglyphic date 13 Flint carved in bas-relief. Caso saw this carving in 1933 in place in the wall of the school building, and he reported it in a 1956 publication. It dates to the period Monte Albán II (300–100 B.C.), as do the glyphs and numerals found on the large blocks at the site. (These dates in the Monte Albán sequence were assigned before the sequence for Huamelulpan itself was established.)

A similar slab with a carved numeral and another with a figure of an iguana are also housed in the museum. In addition, there are glass cases containing ceramic specimens from the site, including some attractive, large, seated figures, a chronological chart showing Huamelulpan's relationship to the Nochixtlán Valley of Oaxaca, and a sign giving a description and chronology of the site.

Labeling in the museum is fairly good, and lighting is fair. Photography is not allowed. There are no rest rooms, food, or drink at the museum. The museum has no set schedule; when a visitor arrives, the guardian will come and open it up. Allow 15 minutes for a visit.

★
YUCUITA
(yoo-KWEE-tah)

Derivation:
    Mixtec for "Hill of the Flowers."
Culture:
    Mixtec.
Location:
    West-central Oaxaca.
Map: 4 (p. 194)

The Site

Two areas of Yucuita have been partly consolidated, are open to the public, and are worth a look. Both lie a few feet off the road that goes from Highway 190 to the modern town of Yucuita, up on the side of a hill.

The first area you reach from the highway is called Area DFK (on the left side of the road). This area is formed of a multilevel platform (facing east) through which runs a tunnel that served not only as a water control feature but also as a passageway leading up to the center of the site. To the right of the tunnel's entrance is a narrow, inset stairway. An unfinished monumental stairway (ascending from the south) is found nearby, to the right of the tunnel and the narrow stairway. Parts of a massive stone wall, the lower portion of which has been consolidated, can be seen to the left.

Tunnel and stairway in Area DFK, Yucuita. Late Classic period.

Monument 1 from Yucuita, on display in the Yucuita town plaza. Late Preclassic period.

From there, drive uphill a short way, following the road as it curves to the left, until you reach Area A (on the right). The remains here are the lower walls of an elite residence. From this area you have a good view of the Cerro de las Flores (Hill of the Flowers) to the north.

Again following the road uphill a short distance, you come to the plaza of the present-day town of Yucuita, up a few steps to the right of the road. A couple of carved stones from the site of Yucuita are displayed there; the more interesting by far is Monument 1, a free-standing stone (possibly a stela) of irregular shape carved on both of its wide sides. It has a U element on each side, possibly a glyph for "hill" or "cave," discs with three dots arranged horizontally across the middle, and amorphous shapes with a double outline that seem to be floating around at odd angles.

The other monument is smaller, boulderlike, and lying in a garden bed. Although the stone seems unshaped and has a low depression in its surface, bas-relief carvings appear on the surface, though they are hard to discern.

The two architectural groups already mentioned and Monument 1 date to around 500 B.C. to A.D. 300, the Early Urban stage of Oaxaca prehistory.

We heard that there was a museum on the town plaza in Yucuita, and indeed we saw a sign saying "Museo" on a room next door to the Municipal Palace. It was closed at the time of our midday visit, and an inquiry to a resident of the town resulted in a denial that it was ever open. Perhaps you will have better luck.

Yucuita is one of the largest archaeological sites in the Nochixtlán Valley, and it had a long but interrupted occupational sequence. It was first inhabited from around 1500 B.C. to around 1200 B.C., then was mostly depopulated. Beginning around 500 B.C. it began to flourish, and by 200 it had a population of 2,000 to 3,000. Around A.D. 100 it again went into decline, and 200 years later the nearby Yucuñudahui became the seat of power in the area. Though Yucuita remained occupied, it served as a second-level center. It continued to be occupied into the colonial period.

Recent History

An archaeological zone that included Chacchoapan, Yucuita, Coyotepec, and Yucuñudahui was surveyed in 1933–34 by Martín Bazán, Juan Valenzuela, and Eulalia Guzmán, and the latter issued a report in 1934. In 1938, Alfonso Caso and his associates excavated for several days in the area.

More recent studies at Yucuita were conducted by Ronald Spores, Patricia Plunket, Gabriela Uruñuela, and Nelly Robles García in the 1970s and 1980s.

Connections

1. Huajuapán de León to Yucuita: 58.7 miles [94.5 kilometers] by paved road (1:35).

2. Oaxaca City to Yucuita: 70.5 miles [113.5 kilometers] by paved road (1:48).

Getting There

1. From Huajuapán de León, take Highway 190 southeast to the cutoff for Yucuita (marked with a sign). Turn left and go 3.1 miles [5.0 kilometers] to Area DFK. Area A is 0.1 mile [0.2 kilometer] beyond, and the town plaza is another 0.7 mile [1.1 kilometers]. The distance given in "Connections" is all the way to the plaza.

2. From Oaxaca City, take Highway 190 northwest to the cutoff for Yucuita, turn right, and follow the directions already given. Alternatively, you could take Highway 135D to Nochixtlán and pick up Highway 190 there.

Allow 35 minutes to see both consolidated areas and the sculptures in the plaza. The three areas are always open. There is no food at Yucuita, nor are rest rooms available. You could probably pick up soft drinks in town.

Getting bus connections to Yucuita would probably be time consuming.

★
HUITZO
(WEET-soh)

Derivation:
　　Zapotec for "Military Lookout."
Culture:
　　Zapotec (see text).
Location:
　　Central Oaxaca.
Maps: 4 (p. 194) and 4A (p. 204)

The Site

According to Ignacio Bernal, the site of Huitzo-Suchilquitongo is nearly as large as Monte Albán and has numerous buildings and great plazas. In earlier times the now independent towns of Suchilquitongo and Telixtlahuaca were considered barrios of Huitzo. The part of interest for visitors, however, is quite small. The main feature, Tomb 1, has two chambers, and there are carved slabs set into its exterior face.

On the far right (as you face the tomb) is a depiction of a stylized animal head with the number one represented by a dot—perhaps representing a date. The head and dot are partly enclosed by a simple border. Below and to the left is a larger slab (a jamb) on which the carvings are difficult to interpret, but it appears to depict a human head coming out of an animal head, or perhaps the human is wearing an animal headdress.

The jamb on the left depicts a lord carrying a shield, atlatl, and darts. This jamb is installed upside down. A couple of feet above it is a fragment showing a realistic animal head—perhaps a coyote—framed by the remains of a border. On the far left is a rather abstract panel. Remnants of red paint remain in the deeper grooves of some of the carvings.

The face of the lintel above the doorway is painted with stylized skulls in red and white in codex style.

The carved stones are Postclassic and were reused even later in this tomb, accounting for why one jamb is inverted and the other stones are rather randomly placed.

The principal occupant of the tomb was judged to be a man in his early twenties; he was accompanied by many offerings, including jade and amethyst beads and a necklace of cast gold beads. Skeletons of other adults, perhaps previous occupants of the tomb, were also found. The tomb is protected by a cement roof and metal bars.

The ethnic identity of the occupants of the tomb is uncertain. The grave goods, carved stones, and codex-style painting seem to point to a Mixtec identity, yet early sources say that the Zapotecs fortified Huitzo while

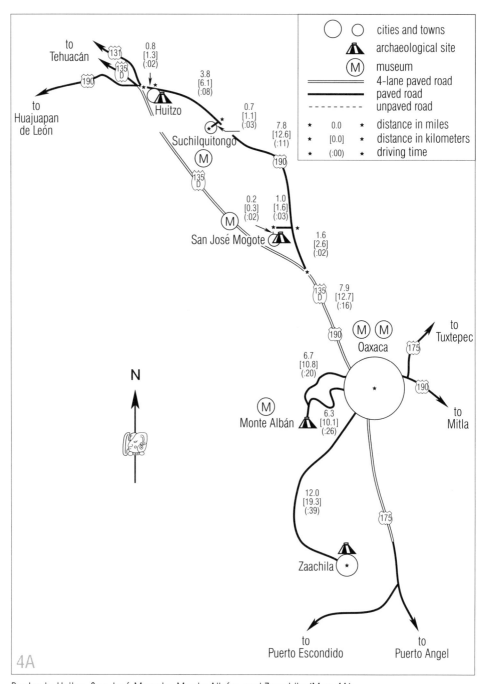

Routes to Huitzo, San José Mogote, Monte Albán, and Zaachila (Map 4A).

Entrance to Tomb 1, Huitzo. Postclassic period.

their Mixtec allies fought the Aztecs in another area.

The rest of the architectural remains visible in this area are not impressive and are partly covered with vegetation. They consist of the lower remnants of walls that formed a hall, which runs a short distance from the left of the tomb. Remains of a stair are found on the side of the mound on which the structure rests.

Huitzo had a long history. Its builders were erecting impressive structures between 850 and 700 B.C., and it was occupied at the time of the Spanish conquest; it remains so even today.

Recent History

Huitzo was formerly known as Cuauhxilotitlan and was mentioned under that name (spelled in various ways) in Spanish chronicles of the sixteenth and seventeenth centuries. These early works refer to the town as having both Zapotec and Mixtec residents.

Huitzo and Suchilquitongo were two of more than 200 sites visited by Ignacio Bernal during a pottery-collecting expedition, and

he noted that ceramics from Suchilquitongo were fundamentally Zapotec, with a thin surface layer belonging to a Mixtec invasion. This invasion occurred shortly before the Spanish conquest and is corroborated by early Spanish writings.

In 1966, John Paddock published photos of some ceramics from Huitzo (called Huitzo Polished Cream) and noted that it was rarely found at other sites in the Valley of Oaxaca. On his chart he dated this ware to A.D. 800.

In 1969, Christopher L. Moser reported on Tomb 1, which he excavated.

Connection

Oaxaca City to Huitzo: 21.1 miles [43.0 kilometers] by paved road (:37), then 0.1 mile [0.2 kilometer] by dirt road (:01).

Getting There

From Oaxaca City, take Highway 190 northwest. You will come to a sign marking a cutoff for the town of Huitzo at kilometer 162. It is possible to get there this way, but it requires negotiating the bumpy streets of the town. It is better to pass up this cutoff and proceed 1.0 mile [1.6 kilometers] to another cutoff. This one is unmarked, but a landmark is a restaurant on the left just beyond the dirt road. Both cutoffs are on the left (south), and the second one is much closer to the tomb. After you turn left, the dirt road crosses a railroad track. The site is located just past the track on a mound on the left of the road. The mound can be spotted by the mesquite trees growing on top. Take the footpath that leads uphill and follow it a short distance to the site. The ruins are not visible from the road.

There is no special time for visiting; the site is not fenced off, so you can go at any time. Allow 15 minutes for a look at the tomb. There are no rest rooms, food, or drink at the site, but food and drink are available at the nearby restaurant. If you are without a car, a bus can drop you off at the cutoff.

★ ★
SUCHILQUITONGO MUSEUM

The Suchilquitongo Museum is in the town of the same name, just off the main plaza, 1.2 miles [1.9 kilometers] off Highway 190. A sign at the highway points out the way to the town, and another, in town, to the museum.

As you enter the museum, the room to the left contains the archaeological material, and the one to the right displays old books and material on community affairs and politics.

The archaeological section has ceramics including an impressive large urn with small handles and engraved designs. There are photographs and a model of Tomb 5 at a site called Huijazoo. Text informs the visitor that the group of murals in the tomb is the largest known for pre-Hispanic Oaxaca. Huijazoo is near Suchilquitongo but was not open to visitors at the time of our last visit.

Other displays include skulls and parts of jawbones, boxes with covers, and date glyphs carved on stones. Labeling is fair, as is the lighting. Photography is not permitted. There are no rest rooms, food, or drink at the museum.

There is no set schedule at the museum. When visitors arrive, the guardian will come and open it. Allow 15 minutes for a visit.

★ ★
SAN JOSÉ MOGOTE
(sahn hoh-SEH moh-GOH-teh)

Derivation:
  Spanish for "Saint Joseph Hummock (Hillock)."
Culture:
  Zapotec.
Location:
  Central Oaxaca.
Maps: 4 (p. 194) and 4A (p. 204)

The Site

Although a number of buildings are known at San José Mogote, only Structure 1, which has been partly restored, is of interest to visitors. A trail from the main plaza of the town leads to it.

This structure is a large pyramidal mound measuring 328 feet (100 meters) on each side, with a height of 52.5 feet (16 meters). On the west side, a narrow inset stairway has been uncovered. It was originally roofed over

The north side of Structure 1, San José Mogote. Middle Preclassic period.

with stone slabs, forming a secret subterranean stairway. On the north side of the mound, a broad stairway to the top of the mound has been restored. Atop the pyramid, several low platforms are the remains of individual structures.

The very important Monument 3 is also found atop the pyramid. Its bas-relief carvings, similar to the *danzantes* at Monte Albán, appear on its broad upper surface and on one narrow side. It dates to 700 to 500 B.C., a little earlier than the *danzantes*. The monument pictures a male figure who has had his heart removed. Below the figure's bent left leg are two glyphs that read "One Earthquake," which is believed to be the victim's personal name. The monument was used as a step between two structures.

Monument 3 is protected by metal doors with a padlock. Check with the guardian about when the doors are open. We got conflicting reports and didn't actually see the carving, but it has been widely published. The glyphs are the earliest known form of Zapotec writing.

San José Mogote lies in the Etla Valley (a subvalley of the Valley of Oaxaca), and it began developing around 1500 B.C. or perhaps

somewhat earlier. The earliest ceramics found in the Valley of Oaxaca come from San José Mogote. By 1150 the site covered an area of 74.1 acres (30 hectares), and from that time until 850 it conducted long-distance trade with San Lorenzo Tenochtitlán, the Basin of Mexico, and Chiapas.

During the period 800 to 500 B.C., San José Mogote covered 172.9 acres (70 hectares). Around 500 B.C., the site was one of three chiefdoms that were, in confederation, the principal founders of Monte Albán. Monumental construction continued at San José Mogote through A.D. 200. From then until 750 the site went into decline and was minimally occupied, and Monte Albán became the most important site in the Valley of Oaxaca.

Recent History

In the early twentieth century, Constantine Rickards, the English consul in Oaxaca, photographed the mounds at San José Mogote. In the 1950s, Ignacio Bernal inventoried 275 sites in the Valley of Oaxaca, including San José Mogote; this was the first mention of the site by an archaeologist.

Kent V. Flannery and Joyce Marcus, both of the University of Michigan, coordinated the most ambitious project at the site—the Prehistory and Ecology Project of the Valley of Oaxaca—from 1966 to 1981. This multifaceted project encompassed studies of geomorphology, human geography, and settlement patterns, among other things. It established the interaction of Zapotec societies from the Archaic period (9025 B.C.) until the decline of Monte Albán as the center of major importance in the central valleys of Oaxaca in the Late Classic period. In the 1990s, the Oaxaca Regional Center of INAH and other Mexican agencies conducted additional work, including the restoration of Structure 1.

Connection

Oaxaca City to San José Mogote: 10.5 miles [16.9 kilometers] by paved road (:21), then 0.2 mile [0.3 kilometer] by dirt road (:02).

Getting There

From Oaxaca City, take Highway 190 (also Highway 135D at this point) heading northwest to where the two highways separate, 7.9 miles [12.7 kilometers]. Take the right fork (Highway 190) and continue 1.6 miles [2.6 kilometers] to the cutoff for San José Mogote, marked with a sign. Turn left for 1.0 mile [1.6 kilometers] to another sign for the museum and turn left again onto the dirt road. Proceed to the town plaza. A parking place can be found nearby.

Visiting hours for the site are not posted, so I can't report what they are. There is no food or drink, but there are rest rooms at the nearby museum. Allow 40 minutes for a visit. Buses go to San José Mogote, and it is close enough to Oaxaca City to make taxiing practical.

★ ★ ★
SAN JOSÉ MOGOTE MUSEUM

The San José Mogote Museum is a nice surprise. Though not terribly large, the collection is impressive and well arranged. In addition, it contains some real gems. A jade statuette almost 20 inches (49 centimeters) tall shares a case with a smaller jade figure. They were found together in an offering box below the floor of one of San José's structures. The large figure dates to around 100 B.C. to A.D. 200.

A large, elaborate effigy *incensario* forms an impressive display; it dates between 100 B.C. and A.D. 200. It was found buried under a temple at the site, and it still retains much of the vermillion pigment with which it was covered. Even earlier is a group of four figurines arranged in a ritual scene. They date to 1150 to 850 B.C.

Also displayed are another double-headed, grotesque *incensario* and a group of four kneeling, grotesque female effigies accompanied by a "flying figure" wearing a mask depicting lightning. The flying figure rests atop a glass case in which a kneeling figure and a bowl are arranged in the same placement as that in which they were originally found in relation to the flying figure. Originally the kneeling figure and bowl were encased in a miniature adobe tomb. Nearby, necklaces, small figurines, and ceramic bowls and pots are exhibited.

One section of the museum is devoted to the historic Hacienda El Cacique, which lies near San José Mogote, and restoration photos are exhibited.

Lighting in the museum is also better than average, and informative signs (in Spanish) provide additional details. Photography without flash is permitted. There is no food or drink at the museum, but there are rest rooms.

The museum has no set schedule; when visitors arrive, the guardian will come and open it. Allow 20 minutes for a visit.

Effigy *incensario* from San José Mogote, displayed in the San José Mogote Museum. Late Preclassic period.

★ ★ ★ ★
MONTE ALBÁN
(MOHN-teh ahl-BAHN)

Derivation:
  Spanish for "White Mountain."
Earlier Names:
  An earlier Aztec name was Ocelotepec, Nahuatl for "Hill of the Jaguar." An even earlier Mixtec name was Yucu-cui. A still earlier Zapotec name may have been Danipaguache or Danipaan, Zapotec for "Sacred Mountain."
Culture:
  Zapotec (see text).
Location:
  Central Oaxaca.
Maps: 4 (p. 194) and 4A (p. 204)

The Site

Monte Albán is perched atop an artificially flattened mountain about 1,200 feet (365.8 meters) above the city of Oaxaca. This superb location makes it a worthy setting for a city of the gods. It is a large site covering 2.5 square miles (6.5 square kilometers) and is one of the most intensively studied in Mexico. Its well-developed chronology covers 13 centuries (500 B.C. to A.D. 800) and forms the basis for the dating of the other sites in the state. A great deal of restoration has been undertaken at Monte Albán, making it extremely rewarding visually.

As you arrive at the site, you enter the northeast corner of the Great Plaza, some 984 feet (300 meters) long and 656 feet (200 meters) wide. Various structures cover the perimeter of the plaza, and more are found on the central axis. A logical tour would be

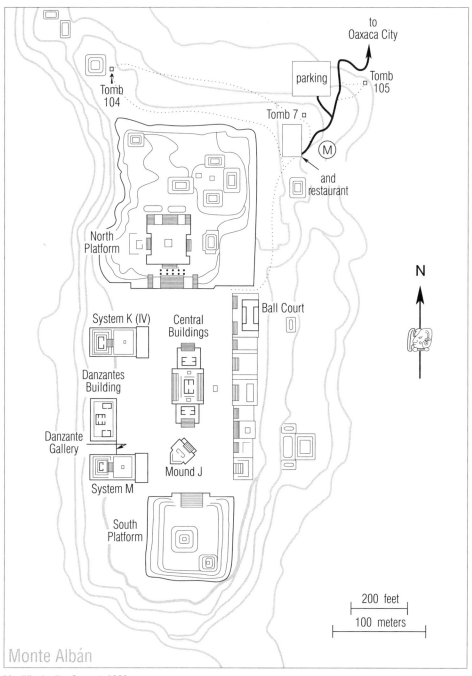

to
Oaxaca City

parking

Tomb 105

Tomb 104

Tomb 7

M

and
restaurant

North
Platform

System K (IV)

Central
Buildings

Ball Court

Danzantes
Building

Danzante
Gallery

System M

Mound J

South
Platform

N

200 feet
100 meters

Monte Albán

Modified after Bernal, 1958.

Ball court at Monte Albán. Late Classic period.

clockwise around the plaza to its southern extremity, then zigzagging between the structures on the central axis and those on the western edge. Then proceed to the northern area. If you wish, you can visit some tombs that are away from the main area.

To enter the Great Plaza, you pass along the east side of the North Platform, which has been partly restored. Access to the top is by stairways on the east and south sides. I recommend visiting this after you tour the other structures.

Following this plan, the first structure you visit is the ball court. This large, well-restored court is in typical Zapotec style. A stair on the north side leads down to the playing level.

To the south of the ball court is an imposing series of Classic period substructures and platforms, one of which was used as a dwelling. They are all approached by broad stairs. Lying between the central structure in this north-south row and the buildings on the central axis of the Great Plaza is a small *adoratorio*. When excavated, it revealed a magnificent mask of the bat god made of 25 pieces of jade, with shell for the teeth and eyes. Pendants hanging from the mask are of a common green stone. The mask is dated between 100 B.C. and A.D. 250 and is now in the Mexico City Museum.

The south end of the Great Plaza is bounded by the South Platform, which is ascended by a broad stair; atop it rest two structures. The stairway has been restored and is worth the climb for a view of the other structures around the plaza. The South Platform is also interesting for the numerous carved stelae incorporated into its base and others found in the surrounding area. (Most, if not all, of the carved monuments at Monte Albán have been removed to the site museum or the Mexico City Museum. What you see at the site are excellent copies.) Alfonso Caso dated these sculptures from A.D. 250 to 650.

From the South Platform continue clockwise to the west for a look at System M and a carved stela found in front that dates between A.D. 250 and 650. System M is composed of a rather large pyramid rising in four terraces; on top are the remains of the lower part of a temple that included four columns. The pyramid is fronted by a patio and, farther east, a low mound with a broad stairway.

To the north of System M is one of the most interesting parts of the site, the Danzantes Gallery and the Danzantes Building. The *danzantes* are figures carved on stone slabs in dynamic poses such that they resemble dancers; hence the name *danzantes* (the Spanish equivalent). We know, however, that the figures are not dancers but probably depict captives—perhaps dead, since the eyes are often shown closed. Almost 300 *danzantes* are known from Monte Albán. Some of the

View of the northeast corner of the Great Plaza with Classic period structures, Monte Albán. The *adoratorio* is in the foreground.

System M, view from the east, Monte Albán. Classic period.

Danzante figure with glyph in the upper right corner, Monte Albán. The original danzante is now in the Monte Albán Museum; a replica has been installed in its place.

slabs are incorporated into the Danzantes Building, and others are lined up between it and System M. Also in the area are copies of Stelae 12 and 13. The originals are in the Monte Albán Museum and date between 500 and 100 B.C. Although the inner building of the *danzantes* is one of the earliest structures at Monte Albán, a restoration was undertaken later, between A.D. 650 and 800. A passageway gives access to the earlier structure.

From the *danzantes,* head east to Mound J, the southernmost structure on the central axis. Mound J differs in both shape and orientation from the other buildings at the site; it resembles an arrowhead and points southwest, whereas the other buildings are rectangular and aligned to the cardinal points.

This interesting building, with a stairway on the northeast side and a vaulted tunnel, is built of large slabs, many of which are carved. A few *danzante*-style figures (500 to 100 B.C.)

have been incorporated, but more prevalent is another style (100 B.C. to A.D. 250). The motif in each is similar: a human head faces downward beneath a glyph for "hill," indicating a place. This is accompanied by glyphs that probably indicate the name of the place, and sometimes by a calendrical notation. These carvings may depict towns conquered by the people of Monte Albán. It is also theorized that Mound J might have been used as an astronomical observatory.

North of this structure on the central axis is a group of three connected buildings approached by stairs on all four sides. From there, head west to System K (IV), which is similar in layout to System M. Under the main pyramid of System K is an earlier structure dating from 500 B.C. to A.D. 250. To the north of the patio of System K is Stela 18 (100 B.C. to A.D. 250), a huge monument that is broken and partly eroded.

Mound J, view from the south, Monte Albán. Late Preclassic period.

Now proceed to the broad stairway that ascends the North Platform. At the level of the plaza, near the center of the stairway, is Stela 9 (A.D. 650 to 800); it is carved on all four sides. Climb the stairway for a look at the sunken patio and the surrounding structures. Stairways lead down to the patio on all four sides, and an altar is found in the center.

From this area you can return to the site entrance via the Great Plaza. If you wish to see some of Monte Albán's famous tombs, however, follow a trail heading north from the rear (north side) of the North Platform and going downhill to Tomb 104. This tomb, built between A.D. 250 and 800, has a niche that contains an urn bearing a depiction of Cocijo, the Zapotec rain god, in the headdress of the figure. There is a slab with carved glyphs, and the interior of the crypt is covered with murals. Unhappily for visitors (though perhaps not for the fragile murals themselves), a gate blocks the entrance to the crypt, and there is no artificial lighting, so the murals cannot be appreciated. Trails lead from there to other tombs in the area, but they are kept locked.

The best access to the famous Tomb 7 (also locked) is via a trail that heads north from the road to Monte Albán (west side) and joins the road near the restaurant. The tomb is of Zapotec construction, but the rich grave goods were deposited by Mixtecs when they reused the tomb.

On the east side of the road, another trail leads to Tomb 105. This tomb can be easily spotted from the restaurant area and is worth a visit to see the huge stone lintel at the entrance, reminiscent of those at Mitla. Tomb 105 also contains murals but it, too, is kept locked. You pass a partly excavated ball court on your way to the tomb.

In the earliest period at Monte Albán (500 to 100 B.C.), the leveling of the plaza began. Contact with Mayas of Chiapas and

Guatemala took place between 100 B.C. and A.D. 250. From 250 to 650, Teotihuacán's influence was felt; it is manifested in the decoration of buildings, ceramics, and tombs.

The major florescence of Monte Albán began around A.D. 650, with the fall of Teotihuacán. It lasted until 800, and most of the buildings were constructed during this time, sometimes covering earlier structures. After 800, the population diminished, and no new monumental constructions were built. From 1325 to 1521, Mixtecs entered the area and reused some of Monte Albán's tombs.

Recent History

Guillermo Dupaix visited Monte Albán in the early nineteenth century and uncovered some of the *danzantes*. The first description of the site, however, was published in Mexico in 1859 by J. M. García, as an appendix to a work by José Murguía. It included a sketch of the Great Plaza. In 1881, A. F. Bandelier visited Monte Albán, as well as other sites in the area; he published a report of his tour in 1884. William Holmes superficially studied Monte Albán in 1895 and left a panorama of the site. The first serious exploration of Monte Albán was undertaken by Leopoldo Batres in 1902.

Most of what we know about the site, however, is due to work that started with Alfonso Caso and his collaborators, including Jorge Acosta and Ignacio Bernal. It began in 1931 under the auspices of the Mexican government and lasted for 18 seasons. This work resulted in many publications in both Spanish and English. Additional work was done in the 1960s, and between 1971 and 1973, Richard Blanton and his colleagues surveyed Monte Albán in what was called the Settlement Pattern Project. In the 1990s, INAH instigated new excavations.

Connection

Oaxaca City to Monte Albán: 6.7 miles [10.8 kilometers] by paved road (:20).

Getting There

Head northwest on Highway 190 (135D) to the outskirts of Oaxaca City, 2.6 miles [4.2 kilometers], and turn left at the sign for Monte Albán. Then follow the road to the site. This road connects with the older route shortly before the parking area for the site. It is a relatively new road to Monte Albán—wide, well engineered, faster, and more comfortable than the old narrow, winding road. I highly recommend it.

Monte Albán is open daily from 8:00 A.M. to 6:00 P.M. Allow three or four hours for a visit. Bring plenty of film; Monte Albán is very photogenic. A wide-angle lens will be useful for shooting some of the *danzantes* in the wall by the passageway. An extra fee is charged to bring a video camera into the site.

A restaurant is found in the service building that also houses the museum, and there are rest rooms as well.

Regularly scheduled bus service to Monte Albán leaves from the Mesón del Ángel Hotel at Calle Mina 518. The site can also be reached by taxi or on bus tours.

★ ★ ★
MONTE ALBÁN SITE MUSEUM (MONTE ALBÁN MUSEUM)

The collection in the Monte Albán Museum, as it now exists, is a far cry from the museum I wrote about in 1982. At that time the major displays were ceramics from the site. Now a huge collection of stone carvings, mostly bas-reliefs, has been moved from the site to the museum, obviously for protection.

The museum is composed of a few rooms. In the first are displayed old photographs and newer ones relating to work conducted at

Stela 12 from the Danzante Gallery at Monte Albán, on display in the Monte Albán Museum. Middle to Late Preclassic period.

Monte Albán from 1992 to 1994, along with site plans and diagrams and a partly reconstructed, modeled stucco decoration that once graced the facade of one of Monte Albán's structures.

The major room houses an array of bas-relief carvings. The lighting in this area is quite good, owing to a centrally located skylight. Other parts of the museum are fairly well lighted. Among the notable pieces are Stelae 9, 12, and 13, as well as the *danzantes*.

In an area off the major room, parts of carved columns, ceramics, and large chunks of mica that originally came from Teotihuacán are displayed, as are skulls in a tomb with offerings of beads. The design on a bas-relief carving of a protective face mask worn by ball players is almost modern and abstract.

In the last room there are architectural models, photographs, and a video showing work at the site. Labeling at the museum is rather general, but all the displays come from the site.

Photography without flash is permitted at the museum, and there are an adjacent restaurant, rest rooms, and bookstore.

The museum is open daily from 8:00 A.M. to 6:00 P.M. Allow 20 minutes for a visit.

★ ★
ZAACHILA
(sah-CHEE-lah)

Derivation:
  Zapotec for "Sky Dragon."
Earlier Name:
  Teozapotlan.
Culture:
  Zapotec (see text).
Location:
  Central Oaxaca.
Maps: 4 (p. 194) and 4A (p. 204)

The Site

Zaachila, the last capital of the Zapotecs, today seems a sad place when compared with the magnificent earlier capital of Monte Albán. Although Zaachila is a relatively large site, only one small area is of interest to visitors. This is the large Mound A, topped by a rectangular patio with remains of low adobe walls and two tombs in the patio floor. Tomb 1 has a stepped fret design over the doorway of the antechamber and remains of sculptured plaster figures on the interior walls, including two figures related to death, an owl, and a figure with a turtle shell. This tomb has several niches that originally contained offerings.

Sometimes the interior of the tomb is lighted and sometimes it is not. It's a good idea to take a flashlight. You could also ask the guardian if you might take a flash photo. This was once allowed, but that may have changed.

Tomb 2 also has a stepped fret at the antechamber, but no interior sculpture. The interiors of the tombs are made of stone slabs, the only stone used in construction at the site.

Mound A is near the church in the center of the town of Zaachila. Park at the rear of the church on the street to the right of the church (as you face it). Then look for a stone stairway opposite the parking area and a sign at its foot, announcing the archaeological zone. The stairway leads to the top of Mound A.

Zaachila was occupied from the Early Preclassic period onward and became one of the most important places in the Valley of Oaxaca during the decline of Monte Albán at the end of the Classic period. Mound A, however, was a pure Postclassic development.

The grave goods found in Tombs 1 and 2 seem to be Mixtec and are similar to objects found in Tomb 7 at Monte Albán. The carved bones and gold jewelry found in both places show that they were very close in time, all belonging to the period Monte Albán V (roughly A.D. 1000 to 1521). The guardian of Zaachila told us that the principal occupant of Tomb 1 was a Mixtec king who was married to a Zapotec woman. Some authorities, however, might disagree.

Recent History

At the time of the Spanish conquest, Zaachila was a living town. Although it was originally Zapotec, by the time of the conquest Mixtecs were in the area as well. The Zapotec king of Zaachila at this time was named Cosijoeza; he died in Zaachila in 1529. By that time the Zapotecs, as well as the Mixtecs and Aztecs, had been crushed by the Spaniards.

In 1947, when Alfonso Caso tried to excavate at Zaachila, the villagers, who strongly

Plaster figure on the wall of Tomb 1, Zaachila. Late Postclassic period.

opposed anyone's digging in their ancient tombs, forced him to flee for his life. The same thing happened to Ignacio Bernal in 1953. Finally, in 1962, Roberto Gallegos managed to do some work at the site, but only under armed guard.

A lot of what we know of the site comes from Gallegos's excavations for the Mexican government, although certain carved stones from Zaachila and the surrounding area were known and studied earlier by Caso. He dated Stone 1, now in the Mexico City Museum, as perhaps from the period Monte Albán IIIa (roughly A.D. 200 to 500).

In the 1970s, a number of scholars studied various subjects related to Oaxaca, including Zaachila. A partial list includes Kent V. Flannery, Joyce Marcus, Richard E. Blanton, John Paddock, and Ronald Spores.

Connection

Oaxaca City to Zaachila: 12.0 miles [19.3 kilometers] by paved road (:39).

Getting There

From Oaxaca City, head south through the city until you reach the *periférico* and turn right. Continue a few blocks along the *periférico* until you come to a bridge across the Atoyac River (on the left). Cross the river and shortly you will come to a fork in the road; the left branch (marked) goes to Zaachila. On the way there you will pass through the village of Xoxocotlán and then Cuilapan. As you drive along, be prepared for multiple *topes* near the towns. Cuilapan, with its fascinating, unfinished Dominican monastery

and church dating from 1555, is worth a stop either before or after you visit Zaachila, as it is most photogenic.

Inside the church is the grave of Donaji, daughter of Cosijoeza, and her husband, the Mixtec prince of Tilantongo. Their tomb is inscribed with the Spanish names they took, "Maioana Cortés" and "Diego Aguilar."

Zaachila is open daily from 10:00 A.M. to 5:00 P.M. Allow 30 minutes to visit the site and one hour or more to visit the monastery at Cuilapan. There are no rest rooms, food, or drink at the site of Zaachila, but soft drinks are available in the town.

★ ★ ★ ★
REGIONAL MUSEUM OF OAXACA
(OAXACA MUSEUM)

Ceramic figure called the Scribe of Cuilapan. Late Preclassic period. On display in the Oaxaca Museum.

The Oaxaca Museum in Oaxaca City fully reopened on July 24, 1998, after undergoing extensive renovation that began in 1994. During this work, only some parts of the collection were on display. The old convent that houses the collection was completely refurbished: the wall paintings and decorations have been lovingly restored, and gold leaf has been reapplied. It is now truly spectacular.

The museum has two stories surrounding a central patio. A large shop with a good collection of books and handcrafted items is found on the first floor. Nearby is an extensive library of old books where a *lienzo* from Zacatepec is displayed.

The second floor contains a number of rooms that exhibit the pre-Columbian collection and colonial period and more modern materials. Some of the more outstanding displays are a *danzante* from Monte Albán, funerary urns (some depicting Cocijo, the Zapotec rain god), and the beautiful Late Preclassic ceramic figure of a young man popularly called the "Scribe of Cuilapan." A number of bas-relief carvings from various periods are exhibited, as are figurines and ceramic vessels. Two stone yokes, an *hacha,* and a *palma* come from San Vicente Mazatan. They are the only examples of this Gulf Coast complex known from Oaxaca.

The museum is justly famous for the priceless jewelry excavated from Tomb 7 at Monte Albán by Alfonso Caso in 1932. This ranks as one of the most spectacular discoveries in Mesoamerican archaeology.

More than 500 items were found in Tomb 7 and catalogued. According to Caso, a single catalogue number at times included "necklaces of gold, pearl, and turquoise, composed of hundred of beads each." A rare rock-crystal urn and more than 300 carved jaguar and deer bones, some inlaid with turquoise, were also part of the treasure trove. Copies of some of the more impressive pieces of jewelry are sold throughout the city.

An appreciated touch at the museum is the inclusion of benches where visitors can stop to rest. Cactus gardens can be seen outside below one of the rest stops.

The museum is now part of the Santo Domingo Cultural Center, which includes Santo Domingo Church, one of the gems of Spanish colonial architecture. Both are on Calle Macedonio Acalá, five blocks north of the Zócalo.

The museum's hours have expanded. It is now open Tuesday through Sunday from 10:00 A.M. to 8:00 P.M. It is closed on Monday. Allow two hours for a visit and some extra time to see Santo Domingo Church. Lighting in the museum is good for viewing and fair for photography, which is permitted without flash. There is an extra charge to use a video camera. Labeling (in Spanish) is good. In many of the rooms there are large cards that explain the displays. Rest rooms are found on the second floor. No food or drink is available, but the museum is close to a number of small restaurants.

★ ★ ★
RUFINO TAMAYO MUSEUM OF PREHISPANIC ART OF MEXICO (TAMAYO MUSEUM)

The Tamayo Museum is a very fine three-star museum. It was tempting to give it four stars; maybe it is best thought of as three and a half stars.

In 1974 the museum opened its doors at Calle Morelos 503 in Oaxaca City. The lovely colonial building houses the collection of the Mexican artist it was named for. Tamayo collected pre-Hispanic art for more than 20 years, "for his own pleasure," but also with the idea of protecting the pieces from exportation and, most importantly, of donating them to the people of his native state of Oaxaca.

The governor of the state of Oaxaca donated the building, but Tamayo bore the cost of its restoration and adaptation. It is admirably done, with black marble floors and attractive lighting, and the pieces are imaginatively displayed.

A sign near the entrance informs you that "this is a museum of art," and the displays bear this out. There are five *salas* (halls) around three sides of a pleasant patio, and each *sala* is a different "color." That is, the background color for the display cases is different from room to room, and this color code is used in the small guidebook for the museum. There are also some pieces displayed on the corridor walls that face the patio.

The collection is surprisingly extensive. It covers everything from Middle Preclassic Olmec pieces to Late Postclassic Aztec. Practically all parts of Mexico where Mesoamerican civilization developed are represented. There is an especially fine selection of ceramic figurines from western Mexico, and Veracruz is well represented with carved stone yokes, *hachas,* and ceramic smiling heads and figures. An extensive collection of Mezcala-

Maya stela from Campeche, Late Classic period. Displayed in the Tamayo Museum.

Usumacinta River region. The one pictured here might also possibly have come from the Palenque area, according to Karl Herbert Mayer in his 1984 book *Maya Monuments*. The two stelae are set on pedestals, and a portion of another—showing the upper part of a figure—is displayed in a showcase. Another case houses a beautiful glyph-carved stone from Chiapas and yet another stela fragment or possibly a lintel or door jamb.

Another Maya monument labeled as coming from Campeche is a bas-relief stone panel with a depiction of Tlaloc. It is so similar to the Tlalocs found in the lower part of the Adivino at Uxmal, Yucatán (unfortunately no longer visible), that it almost certainly belongs to the corpus of Tlalocs from that site, according to Mayer's 1995 supplement to *Maya Monuments*.

This brings up the one flaw in an otherwise fine museum—most of the pieces are rather vaguely labeled. Some Maya pieces are labeled "Classic Maya, seventh to eighth century," and occasionally the state from which they come is mentioned, but rarely is a specific site given.

style greenstone carvings, both large and small, is impressive.

For me, the most exciting part of the collection is in the Green Sala (Number 4), where much of the Veracruz material is displayed; also in this *sala* are several major Maya monuments. There are two complete Classic Maya stelae labeled as coming from Campeche but which may come from the

The Tamayo Museum is open on Monday and from Wednesday through Saturday from 10:00 A.M. to 2:00 P.M. and 4:00 P.M. to 7:00 P.M. On Sunday it is open from 10:00 A.M. to 3:00 P.M. It is closed on Tuesday. Allow 1.5 hours for a visit. Lighting is good in the museum, and photography without flash is permitted. The museum has a small bookstore and rest rooms, but no food or drink.

★ ★ ★
DAINZÚ
(dah-een-SOO)

Derivation:
    Zapotec for "Hill of
    Tlacochahuaya."
Culture:
    Zapotec.
Location:
    Central Oaxaca.
Maps: 4 (p. 194) and 4B (p. 222)

The Site

Dainzú reportedly occupies the southern section of a huge archaeological area. It may have actually been an independent site. The area of interest for visitors is the relatively small excavated part. The road that enters the site divides it into two sections. Structure A (the main pyramidal mound) lies to the left (east) of the road, and Group B, the adjacent Group C, and Group J (the ball court) lie to the right (west).

Structure A measures 164 feet (50 meters) along its north-south axis, stands some 25 feet (7.5 meters) high, and has been partly restored. It rises in three stepped tiers and is divided by a stairway on the west. The southern wall of the stairway and the lower tier of the mound have inlaid stones with bas-relief carvings. Most are found to the right (south) of the stairway.

Part of Group B in the foreground, Dainzú. Late Preclassic period. Structure A in the background. Middle Preclassic period with Classic period additions.

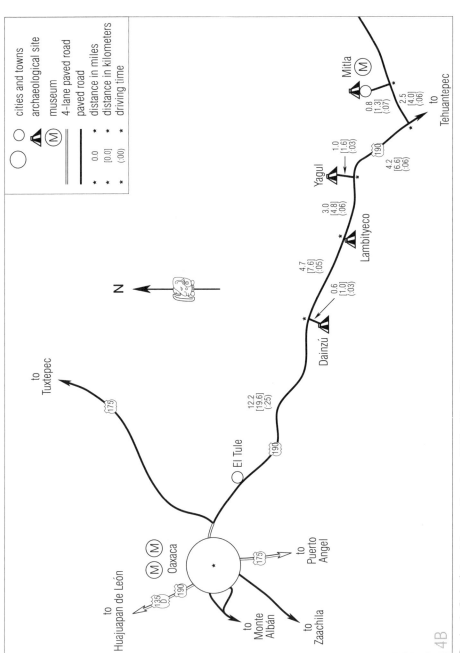

Routes to Dainzú, Lambityeco, Yagul, and Mitla (Map 4B).

cities and towns
archaeological site
museum
4-lane paved road
paved road
* distance in miles
** distance in kilometers
*** driving time

0.0   *
[0.0] **
(.00) ***

N

to
Tuxtepec

175

El Tule

190

12.2
[19.6]
(.25)

Oaxaca

M M

to
Huajuapan de León

135
D

190

to
Monte
Albán

to
Zaachila

175

to
Puerto
Angel

Dainzú

0.6
[1.0]
(.03)

4.7
[7.6]
(.05)

Lambityeco

3.0
[4.8]
(.06)

Yagul

1.0
[1.6]
(.03)

190

4.2
[6.6]
(.06)

to
Tehuantepec

2.5
[4.0]
(.06)

0.8
[1.3]
(.07)

Mitla

M

Carved slab representing a god, reset in the south wall of the stairway of Structure A, Dainzú. Middle Preclassic period.

Fifty carvings in all have been discovered, 27 of which were found in place. One represents a seated figure, possibly a god, and two others depict humanized jaguars.

It seems fairly certain that the figures on the remainder of the slabs depict Middle Preclassic ball players. Each of these figures wears a mask or face shield, and most have a collar and protective gear on their hands and sometimes on their knees. Each holds a small ball in his right hand, which would indicate a different kind of ball game from that played during the Classic period, when players were not allowed to touch the ball with their hands. The figures' dynamic poses also support the theory that they are ball players. The carvings are most interesting, and many are well preserved. They are protected by a roof, so photographing them is not as easy as it once was.

The carved slabs and most of Structure A date to the end of the period Monte Albán I (ca. 300 B.C.). A tomb is also found in the structure, and the whole is built into the side of a hill. There are nice views from the top of the structure.

Group B, also dating to around 300 B.C., has been partly excavated and restored. The first excavations in the central and southern part of Group B uncovered remains of a stairway and the lower portions of low walls. Work in the northern part of the group brought to light a tomb, the facade of which is made of three large stones (the lintel and two jambs) carved in bas-relief with a frontal depiction of a crouching jaguar. The relief is in excellent condition. It is now protected by bars.

A bit to the north of the tomb is an eroded carved boulder, and nearby, to the east, is a stairway that descends to a lower chamber. On a portion of a wall abutting the stairway on the north is a carved slab, and two more carved slabs are found inlaid in the walls of the lower chamber. One slab (Relief 86) depicts a ball player.

Return to the upper level and head west and then south for a look at some restored stairs, a sunken patio, and the lower walls of a plastered structure with two columns in the doorway, called the Yellow Temple. Father south are the remains of what appears to be a sunken chamber, and nearby is a sort of drain.

From there, head west to the ball court, found on a lower level. The south half of the ball court has been restored, and it is interesting to compare this part with the unrestored, amorphous mound that faces it and forms the other half. This court is similar to

Representation of a jaguar decorating the entrance to a tomb, Dainzú. Middle Preclassic period.

Relief 86, depicting a ball player, in place in the lower chamber in the northern part of Group B, Dainzú. Middle Preclassic period.

Ball court, Dainzú. Early Postclassic period.

the one found at Yagul and dates to around the same time period, A.D. 1000.

Ignacio Bernal considered the ball-player carvings at Dainzú part of the Olmec world, like the danzantes at Monte Albán. He found both sets of images "Olmec in spirit, if not in detail." He labeled them "Olmecoid," referring to a high culture showing Olmec influence but not being purely Olmec. The danzantes and ball-player carvings date roughly to the same time period.

Recent History

Dainzú was reportedly discovered in the 1960s, and excavations began under the direction of Bernal in late 1966, for the Mexican government. The site has been open to visitors since 1970. INAH conducted additional work there in the 1980s.

Connection

Oaxaca City to Dainzú: 12.8 miles [20.6 kilometers] by paved road (:28).

Getting There

Take Highway 190 southeast from Oaxaca City to the cutoff for Dainzú (marked with a sign), 12.2 miles [19.6 kilometers]. Turn right and proceed to the site's parking area. If you are without a car, you can get a bus to drop you off at the junction and walk from there, or you can get a taxi in Oaxaca.

Dainzú is open daily from 8:00 A.M. to 6:00 P.M. Allow 1.5 hours for a visit. There is no food or drink at the site, but there are rest rooms. A fee is charged to bring a video camera into the site.

★
LAMBITYECO
(lahm-beet-YEH-koh)

Derivation:
A hybrid name of Spanish and Zapotec words meaning "Distillery Mounds," according to Marcus Winter.
Culture:
Zapotec.
Location:
Central Oaxaca.
Maps: 4 (p. 194) and 4B (p. 222)

The Site

Lambityeco is part of a large archaeological zone called Yegüih, with an area of 185 acres (75 hectares). Only a small part on the edge of the site has been excavated. The whole site comprises hundreds of mounds, some of which extend to the nearby village of Tlacolula. An accurate count is impossible, because some of the mounds in the village have been leveled.

The excavated portion is made up of an architectural assemblage running in an east-west line, and a separate structure a bit to the south. The whole is part of a residential construction. The architectural remains are not terribly impressive, but the sculptural decorations make a visit worthwhile.

On the east end of the main assemblage is a patio bordered on one edge by two carved stone friezes, each depicting an aged couple and their accompanying name glyphs. Between the two friezes is a small, altarlike structure. In front of and below the altar, a tomb was sunk into the patio floor, and another old couple is represented in stucco on its facade. Some remains of red paint border the faces. It is theorized that the couple depicted on the tomb were the owners of the house. The area around the friezes and tomb is kept fenced off, so bring a telephoto lens if you want photographs of the sculptures.

Carved stone frieze in the patio on the east, Lambityeco. Late Classic–Early Postclassic period.

Stucco facade on the tomb entrance in the patio on the east, Lambityeco. Late Classic–Early Preclassic period.

Lambityeco was occupied for a relatively brief time during the period Monte Albán IV (A.D. 700 or 750 to 950 or 1000), although other parts of Yegüih began as early as the Middle Preclassic period. Even so, the excavated house shows several construction phases. It is thought to have been built during the population peak of the community.

Now go to the structure to the south of the main assemblage, which also contains a tomb. Of more interest here, however, are nearby stucco heads of Cocijo. One of these large sculptures is in almost pristine condition. You will want a telephoto lens here as well.

The west end of the main assemblage is occupied by a fair-sized plaza with low stepped platforms bordering three sides, and on the fourth (east) side, a taller pyramidal base with a stairway. There is a low rectangular altar in the plaza.

Both stone and adobe were used in the construction at Lambityeco, and some cut-stone, stepped fret designs are found on the wall facing the east patio.

Recent History

The archaeological zone of Yegüih, including the part called Lambityeco, was recorded by Ignacio Bernal in 1953. Excavations began in the 1960s under the direction of John Paddock for the University of the Americas, which is connected with the Institute of Oaxacan Studies. Intermittent work by the institute continued until 1975.

Connection

Oaxaca City to Lambityeco: 16.9 miles [27.2 kilometers] by paved road (:30).

Getting There

From Oaxaca City, take Highway 190 southeast to the site, which is right on the road

Stucco head of Cocijo, the Zapotec rain god, Lambityeco. Late Classic–Early Preclassic period.

(right side) and visible from it. It is also marked with a sign. Lambityeco is located 1.2 miles [1.9 kilometers] before (northwest of) the town of Tlacolula as you drive away from Oaxaca City. If you are without a car, a bus could drop you off there.

Lambityeco is open daily from 9:00 A.M. to 5:00 P.M. Allow 30 minutes for a visit.

There are no rest rooms, food, or drink at the site, but these are available nearby. Try La Fiesta Restaurant on the highway at the cutoff for Tlacolula. It serves good regional food. Another possibility is the Centeotl Restaurant on the access road to Yagul. It also serves regional food.

YAGUL
(yah-GOOL)

Derivation:
Zapotec for "Old Tree."
Earlier Name:
Gui-y-Baa.
Culture:
Zapotec (see text).
Location:
Central Oaxaca.
Maps: 4 (p. 194) and 4B (p. 222)

The Site

A relatively large site, Yagul is set in lovely surroundings. It lies at the base of a hill that was partly leveled to accommodate the buildings forming the Acropolis.

The other group of interest, the Great Fortress, is located on the highest point of the hill overlooking the valley and can be reached by a rather steep trail. It is definitely worth the effort for the views of the Acropolis and the surrounding countryside. The builders of Yagul certainly had an eye for beauty when they selected their location.

Entrance to Tomb 30, Yagul. Postclassic period.

View of the ball court, Yagul. Postclassic period.

When you arrive at the site's parking area, proceed first to Patio 4, a bit to the southwest. There are several tombs in the floor of the patio; the most interesting is Tomb 30, which, with the adjoining Tombs 3 and 29, forms one of several triple tombs found at Yagul. Its facade is carved with stepped fret designs and small three-dimensional heads. You may have to ask the guardian to open the door to the tombs for you. Patio 4 also has a squat statue of a toad near the mound on the east end.

From Patio 4, a short climb to the northwest will get you to the ball court. This court, larger than that at Monte Albán, has been completely excavated and restored, and it is a beauty. It differs from the one at Monte

Stone mosaic panel at the rear of the Council Hall, Yagul. Postclassic period.

Partial view of the Palace of Six Patios, Yagul. Postclassic period.

Albán in that there are no niches or central marker stones.

West of the ball court is Patio 1 and its surrounding buildings. The best preserved are those bordering the patio on the west and north. The northern structure, called the Council Hall, is similar in design to the Hall of the Columns at Mitla, but no columns were used.

When you leave this area, make sure you see the back of the Council Hall. Here are the remains of a stepped fret design that is over 120 feet (36 meters) long. There are two variations of the motif, both of which are also found in the Group of the Columns at Mitla.

From the rear of the Council Hall, head north across a narrow street to the Palace of Six Patios. This is a veritable maze of residential structures that were altered and added to several times. The trail to the Great Fortress takes off from the north of the Palace of Six Patios and goes up the hill.

Certain stone implements collected at Yagul may indicate that the site was occupied in preceramic times. By the Monte Albán I period, occupation is certain. A carbon-14 date for Yagul of 390 B.C. came from material associated with the later part of the period. Yagul continued to be occupied sporadically until around the Spanish conquest.

The similarities between Yagul and Mitla are pronounced, though the structures and decorations at Yagul are less refined. The use of stepped fret mosaics was also less extensive, and Yagul probably lacked the huge stone lintels used at Mitla. This probably partially accounts for the structures' poorer state of preservation. It is possible that some of the latest Mitla-style constructions at Yagul are a little later than those at Mitla. As at Mitla, the preponderance of the architecture is civic and residential rather than religious in nature.

Some authorities believe that, like Mitla, Yagul had an earlier Zapotec occupation followed by a Mixtec one or a Zapotec-Mixtec blend. Other scholars hold that both sites were Zapotec throughout their existence. For more details on this controversy, see the articles by John Paddock, Kent Flannery, and Joyce Marcus in Flannery and Marcus's 1983 book, *The Cloud People.*

Recent History

The first report of Yagul was that of A. F. Bandelier in 1884. He had visited the site some three years earlier, when he also visited Mitla, Monte Albán, and several other places. It was he who was told the name of the site was Gui-y-Baa, Zapotec for "Heaven."

There is nothing to note about Yagul from that time until the 1953 investigations of Ignacio Bernal. He began excavating Yagul in 1954, and because it proved to be a particularly interesting site, work continued for over a decade. Students at the University of the Americas assisted in the work, under the direction of Bernal, Paddock, and Charles R. Wicke.

In 1960, three tombs in Monte Albán I style were excavated by Bente Bitman Simons, David Sanchez, and Robert Chadwick for the University of the Americas. They are located near the Great Fortress and are the only Period I tombs known at Yagul. An unusual feature is their adobe construction. In the 1990s, additional work was undertaken in the Patio 4 area.

Connection

Oaxaca City to Yagul: 20.9 miles [33.6 kilometers] by paved road (:39).

Getting There

Take Highway 190 southeast from Oaxaca City to the Yagul cutoff, 19.9 miles [32.0 kilometers], and turn left (north) for 1.0 mile [1.6 kilometers] to the site. A bus could get you as far as the junction, which is marked, although you would have to walk the last part, uphill. A car or taxi would be easier.

Yagul is open daily from 8:00 A.M. to 5:30 P.M. Allow about two hours for a visit (if you plan to include a trip to the Great Fortress). Bring a wide-angle lens for front shots of Tomb 30.

There are no rest rooms, food, or drink at the site, but these are available nearby at the Centeotl Restaurant along the access road to Yagul.

Note: As you turn off the highway onto the Yagul access road, look to the right (east)

Large pictograph on the face of the cliff, Caballito Blanco. End of the Middle Preclassic period.

at the upper part of a nearby cliff. On the face is a white pictograph that is part of the archaeological site of Caballito Blanco. According to Alfonso Caso, the pictograph is diffi- cult to interpret but is probably one of the oldest paintings known in Oaxaca. You can get good photographs of it with a telephoto lens from the access road.

MITLA

(MEET-lah)

Derivation:
From the Nahuatl Mictlán ("Place of the Dead").

Earlier Name:
Lyobaa, Zapotec for "Tomb" or "Place of Rest."

Culture:
Zapotec (see text).

Location:
Central Oaxaca.

Maps: 4 (p. 194) and 4B (p. 222)

The Site

Of the five groups of structures at Mitla, the two most important are the Group of the Columns and the Group of the Church. These two groups are of prime interest to all visitors; the enthusiast, however, might also want to take a look at the Arroyo Group and the Adobe Group in different parts of the site.

A parking area lies northeast of the Church Group. From it, go to the service building to buy your ticket and proceed south.

The Church Group is composed of three patios with their surrounding rooms in a

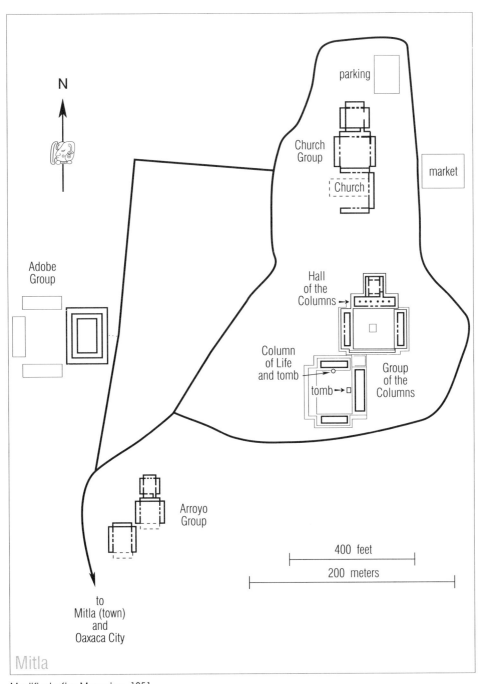

N

parking

Church
Group

Church

market

Adobe
Group

Hall
of the
Columns →

Column
of Life
and tomb →

tomb → □

Group
of the
Columns

Arroyo
Group

400 feet

200 meters

to
Mitla (town)
and
Oaxaca City

Mitla

Modified after Marquina, 1951.

Hall of the Columns, main (south) facade, Mitla. Late Postclassic period.

north-south line. The colonial church, built of stones from the pre-Columbian structures, occupies most of the southernmost patio. The center and north patios have some remains of stepped fret designs in stone mosaics. The north patio also has remains of Mixtec-style paintings in the inset panels above the doorways.

The Group of the Columns, the most interesting part if the site, lies to the south of the Church Group. It, too, is an arrangement of three patios and their surrounding rooms. Entry to the group is from the middle patio, from which you get a gorgeous view of the Hall of the Columns.

The facade of the Hall of the Columns is broken by three centrally located doorways separated by panels of stepped fret designs in the many variations for which Mitla is duly famous. This long, low building rests atop a platform with vertical walls and a central inset stairway. The stairway takes you into the hall itself, a room some 120 feet (36 meters) by 21 feet (6.3 meters), with 6 monolithic columns, each 3 feet (0.9 meters) in diameter, arranged along the long axis. These originally helped support the roof. The interior of the room is undecorated.

Near the eastern end of the room, a low doorway formed by huge stone jambs and a lintel gives access to the small north patio. This patio is surrounded by four rooms in an excellent state of preservation, all decorated (both inside and out) with panels of stepped fret designs. The designs were formed by inlaying the cut stone in mosaic fashion into the core of the wall. This was done with great precision, and the mosaic was then painted. A few remnants of paint are still visible. The whole effect is sometimes referred to as "frozen lace."

In a few places, the stepped fret design was carved into large stone blocks, but the mosaic form is decidedly more prevalent. It is generally agreed that the motif is a stylized version of the sky serpent and therefore a symbol of Quetzalcóatl. The beam, pole, and mortar roof of one of the rooms around the small patio has been restored to give visitors an idea of the original construction.

Hall of the Columns, interior room showing the columns, Mitla. Late Postclassic period.

Interior of the north patio, Mitla. Late Postclassic period.

Detail of the tomb entrance of the north building of the south patio, Mitla. Late Post-classic period.

From there you return to the middle patio for a look at the other architectural remains surrounding it. Then proceed to the south patio, adjacent to the southwest. The structures around this patio are less well preserved but are worth some time to see. Especially impressive are the enormous stone lintels and jambs, some of which are still in place. The decorations are similar to those already described.

Also of interest in this area are two cruciform tombs (in front of and below the east and north buildings), which are accessible from the patio floor. The interiors of both are decorated with carved stepped fret designs, and a large monolithic column is found in the tomb of the north building.

You now return to the parking area and drive south and west around the groups you just visited. You can park near a junction from which you can see the Arroyo Group (on the left). Again this is an assemblage of three patios and surrounding rooms. The rooms are also decorated with stepped fret designs, though the architectural remains are not as well preserved as those in the Group of the Columns.

From the junction you can walk north something over a block and turn left. You will be facing the greatly ruined Adobe Group, where some of the adobe construction of a fair-sized mound is still visible. The mound is the largest of four around a quadrangular plaza; a church has been built on top.

Ceramic evidence indicates that Mitla was occupied from early in the Middle Preclassic period, but the structural remains date to later times. The structures in the Church Group and the Group of the Columns belong to the last period (A.D. 1300 to 1521), before the Spanish conquest. The Arroyo Group is similar in construction and dates to the same period. The Adobe Group is believed to date to an earlier time. The greatly ruined South Group (not shown on the site plan) provides a longer sequence. It contains a burial dating to Early Classic times as well as offerings that were interred during the last period.

The earlier structures at Mitla were built by Zapotecs, but there is still some question about the structures built during the last period. According to John Paddock, "one of the most controversial topics in the history of Oaxaca archaeology is the nature of the Mixtec presence in the Late Postclassic in the Valley of Oaxaca." Some authorities believe that a good deal of Mixtec influence was present at Mitla (and Yagul), whereas others think that both sites were Zapotec throughout their history.

Some of Mitla's buildings were still occupied at the time of the Spanish conquest and continued in use during part of the sixteenth century.

Recent History

Spanish friars made mention of Mitla just a few years after the conquest. The earliest account is apparently that of Fray Martín de Valencia, who visited the site and in 1533 gave a brief description. Better known is the seventeenth-century work of Fray Francisco de Burgoa. This native of Oaxaca praised the skill of the ancient architects and commented on the monolithic columns and stone mosaics. Equally enthusiastic were eighteenth-century reports by Fray Juan de Torquemada.

In the nineteenth century, Mitla received many visitors. Although Alexander von Humboldt did not personally visit the site, in 1810 he published plans made in 1802 by Luis Martín and Pedro de Laguna, working for the Mexican government. Then came Guillermo Dupaix, A. F. Bandelier, Désiré Charnay, Eduard Seler, William Holmes,

Marshall Saville, and many others. Mitla became one of the most visited sites in Mexico.

Although a few attempts at preserving the structures were made at the end of the nineteenth century, it was not until the work of Leopoldo Batres in 1901 that restoration was carried out. Although imperfect, it succeeded in preserving the buildings.

The bulk of this work was exploratory and descriptive. The first modern excavation of the site was that of Alfonso Caso and Daniel F. Rubín de la Barbolla in 1934 and 1935. In the early 1960s, additional work was carried out by Ignacio Bernal and John Paddock, under the sponsorship of the Mexican government. In 1990, Nelly M. Robles García and Alfredo Moreira Quirós published a paper on a newer restoration project that they had undertaken.

Connection

Oaxaca City to Mitla: 27.4 miles [44.1 kilometers] by paved road (:55).

Getting There

Take Highway 190 southeast from Oaxaca City for 24.1 miles [38.8 kilometers] to a junction on the left for Mitla. This road continues 2.5 miles [4.0 kilometers] to the town of Mitla and on to the site.

Mitla is open daily from 9:00 A.M. to 5:00 P.M. Allow 1.5 hours for a visit. There are rest rooms and soft drink stands at the site; nearby is a restaurant and craft market. An extra fee is charged to bring a video camera into the site.

Frequent buses run between Mitla and Oaxaca City, and from the latter, tours to the site can be arranged.

In addition to the archaeological sites between Oaxaca City and Mitla, you should also stop for a look at the giant tree called El Tule. It is located in a churchyard off the north side of the highway 5.8 miles [9.2 kilometers] out of Oaxaca City. It is a species of cypress called *ahuehuete* and is reputed to be 2,000 years old. The circumference at its base is 160 feet (48.8 meters). A 10-minute stop should do it.

★ ★
MITLA MUSEUM OF ZAPOTEC ART
(FRISSEL MUSEUM)
(MITLA MUSEUM)

The Mitla Museum's collection is displayed along corridor walls facing a patio and in a room off the patio. At the time of our last visit, another room was undergoing reconstruction.

Bas-relief carvings, some with remnants of red paint, are exhibited in the corridor. Some represent genealogical registers, and some carvings are accompanied by dates. In a large glass case, a huge selection of clay figurines, figurine heads, and greenstone figures is exhibited. Another display shows ceramic molds and items made from the molds. Another case houses polychrome pottery, more figurines, and stone bark beaters. There are also carved vases and engraved ceramics.

Highlights inside the museum include a couple of large urns with seated figures and another urn with a crouching figure of the jaguar god. Additional urns and ceramic pots and figurines make up other displays. Most of the items in the collection are in excellent condition.

This was originally a private museum based on the collection of the late Ervin Frisell, but it is now operated by the University of the Americas Center of Regional Studies. The items come mainly from the state of Oaxaca, and most are from the Valley of Oaxaca. They were purchased and donated over a period of years.

Ambient light along the corridors is good, as is the artificial light inside. The exhibits are labeled in Spanish and English. Photography is not allowed in the museum or along the corridors.

There is a restaurant with rest rooms in the building that houses the museum. The address is Calle Juárez 2 in the town of Mitla; it is across the street from the main plaza. The museum is open on Monday and Tuesday and from Thursday through Sunday from 10:00 A.M. to 5:00 P.M. It is closed on Wednesday. Allow 15 minutes for a visit.

SECTION 5

• • • •

CENTRAL GULF COAST

Ball-player panel from Aparicio. Late Classic period. On display in the Jalapa Museum.

GENERAL INFORMATION FOR SECTION 5, CENTRAL GULF COAST

Mexico's central Gulf Coast is made up of the southern part of the state of Tamaulipas and the northern part of Veracruz. It is mostly flat, though in some areas the inland mountains and foothills come close to the shore. It is basically hot and humid except for some inland sections (such as Cuetzalan and Jalapa), which are cooler because of their altitudes.

Places for stopovers abound in this section, both along the coast and inland. From north to south they are Tampico, Valles (inland), Tuxpan, Poza Rica, Papantla, some beachfront places about 30 to 35 miles [48.3 to 56.3 kilometers] south of Papantla, Cuetzalan (inland), Jalapa (inland), Veracruz, Santiago Tuxtla, and Catemaco.

Tampico, Poza Rica, Jalapa, and Veracruz have hotels in all price ranges. The best in Poza Rica is the Hotel Poza Rica Inn, and the relatively new Fiesta Inn on the east end of Jalapa is conveniently located. Decent to fairly good accommodations can be found in the other places. The best for each place is the Hotel Valles in Valles, the Plaza Palmas on the bypass around Tuxpan, the Hotel El Tajín in Papantla (modest), the Hotel de la Playa El Palmar and the Torre Molino along the coast, the Posada Cuetzalan in Cuetzalan, the Hotel Castellanos in Santiago Tuxtla (modest), and the Hotel La Finca in Catemaco (conveniently located). The beachfront hotels and those in Cuetzalan and Veracruz tend to fill up on Friday and Saturday nights. Try to arrive early to get a room at any of these places on weekends. There are restaurants at all of the stopovers mentioned.

Highway 180 runs the length of the Gulf Coast, and most of it is good. Between Tampico and Tuxpan, however, there is a stretch of about 50 miles [80.5 kilometers] that is only fair, with a few spots that are poor. This is in a swampy area where roads deteriorate rapidly. Along Highway 70 from Tampico to the cutoff for Tamuín there is a section that is poor (and a few miles that are bad) near El Ébano.

The only real mountain driving in this section is on Highway 129 from Tezuitlán to the cutoff for Cuetzalan and Highway 575 to Cuetzalan. This last part is also prone to fog in spots. There is a little hilly driving between Poza Rica and Papantla and for a short distance beyond, and in the area of the Tuxtla Mountains from northeast of Santiago Tuxtla to Catemaco and about 25 miles [40.2 kilometers] farther. The condition of roads (paved and unpaved) going to a specific site or museum is given in the text for that site or museum.

The major airports in the region are at Tampico (with direct flights to Harlingen, Texas) and Veracruz. Flights from these airports connect with Mexico City and other destinations within the country.

The points of reference for distances and driving times are the following: (1) in Tampico, the junction of the *libramiento* (bypass) that goes around the west edge of the city and Highway 70; (2) in Valles, the junction of Highways 70 and 85; (3) in Tuxpan, the bridge over the Tuxpan River; (4) in Poza Rica, the bridge over the Cazones River at the north end of town; (5) in Papantla, the junction of Highway 180 and the road that goes south to El Chote; (6) in Veracruz, the bridge over the railroad yard at the north end of town; and (7) in Santiago Tuxtla, the junction of Highways 180 and 179.

Vehicles can be rented at the airports already mentioned and through major hotels in Tampico, Poza Rica, Jalapa, and Veracruz. There are travel agencies in these four places as well.

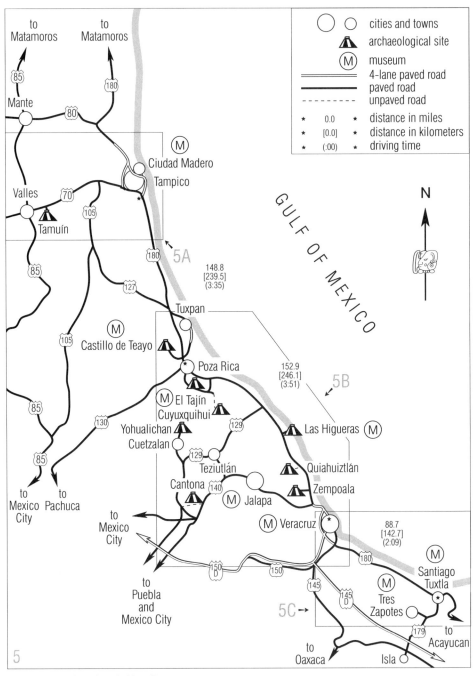

cities and towns
archaeological site
museum
4-lane paved road
paved road
unpaved road
0.0   distance in miles
[0.0] distance in kilometers
(:00) driving time

to Matamoros
to Matamoros

85
180

Mante
80

Valles
70
105

Tamuín

180   5A

85

148.8
[239.5]
(3:35)

127

Tuxpan

105
Castillo de Teayo

Poza Rica

152.9
[246.1]
(3:51)

5B

El Tajín
Cuyuxquihui

130
Yohualichan
Cuetzalan

129
Teziutlán

129

Las Higueras

85

Quiahuiztlán
Zempoala

85

to Mexico City
to Pachuca

Cantona
140
Jalapa

to Mexico City

Veracruz

88.7
[142.7]
(2:09)

180

Santiago Tuxtla

150
D
150

145
145
D

Tres Zapotes

5C →

to Puebla and Mexico City

to Oaxaca
Isla

179
to Acayucan

N

GULF OF MEXICO

Ciudad Madero
Tampico

5

North-central Gulf Coast (Map 5).

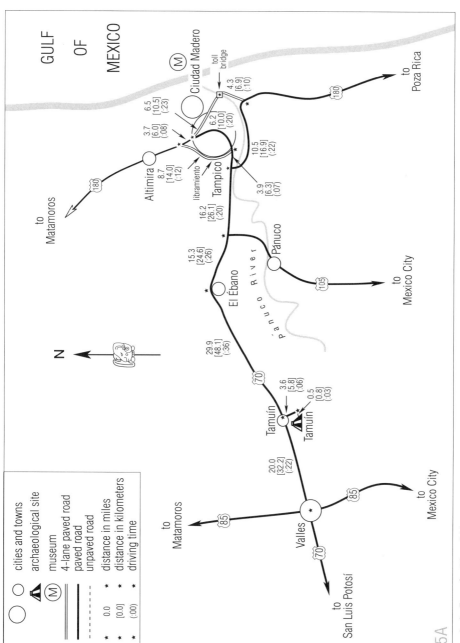

GULF

OF

MEXICO

Ⓜ Ciudad Madero

toll bridge

4.3 [6.9] (.10)

to Poza Rica

⑱⓪

6.5 [10.5] (.23)

3.7 [6.0] (.08)

6.2 [10.0] (.20)

Altimira

8.7 [14.0] (.12)

libramiento

Tampico

10.5 [16.9] (.22)

3.9 [6.3] (.07)

to Matamoros

⑱⓪

16.2 [26.1] (.20)

15.3 [24.6] (.26)

Pánuco

El Ébano

P a n u c o   R i v e r

⑩⑤

to Mexico City

N

29.9 [48.1] (.36)

⑦⓪

Tamuín

3.6 [5.8] (.06)

0.5 [0.8] (.03)

Tamuín

20.0 [32.2] (.22)

to Matamoros

⑧⑤

Valles

⑧⑤

to Mexico City

⑦⓪

to San Luis Potosí

cities and towns
archaeological site
Ⓜ museum
4-lane paved road
paved road
unpaved road
distance in miles
distance in kilometers
driving time

★ 0.0
★ [0.0]
★ (.00)

5A

Route to Tamuín (Map 5A).

★ ★
MUSEUM OF HUASTEC CULTURE
(CIUDAD MADERO MUSEUM)

Huastec stone figure in the Ciudad Madero Museum. Classic period.

The Ciudad Madero Museum is located in that city's Technological Institute on Calle 1° (Primero) de Mayo at Calle Justo Sierra. When you walk through the gate at the institute, turn right and follow an outside corridor for a while until you come to the museum entrance (on the left).

The first display is a map of the Huastec region with archaeological sites pinpointed. The next display shows different physical types through photos of living people and pre-Columbian figurines. Implements, including manos and metates and arrow and lance heads, are exhibited along with ceramic bowls and figurines from various periods. Some of the ceramics are polychromes. Jewelry, copper bells, and objects of hammered gold and shell are displayed, as is a fine carved Totonac yoke.

There are copies of a fresco from Tamuín and a plan of the site, and models of conical temples typical of Huastec architecture. Several typical Huastec carved stone figures form an important part of the collection. An interesting monument called the Slab of Texupezco, after a site in Veracruz, is carved in bas-relief with symbols having to do with water.

The Ciudad Madero Museum is open Tuesday through Friday from 10:00 A.M. to 5:00 P.M. and on Saturday from 10:00 A.M. to 3:00 P.M. It is closed on Sunday and Monday. There is a small area at the museum where publications are sold. There are no rest rooms at the museum and no food or drink, but these can be found at restaurants in Ciudad Madero and Tampico. The lighting is fair, and photography without flash is permitted. Labeling is rather poor, but happily, a guidebook for the museum, which gives some good information, is available there. Allow 20 minutes to view the collection.

TAMUÍN
(tah-moo-EEN)

Derivation:
   A corruption of the Huastec Tamohi, meaning "Place of Ramón Trees."
Culture:
   Huastec.
Location:
   Southeastern San Luis Potosí.
Maps: 5 (p. 242) and 5A (p. 243)

The Site

Tamuín is recognized as one of the major Postclassic centers of Huastec culture. Only one section of the site is open to visitors.

You begin your tour at the foot of a huge platform faced with river boulders and originally stuccoed—the type of construction used for all the buildings at Tamuín. A broad stairway with unusually wide *alfardas* ascends the platform. Remains of stucco can be seen on the north side wall of the stairway.

The top of the platform supports several buildings around a plaza. Those on the north, south, and west sides of the plaza are platforms of varying sizes; all have stairways facing the plaza. The west building is the largest and appears to have had a stairway on the west side as well, facing the Tamuín River, a tributary of the Pánuco. This structure rises in a couple of tiers, and small circular constructions are found at ground level on the north side of the east stairway.

The south platform has some remaining (or restored) stucco, and stairways on the west and north sides. The stairs of this structure have *alfardas* with vertical upper zones.

The most interesting structure is in the center of the plaza. It is formed of two conical altars connected by a bench, and another bench that connects to an eastern stair bordered by *alfardas*. The stair ascends a small pyramidal base with the remains of merlons on top. The altar near the steps is smaller at the top, while the reverse is true of the other. The pyramidal base, benches, and altars retain much of their stucco surfaces, and red and yellow paint, the remnants of frescoes, are found on the altars and parts of the sides of the benches.

Other small structures include a low square platform to the south of the conical altars, a circular depression best appreciated from the top of the west platform, and remains of a low, altarlike platform to the north of the conical altars.

Some authorities feel that the style of the frescoes is related to the style used in the Mixtec codices. Others see a more Toltec influence. The Huasteca, where Tamuín is located, is known to have received influences from both groups.

The Gulf Coast of Mexico and the Yucatán Peninsula are believed to have been occupied in ancient times by a people speaking a common Maya language. At some point, another group (or groups) of Totonac-Zoquean speakers intruded, pushing into the southern Gulf Coast area and effectively splitting the Maya group into two—the Huastec Mayas on the northwest and the Yucatec Mayas on the east. On the basis of glottochronology, it is believed that the Huastecs were separated from the rest of the Maya group as early as 1400 B.C. and that other groups intruded into the area at a later date. The stratigraphic sequence for the Huasteca runs in an unbroken line from 1100 B.C. up to the Spanish conquest.

Architecturally, the Huastecs were no match for their southeastern Maya cousins. Nevertheless, they developed their own characteristic architectural style—notable for many circular structures—and an important culture of their own, distinguished by fine stone statuary, beautifully carved shell, and excellent pottery.

One of the gems of Huastec sculpture was found at El Consuelo ranch, near Tamuín. Popularly called the "Adolescent," it is now

Conical altars and bench with remains of red-painted frescoes, Tamuín. A small pyramidal platform is at the rear. Postclassic period.

in the Mexico City Museum. This figure, carved in the round, depicts a nude young man with tattoos covering almost half his body; some of the tattoos are glyphs. He carries on his back an infant who is perhaps associated with the sun or wind god, Ehécatl, a manifestation of Quetzalcóatl.

Quetzalcóatl was a major deity in the Huasteca, and it may be Quetzalcóatl or his priests who are depicted in the frescoes at Tamuín. Some authorities believe that Quetzalcóatl had his origins in the Huasteca.

Recent History

The early major work at Tamuín was that of Wilfrido du Solier, who explored the site in 1946 under a project sponsored by INAH. Du Solier is known for his work in the Huasteca, and he reported on the frescoes at Tamuín in 1946.

In 1978, the conical altars were restored by Noe Martínez González. Major excavation at Tamuín began in 1990, directed by José Maurilio Perea, and the work continued for several years.

The statue of the Adolescent was discovered many years before the early major work at the site and was in a local collection in 1918. Later it was sent to the Mexico City Museum.

Connections

1. Valles to Tamuín: 23.6 miles [38.0 kilometers] by paved road (:28), then 0.5 mile [0.8 kilometer] by rock road (:06).

2. Tampico to Tamuín: 68.9 miles [110.9 kilometers] by paved road (1:35), then 0.5 mile [0.8 kilometer] by rock road (:06).

Getting There

1. From Valles, take Highway 70 heading east to the town of Tamuín and the cutoff for the site, 20.0 miles [32.2 kilometers], and turn right. A sign saying El Consuelo marks the

junction. Proceed 3.6 miles [5.8 kilometers] to the gate for the site and a sign saying Tamohi. Turn right onto the rock road and continue to the base of the site and the parking area.

2. From Tampico, head west on Highway 70 to the cutoff for Tamuín, 65.3 miles [105.1 kilometers], and turn left at the sign for El Consuelo. Then follow the directions already given.

Tamuín is open daily from 7:00 A.M. to 6:00 P.M.—at least that was the schedule when the archaeologists were working. Allow one hour to visit the site. There is no food or drink at the site, nor are there rest rooms.

★ ★

CASTILLO DE TEAYO

(kahs-TEE-yoh deh teh-AH-yoh)

Derivation:
  "Castillo de" is Spanish for "Castle of," and Teayo is Huastec for "In the Stone Turtle."
Culture:
  Huastec.
Location:
  North-central Veracruz.
Maps: 5 (p. 242), 5B (p. 248), and 5B1 (p. 249)

The Site

The feature of interest at Castillo de Teayo is the three-tiered pyramid next to the plaza in the town of the same name. This imposing structure rises 42.7 feet (13.0 meters) and faces a little west of south; it has a stairway on that side. The tiers of the structure are sloped, and the stairway is bordered by *alfardas* with vertical upper zones. Atop the pyramid is a one-room masonry temple covered with a thatch roof. The surface of the pyramid was originally covered with stucco.

It is possible that the stairway seen today at Castillo de Teayo was actually part of an earlier construction. Some believe that after the arrival of the Spaniards, the indigenous population undertook a new construction stage of the pyramid but never completed a new stairway that would have covered the existing one. Although the pyramid has been studied and consolidated, it has never been thoroughly excavated or tunneled.

The modern town of Castillo de Teayo was founded in 1872, and it surrounds the pre-Columbian pyramid. Embedded in a modern wall in front of the pyramid is a bas-relief sculpture depicting Tlaloc and another deity.

Recent History

Much of the archaeological work at Castillo de Teayo was conducted by José García Payón, who published his reports in the 1950s and 1960s. Earlier, Eduard Seler studied the site and believed the remains were Aztec. Apparently the ceremonial precinct was never wrecked by the Spaniards.

Connections

1. Poza Rica to Castillo de Teayo: 23.4 miles [37.6 kilometers] by paved road (1:05), but see "Getting There."

2. Papantla to Poza Rica: 14.2 miles [22.9 kilometers] by paved road (:37).

3. Tuxpan to Castillo de Teayo: 37.1 miles [59.7 kilometers] by paved road (1:19).

Getting There

1. From Poza Rica, head north on Highway 180 (and for a short distance beyond it on Highway 127) to the cutoff for Castillo de Teayo. The cutoff is marked with a sign for

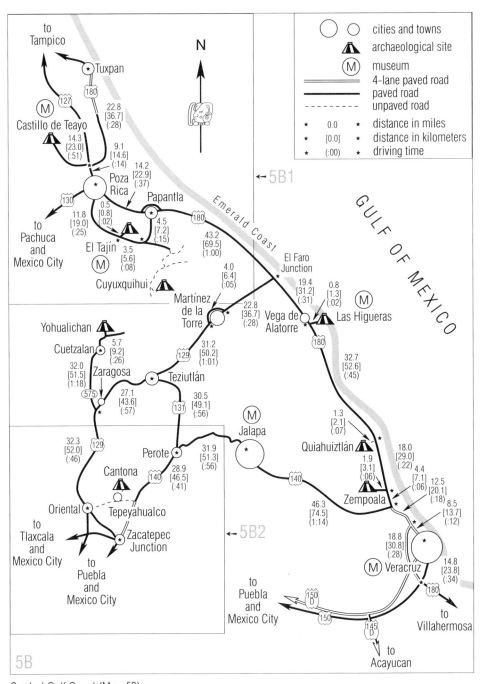

←5B1

←5B2

Central Gulf Coast (Map 5B).

5B

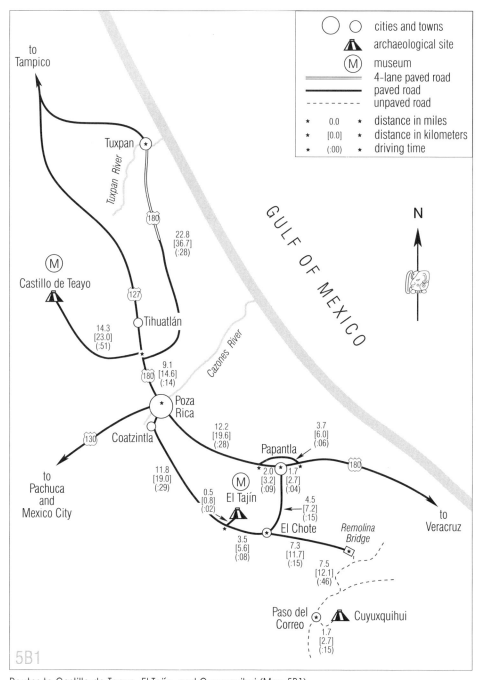

Routes to Castillo de Teayo, El Tajín, and Cuyuxquihui (Map 5B1).

The pyramid, Castillo de Teayo. Postclassic period.

Zapotalillo; however, the sign faces the other way. The best landmark is the end of the new road that you will pass (a continuation of Highway 180 as it turns to the east); it comes in on the right (from Tuxpan). The cutoff for Castillo de Teayo is just past this on the left (west). Turn left at the junction and follow the road to the plaza and pyramid.

Although the road from the highway to Castillo de Teayo is listed as paved, its surface has been poor for a long time. It deteriorated further when heavy rains from a hurricane washed away the edges. Perhaps by now it has been repaired; if so, you will be able to drive the 14.3 miles [23.0 kilometers] in less than the 51 minutes indicated on the accompanying maps.

2. From Papantla, head northwest on Highway 180 to Poza Rica, then follow the directions already given.

3. From Tuxpan, head south on Highway 180 to the junction with Highway 127. This is the end of the new road mentioned earlier. Turn right for a short distance on Highway 127 to the cutoff for Castillo de Teayo. Then turn left and continue to the plaza and pyramid. Note: The first 11.5 miles [18.5 kilometers] of Highway 180 south of Tuxpan are four lanes. A projection shows that the entire section from Tuxpan to Highway 127 will eventually be four lanes and that a continuation to the southwest, also four lanes, will extend all the way to Teotihuacán.

Castillo de Teayo, being right next to the town's plaza, is open every day, all day. Food and cold drinks are available in shops near the pyramid. There are no other facilities.

★ ★
CASTILLO DE TEAYO MUSEUM

The Castillo de Teayo Museum is to the left of the pyramid (as you face it). It is a fenced and roofed area that houses several dozen carved stone monuments. The gate is kept locked until visitors arrive. The caretaker can generally be found sitting on a bench near the pyramid, wearing an INAH cap; he will open the gate to the museum for you.

Some of the more interesting monuments in the collection are a bas-relief stela bearing a depiction of Tlaloc, a Huastec sculpture of a female wearing a *quechquémitl,* a serpent's head with a human head emerg-

ing from its mouth, and a three-dimensional, headless statue of Xipe Totec standing with his legs crossed.

At one time the monuments now in the museum stood around the base of the pyramid. In the early 1980s, INAH moved them to the museum for protection. Although unlabeled, the sculptures came from the site or its immediate surroundings and date to the Postclassic period.

The museum is opened as requested daily. Allow 15 minutes for a visit. There is enough ambient light for photography.

Stone sculpture of a serpent with a human head emerging from its mouth. Postclassic period. Displayed in the Castillo de Teayo Museum.

★ ★ ★ ★
EL TAJÍN
(ehl tah-HEEN)

Derivation:
Totonac for "Lightning."
Culture:
Classic Veracruz (or El Tajín)
(see text).
Location:
North-central Veracruz.
Maps: 5 (p. 242), 5B (p. 248),
and 5B1 (p. 249)

The Site

El Tajín is the most spectacular site on the Gulf Coast of Mexico. A great deal of clearing, consolidation, and restoration was undertaken during the Tajín Project from 1984 through 1992, revealing structures that had previously been simply emerald green mounds. There is more to see at El Tajín today than ever before in its modern history. The dates used here are taken from S. Jeffery K. Wilkerson's *El Tajín: A Guide for Visitors* and José García Payón's *El Tajín: Official Guide.*

The first small constructions at El Tajín were inaugurated around A.D. 100, and the site grew to its peak in the Late Classic period, when it reached its maximum extent of over 3.9 square miles (10 square kilometers). It was abandoned around 1100. Some areas near El Tajín, however, were occupied by hunters and gatherers as early as 5600 B.C. An example is La Conchita, about 15.5 miles [24.9 kilometers] east of El Tajín. Another, the nearby riverbank site of Santa Luisa, 19.0 miles [30.6 kilometers] to the east of El Tajín, was occupied before 4000 B.C.

People called Totonacs live in the area of El Tajín today, and it was once thought that El Tajín was a Totonac site. When this idea was discarded (after it was discovered that the Totonacs probably entered the area only in the Postclassic period), the preferred nomenclature for the builders of El Tajín became the culture of Central Veracruz or the culture of El Tajín. Later it was learned that the earliest identifiable culture of the region was Huastec. The Huastecs arrived in the area around 400 B.C. El Tajín was the recipient of influences from other cultures throughout its history—Teotihuacán, Maya, and Toltec. In some cases the influence was reciprocal, especially in the case of Teotihuacán. Even while incorporating foreign traits, however, El Tajín retained its identity.

Entrance to El Tajín is through a new visitors' center that houses the site museum, ticket office, and cafeteria. As you leave the building and head to the site, you come first to the Arroyo Group, where four major pyramidal structures surround a large plaza. The plaza covers more than 86,000 square feet (7,990 square kilometers) and is believed to have been used as a marketplace in ancient times. Sculptures were found in the buildings of the Arroyo Group, some depicting figures that are strongly reminiscent of the merchant deities of central Mexico, in a style not fully typical of El Tajín, according to Wilkerson.

You reach Building 19 first; it rises in numerous tiers and has stairways on all four sides. Those on the north and south are wider than those on the east and west. Building 19 borders the south side of the plaza.

Building 20 lies on the west side of the plaza and has a stairway on its east side. Buildings 16 and 18 border the north and east sides of the plaza, respectively, and also have stairways facing the plaza. Building 16 rises in five tiers, each topped by a cornice with niches below. The tiers of Building 18 are plain, but its three stairways have niches covered with projecting cornices on the centerline of each stairway. All four buildings of the Arroyo Group had superstructures originally.

You then follow the trail north, along the east side of Building 16. Opposite, on the

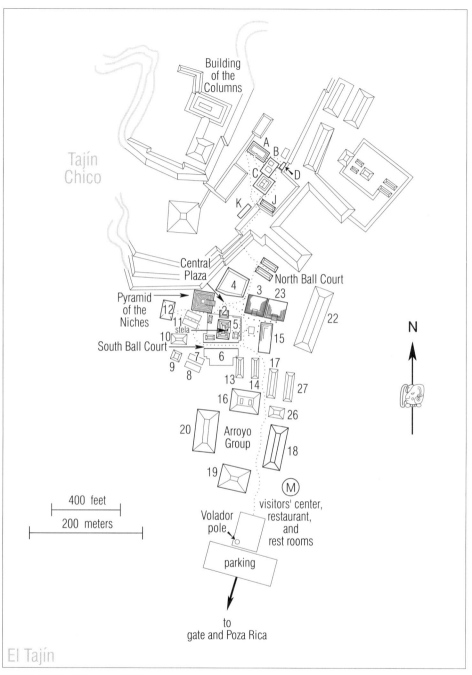

Building
of the
Columns

Tajín
Chico

A
B
C
D
J
K

Central
Plaza

North Ball Court

Pyramid
of the
Niches

12
11
stela
10

4
2
3
23

5
15

22

South Ball Court

7
9
8
6

13
14

16

17
27

26

20

Arroyo
Group

18

19

N

M
visitors' center,
restaurant,
and
rest rooms

400 feet
200 meters

Volador
pole

parking

to
gate and Poza Rica

El Tajín

Modified after Wilkerson, 1987.

Bas-relief carving in the South Ball Court, El Tajín. The figure at lower right is practicing self-sacrifice. Early Postclassic period.

east side of the trail, is Building 26, and north of that is one of El Tajín's 17 ball courts (Buildings 17 and 27). Another ball court lies nearby to the northwest (Buildings 13 and 14). El Tajín's most impressive court lies northwest of the one just mentioned. The north wall of the platform of Building 6 forms the south wall of the South Ball Court; the south wall of the platform that supports Building 5 forms the north wall of the South Ball Court. Each wall is carved on each end and in the center for a total of six panels, each elaborately ornamented with scenes related to the ritual ball game. Buildings 5 and 6 and the South Ball Court date to a little after A.D. 900. A detailed description of the story told by the panels, and their reading order, can be found in Wilkerson's book.

Walk through the South Ball Court (from east to west) and then go northwest for a look at Buildings 10, 11 (which forms the south side of another ball court), and 12, all of which are interesting. When you look through the playing alley of the ball court, from east to west, you are looking directly at the front of Building 12, which rises in two levels. There are niches at the top of each level, and cylindrical columns support the projecting cornices at the front of the niches.

From there you can retrace your steps going west to east through the South Ball Court, then north to the front of Building 5. Alternatively, you can get to the front of the Pyramid of the Niches by taking the path that leads past the building's southeast corner, near where it almost touches the platform of Building 5. The latter way brings you to the Central Plaza, the core of the site and the part that was excavated, consolidated, and restored first. I will describe the

Front (east side) of Building 5, El Tajín. Late Classic period.

structures around the plaza, but the order in which you visit them is up to you. By following the wide paths at El Tajín, you won't miss anything of importance.

Building 5 is an imposing pyramidal structure that faces east and rests on a platform more than 32,000 square feet (2,973 square meters) in area. Building 5 served as a temple, and a freestanding sculpture or stela can be seen on the centerline of the stairway at the top of the first level of the structure. The stela, which depicts the god Tajín or a death deity, once stood in the temple atop the building. Building 5 shares the platform with other, smaller structures, notably Building 2, which will be described later.

Building 15 lies across an open space to the east of Building 5. Building 15 is a civil structure probably dating to around A.D. 950; it has a broad western stair. In the center of the open space lies a low platform with a western stair. To the north of the platform is Building 3, and adjacent to it on the east, Building 23. Both structures face south.

Building 3 has some features unusual for El Tajín. Although it rises in tiers (in this case seven), as do most of El Tajín's other structures, each tier is divided into panels of different widths. The building was originally painted blue—on several occasions—rather than the more common red. The remains of blue paint can best be seen on the base of the stairway and on the eastern wall. It is believed to have been constructed around A.D. 500.

Building 23 is nearly identical in plan to Building 3, but it differs from it in being one of the last constructions at El Tajín, probably dating to around A.D. 1050. This structure was painted red, rises in five tiers, and originally had stepped merlons on top—a common feature in Postclassic Gulf Coast architecture, seen at such sites as Quiahuiztlán and Zempoala. The lower part of the stairway has a divider that is actually a buttress added after the original stairs were greatly destroyed, perhaps by an earthquake. The purpose of the buttress was to hold the fill behind the stairway in place. From the front of Building 23, look to the right (east) for a view of the front part of the partly cleared Building 22.

Freestanding sculpture on the steps of Building 5, east side, El Tajín. Late Classic period.

From there, head west past the fronts of Buildings 23 and 3 and enter the Central Plaza. You will be facing the Pyramid of the Niches, also called Building 1, which borders the west side of the plaza. This is the most spectacular building at the site, the first structure discovered, and one of the best preserved. It is the construction that everyone thinks of as symbolizing El Tajín.

The Pyramid of the Niches rises in six tiers, and there are a few remains of a crowning temple, bringing it to a height of 67 feet (20.4 meters). When its temple was intact, obviously it was somewhat taller. The construction style is *talud-tablero,* with niches in the *tableros* and a projecting cornice on top of each tier. Although most of El Tajín's structures have some niches, the Pyramid of the Niches has 365 covering all four sides of the building, plus more in projections from the centerline of the stairway. The number 365 may refer to the days of the solar year, but it is believed that the primary purpose of this number of niches was not calendrical. Some people have theorized that idols were placed in the niches, but this idea is not supported by the archaeological evidence.

The *alfardas* of the structure's stairway each have two borders, and in between there are stepped frets, which may have been painted blue against a red background. The quality of the stone-cutting in the Pyramid of the Niches is of the highest order; the stone slabs, especially in the niches, exhibit superior craftsmanship. Within the structure there is an earlier one that had *taludes* but no niches. The earlier building dates to around A.D. 250, while the structure seen today was built around 600.

The south side of the Central Plaza is bordered by the platform of Building 5. Building 2 rests on the platform and juts into the plaza from it; it has a divided northern stairway that ascends to the top of the first level and a single broader stair that goes to the top. The top of the first level of the stairway is crowned with a single row of niches topped by a projecting cornice. An earlier building can be seen inside the top of the structure. A smaller two-level building lies to the west of Building 2.

Building 4 borders the north side of the Central Plaza, and although it has been investigated, it has not been restored. It has a stairway on the north side, away from the Central Plaza.

Now follow the path that heads north between Buildings 4 and 3; this takes you to the North Ball Court. It is smaller than the South Ball Court, but its walls, too, are each carved with six panels in the same relative positions as those in the south court's walls. Unfortunately, the carvings are not as well preserved, but they are still worth some study. The North Ball Court dates to around A.D. 600.

To the northwest of the North Ball Court, a stairway leads up over terraces to the

The Pyramid of the Niches (background) and Building 2 (at left), El Tajín, before restoration. *Voladores* (fliers) are performing in the Central Plaza; the *volador* pole is now at the entrance to the site.

level of the part of the site called Tajín Chico. After you climb the stair, you head northeast, climb a bit more, and come to Building J, covered with a thatch shelter. There you will see some remnants of blue paint and a stucco panel with a zigzag design. From Building J, a few steps up toward the northwest bring you to the plaza of Tajín Chico.

To the southwest of this stair is Building K, with ornately decorated niches and projecting cornices at the top of the structure. From Building K, head northeast to the west side of Building C. It is believed to have served a civil function. It rises in three tiers and bears a few remains of its crowning superstructure of three rooms. Its niches contain stepped frets, and the structure has stairways on both east and west sides. Building B is adjacent to the north.

Building B, with two stories and stairways on its east and west sides, is believed to have been a palace. There is one room on the first story and two on the second. The second story is reached by a narrow stair from the room on the first story. This is the only palace at El Tajín with one story placed directly above the other, a feature rare outside the Maya area.

To the west of Building B is Building A. Its entrance, on the south (plaza) side, is through a stairway covered with a corbeled vault, also an unusual feature outside the Maya area. On each side of the opening for the stairway are walls with indications of false steps, and beyond these are decorative double borders with stepped frets in between, reminiscent of the *alfardas* flanking the stairway of the Pyramid of the Niches. The real

Front (west side) of Building C at Tajín Chico, El Tajín. Early Postclassic period.

stairway of Building A leads to an upper level, the walls of which bear many well-preserved stucco decorations in the stepped fret pattern and other geometric motifs. Buildings A, B, and C were built around A.D. 800, although there is an earlier structure beneath Building A that dates to around 700.

Leave Building A from its south stairway and walk around the east side of the structure along a narrow passage between Buildings A and B, then turn right and go to Building D. Remains there include stucco decorations in a geometric pattern and a stair that leads to a terrace on a lower level. Building D dates to around A.D. 950.

The various buildings at El Tajín face different directions, but two of the most important structures, the Pyramid of the Niches and Building 5, face east, making the morning hours the best time to photograph them. If time allows, plan for some afternoon hours as well, especially for Tajín Chico. There is no reason to visit the Building of the Columns, because the columns have been moved to El Tajín Museum, and the trail to the building has become overgrown.

Recent History

El Tajín was discovered by Diego Ruíz, an officer of the tobacco guard, in March 1785 while he was searching for growers of illegal tobacco in the Papantla region, an area under his jurisdiction. He published a description of the Pyramid of the Niches in a Mexican journal in July of the same year. The site was later visited by Guillermo Dupaix (better known for his work at Palenque), Alexander von Humboldt, and Carlos Nebel, all in the nineteenth century. Nebel was the first visitor to realize that there was more to El Tajín than just the Pyramid of the Niches.

Many others visited and wrote about El Tajín in the early twentieth century. For detailed coverage, see the 1992 book *Tajín*, by Brueggemann, Ladrón, and Sanchéz. The first phase of archaeological work at the site was that directed by Agustín García Vega, who published his findings starting in 1929. Enrique Juan Palacios studied the sculptures found at the Pyramid of the Niches and in 1932 published his findings. During the 1936 field season, in addition to continuing exploration and conservation efforts, Wilfrido du Solier studied El Tajín's ceramics. He published his conclusions in 1939 and 1945. In 1938, José García Payón visited El Tajín, and the following year he continued the work of consolidation and restoration that had begun under García Vega. García Payón continued his work on El Tajín, in one form or another, until his death in 1977. In 1960, Román Piña Chan began the construction of a provisional site museum, where the sculptures from the site were placed. He also studied the architecture.

Others also worked at the site, studied the ceramics, and studied nearby sites in order to place El Tajín in a more regional context. In 1983, INAH and the government of the state of Veracruz joined forces for work at the site, and this began the real multidisciplinary efforts, which included investigators from the Institute of Anthropology of the University of Veracruz, coordinated by Alfonso Medellín Zenil as representative of the Veracruz state government.

From 1984 through 1992, work carried out by members of the Tajín Project, under the coordination of Juergen K. Brueggemann, completely changed the look of the site. Thirty-four buildings were repaired or thoroughly explored. During the project, a post-Tajín occupation was discovered; it represents an occasional reoccupation of the site in pre-Hispanic times, but after the fall of the site in the Postclassic period. The visitors' center and the new museum were also constructed during the project.

Connections

1. Papantla to El Tajín: 8.5 miles [13.6 kilometers] by paved road (:25).

2. Poza Rica to El Tajín: 12.3 miles [19.8 kilometers] by paved road (:31).

Getting There

1. In Papantla there is a sign on Highway 180 marking the way to El Tajín; take this road south to El Chote, 4.5 miles [7.2 kilometers]. (After you leave Highway 180, but while you are still in Papantla, you will pass a rather unattractive statue at 1.3 miles [2.1 kilometers]. The street from the highway to the statue is one way, so if you return this way, you will have to use another route to get back to the highway from the statue, not an easy task with Papantla's winding streets.)

When you reach El Chote, turn right at an unmarked junction and go 3.5 miles [5.6 kilometers] to the entrance to El Tajín, marked with a large sign. Turn right and proceed to the parking area in front of the visitors' center.

2. From Poza Rica (at the junction of Highways 180 and 130 by the bridge over the Cazones River), follow Highway 180 south and then east for 1.6 miles [2.6 kilometers] to a sign for El Tajín and turn right. Proceed to Coatzintla, 0.6 mile [1.0 kilometer], and turn left at the sign for El Tajín. Go 9.6 miles [15.4 kilometers] to the entrance for El Tajín and turn left. Proceed to the parking area.

At El Tajín there are rest rooms in the visitors' center. In addition to the cafeteria there, food and drink are sold from stands next to the parking area; some stands sell souvenirs. When visiting El Tajín, carry a canteen of water and wear a sun hat.

The site is open daily from 9:00 A.M. to 5:00 P.M. Allow three hours for a visit. Guides can be hired at the site if you would like to have someone show you around. Buses pass the entrance to El Tajín, and tours to the site can be arranged in Poza Rica; check at the better hotels. You could also taxi to the site from either connection.

Postscript

While you are at El Tajín you will likely get a chance to see a performance by the famous Voladores ("Fliers")—don't miss it. Years ago the *volador* pole was set up in the Central Plaza in front of the Pyramid of the Niches. Later it was moved to a spot south of the Arroyo Group, and now it stands just outside the visitors' center. Over the years, performances have become more frequent. Also over the years, the number of visitors to the site has increased dramatically. So far as I can tell, a performance takes place whenever there are enough people around. You might try asking at the ticket desk, however, to see if there is a specific schedule.

This acrobatic "dance" has pre-Columbian roots and a religious and ritual significance. Five costumed men climb a tall metal (formerly a wooden) pole. Four are attached to the top with ropes, and the fifth performs a stomping dance, accompanied by flute music and drum beats, atop a small platform. As the dance progresses, the four men "fly" from the top of the pole by their ropes, slowly descending while upside down, in ever widening circles as the platform atop the pole gradually turns.

They represent macaws, which symbolize the sun, and they make 13 revolutions as they descend, before righting themselves at ground level. The 4 flying men times 13 revolutions equals 52—a number that represents a major cycle of time (in years) in the Mesoamerican calendar.

A sixth costumed young man circulates among the viewers and collects donations, perhaps a modern addition to the ceremony.

The area around El Tajín is noted for the production of vanilla by the present-day Totonacs. Vanilla is actually the seed pod of a certain orchid that is hand pollinated. A popular regional curio is made from the pods, which are woven into various forms—flowers, scorpions, vases, and so forth. These are locally called *figuras de vainilla,* and they make unusual souvenirs. They can be found at El Tajín and at stores in Papantla. It is sometimes suggested that you place the *figuras* in your sugar bowl to impart a vanilla aroma.

★ ★
EL TAJÍN MUSEUM

When you enter the visitors' center at El Tajín, you will find the museum inside on the right. It was inaugurated in November 1992. Some highlights of the collection are drum-shaped discs that made up columns at the Building of the Columns above Tajín Chico. They are carved in bas-relief and relate rituals involving Thirteen Rabbit, an

Detail of a carved column from the Building of the Columns, El Tajín. Early Postclassic period. Displayed in El Tajín Museum.

El Tajín ruler who probably constructed the Building of the Columns. The columns date to the Early Postclassic period.

Another interesting display is a partly defaced bas-relief panel of a standing male figure in frontal view; he holds an incense bag and a fan (or a plumed staff). He may represent a ball player or a priest. The carving comes from the Pyramid of the Niches, according to some early sources, whereas other, more recent writers say it was found in the Arroyo Group. Although the accoutre-ments depicted are typical of El Tajín, the style of the carving is not.

Other bas-relief panels, a model of El Tajín, and another of the Building of the Columns form other exhibits. There are remains of a mural painting, a burial, and display cases housing ceramics.

Photography without flash is allowed. Lighting is fairly good in some areas and rather poor in others. There is some labeling. The museum is open daily from 9:00 A.M. to 4:00 P.M. Allow 30 minutes for a visit.

★ ★

CUYUXQUIHUI

(koo-yoosh-KEE-wee)

(COYOXQUIHUI)

Derivation:
Totonac for "Armadillo Tree (Wood)" (see text).
Culture:
Probably Totonac, later Huastec and Aztec.
Location:
East-central Veracruz.
Maps: 5 (p. 242), 5B (p. 248), and 5B1 (p. 249)

The Site

In the mountains near Cuyuxquihui grows a certain tree, the bark of which resembles an armadillo shell—hence the name of the site. It is not known whether this was its original name. The site lies on graded terraces that rise from north to south; you begin at the north end and climb to the south. Some spots at the site give nice views of the landscape below.

The first structure of interest is a platform with a broad stairway on the west side. After looking at this and nearby grass-covered mounds, climb the stairway and turn right (south). A little farther along you come to another stairway that ascends a terrace, and then you arrive at the main plaza, the most interesting part of the site. As you enter the plaza you can see three important buildings: Structure I on the right (west), Structure III straight ahead, and Structure IV on the left.

Structure I, the major building at the site, rises 32.8 feet (10.0 meters) in four tiers. On the east side it has a stairway of 37 steps bordered with *alfardas* topped with vertical upper zones. At the top of the structure is a low vertical wall that forms a platform. The tiers of the structure are sloped, and they originally had a thick coating of stucco painted predominantly in red and blue. The structure, believed to have served a ceremonial function, has been consolidated, and a fair amount of its stucco finish remains.

Structure III, on the south end of the main plaza, is a platform with three stairways. It was constructed in three stages, and in the third stage the *alfardas* with vertical upper zones were added. A thatch roof near the center of the platform shelters the fragmentary remains of paintings that date to the first building stage. The paintings were covered by later construction but were revealed during excavation; a few traces of red are still discernable. At some spots along the stairways

Structure I, the main building, Cuyuxquihui. Postclassic period.

Structure IV, Cuyuxquihui. Postclassic period.

you can see the last two construction stages. Atop the platform is a plain upright stone, 6 feet (0.9 meter) high, that appears to be a stela.

Structure IV, rising in three tiers and with a western stair, backs up to a hill on the east side of the main plaza. It has been cleared and consolidated and is backed by luxuriant greenery. It retains some remains of stucco.

Structure V, adjacent to Structure IV on the north, has not yet been cleared, but it has been studied; it is much like Structure IV. Both structures are similar to but smaller than Structure I.

Another important structure at Cuyuxquihui is a ball court that lies about 0.5 mile [0.8 kilometer] south of the main plaza. It has been studied but not excavated. It is not shown to visitors.

Cuyuxquihui is a relatively late site, but exactly how late seems to be in question. Some authorities believe it was probably built in the Terminal Classic period, around A.D. 900, in which case it would have overlapped the last phase at El Tajín, 12.5 miles [20.1 kilometers] to the northwest. Others believe that Cuyuxquihui was constructed after the abandonment of El Tajín around 1100, and possibly as late as 1250. S. Jeffery K. Wilkerson believes that the structures at Cuyuxquihui show a clear post–El Tajín style of unembellished architecture.

The Totonacs are believed to have been the original builders of Cuyuxquihui. Excavations, however, have turned up Huastec ceramic wares and objects of Aztec origin. The Huastec materials are of Postclassic date. Around 1465, the Triple Alliance of Texcoco, Tlacopan, and Tenochtitlán took over the general area and set up a garrison at Cuyuxquihui. This transformed the local culture into a new hybrid that lasted until the Spanish conquest in 1519.

Recent History

Although Cuyuxquihui has been known for a long time, archaeological studies began only in 1981, continuing in 1983. The work included clearing the site and mapping it, excavating and consolidating some of the structures, and creating an access road. The project was conducted by the Veracruz Regional Center of INAH with the support of the Program for the Defense and Development of Totonac Culture. It was directed by J. Omar Ruíz Gordillo, an archaeologist with the Veracruz Regional Center.

The main plaza at the site and the trails leading to it are kept well cleared.

Connections

1. Papantla to Cuyuxquihui: 11.8 miles [19.0 kilometers] by paved road (:30), then 9.2 miles [14.8 kilometers] by rock road (1:01).

2. Poza Rica to Papantla: 14.2 miles [22.9 kilometers] by paved road (:37).

Getting There

1. From Papantla, head south on the road going to El Chote. Admittedly, this is not as quite as easy as it sounds, owing to some one-way streets in Papantla. (When you return to Papantla, you will have to follow a slightly different route through town to get to the highway.) If you follow the signs for El Tajín out of Papantla, however, you will find your way to El Chote (not marked with a sign). In El Chote, at the junction with the road to the Remolina Bridge, a sign for El Tajín points right; you turn to the left. Ask if in doubt.

Go straight to the bridge (over the Tecolutla River); along the way, bypass a possible fork to the right that goes to Agua Dulce. Immediately after the bridge, turn right onto a rock road (unmarked) that goes to Paso del Correo. Partway there you will come to an unmarked cross road where you must turn right or left; turn right and follow the road to Paso del Correo. As you enter the near (north) end of the village, take a left at a small sign that indicates the way to Cuyuxquihui. Follow the road (uphill) to another sign that indicates a right turn. From there you drive over a grassy track for 0.2 mile [0.3 kilometer] to a parking area near the caretaker's house. You will have to stop at a barbed-wire fence along the way; someone will open this for you. Then proceed to the parking area.

2. From Poza Rica, take Highway 180 southeast to Papantla; do not take the bypass around Papantla. Then follow the directions already given.

There are no facilities, food, drink, or rest rooms at Cuyuxquihui. The woman who is the site's caretaker (plus a couple of kids) will show you around. The site is open daily from 9:00 A.M. to 5:00 P.M. Allow 45 minutes for a visit.

The only recommended way to reach Cuyuxquihui is in a private vehicle. You can drive as far as Paso del Correo in a standard vehicle, though the rock road is bumpy and you will have to drive slowly. From there to the site, a high-clearance vehicle may be needed, especially if it has been wet. If you can't make it all the way in your vehicle, you could park when you reach an escarpment and walk in the rest of the way. If you are without a vehicle, you might be able to get a bus to Paso del Correo and walk to the site from there. This method, however, can hardly be recommended. It would be time consuming and tiring.

★ ★
YOHUALICHAN
(yoh-wah-LEE-chan)

Derivation:
 Nahuatl for "Dark House."
Culture:
 El Tajín.
Location:
 Northeastern Puebla.
Maps: 5 (p. 242) and 5B (p. 248)

The Site

Yohualichan is believed to have been a sort of satellite of El Tajín, which lies about 28.0 miles [45.0 kilometers] to the north-northeast. Though Yohualichan is much smaller than El Tajín, its architecture is quite similar to the latter's, especially in the use of *talud-tablero* construction and El Tajín–style decorative niches. Authorities comment that the quality of the stone cutting at Yohualichan is inferior to that at El Tajín. Data are lacking to fix a definite date for Yohualichan's apogee, but studies that have been conducted suggest a time around A.D. 400. The site was abandoned during the Aztec expansion in the Late Postclassic period.

Yohualichan occupies four terraces that slope downward from south to north, although visitors today see only the two upper terraces. They form the most important part of the site, however, and the section that has been partly restored. The structures on the lower levels of the site have not been cleared or consolidated.

The site is in the town of Yohualichan, which partially surrounds it. The town's main plaza lies adjacent to the back (east side) of the Main Structure at the site. When you arrive at the site, you can park outside the fence that encloses it. You enter at the south end, which is the uppermost level. You can tour Yohualichan more than one way; the following is what we did. We headed

The Main Structure (right) and the building of the Grecas (left), Yohualichan. Classic period.

Stucco decorations on the Building of the Grecas, Yohualichan. Classic period.

north along the outside of the ball court (west side) and descended to the principal plaza down a stairway.

Five structures surround the plaza; the Main Structure is on the west side, and the Building of the Grecas is on the south. They join at right angles on the southwest corner, the stairway of which was our access to the plaza. The Main Structure rises in five tiers with a few remains of a sixth, all adorned with niches. It has a central stairway on the east (plaza) side, bordered by *alfardas*.

The Building of the Grecas has a northern stair bordered by *alfardas*. I recommend climbing the stair for a look at some stepped frets (*grecas*) made of stucco on the east side of the stairway near the top, and for a view of the East Building. The Building of the Grecas also has five tiers and parts of a sixth. If you walk around to the back of the struc-

ture, near the top, you get a good view of the ball court to the south. You now return to plaza level and head east. The structure adjacent to the Building of the Grecas on the east (but still on the south side of the plaza) has not been consolidated or restored, but even there you can see the remains of a few niches.

Next you might cross to the north side of the plaza. It is simply a mound today, but I recommend climbing it for the view you get of the Main Structure. At any rate, your last stop in the Main Plaza will be the East Building, which borders the east side of the plaza. It is smaller than those already described, with two tiers, again with niches, and a two-part western stair. The *alfardas* on the lower level stair have vertical upper zones.

From there, head south to a paved area, where you will see the opening to a tomb. You then go west to the north end of the ball

The East Building, Yohualichan. Classic period.

court and head south through it. The lower walls of the court have been restored; they are made of large stone blocks. When you leave the south end of the ball court, you will be near the site entrance.

Recent History

The ruins of Yohualichan have no doubt been known to inhabitants of the area for quite some time. The first work at the site, however, was that of Enrique Juan Palacios, who cleared parts of it, notably the east stairway of the Main Structure. He also photographed the buildings and produced a site plan. His work was published in 1926.

In 1979 and 1980, new clearing, consolidation, and restoration were undertaken by Daniel Molina Feal, of the Veracruz Regional Center of INAH. He published a report in 1986. Additional restoration was carried out after 1987. The site is kept nicely cleared.

Connections

1. Cuetzalan to Yohualichan: 5.7 miles [9.2 kilometers] by paved road (:26).

2. Papantla to Cuetzalan: 160.3 miles [257.9 kilometers] by paved road (4:49).

Getting There

1. From Cuetzalan (at the parking lot of the Posada Cuetzalan), take Calle Carmen Serdán heading northwest and then north. This street ends at Calle Miguel Alvarado Ávila, where you turn left. Continue until you can make a right turn onto the road for Yohualichan. Take this turn, and soon you will pass an airport. After that the road branches; take the right fork. Continue until you come to the final cutoff for Yohualichan. This is 4.5 miles [7.2 kilometers] from the parking lot in Cuetzalan. This final junction is hard to spot; it is marked with a sign, but it faces the other way. Make a sharp left (almost a U-turn) and proceed to the site, 1.2 miles [1.9 kilometers]. This last part is made of flagstones.

Although a guide is not *essential* to reach Yohualichan, it is better to have one. Not all of the junctions along the way are marked. Ask for a guide at your hotel in Cuetzalan.

2. From Papantla, take Highway 180 east and then southeast to El Faro Junction, 43.2 miles [69.5 kilometers]. Turn right onto Highway 129 and follow it—taking the bypass around Martínez de la Torre—for 85.1 miles [136.9 kilometers] to a junction with Puebla State Highway 575 and turn right. This cutoff is a little past Zaragosa. Follow Highway 575 to Cuetzalan, 32.0 miles [51.5 kilometers]. This part has lots of curves and sometimes low hanging clouds on the road. Drive with caution.

The distance given for this stretch applies if you stay on the highway, go around the east part of Cuetzalan, and enter it near the church in the center of town. There is another entry that is better if you want to go to the Posada Cuetzalan; this is a cutoff marked with a sign saying "Centro." It is 0.6 mile [1.0 kilometer] *before* the highway ends at the church; that is, it is 31.4 miles [50.5 kilometers] from the junction of Highways 129 and 575. This entry forks left from the highway and is a two-way cobblestone street that goes steeply downhill. Follow it for 0.4 mile [0.6 kilometer] to the front of the Posada Cuetzalan (on the left).

Yohualichan is open Wednesday through Sunday from 10:00 A.M. to 5:00 P.M. It is closed on Monday and Tuesday. There are no rest rooms, food, or drink at the site. Allow one hour for a visit.

The Posada Cuetzalan is probably the best hotel in town, and it also has a good restaurant. There are several other modest hotels in Cuetzalan and another, the Villas Cuetzalan, on the highway (right side) shortly before you reach the cutoff for "Centro" as you are driving north. Cuetzalan is an interesting town with a big Sunday market, and the hotels there tend to fill up on weekends. Try to arrive early on those days.

Along the Emerald Coast, northeast of El Faro Junction on Highway 180, there are a number of beachfront hotels, motels, and trailer parks, some with hookups. Most of the facilities are modest. One of the best is the Torre Molino, a hotel with some bungalows and a trailer park; the management is accommodating. It is 7.4 miles [11.9 kilometers] northeast of El Faro Junction (:11). Another is the Hotel de la Playa El Palmar, with some recently refurbished rooms, 10.2 miles [16.4 kilometers] northeast of El Faro Junction (:16). Both would be closer stopovers to Cuetzalan than Papantla is, so you might use one of them if you want to get to Cuetzalan early the next day. Driving time from El Faro Junction to Cuetzalan is 3:49.

Cuetzalan can also be reached from Jalapa in 4:07 via Perote and Teziutlán, or from various points of departure in central Mexico.

★ ★
LAS HIGUERAS
(lahs ee-GEH-rahs)

Derivation:
Spanish for "The Fig Trees."
Culture:
Totonac (see text).
Location:
North-central Veracruz.
Maps: 5 (p. 242) and 5B (p. 248)

The Site

Las Higueras lies on a plain along the Gulf Coast, near the Colipa River. It is known for its polychrome murals and has one structure of interest for visitors, Building 1. This is the largest and most important structure at the site, and during its history it was stuccoed and painted with murals 29 times, one layer on top of another.

Building 1, east side, Las Higueras. Postclassic period.

Building 1 has a pyramidal base formed of sloping tiers and a cruciform shrine on top. It is approached by an eastern stairway. Climb a path on the south side of the building; the guardian will lead the way. At the top you can see the remains of the shrine and of some of the many layers of stucco at the base of a low wall.

After you return to ground level along the path, walk around the base of the structure for a look at the stairway and the adjacent sloped tiers on the northwest corner of the base. This part of the base is better preserved than the other corners.

Building 1 was constructed of an earthen core covered with a facing of river cobbles. These were held in place with a lime and mud mortar, and the surface of the shrine was then stuccoed and painted. Each of the building's two major construction phases had mural decorations. According to Felipe Solís, writing in the 1992 book *Museum of Anthropology of Xalapa,* the paintings span

the time from A.D. 600 to 900. Some other authorities, however, believe that most of the paintings date to the Early Postclassic period. The style of the paintings changed over time, and the later paintings display a more extensive palette of colors. It is believed that the murals show influence from El Tajín and Teotihuacán. Some 984 linear feet (300 linear meters) of murals were lifted from the surfaces of the shrine and sent to Jalapa for restoration, since they could not be preserved in place. For a description of some of the fragments, see "Las Higueras Museum."

Although the generic name "Totonac culture" is applied to sites in central Veracruz, including Las Higueras, it is known that the Totonacs themselves arrived in the area only around A.D. 900. If some of the murals date to the Postclassic, then they are perhaps Totonac.

The 27 other structures that form the site are simply mounds today, some of them under part of the modern town. You can see one of them 0.2 mile [0.3 kilometer] past Building 1 and the museum when you continue along the road on which you came in. It is on the left, behind a fence in someone's yard. There really isn't a lot to see.

Recent History

At the time of the Spanish conquest, there was a town called Yetla-Acalco or Acacalco near where Las Higueras stands today. The town was apparently abandoned shortly after the conquest.

Undoubtedly the modern residents of the village of Las Higueras were aware of the pre-Columbian mounds there for a long time, but it was only in 1968 (or 1967, according to some sources) that the chance discovery of figures painted on a wall was made. The local authorities reported the find to the Institute of Anthropology of the University of Veracruz. The university undertook excavations of Building 1 in 1968, under the direction of Alfonso Medellín Zenil, with the assistance of graduate students. The work continued for four field seasons. Deposits near the river were also studied, and the artifacts recovered indicate that the area was occupied as early as the Middle Preclassic period. An engineer, Ramón Kroster, made a topographic plan of the site, the murals were lifted from the walls and floor of the Building 1 shrine, and the structure was consolidated.

Connections

1. Papantla to Las Higueras: 63.4 miles [102.0 kilometers] by paved road (1:33).

2. Veracruz to Las Higueras: 76.9 miles [123.8 kilometers] by paved road (1:45).

Getting There

1. From Papantla, take Highway 180 east and then southeast to the cutoff for Las Higueras, 62.6 miles [100.7 kilometers], and turn left. The junction is marked with a sign and is found just after you leave the southern outskirts of Vega de Alatorre. From there the road goes to the town, museum, and site of Las Higueras. The site and museum are behind a fence, and there is a place to park outside.

2. From Veracruz, head northwest on Highway 180 to the cutoff for Las Higueras, 76.1 miles [122.5 kilometers], turn right, and proceed to the site. If you approach this way you will spot the cutoff shortly after you cross a bridge over the Colipa River.

There are rest rooms at the site, but food and drink are not available. The site is open Tuesday through Sunday from 9:00 A.M. to 5:00 P.M. It is closed on Monday. Allow 35 minutes to visit Las Higueras.

★ ★

LAS HIGUERAS MUSEUM

Las Higueras Museum is small but nicely done, and it has good ambient light. The major displays include excellent copies of a dozen restored mural fragments from the shrine of Building 1. (The original fragments are in the Jalapa Museum.) Many represent men and women walking in procession, whereas other figures are taking part in some kind of ritual. One fragment depicts three standing musicians playing long, trumpetlike instruments; another is a floor fragment representing the sun.

In addition to the copies of the fragments, a restoration model of the Building 1 shrine is displayed. A plan of the whole site and a few stone and ceramic pieces are also exhibited. There is some labeling in the museum. Outside it, some simple stone objects (unlabeled) are arranged.

The museum is open Tuesday through Sunday from 9:00 A.M. to 5:00 P.M. It is closed on Monday. Allow 15 minutes for a visit. Photography without flash is permitted.

Copy of a mural fragment from Building 1, Las Higueras. Post-classic period. On display in Las Higueras Museum.

★ ★
QUIAHUIZTLÁN
(kee-ah-wees-TLAN)

Derivation:
Nahuatl for "Rainy Place."
Culture:
Totonac (see text).
Location:
Central Veracruz.
Maps: 5 (p. 242) and 5B (p. 248)

The Site

Quiahuiztlán is now a very good two-star site; two and a half stars might be a more accurate rating. The improvements from some years ago include better access (a road now goes almost all the way up to the site) and the clearing, consolidation, and restoration of some of the structures. Quiahuiztlán served three purposes: it was a city of 15,000 people, a cemetery (with 78 tombs), and a stronghold ringed with defensive walls. Visitors today can see the three cemetery groups and the adjacent structures. A civic section to the east and a residential section to the south are not open and have not been restored.

From the parking area just below the Central Cemetery, a stone stepped path goes up to that part of the site and enters it adjacent to the south side of Building 3, which was built in two construction stages, both during the Postclassic period. A broad divided stairway on the southeast side gives access to the top of Building 3, where low walls of a structure are found. It was once topped by a building of perishable materials and is believed to have been used for performing rituals.

To the southeast and bordering a plaza on the south, a group of miniature temples is arranged in a couple of irregular rows with

Miniature structures in the Central Cemetery, Quiahuiztlán. Postclassic period.

an east-west alignment. Another miniature temple is found near the center of the plaza. The temples functioned as shrines for tombs, and they were coated with an unusually hard stucco. Upon excavating them, archaeologists found human skulls and bones in burial chambers behind the stairs and under the floors of the temples. The bones were accompanied by elaborate ceramic offerings.

All of the miniature temples are of similar size and design; they generally do not exceed four feet in height, and many are smaller. Each temple sits on a platform approached by a single stairway bordered by *alfardas* with vertical upper zones. Above the platform is the plain temple, with its doorway at the top of the stair. Each temple has a two-part roof with sloping sides and a flat top. There are 34 temple-tombs in the Central Cemetery.

At the east end of the row and to the north are Tombs 1 and 2. They are larger and of a different configuration; both have western stairs. Tomb 1 has its stair bordered with *alfardas* with vertical upper zones. There is no structure at the top of the stairway, but there are remnants of merlon decorations. Two burials were found in Tomb 1. Tomb 2 is similar but less well preserved.

A rather poor trail (part of it seems to be a gully) from the southeast part of the Central Cemetery leads uphill to the South Cemetery. More miniature temples are found here, including one that is unusual. It has three doorways instead of one; its single stairway is broader; and it rests on a wider base. From the South Cemetery there are good views of Pyramid 1 below, which you will see later at close range. You now return to the Central Cemetery and continue your tour.

A short distance to the northeast, a stairway goes up to the slightly higher level of the Central Plaza and its adjacent buildings. The largest structure facing the plaza is Pyramid 1, on the north side. This is a three-tiered platform with a stairway on the south. There are remains of low walls atop the upper platform. Two Early Postclassic structures that underlie the final Late Postclassic one reportedly show finer workmanship than the latter. Within the Central Plaza are found three small stone platforms that presumably functioned as altars.

Pyramids 2 and 2a border the east side of the Central Plaza. Pyramid 2 is the larger and more northerly, and it was constructed in two stages. On top, the low walls and columns of a shrine remain. Pyramid 2a, with a single construction stage dating to the Late Postclassic period, has an eastern stair, facing the sea. It also functioned as a tomb.

Tomb with three doorways in the South Cemetery, Quiahuiztlán. Postclassic period.

Just to the southeast is found another lone miniature temple-tomb; it differs from those already described in the more complex shape of its platform base and in the shape of its roof, which resembles that of a thatch-roof dwelling, rather than being flat.

From there, head north along the east sides of Pyramids 2a, 2, and 1 to the East Cemetery, on a still higher level. Along the way you will pass a low-lying structure on the east side of Pyramid 1. Its function is unknown, but it seems to have a drain installed in the floor.

In the East Cemetery, a group of minia-ture temple-tombs like those already described faces south and west near a stairway, appar-ently part of an Early Postclassic Toltec-influenced structure. This vantage point affords beautiful views of the Gulf of Mexico to the east, as well as views of the lower levels of the site to the southwest.

Quiahuiztlán was apparently first settled in the Late Classic period. Later in that period the town was overrun by Toltecs, whose remains have been found at the site. In the early part of the Late Postclassic, Quiahuiz-tlán was again invaded, this time by Aztecs. Most of the structures got their distinctive stucco coatings after the Aztec incursions.

Recent History

Quiahuiztlán is mentioned in the account of the conquistador Bernal Díaz del Castillo as a fortified town "which stands amid great rocks and lofty cliffs." It was a living city at the time of the Spanish conquest, and it was near here that Cortés founded the first Span-ish settlement on American soil. He called it Villa Rica de la Vera Cruz.

The tombs of the Central Cemetery were excavated and restored between 1951 and 1953, and the lower levels of the site were mapped. The work was conducted under the direction of Alfonso Medellín Zenil. Addi-tional work undertaken in the early 1990s included the building of the road to the site and the clearing, consolidation, and restora-tion of some of the structures.

Connections

1. Veracruz to Quiahuiztlán: 43.4 miles [69.9 kilometers] by paved road (:58), then 1.3 miles [2.1 kilometers] by fair rock road (:07).

2. Papantla to Quiahuiztlán: 95.3 miles [153.3 kilometers] by paved road (2:16), then 1.3 miles [2.1 kilometers] by fair rock road (:07).

Getting There

1. From Veracruz, head northwest on Highway 180 to the cutoff for Quiahuiztlán and turn left onto the rock road (marked with a sign). The road is just past a house on the same side of the highway. After you go a short distance on the rock road, you will pass through the entrance gate and by another house (on the right). From there, follow the road up to the parking area.

2. From Papantla, take Highway 180 east and then southeast to the cutoff and turn right. The cutoff is just before the house on the highway. From there, follow the directions already given.

Quiahuiztlán is open Tuesday through Sunday from 9:00 A.M. to 5:00 P.M. It is closed on Monday. Spanish-speaking guides are available if you wish to have someone show you around. They are generally to be found near the Central Cemetery, where you enter the site. There is no food or drink at the site, nor any rest rooms. Allow one hour for a visit.

Buses pass the cutoff for the site going both ways and could drop you off there, from where you could hike up to the site on the rock road. If you plan to try this, wear a sun hat and carry a canteen of water.

If you have a vehicle and are leaving from and returning to Veracruz, Quiahuiztlán and Zempoala can be visited in one day. Carry your own food and drink.

★ ★
ZEMPOALA
(sehm-POAH-lah)
(CEMPOALA)

Derivation:
  "Place of Twenty," derived from the Nahua (see text).
Original Name:
  Zempoala.
Culture:
  Totonac.
Location:
  Central Veracruz.
Maps: 5 (p. 242) and 5B (p. 248)

The Site

Zempoala was founded by the Totonacs in the Postclassic period, probably around A.D. 1200. It was a living city of considerable size at the time of the Spanish conquest in 1519.

There at least three possibilities for the significance of the name Zempoala. It could refer to the 20 tributaries of the Actopan River that pass nearby; it might be a refer-ence to the fact that markets were held there every 20 days; or it might refer to the 20 towns that were once a part of Zempoala's domain.

Although everything visible at Zempoala today dates to the Late Postclassic period, ceramics dating to the Late Preclassic were discovered in a mound cut through by the Actopan River.

The ruins of Zempoala cover about 2 square miles [5.2 square kilometers] and encompass 10 groups of buildings. Visitors today, however, see only the central area, called Walled System IV, and one temple outside it. This is but a small portion of the site.

As you enter the site from the south, you are entering Walled System IV, a plaza with major buildings on the east, north, and west sides; smaller structures are found within the plaza. The whole is surrounded by a merlon-topped wall. Step-shaped merlons are a typical feature of Totonac architecture.

On the east side of the plaza, you come first to two circular structures. The larger one is simply an enclosure; both have merlon

Large circular enclosure with merlon decorations, near the Temple of the Chimneys, Zempoala. Late Postclassic period.

decorations on the tops of the walls. The enclosure may have been associated with Aztec warrior worship.

Behind these structures, the Temple of the Chimneys rests on a long F-shaped platform. The building itself rises in seven sloping tiers; it has a western stair bordered by *alfardas* with vertical upper zones. There are merlons on top on the north, east, and south sides. At the foot of the stairway are found remains of low temple walls and hollow columns, which give the temple its name. When the Temple of the Chimneys was excavated, a clay figure in a reclining pose, resembling a *chacmool,* was discovered.

From the top of the Temple of the Chimneys you get a good view of the structures around the plaza, including a similar but smaller temple to the south. Also visible (to the east) is the Temple of the Little Faces, some 240 yards (220 meters) away and accessible by foot trail.

Along the north side of the Temple of the Chimneys, the trail leads east and then northeast to an exit from Walled System IV, where you go through an open gate. From there, follow the path to the Temple of the Little Faces, so named because of many small clay faces that once decorated interior panels

in the room at the top of the structure. The trail is easy to follow and goes through sugarcane fields. It is definitely worth the short walk to the temple, as there are painted decorations on both inside and outside walls. The Temple of the Little Faces is composed of a two-tier platform, each tier approached by a broad stairway, and a single room on top. The remaining walls of the room stand a little over 6.5 feet (2.0 meters) high—higher than the walls remaining on most other structures at Zempoala. The designs painted on the lower parts of the walls are said to represent the sun, moon, and Venus.

You now return to the plaza the way you came. To the west is a square altar, and to the north, the Great Temple, which borders the north side of the plaza. It is the most impressive structure on the plaza, rising in 13 tiers with a southern stairway bordered by *alfardas* with vertical upper zones. It was constructed in four stages. On the south side of the base, and west of the stairway, some of the earlier construction can be seen. The remains of columns and stepped merlon decorations are found on top of the Great Temple.

To the southwest of the Great Temple, a small temple with the remains of lower

Temple of the Little Faces, Zempoala. Late Postclassic period.

The Great Temple, Zempoala, from the southeast. Late Postclassic period.

walls on top is found resting on a low platform. From there, head southwest to visit more structures that face east. One structure with a circular extension at the rear is believed to have been dedicated to Ehécatl.

To the south lies the Great Pyramid, with a divided stairway. At the base of the stairway, in the center, is a circular construction, perhaps a basin. At a somewhat higher level, along the stairway's division, another is found. The pyramid is believed to date to the sixteenth century and to be one of the latest constructions at Zempoala. Another, smaller structure lies to the south.

Temple dedicated to Ehécatl, Zempoala. Late Postclassic period.

The earliest construction stage at Zempoala shows some Toltec remains, and the latest exhibits strong influence from central Mexico, manifested in both Aztec-style architecture and the Mixteca-Puebla-style ceramics typical of Cholula. All the structures are faced with river cobbles.

Zempoala occupies an ecological niche in the form of an arid wedge that interrupts the tropical rain forest along the coast of Veracruz. It is probably for this reason that irrigation was necessary to support the site's residents. There is both documentary and archaeological evidence for an elaborate drainage system consisting of canals, aqueducts, and subterranean masonry, although this is not readily discernible today.

The central area of Zempoala is kept well cleared, and it is easy to roam around the various structures.

Recent History

Shortly after Cortés landed on the coast of Veracruz, he visited Zempoala. At the time it was the largest native city he and his men had seen, with a population of about 30,000.

The conquistadors were much impressed with what they saw. In the words of Bernal Diáz del Castillo: "We were struck with admiration. It looked like a garden with luxuriant vegetation, and the streets were so full of men and women who had come to see us, that we gave thanks to God at having discovered such a country." The freshly whitewashed structures gleaming in the tropical sunlight led one of Cortés's scouts to believe that the buildings were covered with silver.

Although Zempoala once represented the apogee of Totonac culture, at the time of the Spanish conquest it had been under Aztec control for some time. The archaeologist José García Payón believed that had the Spanish conquest occurred 50 years later, Totonac culture probably would already have been extinguished. Aztec exploitation of the Totonacs made the latter receptive to an alliance with Cortés. This alliance—Cortés's first with a native group—was one of the major factors contributing to the success of the conquest of the Aztec capital of Tenochtitlán, and thereby all of Mexico.

Just sixty years after the conquest, Zempoala consisted of only 30 households, most of the inhabitants having been killed by smallpox brought in with the conquistadors. By 1600, only two inhabitants survived.

The site was explored and reported upon by Francisco del Paso y Troncoso in 1891, but the bulk of the work at the site was done in the 1940s by García Payón.

Connections

1. Veracruz to Zempoala: 27.3 miles [44.0 kilometers] by paved road (:42).

2. Papantla to Zempoala: 115.2 miles [185.4 kilometers] by paved road (2:44).

Getting There

1. From Veracruz, head northwest on Highway 180 to the cutoff for Zempoala (marked with a sign), 25.4 miles [40.9 kilometers], and turn left. Go straight ahead 1.8 miles [2.9 kilometers] to another sign and turn right onto a cobblestone street. Proceed straight ahead for the final 0.1 mile [0.2 kilometer] to the site entrance, where you park outside.

2. From Papantla, take Highway 180 heading east and then southeast to the cutoff for Zempoala, 113.3 miles [182.3 kilometers], and turn right. Then follow the directions already given. In addition to the sign on the highway, a landmark for the cutoff is a Pemex station immediately south of the cutoff.

There are rest rooms at the site; food and drink are not available. Zempoala is open daily from 9:00 A.M. to 6:00 P.M. Allow 1.5 hours for a visit. Wear a sun hat.

The town of Zempoala can be reached by bus. If you have your own vehicle, a visit to Zempoala can be combined with a visit to Quiahuiztlán in a day trip out of Veracruz.

★ ★ ★ ★

MUSEUM OF ANTHROPOLOGY OF JALAPA
(JALAPA MUSEUM)

The Jalapa Museum is truly a world-class facility, housing an incredible collection of pre-Columbian art. It is one of the superb regional museums in Mexico, and its design and layout are the best of them all. It boasts over 145,000 square feet (13,500 square meters) of exhibition space and is built on land totaling 322,000 square feet (30,000 square meters). The collection contains 27,000 pieces, of which 2,500 are on display. Inaugurated on October 30, 1986, the museum replaced an older one that had run out of space. The new museum occupies the same site as the old one, on the northern outskirts of Jalapa on Avenida Jalapa (spelled Xalapa in Mexico).

Native vegetation is incorporated into many of the displays, giving them the feeling of a natural setting, and the grounds outside are attractively landscaped. Natural light is integrated into many of the areas, augmented by artificial lighting. In other areas, only artificial light is used, and in these places it is almost impossible to photograph the pieces. Labeling in the museum is generally good.

The museum is laid out on several levels that descend gradually as you progress through it. It would be impossible to describe all the outstanding exhibits in the collection, but I will mention some of the highlights, as well the general sections and the cultures to which they pertain.

As you enter the museum, the ticket booth is to the left, and beyond that is a gallery for temporary exhibits. Opposite the entrance is a vestibule where San Lorenzo colossal head number 8 is exhibited on a double platform. It is one of the best-preserved heads from the site.

San Lorenzo colossal head 8, displayed in the Jalapa Museum. Early Preclassic period.

All of the San Lorenzo monuments, including many not mentioned here, date to the Early Preclassic period. A room to the left of the vestibule contains another San Lorenzo head, number 5. In the same room there are informative charts, one chronological and the other giving information about the museum. From there you turn right and gradually descend through the galleries to the end. There are additional *salas* and patios off to the right of this main corridor. Make sure you see them all.

The next several galleries and a patio are devoted to Olmec remains. San Lorenzo head number 1, El Rey, is in the patio, along with a San Lorenzo large tabletop altar with a figure seated in a niche. Also in the patio is Stela 1 from El Viejón, possibly of Middle Preclassic date.

The remarkable Las Limas seated green-stone figure holding a were-jaguar baby is in the Olmec section. It dates to the Middle Preclassic period and is in pristine condition. Farther along is an Early Preclassic basalt seated figure holding a bar; it comes from the summit of San Martín volcano. In a side *sala,* more San Lorenzo heads are displayed. The art of jade carving is beautifully exemplified by sensitive, naturalistic masks from Arroyo Pesquero and by incised celts, one of which may be from the same site. All date to the Middle Preclassic period.

You then come to the Totonac section. Highlights here are a basalt stela from Piedra Labrada and a basalt head wearing a rain god mask from Cerro de las Mesas. Both date to the Late Classic period. There are bas-relief panels of Late Classic date from El Tajín and a magnificent collection of elaborate *palmas* and *hachas* from various parts of central Veracruz. A bas-relief slab from Aparicio depicts a decapitated ball player seated on a throne, his neck spurting seven entwined serpents symbolizing blood. All of these are of Late Classic date.

Among the clay items in the Totonac section, the larger-than-life-size hollow figures of deified females from El Zapotal are

Hollow figure of a deified female from El Zapotal, Late Classic period. On display in the Jalapa Museum.

magnificent. They date to the Late Classic period, as do the remarkable smiling heads that come from various sites in central Veracruz. The Late Postclassic period is represented by a figure of Xipe Totec, 4.9 feet (1.5 meters) tall, that is in pristine condition.

The Huastec section comes next; it is smaller than the Olmec and Totonac sections but has some impressive pieces. They are mostly typical flat, slablike stone figures with some three-dimensional parts such as faces, hands, and, on the female figures, breasts. Many of the figures represent deities. They come from several Huastec sites in northern Veracruz and date to the Postclassic period. Another Postclassic piece is more stela-like and is carved in bas-relief; it displays traits associated with Tlaloc.

The last section of the museum exhibits contemporary arts and crafts of Veracruz.

In addition to the archaeological pieces, there are charts and maps with sites shown for the various areas, ceramic pots from different parts of Veracruz, photo displays, and a model of El Tajín.

The Jalapa Museum is open Tuesday through Sunday from 10:00 A.M. to 5:00 P.M. It is closed on Monday. Photography without flash is permitted, but there is a small charge to bring a camera into the museum. There are rest rooms and a cafeteria at the museum. There is also a bookstore that sells souvenirs as well as publications. Allow two hours for a visit and more if you plan to take a lot of photos.

Unrated
CANTONA
(kahn-TOH-nah)

Derivation:
   Possibly from the Spanish *cantón* (region) or *cantona* (great house).
Culture:
   See text.
Location:
   Far eastern Puebla.
Maps: 5 (p. 242), 5B (p. 248), and 5B2 (p. 280)

The Site

Cantona is unrated because when we visited the site, we arrived too late in the day to tour all of it, although we did see some of the lower sections. It would certainly rate two stars, and possibly three, if all of the open part of the site were visited.

Cantona is reported to have been one of the most urbanized sites in ancient Mexico. It covers 4.6 square miles (11.9 square kilo-meters) and encompasses some 3,000 residential courtyards and 24 ball courts, the greatest number of ball courts found at a Mesoamerican site to date. It has an extensive network of causeways (more than 500 have been located). There are also streets and passageways. The site lies at an altitude of 8,200 feet (2,500 meters) to 8,530 feet (2,600 meters), and the *calzadas* (causeways) climb from the entrance to the site to increasingly higher levels of the mountain.

The structures in the lower sections are mostly residential platforms arranged around patios that are connected by *calzadas*. The upper levels of the site support the ceremonial precincts, where pyramids, ball courts, and elite residential units are found. The pyramids are stepped, and their stairways are sometimes bordered by *alfardas*. Often the platforms are stepped as well.

The construction methods at Cantona are unusual. The site rests on a lava field, and lava blocks were used in the buildings and low walls that border the *calzadas*. The blocks seem mostly untrimmed. No mortar

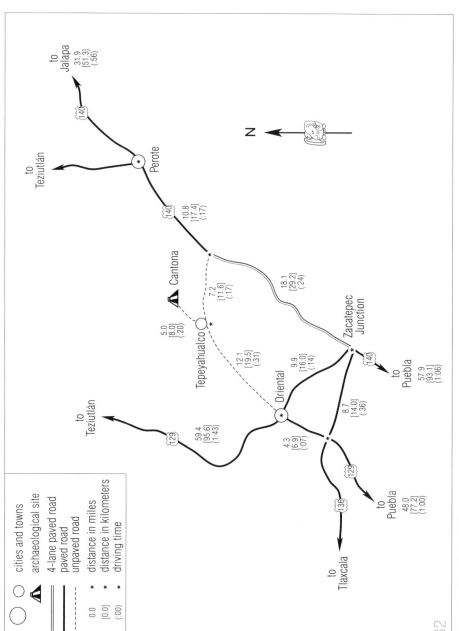

Route to Cantona (Map 5B2).

Legend:

○ cities and towns
▲ archaeological site

═══ 4-lane paved road
━━━ paved road
---- unpaved road

0.0   distance in miles
[0.0]   distance in kilometers
(:00)   driving time

to Jalapa
31.9
[51.3]
(:56)

[140]

Perote

to Teziutlán

[140]
10.8
[17.4]
(:17)

Cantona

7.2
[11.6]
(:17)

18.1
[29.2]
(:24)

Zacatepec Junction

5.0
[8.0]
(:20)

Tepeyahualco

12.1
[19.5]
(:31)

9.9
[16.0]
(:14)

Oriental

[140]

to Puebla
57.9
[93.1]
(1:06)

8.7
[14.0]
(:36)

4.3
[6.9]
(:07)

to Teziutlán

[129]
59.4
[95.6]
(1:43)

[129]

to Puebla
48.0
[77.2]
(1:00)

[136]

to Tlaxcala

N

Beginning of Calzada 1, Cantona. Late Classic period.

was used to bind the blocks together, nor was any stucco used to finish the surface. The low walls of the causeways resemble nothing so much as the dry-laid stone field walls that are seen everywhere in the mountainous areas of Mexico today. These are generally used to mark property boundaries.

At the entrance to the site you will see two *calzadas*. The one to the left is Calzada 1, the one you should take. The other is Calzada 2, the one on which you will return. Calzada 1 climbs over steps and then becomes a ramp. Just follow the *calzadas* to the upper levels of the site.

Cantona was occupied from around A.D. 600 and reached its apogee from 700 to 900 or 950. During this period—after the demise of Teotihuacán and Cholula but before the rise of Tula—it was the largest and most important city in the central highlands. Cantona then declined and was abandoned around 1000 to 1050.

Ancient Cantona lay on a commercial route called the "Teotihuacán Corridor" that connected the high plateau of central Mexico with the southern Gulf Coast. The route crossed the northern and northeastern parts of Tlaxcala (where a branch went south to Oaxaca) and continued on to the sea. Along these routes, products from various regions were funneled into Teotihuacán. Nothing I have read about Cantona indicates exactly which culture built this great city, but that it had connections with various parts of central Mexico, the Gulf Coast, Oaxaca, and the Maya lowlands is undeniable.

Recent History

Cantona has been known for more than 200 years. It was mentioned in the *Gacetas* (Gazettes) of Alzate in 1790, although this was apparently not widely known until many years later. Henri de Saussure is generally considered to be the site's discoverer; he pointed out the location of Cantona in 1855. A text about the archaeological monuments of Cantona was published by Nicolás León in 1903. Many others visited the site throughout the twentieth century, and reports on some of the explorations were published over the years.

In 1992 the Cantona Archaeological Project began, and work continued until 1994

A patio group, Cantona. Late Classic period.

under the direction of Ángel García Cook. During this project a small part (less than 1 percent) of this large site was restored; it opened to the public in 1994.

Connections

1. Puebla to Cantona via Highway 129: 52.3 miles [84.1 kilometers] by paved road (1:07), then 17.1 miles [27.5 kilometers] by mostly poor unpaved road (:51).

2. Puebla to Cantona via Highway 140: 76.0 miles [122.3 kilometers] by paved road (1:30), then 12.2 miles [19.6 kilometers] by mostly fair unpaved road (:37).

3. Perote to Cantona: 10.8 miles [17.4 kilometers] by paved road (:17), then 12.2 miles [19.6 kilometers] by mostly fair unpaved road (:37).

4. Jalapa to Perote: 31.9 miles [51.3 kilometers] by paved road (:56).

Getting There

1. From Puebla, take toll Highway 150D heading east to the junction with Highway 129 (Amozac junction), 13.5 miles [21.7 kilometers]. Head northeast on Highway 129 to and through Oriental, 38.8 miles [62.4 kilometers]. There you pick up a poor, unpaved road that goes pretty much straight ahead as the paved Highway 129 curves to the left. The unpaved road goes northeast to the cutoff for Tepeyahualco, on the left, 12.1 miles [19.5 kilometers] from Oriental. There are many turns to make along this road, going through or around small villages; the way is well marked, so just follow the signs. Shortly after you turn left at the junction for Tepeyahualco, you will cross a railroad track and

then enter the town itself; go through it and on to the parking lot at Cantona, 5.0 miles [8.0 kilometers]. This last part is dirt and is poor, but you can drive it in a standard vehicle if you take it slowly.

2. To use the other route from Puebla, take Highway 150D east to Highway 140 (Acatzingo junction), 29.0 miles [46.7 kilometers]. Then head northeast on 140, pass Zacatepec junction, and go on to the first cutoff for Tepeyahualco, 47.0 miles [75.6 kilometers]. Turn left onto a fair rock road and continue to the second cutoff for Tepeyahualco (and Cantona), 7.2 miles [11.6 kilometers]. Turn right and go on to Cantona. This route takes a few minutes longer than the first, but it avoids the 12.1 miles [19.5 kilometers] of poor road between Oriental and the final cutoff for Cantona at Tepeyahualco. Another advantage is that this route has 18.1 miles [29.2 kilometers] of four lanes on Highway 140. It is a more pleasant drive than the first way.

3. From Perote, take Highway 140 southwest for 10.8 miles [17.4 kilometers] to the junction with the rock road that heads to Tepeyahualco. This junction is found very shortly after you see a sign saying you have entered the state of Puebla. Then follow the directions given under Connection 2.

4. From Jalapa, head west to Perote on Highway 140, then follow the directions already given.

All of the roads to Cantona are well marked. We had to ask directions only once, at an unmarked fork in the road just a short distance from the site. Actually, either branch would have taken us to Cantona. The town of Tepeyahualco and the road from Oriental to Highway 140 are shown on current detailed maps of Mexico.

Driving your own vehicle is the recommended way to reach Cantona. You could surely reach Oriental by bus, but we saw none between there and Tepeyahualco. Inquire before attempting to reach Tepeyahualco this way. Once there, you might be able to find a taxi to get you to the site. Remember to arrange for it to pick you up later.

Cantona is open daily from 10:00 A.M. to 4:00 P.M. There is a good rock-surfaced parking lot, a service building with rest rooms, and some tree stumps set up in the shade where you could eat a picnic lunch. Bring your own—there is no food or drink at the site. It would be wise to carry a canteen of water if you plan to tour all of the site.

A guidebook for Cantona suggests that you allow two hours to visit it. But considering the altitude and the amount of climbing involved, I would guess that it might take longer if you plan to visit all of the site that is open.

★ ★ ★

MUSEUM OF THE CITY OF VERACRUZ (VERACRUZ MUSEUM)

The Veracruz Museum is near the center of the city, at the corner of Calles Zaragosa and Morales. The collection is housed in an interesting old building of typical Mexican design, with rooms around a central patio.

Several pre-Columbian stone carvings, none of them labeled, are arranged around the patio. You then enter Sala 1, where there is a model of the Pyramid of the Niches from El Tajín and photo displays. Sala 2 houses the Spanish colonial materials—old maps, *lienzos,* and cannons. Sala 3 is devoted to Africans in Veracruz, mostly through photo displays. Off of this *sala* is a copy of colossal Olmec head number 5 from San Lorenzo. You then go upstairs to the second floor.

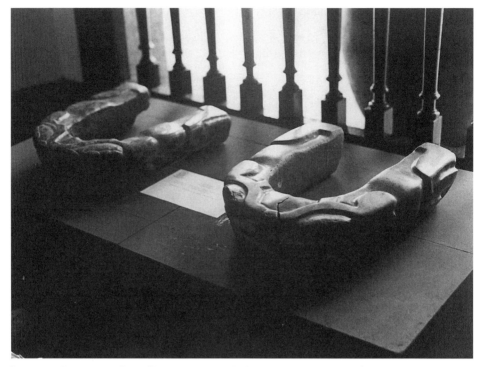

Two carved yokes from Torrecilla, on display in the Veracruz Museum. Late Classic period.

The displays on this floor include carved panels, some in the style of El Tajín, and Huastec sculptures, some of which are labeled as originals and others of which are possibly copies. Salas 6 and 7 on this floor display photos of cemeteries, *tran vias* (narrow-gauge railways), and ship building. There are food exhibits and photos of elaborately dressed people from an earlier time, as well as manikins dressed in costumes, old-style park benches, medical instruments, shells and jewelry made from shell, and a king's carnival costume.

You now return to the first floor and continue around the patio through Salas 4 and 5. Exhibits include political photos and more pre-Columbian artifacts, some of which

may be copies. Some of the items are in cases and others are on low platforms. Ceramic pots, figurines, and heads are exhibited, as are *incensarios*. Two outstanding items are Classic period carved Totonac stone yokes from Torrecilla. They bear representations of Tlaltecuhtli, the earth monster, pictured as a fantastic toad.

The Veracruz Museum is open Monday through Saturday from 9:00 A.M. to 4:00 P.M. It is closed on Sunday. The patio displays get natural light, and the indoor exhibits are fairly well lighted artificially. Photography without flash is permitted. There are rest rooms at the museum and restaurants nearby. Allow one hour for a visit.

★ ★
TUXTECO MUSEUM
(toosh-TEH-koh)
(SANTIAGO TUXTLA MUSEUM)
(TOOSH-tlah)

The Santiago Tuxtla Museum faces the main plaza in the center of the town of that name. It has both indoor and outdoor sections. On the inside there are nicely arranged and well-lighted displays of ceramics, including a large selection of the famous Veracruz smiling heads. Jade and other greenstone jewelry is displayed in cases, as is an interesting ceremonial knife made of clay; its designs represent ritual sacrifice. Small stone artifacts, some carved in bas-relief, are exhibited inside, whereas the larger stone pieces are in the outdoor section. The indoor displays are fairly well labeled—an improvement from some years ago.

The most impressive piece outside is one of the colossal Olmec heads, called Cabeza Nextepetl, formerly designated Tres Zapotes Monument Q or 2. Tenoned figures, carved boxes, and zoomorphic and anthropomorphic pieces are included. The carved stones displayed outside come from various sites, but most of them pertain to Olmec culture. Only some of them are labeled.

In the town's main plaza is another important monument, the Cobata head, the largest of the known colossal Olmec heads. It stands almost 10.8 feet [3.5 meters] tall and is installed under a shelter. It is one of

The Cobata head, Middle Preclassic period. On display in the plaza of Santiago Tuxtla.

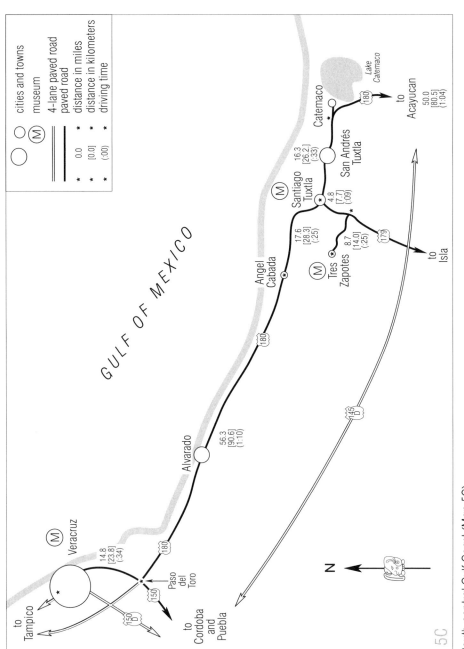

Legend:

○ cities and towns
Ⓜ museum
═══ 4-lane paved road
━━━ paved road
* 0.0 distance in miles
* [0.0] distance in kilometers
* (.00) driving time

GULF OF MEXICO

to Tampico

Ⓜ Veracruz
*

14.8
[23.8]
(.34)

to Cordoba and Puebla

Paso del Toro
*
150

150 D

180

Alvarado
○

56.3
[90.6]
(1:10)

180

Angel Cabada
*

17.6
[28.3]
(.25)

Ⓜ Santiago Tuxtla
*

4.8
[7.7]
(.09)

16.3
[26.2]
(.33)

San Andrés Tuxtla
○

Catemaco
○
*

180

Lake Catemaco

to Acayucan

50.0
[80.5]
(1:04)

Ⓜ Tres Zapotes
*

8.7
[14.0]
(.25)

179

to Isla

145 D

N

South-central Gulf Coast (Map 5C).

5C

the most unusual heads in that the eyes are shown closed. The head gets direct sunlight early in the morning, when all but the very top is illuminated. If you want to photograph it later in the day when it is totally shaded, try "overexposing" a stop if you are using a camera with an averaging meter. This will better bring out the details.

The Santiago Tuxtla Museum is open Monday through Saturday from 9:00 A.M. to 6:00 P.M. and on Sunday from 9:00 A.M. to 3:00 P.M. Photography, including the use of flash, is permitted. For photographing items in glass cases, however, it is better to forgo the flash, because of the glare it causes. There are rest rooms at the museum. Restaurants nearby can provide food and drink. Allow 30 minutes to see the museum and a little more to see and photograph the head in the plaza.

Santiago Tuxtla is 88.7 miles [142.7 kilometers] by paved road southeast of Veracruz (2:09).

Note: If you are driving Highway 180 between Veracruz and Santiago Tuxtla, you will pass through the town of Ángel Cabada, where an interesting stela is displayed in the main plaza. The plaza is north of the highway and separated from it by a row of soft drink and snack stands, which tend to hide it. You may have to ask. This large monument is known as El Mesón stela, and it dates to the Late Preclassic period. The American archaeologist Matthew Stirling believed it was probably late Olmec and noted that it showed some Izapan traits. It is definitely worth a look and a few photos when you are passing by.

El Mesón stela, Late Preclassic period. On display in the plaza of Ángel Cabada.

★ ★
TRES ZAPOTES MUSEUM
(trehs sah-POH-tehs)

The Tres Zapotes Museum, in the town of the same name, was inaugurated in July 1975. It consists of four small wings, open on all sides. This affords enough ambient light for photography.

The collection consists of large and small stone monuments, all from the site of Tres Zapotes, though none is labeled. The Tres Zapotes colossal head (Monument A) is the prize of the collection, but it shares honors with some other major monuments, including Stelae A and D and the upper portion of Stela C, discovered in 1969.

The Tres Zapotes head was the first colossal Olmec head to be discovered (17 colossal heads are now known). It was seen

Monument A from Tres Zapotes, Middle Preclassic period. On display in the Tres Zapotes Museum.

by the Mexican scholar José María Melgar in 1862 when he was visiting the region of San Andrés Tuxtla. He had heard of the unearthing of the head in 1858 by a workman on a nearby hacienda and went to see it. In 1869 he published a short note in the *Bulletin of the Mexican Society of Geography and History,* accompanied by an engraving of the head.

In 1905, Eduard Seler and his wife visited the Tres Zapotes region and saw and photographed the head and an elaborately carved stone box. They reported their findings in 1922.

The most serious work at Tres Zapotes was undertaken by Matthew Stirling, who did perhaps more than any other person of his time literally to "uncover" the Olmec. He visited the site in 1938 and found, uncovered, and photographed the head. These photos won him the support of the Smithsonian Institution and the National Geographic Society, which sponsored further investiga-

tions. Stirling worked at Tres Zapotes in 1939 and at La Venta, San Lorenzo, and Cerro de las Mesas in the following years, making one stupendous discovery after another.

One outstanding monument discovered during the 1939 season was the lower portion of Stela C, with a bar-and-dot date in the Maya style but without the usual period glyphs. Although the top of the monument was missing, Stirling was able to calculate a date of 31 B.C. for the stela. (Actually, Mrs. Stirling did the initial calculation.) More recently the date was revised to 32 B.C. In any case, the stela's date created a great deal of controversy because it was earlier than any date from the Maya lowlands, where dating was then thought to have originated. When a farmer found the crucial missing portion of Stela C, it confirmed beyond doubt the date that Stirling had calculated, though by this time most authorities tended to agree with his interpretation.

Oddly enough, at the Tres Zapotes Museum, the side of the stela with the Cycle 7 date is displayed toward the outside of the museum; facing the interior is the side of the stela with remains of a bas-relief figure. With a wide-angle lens you can get a photograph of the date on the back while standing "in" the museum, or, with a normal lens, you could step down to the grass below for a shot.

Other displays include numerous basalt columns, tenoned figures, metates, and other stone carvings. A few pieces lie on the lawn around the museum.

The Tres Zapotes Museum is open daily from 9:00 A.M. to 5:00 P.M. There are rest rooms, but food and drink are not available. Allow 45 minutes to see the collection. Photography without flash is permitted.

To reach the museum from Santiago Tuxtla (on Highway 180), head southwest on Highway 179, marked for Villa Isla. The junction is just east of a bridge near the main entrance to Santiago Tuxtla. Follow Highway 179 for 4.8 miles [7.7 kilometers] to a cutoff on the right (unmarked). Although the road from Highway 179 to Tres Zapotes was once paved, it is narrow and full of potholes. Go 8.4 miles [13.5 kilometers] to the town of Tres Zapotes, where the road becomes a double boulevard. Go straight in for 0.1 mile [0.2 kilometer] to a *glorieta* and turn left, then another 0.2 mile [0.3 kilometer] to the museum, where you park outside the gate. Total driving time from Santiago Tuxtla is 34 minutes.

SECTION 6

• • • •

SOUTHERN GULF COAST

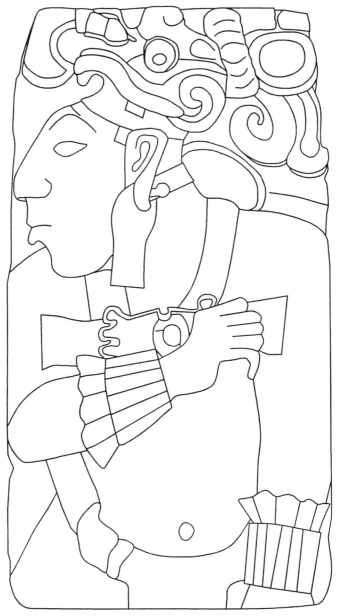

Figure 4 on the west side of the East Court of the Palace, Palenque. Late Classic period.

GENERAL INFORMATION FOR SECTION 6, SOUTHERN GULF COAST

Mexico's southern Gulf Coast is made up of southern Veracruz, Tabasco, northern Chiapas, and southwestern Campeche. The archaeological sites in Campeche are not included in this book since they were covered in my previous *An Archaeological Guide to Mexico's Yucatán Peninsula*. The southern Gulf Coast is a lowland area except for the foothills around Palenque and the higher mountains to the south. It is hot and humid throughout.

The best stopovers, from west to east, are Acayucan, Cárdenas, Villahermosa, Palenque, and Emiliano Zapata. There are restaurants and modest hotels in all these places. In Acayucan, the Kinaku is the best hotel; in Cárdenas, try the Hotel Tlahuasco; and in Emiliano Zapata, the Hotel Maya Usumacinta is the recommended choice. Both Villahermosa and Palenque also have a variety of very good hotels.

There are hotels in Minatitlán and Coatzacoalcos as well, but I do not recommend these cities as stopovers. They are difficult to get into, around, and out of, owing to heavy truck traffic that supports the industrial complexes in the area.

If you are prepared to sleep in your vehicle, another possibility is Rancho Hermanos Graham RV Park on the north side of Highway 180. It is 2.9 miles [4.7 kilometers] east of where the four lane highway ends (driving east from the suspension bridge across the Coatzalcoalcos River) and 4.4 miles [7.1 kilometers] west of the cutoff for La Venta. The park's amenities include a restaurant, recreational facilities, showers, and toilets.

The major roads along the southern Gulf Coast are good, and some sections are four lanes. The condition of unpaved roads is given in the text pertaining to the site or museum involved.

Villahermosa has the major airport in the area; flights arrive from and depart for Mexico City, Mérida, Cancún, Oaxaca, and Tuxtla Gutiérrez. There is also an airport at Palenque with scheduled service.

The points of reference for distances and driving times in this section are the following: (1) in Acayucan, the junction of Highway 180 with the center entrance to town; (2) in Cárdenas, the junction of Highways 180 and 187 on the east end of town; (3) in Villahermosa, the bridge across the Grijalva River; (4) in Palenque, the *glorieta* with the large Maya head at the west entrance to town; and (5) in Emiliano Zapata, the main plaza in town.

Vehicle rentals are available at the Villahermosa airport, east of town, at agencies in town, and through some of the large hotels.

There are travel agencies in Villahermosa and Palenque. At the latter, Viajes Shivalva can be recommended. They specialize in trips to Yaxchilán and Bonampak but can arrange trips to other sites as well. The agency is operated by Marco Morales Fimbres at Calle Merle Green No. 1, in La Cañada section of Palenque on the west end of town. The telephone number is (943)5-04-11; fax is (943)5-03-92. They also have an office in downtown Palenque.

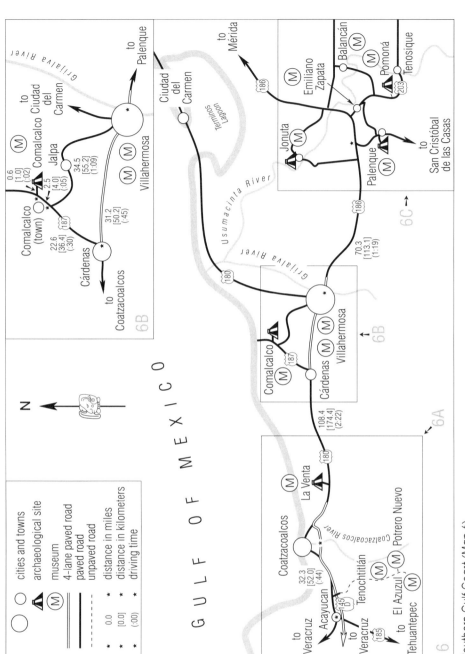

Southern Gulf Coast (Map 6).

MUSEUMS OF OLMEC CULTURE

★ ★

TENOCHTITLÁN MUSEUM

★

POTRERO NUEVO MUSEUM

★ ★

EL AZUZUL MUSEUM

These three museums lie close together, and if you go to the trouble to reach the first one (Tenochtitlán), you should see the others as well, since getting there will take more time than visiting. All three are near the large site of San Lorenzo, which we did not attempt to visit after being told that there was little to see there. Tenochtitlán is a separate site that underlies the village and orchards of the modern town of that name, and Potrero Nuevo is a minor but separate site. As a group they are called San Lorenzo Tenochtitlán, or the Río Chiquito sites. El Azuzul is the most recently identified site in this group.

Matthew W. Stirling discovered the sites of Río Chiquito (Tenochtitlán), San Lorenzo, and Potrero Nuevo in 1945 and conducted a full field season's work in 1946, accompanied by Philip Drucker and others. Working under the auspices of the National Geographic Society and the Smithsonian Institution, they located many monuments.

Michael D. Coe, Richard A. Diehl, and others studied the Olmec remains in the same area from 1966 through 1968 during a project carried out under the sponsorship of Yale University (with which Coe is affiliated) and INAH, with the cooperation of the Institute of Anthropology of Veracruz. Funding came from the National Science Foundation.

In 1990, Ann Cyphers Guillén, of the National Autonomous University of Mexico, began another project to study San Lorenzo, concentrating on the residents' living areas and the workshops of sculptors and other specialists. Later the project's goals were expanded to include settlement patterns and extensive regional surveys. The monuments you will see at the museums were discovered during the various projects mentioned.

The Tenochtitlán Museum, conceived of by Cyphers Guillén and constructed under her supervision, has two enclosed rooms with a roofed but open-sided area between them. Displayed on a platform in the center area is the prize of the collection, a colossal head from San Lorenzo discovered in 1994 and excavated by Cyphers Guillén. The head was found in a ravine with the help of a magnetometer (as was another San Lorenzo head). Pemex, Mexico's national oil company, provided heavy equipment to move the head to Tenochtitlán, where this museum was constructed to house it. A previous museum had been a simple thatch shelter that protected some other sculptures from San Lorenzo.

This was the tenth colossal head discovered at San Lorenzo; it stands 5.9 feet (1.8 meters) tall and weighs nearly 8 tons. It is made of basalt and is in pristine condition. The helmet worn by the head is made of multiple rectangles with rounded corners; each rectangle has a central circular hole. On the floor nearby is San Lorenzo Monument 8, the remains of a rectangular stone altar with slots carved into it.

A few other monuments are nearby, and a couple of dozen are found in the room to the left. Two of the most interesting inside are, first, San Lorenzo Monument 47, a seated, headless human figure wearing a cape (the figure holds a large serpent head in his left

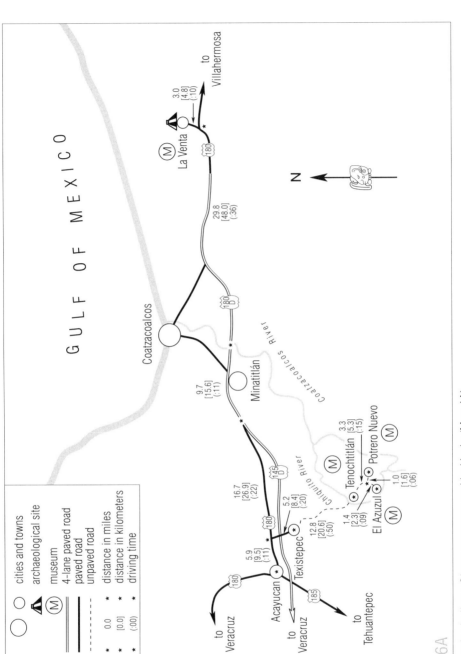

GULF OF MEXICO

N

to
Villahermosa

3.0
[4.8]
(.10)

La Venta

180

29.8
[48.0]
(.36)

Coatzacoalcos

180
D

Coatzacoalcos River

9.7
[15.6]
(.11)

Minatitlán

3.3
[5.3]
(.15)

Tenochtitlán

Potrero Nuevo

1.0
[1.6]
(.06)

El Azuzul

1.4
[2.3]
(.09)

Chiquito River

16.7
[26.9]
(.22)

145
D

5.2
[8.4]
(.20)

12.8
[20.6]
(.50)

180

Texistepec

5.9
[9.5]
(.11)

Acayucan

180

to
Veracruz

to
Veracruz

185

to
Tehuantepec

○ ○   cities and towns
★   archaeological site
Ⓜ   museum
        4-lane paved road
        paved road
        unpaved road

★   0.0   distance in miles
★   [0.0]   distance in kilometers
★   (.00)   driving time

6A

Routes to three Olmec museums and La Venta (Map 6A).

Colossal head 10 from San Lorenzo, Early Preclassic period. Displayed in the Tenochtitlán Museum.

hand and caresses it with his right), and second, San Lorenzo Monument 37, a crouching animal, probably a jaguar, that is also headless. Both of these monuments were discovered during Coe and Diehl's work. Several trough-shaped stones (with covers) that were part of the drainage system at San Lorenzo are also displayed.

The objects in the room on the other side were wrapped in cloth at the time of our visit, and the room was not open, though you could look into it through iron bars. Presumably, these sculptures will one day be displayed.

Outside the museum, under a thatch shelter, is a large tabletop altar, San Lorenzo Monument 20. In a niche on the front, a seated figure holds what is probably a were-jaguar baby; both the were-jaguar and the way the figure holds it are typically Olmec. Both the figure and the baby were severely mutilated in ancient times. There is also a large boulder outside that seems to be uncarved.

Cyphers Guillén was also largely responsible for the Potrero Nuevo Museum, a small, one-room building that houses two interesting fragmented sculptures. One, a magnificent stone torso, was found in 1992. It wears a woven tie-belt, a feathered loincloth, and a spoonlike pectoral "strikingly similar to the jade and jadeite spoons reported from La Venta and other sites," according to Cyphers Guillén. The other sculpture, Potrero Nuevo Monument 1, is in two parts; the top part is greatly damaged. The sculpture depicts a seated figure (now headless) grasping a snake that is draped around him. Matthew Stirling found this monument in front of the principal mound in the village of Potrero Nuevo.

The monuments at El Azuzul Museum are on El Azuzul acropolis, near where they were found in 1987 by a laborer cutting grass. His machete hit a stone object that, when investigated, turned out to be one of the sculptures. He and his friends dug further and uncovered the other monuments. A local

Two kneeling figures at El Azuzul Museum, Early Preclassic period.

landowner erected two shelters to protect them; these are what is now the museum.

Under the larger shelter are two nearly identical kneeling figures (called the twins) wearing flat headdresses from which long trains trail to the ground in the rear. Each figure holds a barlike object on the ground in front, and each wears a rectangular pectoral. Oddly, each was apparently damaged in the same way in ancient times: both are missing the same parts of their headdresses. The remainder of each figure is in excellent condition. One figure sits behind the other, and together they face a seated jaguar, perhaps a supernatural since it has a cleft head. The jaguar, also in excellent condition, is 3.6 feet

(1.1 meters) tall, somewhat taller than the kneeling humans.

Another sculpture, designated Potrero Nuevo Monument 3, is found under the same shelter; it was discovered, badly damaged, somewhere other than El Azuzul by Stirling in 1946. Although it carries the Potrero Nuevo designation, Coe (writing with Diehl in their 1980 book *In the Land of the Olmec*) believed the monument probably had nothing to do with the site of that name. Stirling described it as an apparent depiction of a human female copulating with a jaguar, an idea that caused a good deal of controversy at the time; some authorities disagreed with his interpretation. Other monuments with this apparent theme are known, and although Coe believed Potrero Nuevo Monument 3 indeed depicted what Stirling first suggested, he was uncertain about the others.

Under a smaller adjacent shelter, another seated jaguar can be seen. It was discovered in 1992, precisely where it now lies. It is 5.4 feet (1.65 meters) tall, and it rests on the ground on its back. It is in good condition.

Generally it is unnecessary for me to give detailed directions to museums, since they are in cities, where a street address suffices, or at an archaeological site to which explicit directions have already been given. These three museums are a special case.

The closest and best point of departure is Acayucan, from which you head east on Highway 180 for 5.9 miles [9.5 kilometers] to the unmarked cutoff for Texistepec (on the right). Ask the first person you see if you are on the road to Texistepec to verify that you are on the right road. Drive on to Texistepec, past its plaza and church, and turn left at 5.0 miles [8.0 kilometers] from the highway junction. Then go 0.2 mile [0.3 kilometer] to an unmarked junction with a rock road. So far you will have been driving over paved roads, although the road from the highway to Texistepec is full of potholes; you won't be able to drive any faster on it than on the rock road that follows. At the junction, take the rock road (on the right). Several roads leave Texistepec, so it wouldn't hurt to ask again to make sure you are on the road to Tenochtitlán (ask for San Lorenzo). From the junction it is 12.8 miles [20.6 kilometers] to the Tenochtitlán Museum. Between Texistepec and Tenochtitlán you may come across someone holding a rope across the road who will ask you to pay a small toll to help maintain the road; you will be given a formal receipt.

When you arrive in Tenochtitlán, drive straight through. Near the far end of the town you will find the caretaker's house on the right and the museum just across the road. There is a small sign at the house announcing museums of Olmec culture and arrows pointing out the way to them. You must stop at the house and register; someone with a key will open the left room of the museum for you. Cold drinks are sold at the care-

taker's house, but no food is available anywhere along the way, so bring your own.

It is best to ask at the house for someone to take you to the other two museums, but if that fails, the following directions should get you there. From the Tenochtitlán Museum, follow the rock road straight ahead for 3.3 miles [5.3 kilometers] to a junction with another rock road on the left (marked with a small sign saying Potrero Nuevo). Take this branch road for 1.0 mile [1.6 kilometers] to the Potrero Nuevo Museum (on the right). If it is not open, you (or whomever you have brought along from Tenochtitlán) will have to ask around for someone with a key to let you in. You then return to the first rock road, 1.0 mile [1.6 kilometers], and turn left; then follow it for 1.4 miles [2.3 kilometers] to the base of El Azuzul acropolis. From there you climb on foot to the shelters that house the monuments.

There is no labeling at any of the museums, but all the monuments you will see were produced by the Olmecs during the Early Preclassic period. At Potrero Nuevo you are (fortunately) allowed to use flash. There were indications that the installation of a light was planned, but that had not yet been accomplished when we were there. At the two other places the ambient light is sufficient for photography.

Allow 30 minutes to visit the Tenochtitlán Museum, 15 minutes for Potrero Nuevo, and 25 minutes for El Azuzul. As a day trip—leaving from Acayucan and returning there—the three museums can be visited in less than six hours, including time for a lunch break and to locate people with keys if necessary.

Although buses run along the rock road to Tenochtitlán and El Azuzul, trying to make connections to get in and out in a reasonable time would be difficult. If you are without a vehicle, you might find someone with a truck in Acayucan who would be willing to take you. You would be best off with a high-clearance vehicle, although we did see a couple of standard vehicles along the way. At the time, the road was dry. When it is wet, a high-clearance vehicle would clearly be necessary.

★ ★
LA VENTA
(lah VEHN-tah)

Derivation:
Spanish for "The Roadside Inn."
Culture:
Olmec.
Location:
Extreme western Tabasco.
Maps: 6 (p. 294) and 6A (p. 296)

The Site

Because of projects carried out at La Venta starting in 1984 and conducted by Rebecca González Lauck, the site has become more interesting to visit, and I have raised its rating from one to two stars. Still, the main feature of interest (that is original) is a fluted, conical clay "pyramid" that rises 100 feet (30.5 meters) above the flat Tabasco plain. It can be seen from Highway 180, 3.0 miles [4.8 kilometers] away. The fluting is very regular, and one theory holds that the Olmecs built this "pyramid" in the form of volcanoes in the Tuxtla Mountains, 60.0 miles [96.6 kilometers] away. It is possible, however, that the fluting was caused by erosion. According to González Lauck, the recent excavations "indicate a pyramidal structure with a series of stepped volumes and inset corners that recede from the sides of the central access."

The entrance to the site is through the site museum; from there it is a short walk to the pyramid. If you climb to the top, you can easily see the ridges that form the fluting. Many of La Venta's monuments discovered from 1925 through the 1940s were moved to La Venta Park Museum in Villahermosa in 1958 (see that section for details). Replicas of these monuments have been placed at the

Fluted conical "pyramid," La Venta. Middle Preclassic period.

site in the locations where the originals were found, so there is more to see at the site now than in years gone by. If you like, someone from the museum will show you around, and that way you will be sure not to miss anything. Otherwise you can follow the trails on your own.

The primary occupation of La Venta spanned the years from 1000 to 600 B.C., and the pyramid may have been built between 800 and 700. The site was in decline by 400 B.C., but there is evidence that at least some occupation continued to around A.D. 1200. Some 100 monuments are known from La Venta (including fragments and complete pieces), as are many exquisite jade carvings and ceramics. The finest pieces are displayed in the Mexico City Museum as well as in the Villahermosa Museum and La Venta Park Museum.

Recent History

Frans Blom and Oliver La Farge, working for Tulane University in 1925, discovered La Venta after they heard local reports about its existence. Their expedition was largely exploratory, but during the one day they spent at the site, they discovered six interesting stone monuments, one of them a colossal head (number 1). They were able to excavate only a portion of the head due to their limited time, but it was enough to suggest to Blom a relationship to the head previously reported from Tres Zapotes.

In 1940, Matthew Stirling, working for the Smithsonian Institution and the National Geographic Society, visited La Venta. He found all the monuments reported by Blom as well as 14 others, among which were 3 more colossal heads (numbers 2, 3, and 4). He returned to do additional excavation in 1942, assisted by Philip Drucker, and 1943, with the help of Waldo Wedel. Other work at the site was undertaken by Drucker, Robert Heizer, and R. J. Squier during the 1950s and 1960s.

In 1968, Heizer briefly excavated the Stirling Group, which lies about 0.3 mile [0.5 kilometer] southeast of La Venta's pyramid. He reported that this group appeared to be separate from and physically unconnected

with La Venta. Twenty-three new sculptures were discovered; one, a head with elaborate headgear, is almost an exact duplicate of the head of a figure found by Blom on the summit of San Martín Pajapan in the Tuxtla Mountains. The Stirling Group seems to be a complex of earth-and-clay fill with basalt columns set in rows, and it probably overlapped La Venta in time.

The work in the 1980s conducted by González Lauck was supported by the government of the state of Tabasco and by INAH, with additional help from the National Autonomous University of Mexico, the National Science Foundation, the University of California at Berkeley, the University of Pennsylvania, and the Sorbonne. During this time the site museum was built and the replicas were placed at the site.

Survey mapping was also undertaken, and it was determined that the urban center was larger than previously believed, having nine architectural complexes plus the Stirling Group. Reconnaissances carried out in the environs of La Venta turned up a series of lesser sites contemporaneous with the primary occupation of La Venta. Nine sculptures were also discovered during this work.

Connections

1. Cárdenas to La Venta: 50.4 miles [81.1 kilometers] by paved road (1:11).

2. Villahermosa to Cárdenas: 31.2 miles [50.2 kilometers] by paved road (:45).

3. Acayucan to La Venta: 65.1 miles [104.8 kilometers] by paved road (1:30).

Getting There

1. From Cárdenas, take Highway 180 west to the cutoff for La Venta, 47.4 miles [76.3 kilometers], and turn right. The junction is marked with a sign. Go 3.0 miles [4.8 kilometers] to the parking area at the site museum.

2. From Villahermosa, take Highway 180 west to Cárdenas, then follow the directions already given.

3. From Acayucan, take Highway 180 east toward Minatitlán and join Highway 180D. Continue east on this highway until it ends, then follow its continuation, Highway 180, to the cutoff for La Venta, 62.1 miles [99.9 kilometers]. Turn left at the junction and go on to the parking area for La Venta.

La Venta is open daily from 10:00 A.M. to 5:00 P.M. There is no food or drink at the site, but these are available in the town of La Venta. There are rest rooms at the site museum. Allow one hour for a visit.

Buses go to the town of La Venta, and from there you can taxi to the site.

★ ★
LA VENTA SITE MUSEUM

Squatting stone figure from La Venta, Middle Preclassic period. Displayed in La Venta Site Museum.

As you approach La Venta Site Museum from the parking area, you will see replicas of two colossal heads on platforms near the entrance. Inside there are replicas of other major monuments, a couple of original monuments, and a model of the site. A map shows archaeological sites in Tabasco, and a chronological chart indicates the time period of La Venta compared with other sites. Display cases exhibit original figurines and ceramic pots from the site and copies of a group of carved jade figurines that formed an offering. If all the large monuments were originals, the museum's rating would clearly be three stars.

The museum is open daily from 9:00 A.M. to 4:30 P.M. Allow 20 minutes for a visit. Still photography without flash is permitted; there is a charge to use a video camera. A fair amount of ambient light reaches the museum from skylights, and the display cases are lighted artificially. Little labeling is provided. The museum has rest rooms.

One unusual feature is the museum's thatch roof; it is the largest I have ever seen.

★ ★ ★
COMALCALCO
(koh-mahl-KAHL-koh)

Derivation:
  Nahuatl for "Place of the House
  of Clay Griddles (Bricks)," a
  rough translation.
Culture:
  Maya.
Location:
  North-central Tabasco.
Maps: 6 and 6B (p. 294)

The Site

Comalcalco is a delightful place to visit, with
an impressive number of consolidated buildings and well-preserved stucco sculptures. A
medium-size site covering 0.28 square mile
(0.72 square kilometer), it lies on the westernmost edge of the Maya area. It is unusual for
a Maya site in that no stone was used in its
buildings. The earlier structures at Comalcalco are stucco-covered earth platforms, and
the later structures were made of fired bricks
so thin they might better be described as slabs.
In one wall of the building called the Palace,
the mortar forms layers thicker than the
bricks it binds together. The use of bricks is
understandable, since no stone is found on
the Tabasco plains where Comalcalco is located.
This is by far the most important Maya site
using fired bricks for construction; the others
that did so are also in the general region.

From the parking area for the site (near
the museum, snack stand, and shop), head
east by foot trail toward the site itself. You
will pass the south side of Temple I, and a
branch trail to the left (which goes between
Temples I and III) takes you to it. (*Note:* In
the text and site plan, I use Roman numerals
for the temples, since that is how they are
labeled in the literature. The signs at the site,
however, use Arabic numbers.)

There are some interesting stucco sculptures on the base of the southeast corner of

Temple I, protected by a roof that transmits
enough light for photography. On the corner
proper are the remains of an unusual web-
footed creature with long body scales; to the
right (north) is a throne with the lower parts
of three seated figures. This is followed by a
reclining human and the lower part of
another who stands. Beyond is the lower
part of a human in a running pose. Continue
north to the North Plaza for a view of the
front of Temple I.

This is the tallest temple-pyramid at
Comalcalco. It rises 65.4 feet (19.6 meters)
in two sections—in essence, a smaller pyramid and temple set back atop a larger pyramid. Each section rises in tiers and has an
eastern stairway; the stair on the lower part
is wider. The lower walls of the crowning
temple are intact, but visitors are not allowed
to climb the pyramid to see them. Other structures are off limits as well. The consolidated
tiers of the pyramid have been reconstructed
mostly with modern bricks that have turned
a darkish brown-black, whereas the original
stuccoed surfaces of the stairway *alfardas*
and some lower tiers of the pyramid are a
light gray.

Temple II lies to the northeast and forms
the western end of a long mound that runs
east to west. The temple itself is smaller than
Temple I, although its plan is similar, as are
the plans of the other temples at Comalcalco.
All the temples have two rooms, one behind
the other, and a sanctuary against the rear
wall that was probably vaulted originally. A
stairway ascends from the North Plaza to
Temple II on the south side, and part of the
base of the pyramidal platform on which
Temple II lies has been consolidated.

To the south, across the short dimension
of the plaza, is Temple III. Both the remains
of the structure and the base on which it rests
have been consolidated. There is a stair on
the north side. Adjacent to the east is a stairway with *alfardas* that divide it into sections;
this is called Temple III A. Still farther east is

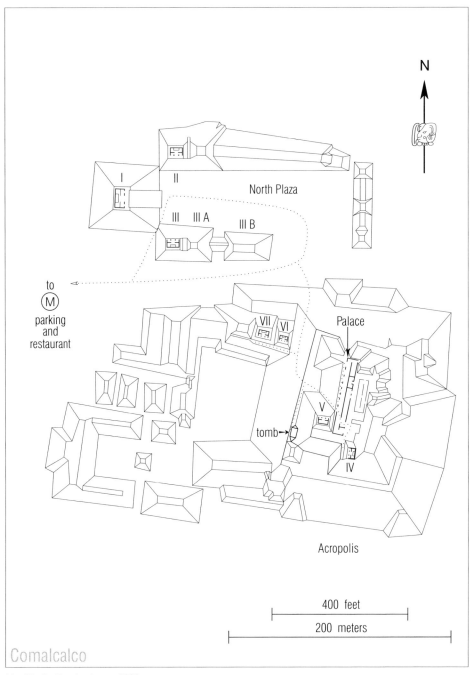

N

North Plaza

I

II

III   III A   III B

to
(M)
parking
and
restaurant

VII VI

Palace

V

tomb →

IV

Acropolis

400 feet

200 meters

Comalcalco

Modified after Andrews, 1989.

Front (east side) of Temple I, Comalcalco. Late or Terminal Classic period.

General view of the Acropolis, Comalcalco. Late or Terminal Classic period.

Temple III B, a low, stepped pyramidal base with a northern stair. This base, made of stucco-covered earth, once supported a brick masonry building that is now totally destroyed.

According to George F. Andrews in his 1989 book about Comalcalco, two of the reasons its brick structures are poorly preserved are the instability of the earthen supporting substructures and the excessive length of the wooden lintels employed in some doorways, which contributed to the collapse of the vaults above.

You now leave the North Plaza at its southeast corner and follow a stepped path that climbs up the Acropolis. At the first level a trail leads west to Temples VI and VII. An

The stucco mask on the front (south side) of Temple VI, Comalcalco. Late or Terminal Classic period.

outstanding and fairly well preserved stucco sculpture representing Kinich Ahau, the Maya sun god, is found on the center of the steps of Temple VI. It is covered by a glass case, but you can get photos through it. The sculpture is part of an earlier substructure discovered when the face of the final substructure was stripped away.

Adjacent to the west is the larger Temple VII, the upper portion of which has been completely destroyed. The base of the structure that is now exposed was also part of an earlier substructure. The base rises in tiers and is divided by a central stairway. The tiers are decorated with stucco sculptures depicting seated humans and other motifs. A roof protects the sculptures, but it transmits enough light for photography.

You now return to the main trail and climb south to a higher level of the Acropolis. Continue straight ahead to a vaulted brick tomb. You will pass a side trail along the way that you will return to later. The north, east, and south interior walls of the tomb are decorated with stucco bas-reliefs of standing human figures accompanied by hieroglyphs. There are three figures on each wall, for a total of nine, and they may represent the Nine Lords of the Underworld. A comparison is often made with the tomb beneath the

Temple of Inscriptions at Palenque, which also has nine figures representing the Nine Lords of the Underworld, though the Comalcalco tomb is smaller. The figures, walls, and floor of the Comalcalco tomb were painted a deep red, but only traces of color remain. A large number of squared and perforated clamshells, also painted red, were found on the floor of the tomb; apparently they were parts of a necklace. A locked chain-link gate prevents entry into the tomb, but you can get photos over or through it.

Return now to the side trail that you passed earlier and follow it upward toward the Palace; you will pass the recently consolidated Temple V along the way. Temple V faces north and was once richly decorated with stucco ornamentation. A chamber—perhaps a tomb—was discovered within the base of the temple.

The Palace, near the top of the Acropolis, is the most imposing building at Comalcalco. It measures 225.1 feet (68.61 meters) long by 26.9 feet (8.2 meters) deep and is composed of two parallel ranges of vaulted rooms. The long axis of the structure runs roughly north to south. The Palace underwent many changes during its lifetime, including extensions to the south and the addition and removal of several cross walls. Its bricks were stuccoed

Stucco decoration on the base of Temple VII, Comalcalco. Late or Terminal Classic period.

and painted red. A curious feature of the Palace vaults is the use of potsherds embedded in the stucco. None of the vaults is intact at present, though one section was in 1880 when the French explorer Désiré Charnay visited Comalcalco; he included an illustration of it in his 1887 book *The Ancient Cities of the New World.* You will enjoy just roaming around the Palace, from the north end of which there are nice views of Temples I and II on the North Plaza and Temples VI and VII on the lower level of the Acropolis.

Near the south end of the Palace, and lying to the east, are the scant remains of another building, an adjacent stair, and a rectangular altar. They are worth a look on your way to Temple IV, which lies farther south. Temple IV is similar in design to Temple V; it, too, has a lower, vaulted interior chamber.

Comalcalco shows a number of similarities to Palenque, 100 miles (160.9 kilometers) southeast. These similarities lie in the plan of its temples, in the use of stucco decorations and their style, and in the tomb with the nine figures. Because much of the work conducted at Comalcalco remains unpublished, there is still some question about the site's exact chronology, though one sequence has it occupied from 100 B.C. to A.D. 1350. It

is believed to have been a trading center. The brick structures are believed to date to the Late Classic or the Terminal Classic and perhaps to both periods.

Recent History

The first official notice of Comalcalco seems to have been taken by C. H. Berendt, who provided a description and a sketch. He may or may not have visited the site in 1869, and the information was published only in 1896 by Daniel G. Brinton.

Charnay published his findings first in 1885 in French and then in an English translation in 1887. The site was further explored by Frans Blom and Oliver La Farge in 1925 for Tulane University. While there, Blom discovered the tomb with the nine figures, and the two men published a report in 1926. In 1956 and 1957, Gordon Ekholm, working for the American Museum of Natural History, conducted investigations, but a full report of the fieldwork was never published.

In 1960, archaeologists from INAH, directed by Román Piña Chan, carried out preliminary investigations and consolidated Temple VII, but this work, likewise, has not been published. George F. Andrews first visited Comalcalco that same year and was deeply impressed with the brick architecture. He returned in the summer of 1966 with a team of four graduate students and carried out an extensive mapping project and architectural survey. The project was funded by the Institute of International Studies of the University of Oregon, the institution with which Andrews is affiliated. He published his findings the following year, and a second edition appeared in 1989.

From 1972 through 1982, archaeologists from INAH conducted excavations and consolidated some of the structures, under the direction of Ponciano Salazar Ortegon. The most ambitious project was the complete excavation and restoration of Temple I. This work remains mostly unpublished. Some time later, Temple V was consolidated.

Connections

1. Cárdenas to Comalcalco: 25.7 miles [41.4 kilometers] by paved road (:37).

2. Villahermosa to Comalcalco (via Cárdenas): 56.9 miles [91.6 kilometers] by paved road (1:22).

3. Villahermosa to Comalcalco (via Jalpa): 37.6 miles [60.2 kilometers] by paved road (1:16).

Getting There

1. From Cárdenas, take Highway 187 heading northeast; go to and past the east edge of the town of Comalcalco to the cutoff for the site. It is on the right and is marked with a sign. Highway 187 joins Highway 180 at the east edge of Cárdenas, at the point where an overpass crosses Highway 180.

2. From Villahermosa, take Highway 180 west to Cárdenas and follow the directions already given.

3. From Villahermosa, head north on Highway 180 for a short distance and pick up an unnumbered highway on the left that goes to Jalpa and on to Highway 187. Then follow the directions already given. This route from Villahermosa is shorter and will take a few minutes less time, but it is not recommended. It goes through several small towns, and the route is poorly marked in some areas. There are a number of cross roads (not shown on the accompanying maps), and it is easy to take a wrong turn. If you enjoy asking directions a lot and driving over innumerable *topes,* you might want to try it. I prefer Connection 2, on which you drive more than halfway to Comalcalco over a four-lane highway.

Comalcalco is open daily from 10:00 A.M. to 4:00 P.M. Allow two hours for a visit. There are rest rooms at the snack stand, where cool (not cold) drinks are sold. There is also a small shop selling booklets and other items nearby. All of this is near the museum, and the three are part of the visitors' center.

Buses run to the town of Comalcalco, and from there you can taxi to the site.

★ ★ ★
COMALCALCO MUSEUM

The Comalcalco Museum is a very good site museum. It is nicely laid out and well lighted with artificial and ambient light (the latter from a skylight), enough for photography. There is little specific labeling, but all the items come from Comalcalco.

In the large single room, glass-enclosed display cases line the walls. They contain a good number of bricks incised with graffiti or modeled with designs in bas-relief. Especially impressive are four bricks modeled, respectively, with lizards, a turtle, and a crocodile. Incised motifs include anthropomorphic and zoomorphic figures, temple architecture, symbols, and linear and geometric designs. According to George F. Andrews, if all the known decorated bricks from Comalcalco were added together—those from the museum, the ones in private collections, and those still in place at the site—the number would exceed 10,000. The designs were not visible once the bricks were laid in mortar. The graffiti on the bricks are thought to be "magical" signs incorporated into the buildings as part of a ritual process.

The graffiti depicting architecture show temples with roof combs. Although no roof combs remain on Comalcalco's temples, the depiction of them on the bricks suggests that the temples once had them. Also, the similarities of the temples to those at Palenque (which have roof combs) hint that roof combs were once present at Comalcalco as well.

Other highlights of the museum are a beautiful carved stone yoke in pristine condition and a baked clay tablet with a hieroglyphic inscription.

In the center of the room is a circular platform where some large stucco heads, both human and animal, are displayed. On two L-shaped islands there are some huge ceramic urns and stucco architectural decorations.

The museum is open daily from 10:00 A.M. to 4:00 P.M. Allow 30 minutes for a visit.

Stucco head from Comalcalco. Late or Terminal Classic period. On display in the Comalcalco Museum.

★ ★ ★ ★
CARLOS PELLICER CÁMARA REGIONAL MUSEUM OF ANTHROPOLOGY (*VILLAHERMOSA MUSEUM*)

Although the Villahermosa Museum is a regional museum, all parts of Mexico are represented in its extensive collection. The displays are housed on three floors (ground floor, first floor, and second floor) and on a mezzanine. You tour the museum by taking the elevator to the upper level (second floor) and beginning there. Then work your way down to the first floor and ground floor, and from there walk up to the mezzanine.

The second floor displays begin with an explanation of the prehistory of the Americas from stone age inhabitants to more recent cultures. A chronological chart covers the time from 1500 B.C. to A.D. 1500, and a map shows the different cultural areas of Mesoamerica.

There are some attractive Early Pre-classic figurines from Tlatilco and a number of displays relating to Teotihuacán, including an alabaster mask and a stone sculpture of the fire god. The Gulf Coast cultures are represented by some Totonac smiling heads and figurines, some beautifully carved *hachas,* and some Huastec sculpture. *Palmas* and yokes are also exhibited. A well-preserved Classic period Zapotec urn depicting Cocijo

Seated stone figure, Monument 11 from La Venta. Middle Preclassic period. On display in the Villahermosa Museum.

is an outstanding display. Western Mexico cultures are represented by ceramic figurines of humans and animals, including a Classic period ball player from Jalisco. Stone and clay sculptures show the art of the Postclassic Mexica (Aztec) culture.

Olmec and Maya pieces are exhibited on the next lower (first) floor, which can be reached by the elevator or a stairway. There are seated basalt Preclassic Olmec figures (including Monument 11 from La Venta), an unusual clay urn depicting a hunchbacked old man, and typical Olmec ceramics. Jade necklaces, ear spools, and ceremonial axes also represent this culture.

The Maya section has an unusual Classic period bas-relief figure of a contortionist from Bellote, Tabasco, part of a seventh-century stela from Cunduacán, Tabasco, and an elaborate Classic period clay incensario from Palenque. Other Maya exhibits are Classic period figurines from Jaina and Jonuta and decorated bricks from Comalcalco.

You now go to the ground floor, where monumental pieces are exhibited. Colossal Olmec head number 2 from La Venta is on a platform in the main room. (You will actually see this when you first enter the museum.) There are other large Olmec sculptures and the Classic Maya Stela 1 from Morales (La Reforma), as well as other Maya pieces.

From there you climb the stairs to the mezzanine, where some of the finest selected Olmec and Maya pieces are displayed. Two Olmec jadeite statuettes are in pristine condition, as are a carved daggerlike or scepterlike greenstone object and a carved ceremonial ax. These items are all from the Preclassic period and all come from La Venta.

Maya pieces include fragments of stucco glyphs from Palenque that date to the Late Classic period and some ceramics of the highest quality. One Early Classic piece from the island of Chablé, Tabasco, is in the form of a snail; one section of it is carved with consummate artistry. The so-called Urn of Teapa, an elaborate Late Classic ceremonial piece, is one of the finest of its kind known.

Among other spectacular displays are a beautiful (though broken) Late Classic polychrome vessel with figures and glyphs and a Terminal Classic cylindrical vessel made of a reddish clay and carved with a scene.

The Villahermosa Museum is on Malecón Carlos A. Madrazo (shown as Avenida Carlos Pellicer Cámara on some maps), south of the center of town. It is one of the buildings forming the CICOM (Centro de Investigaciónes de las Culturas Olmec y Maya) complex. The museum was inaugurated in 1980 in a modern building on the Grijalva River. It replaced the smaller and older museum on the plaza, which had opened in 1952.

The Villahermosa Museum is named for the Tabascan poet Carlos Pellicer Cámara, who founded the old museum, served as its director for 26 years, and donated his own collection to it. The museum is open daily from 9:00 A.M. to 8:00 P.M. There are rest rooms on each level. Photography without flash is permitted. Lighting is fairly good on some objects but poor on others; labeling is fair. Allow 1.5 hours for a visit.

★ ★ ★ ★
LA VENTA PARK MUSEUM

This unique park-museum in Villahermosa, planned and executed under the able direction of Carlos Pellicer Cámara, was inaugurated in 1958 when 33 monuments were transported 80 miles [128.7 kilometers] to it from La Venta. The museum is located along the service road that parallels Highway 180 (Paseo Grijalva) as it goes around the city of Villahermosa. It is a short distance northeast of the junction of Highway 180 and Paseo Tabasco. Although the outside displays have remained the same, inside the museum has improved its facilities a great deal over the years.

After you go through the ticket booth, you come to a covered area—cooled with fans—that has photo displays of sites in Tabasco along with ceramics, obsidian pieces, and other stone artifacts, and where a video covering Olmec culture is shown. There is a model of a large buried mosaic pavement from La Venta, the original of which you will see outside. The large stone sculptures in this area are mostly copies; again, the originals are outside.

Outside, the original monuments are set in a jungly park environment. Included are three colossal heads (numbers 1, 3, and 4), seven huge altars, four stone stelae, two huge floor mosaics (each consisting of 485 pieces of serpentine), and many other interesting sculptures. Before the mosaics were transported, each piece was carefully numbered so they could be accurately reassembled when they were installed in the park.

What the floor mosaics depict is a matter of controversy—and it partly depends on which way they are viewed. Each of the identical mosaics has four tassel-like motifs on one end and a rectangular cutout on the opposite end. If the cutout was meant to be at the top, it could represent the cleft head typical of Olmec deities, in which case the mosaic might represent a jaguar mask. If the tassels were meant to be at the top—as Kent Reilly of Southwest Texas State University believes—then the central column could symbolize the sacred tree of life.

In any case, the floor mosaics were apparently of a sacred nature; they were buried almost immediately after completion. Colored clays originally filled the spaces between the serpentine slabs. Some authorities believe the serpentine came from the Pacific Coast, 150 miles [241.4 kilometers] away.

It is now generally agreed that the basalt used for the colossal heads, altars, and stelae

Altar 4 from La Venta, Middle Preclassic period. Displayed in La Venta Park Museum.

at La Venta came from the Cerro Cintepec in the Tuxtla range, 60 miles [96.6 kilometers] west of the site. Undoubtedly, the Olmecs were excellent engineers as well as artists; moving basalt boulders averaging 18 tons apiece through such terrain would be difficult even today. It is still uncertain whether the boulders were moved while in their original state or after they were partly carved.

When you visit the park, simply follow the well-marked gravel trails. Take any short side trails that you see, as they all lead to interesting monuments—signs point out the way.

Other signs are posted identifying each monument and giving additional information in Spanish and English. Still others identify the flora and fauna in the area. Trees are labeled with the popular name, botanical name, family, and use to which they can be put. Along the trails you will see pens with crocodiles, cages with other animals, and an artisans' market. There are rest rooms and

shelters at several locations and benches for resting near some of the monuments. Trash cans and the walls of buildings are painted with foliage designs so that they blend in with the surrounding vegetation. Everything is well done.

Having the monuments in this jungle setting is appropriate, since it was in this sort of environment that they were found. Huge pieces of sculpture seem to be at their best in an outdoor setting instead of confined within museum walls. It is altogether an excellent idea.

Still photography without flash is permitted, and since the monuments are outside, you really don't need flash. To use flash or a video camera you must get a special permit.

Allow 1.5 hours to tour the park, which is open daily from 9:00 A.M. to 4:00 P.M. Bring insect repellent. Cold drinks are available in the park, and there are food vendors in the parking area just outside.

JONUTA
(hoh-NOO-tah)

Derivation:
Originally Xonotlan, Nahuatl for "Place of Jonote Trees."
Culture:
Chontal Maya.
Location:
Extreme northeast part of Tabasco, near the border with Campeche.
Maps: 6 (p. 296) and 6C (p. 314)

The Site

Jonuta was an important mercantile center in pre-Columbian times and a principal manufacturing center for ceramics, some of which were exported to other parts of the Maya area and even to more distant parts of Mesoamerica. Today, however, there is only one large mound to be seen. It stands near the center of the town of Jonuta and is surrounded by a wall and fence. The town lies on the main branch of the Usumacinta River, but another arm of the river flows to the east. According to Frans Blom, writing in 1926, "this large mound lies so that it has a dominant view of both arms of the river."

When we visited Jonuta, the gate in the fence was locked, but we probably would not have seen much more had it been open.

Once, other mounds existed in Jonuta, but they are mostly gone today, owing to the development of the town. Many were destroyed when the streets were put in and house foundations were dug. Perishable structures, some of which were modest habitations, once topped the mounds; other perishable structures probably served as temples. The mounds have, however, yielded bountiful artifacts over the years, some of which can be seen in the Jonuta Museum. Jonuta's heyday was in the Late Classic period and during the Late Classic to Early Postclassic transition.

Recent History

Jonuta has been known since the early sixteenth century, and the Spaniards relocated people from Xicalango, on the Gulf Coast, inland to Jonuta late in that century. The area was mapped in the late seventeenth century. In 1869, a brief note about the antiquities of Jonuta appeared in print in Mexico.

Désiré Charnay stopped at Jonuta briefly in 1880 on his way to Palenque. He commented on the pyramids that occupied part of the village and on the antiquities that had been unearthed, a collection of which he saw. Charnay's work reached a wider audience than the note printed in Mexico.

In 1926, Blom's work appeared, and in 1956, the Carnegie Institution of Washington published a work on the ceramics of Jonuta, written by Heinrich Berlin. Carlos Álvarez and Luis Casasolo wrote about the Jonuta figurines in 1985.

Connections

1. Palenque to Jonuta: 59.5 miles [96.0 kilometers] by paved road (1:16).

2. Villahermosa to Jonuta: 96.9 miles [155.9 kilometers] by paved road (1:53).

Getting There

Two paved roads connect Jonuta to Highway 186. The one used in both the connections given is the more westerly and is the shortest way to Jonuta from the places listed.

1. From Palenque, take Highway 199 north to Highway 186 and turn left. Go to the junction for Jonuta (marked with a sign) and turn right. After you cross the Usumacinta near Jonuta, make a U-turn to reach the town. Turn left in town at a small *glorieta* and proceed to the Jonuta Museum. The large mound is a block or so away.

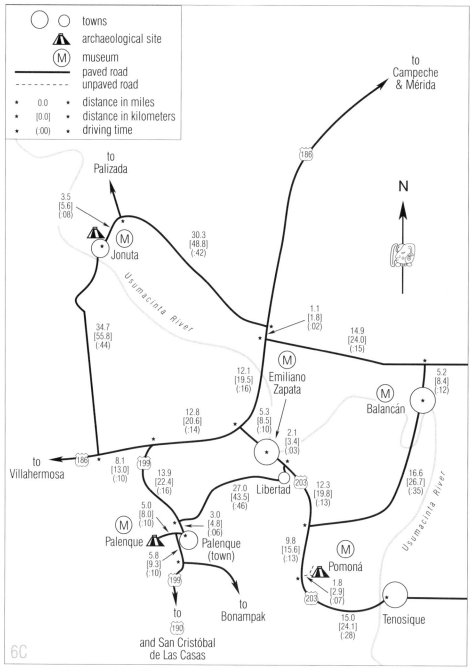

Legend

- ○ ○ towns
- 🔺 archaeological site
- Ⓜ museum
- ——— paved road
- - - - - - unpaved road
- ★ 0.0 ★ distance in miles
- ★ [0.0] ★ distance in kilometers
- ★ (:00) ★ driving time

to
Campeche
& Mérida

186

N

to
Palizada

3.5
[5.6]
(:08)

🔺 Ⓜ
Jonuta

30.3
[48.8]
(:42)

Usumacinta River

1.1
[1.8]
(:02)

14.9
[24.0]
(:15)

34.7
[55.8]
(:44)

12.1
[19.5]
(:16)

Ⓜ
Emiliano
Zapata

5.2
[8.4]
(:12)

12.8
[20.6]
(:14)

5.3
[8.5]
(:10)

2.1
[3.4]
(:03)

Ⓜ
Balancán

to
Villahermosa

186   8.1
[13.0]
(:10)

199

13.9
[22.4]
(:16)

27.0
[43.5]
(:46)

Libertad

203   12.3
[19.8]
(:13)

16.6
[26.7]
(:35)

Usumacinta River

5.0
[8.0]
(:10)

3.0
[4.8]
(:06)

Ⓜ
Palenque 🔺

5.8
[9.3]
(:10)

Palenque
(town)

9.8
[15.6]
(:13)

Ⓜ
Pomoná

🔺

1.8
[2.9]
(:07)

203

199

to
190

to
Bonampak

15.0
[24.1]
(:28)

Tenosique

and San Cristóbal
de Las Casas

6C

Area around Palenque (Map 6C).

2. From Villahermosa, take Highway 186 east to the junction for Jonuta and turn left. Then follow the directions already given.

Depending on your travel plans, you could also use the other connection between Highway 186 and Jonuta as detailed on Map 6C.

You need only a few minutes to see the mound. There are restaurants in town near the museum.

★ ★

ARCHAEOLOGIST OMAR HUERTA ESCALENTE MUSEUM (JONUTA MUSEUM)

The Jonuta Museum, inaugurated in 1985, is composed of two nicely arranged rooms at ground level that display the archaeological collection and a couple more upstairs that house the history section. The museum is named for the professor who was the principal promoter of the creation of the museum.

The first room of the archaeological section has maps, diagrams, and information on Maya culture and the province of Tabasco. The items in the second room are not individually labeled but include ceramics from various periods at Jonuta, flint spearheads, manos and metates, and figurines, many of

Fragments of inscribed and painted pottery from Jonuta. Late Classic or Late Classic–Early Postclassic transition period. Displayed in the Jonuta Museum.

which are whistles depicting humans and animals. Most of the artifacts are Maya and come from Jonuta, but there is an Olmec piece and another, a vase with a depiction of Tlaloc, that is Zapotec—apparently an import.

In one case, fragments of Classic period inscribed ceramic vases are displayed. They show especially fine workmanship. Most of the items in the collection date to the Late Classic period or to the Late Classic–Early Postclassic transition.

The Jonuta figurines are stylistically similar to those from Isla Jaina and to others from the Usumacinta area. Similarities include facial tattooing or scarification and elaborate turbans.

The Jonuta Museum is in the center of the town of the same name on Calle Álvaro Obregón between Calles Hidalgo and Juárez. It is open every day—on Sunday from 9:00 A.M. to 1:00 P.M. and on the other days from 9:00 A.M. to 7:00 P.M. Allow 20 minutes for a visit. Photography without flash is permitted; lighting is only fair. There are no rest rooms, food, or drink at the museum, but there are restaurants nearby.

Ask at the museum for a guidebook about it and the region.

★ ★ ★ ★
PALENQUE
(pah-LEHN-keh)

Derivation:
  Spanish for "Palisade."
Original Name:
  Lakam Ha, Maya for "Big Water."
Culture:
  Maya.
Location:
  Northeastern Chiapas.
Maps: 6 (p. 294), 6C (p. 314), 7 (p. 338), and 7A (p. 340)

The Site

Many archaeologists, art historians, and other scholars, as well as visitors, consider Palenque the most beautiful Maya city. Though it is neither the largest nor the oldest, its setting against the green foothills of the Sierra of Chiapas and the delicacy and refinement of its architecture and sculpture make it the prime gem in the crown of the ancient Maya sites. It was found in a fair state of preservation, and the work undertaken there has rendered it even more inter-esting as the years have passed. There is a great deal to see and photograph, so plan on spending at least two days.

Palenque was occupied from around 500 B.C., in the Middle Preclassic period, though this and the following Late Preclassic are poorly represented. In the Early Classic, the center of Palenque was about 0.6 mile [1.0 kilometer] to the west, where the Olvidado, Palenque's earliest known building, was erected. In the middle to late part of the Early Classic, the site center shifted to where it is today. The Late Classic period was the time of florescence at Palenque, and the site collapsed around A.D. 800 to 830.

When you enter Palenque and follow the path from the parking area (on the west) to the site, you come first to Structure XII. Its temple rises above a tiered base with a northern stair. Half of the front of the building has fallen, but at the bottom of one of the piers on the left (as you face the temple) is found a stucco bas-relief depicting the skeletal mask of a rabbit identified with the moon.

To the east of Structure XII is a platform, and again to the east you come to Structure XIII, which contains the Red Queen's Tomb, discovered in 1994. Her body and burial chamber had been daubed with red—hence

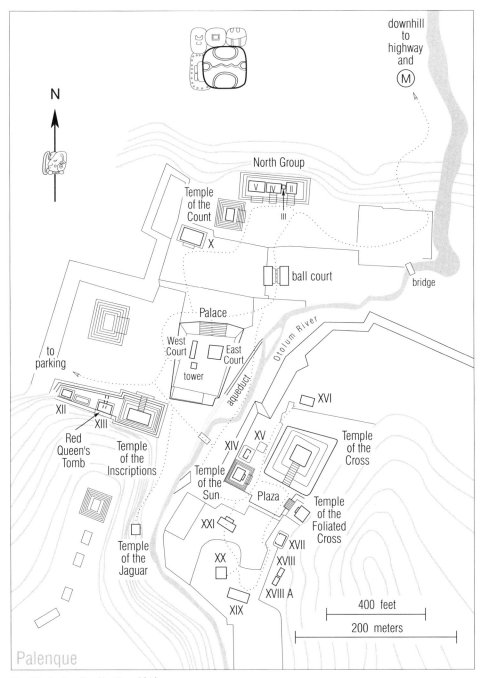

downhill to highway and (M)

N

North Group

Temple of the Count

V IV III II

III

X

ball court

bridge

Palace

to parking

West Court

East Court

tower

Otolum River

aqueduct

XII

XIII

Red Queen's Tomb

Temple of the Inscriptions

XIV

XV

XVI

Temple of the Cross

Temple of the Sun

Plaza

Temple of the Foliated Cross

XXI

XVII

Temple of the Jaguar

XX

XVIII

XVIII A

XIX

400 feet

200 meters

Palenque

Modified after Ruz Lhuillier, 1960.

Temple of the Inscriptions, front (north side), Palenque. Temple XIII is on the far right. Both date to the Late Classic period.

her name. About this royal woman little is known, and no carved inscriptions were found on her sarcophagus.

Next is the Temple of the Inscriptions, one of Palenque's more famous and impressive buildings. The base of the structure is pyramidal and rises in nine tiers. The temple on top, its floor 75 feet (22.9 meters) above the level of the plaza, faces north and is entered by five doorways. The back of the pyramid is partially supported by hills covered with tropical green, which contrasts nicely with the pale gray architecture.

This structure has been known for as long as the site has been known, but it gave up one of its secrets only in 1952. The Mexican archaeologist Alberto Ruz Lhuillier, while investigating the structure, noticed some holes in a large slab that formed part of the floor of the temple. He also noted that the walls of the temple did not end at floor level, but went deeper. This suggested that there was some sort of chamber beneath the floor. And indeed there was.

When the floor slab was lifted, a rubble-filled stairway was revealed. It took four field seasons of two and a half to three months each to remove the rubble. The stairway was

found to make a U-turn partway down, and the remains of five or six youths were found near the end. They probably had been sacrificed to accompany their master. Beyond this was a large triangular stone slab, fitted neatly into the slope of the vault. When this was removed, a fantastic sepulchral chamber came into the view of human eyes for the first time in over 1,200 years.

The chamber measures 30 by 13 feet (9.1 by 4.0 meters) and has an unusually high vault—23 feet (7.0 meters) above the floor—reinforced by stone beams. The bottom of the chamber lies 80 feet (24.4 meters) below the floor of the temple and some 5 feet (1.5 meters) below the level of the plaza. Its walls are covered with bas-reliefs of nine figures, sometimes said to represent the Nine Lords of the Underworld, but this has never been proven. The figures no doubt formed a royal guard for the deceased king who was buried here.

Most of the area of the chamber is taken up by a stone slab measuring 12.5 feet (3.8 meters) long, more than 7 feet (2.1 meters) wide, and 10 inches (25.4 centimeters) thick, and weighing some 5 tons (4,536.0 kilograms). This was the lid of a sarcophagus, beautifully carved in low relief and resting upon a stone block. When the lid was raised—a difficult job in these cramped quarters—a smooth stone slab was found fitted into the stone block. This slab had holes fitted with stone stoppers; these were removed and the slab was duly lifted. In the interior of the hollow stone block lay the remains of a tall man literally covered with jade. He wore jade rings on each finger, multiple jade necklaces made of hundreds of pieces—many in the form of flowers and fruits—many jade bracelets, earplugs, and a jade mosaic mask over his face. A small jade statue of the sun god was found, and the personage held a large jade in each hand and one in his mouth.

On the floor of the crypt under the sarcophagus were found clay vessels, apparently containing food and drink for the deceased, and two beautiful, life-size stucco heads that were originally part of the decoration of some other temple at Palenque. On the sides of the sarcophagus appeared bas-relief depictions of the deceased's ancestors.

The objects found in this tomb, except for the carved stone sarcophagus lid, are now on display in a replica of the tomb in the Mexico City Museum. The tomb itself was built before the pyramid; otherwise, it would have been impossible to get the lid down the stairway.

The glyphs on the edge of the sarcophagus lid, along with recent physical anthropological studies, indicate that the man entombed died at age 80. This individual was Pacal (now called K'inich Janahb' Pakal), meaning Shield. (I have retained the name Pacal, the first given to this ruler, because it is embedded in the literature, especially the popular literature. For other rulers I use the most recent name, followed by the former name or names, since the earlier names are less well known.)

Pacal was the greatest ruler of Palenque; he reigned from age 12 until his death. He was born in A.D. 603, acceded to the throne in 615, and died in 683. The tomb and the Temple of the Inscriptions were completed shortly after his death. Glyphic evidence found elsewhere at Palenque corroborates this decipherment. One of the stucco heads found under the sarcophagus almost certainly portrays Pacal.

Along the stairway that descends to the tomb is a rectangular duct that connected with the sarcophagus. It is believed that this was a sort of magic connection or "psychoduct" enabling the dead lord to communicate with those in the temple above.

The temple itself is also of great interest. It contains three large stone panels carved with 617 hieroglyphs, some of which have been deciphered. They record some of the historical events of Pacal's life. These inscriptions give the temple its name.

The pillars on the outside of the temple are decorated with stucco bas-reliefs of human figures carrying small "children," who probably are representations of God K. Some of Palenque's rulers are depicted on these piers.

South of the Temple of the Inscriptions you will find the Temple of the Jaguar, reached by a trail that goes along the east side of the Temple of the Inscriptions. This small temple has lost its front facade, but it is worth a look for the remains of a stucco relief on the rear wall. Unfortunately, much of this was destroyed during the twentieth century. It represented a personage seated on a throne decorated with two jaguar heads. At the rear of the room, a stairway leads to a lower chamber that probably once contained a burial, although no traces of such have been found.

You now return toward the Temple of the Inscriptions. From that point there are a few possibilities for visiting the other structures. What follows is but one of those. When you reach the Temple of the Inscriptions, take a trail to the right that crosses the Otolum River; follow a branch trail to the right that winds around and enters the plaza of the Cross Group. Facing the plaza on the west is the Temple of the Sun; Temple XIV lies to the northeast (off the plaza); the Temple of the Cross bounds the north side of the plaza; and the Temple of the Foliated Cross is on the east.

All four structures are similar in design and rise on pyramidal bases. The Temple of the Sun—the best preserved—is one of the most beautiful small temples ever erected by the Mayas. This elegantly proportioned structure is sheer perfection, making it one of the most photographed buildings at Palenque. On the back wall of the interior shrine is a

Temple of the Sun, northeast corner, Palenque. Late Classic period.

magnificent carved panel depicting the accession of K'inich Kan B'alam II (formerly called Chan Bahlum II), son and successor of Pacal, in A.D. 684. Pacal is the figure on the left; he is shown deified and acting after death (according to his dress and certain symbols that accompany him). K'inich Kan B'alam II is on the right, receiving his dynastic rights. The panel was dedicated in A.D. 692, as were those in the Temple of the Cross and the Temple of the Foliated Cross.

There are remnants of stucco decorations on the exterior pillars of the Temple of the Sun, as well as on the mansardlike roof and on the perforated roof comb.

Temple XIV has had its two-tiered base and some of its walls restored, although it lacks a roof. It houses another beautifully carved panel in its inner chamber. This is protected by metal bars, but you can get photographs from over the bars or in between

them. There are some remnants of paint on this panel.

The Temple of the Cross rises on the tallest pyramidal base in this group. The only carved stela found at Palenque was discovered on the upper part of the slope in front of the temple. This eroded, rather three-dimensional monument depicts a figure standing on a large hieroglyph.

The base of the Temple of the Cross has been partly restored, though most of the front of the temple itself has collapsed. The carved panel that originally graced the rear wall and gave the temple its name is now in the Mexico City Museum, though two carved slabs flanking the door of the shrine are in place.

From here you get excellent views of the rest of the site and an especially nice one of the Temple of the Sun. Try for morning hours for front-lighted shots of that structure.

Front (east side) of Temple XIV, Palenque. Late Classic period.

Front (south side) of the Temple of the Cross, Palenque. Late Classic period.

Front (west side) of the Temple of the Foliated Cross, Palenque. Late Classic period.

Behind (north of) the Temple of the Cross, a few remains of Structure XVI can be seen.

The Temple of the Foliated Cross has also lost its front facade, but its carved panel is still in place, and it, too, is a beauty. This temple and its base are unrestored.

From the plaza of the Cross Group, two trails lead to other structures on a higher level. One trail starts from near (southwest of) the front of the Temple of the Foliated Cross. The other begins south of the Temple of the Sun along the entrance trail to the Cross Group. From the Temple of the Sun you come first to Structure XXI. The base of this building is made of large, quadrangular, finely cut stones laid in a stepped pattern. Little remains of the structure on top. To the south you come to Structure XX, with stairs on the north and east sides and some remains of walls on top. From there, head southeast to Structure XIX. See "Recent History" for details of important recent discoveries in this area. From there, the trail curves around and heads northeast, passing the fronts of Struc-tures XVIII A and XVIII, twin buildings that face west.

When Structure XVIII was first explored, an inscription made of stucco glyphs was discovered on the back wall of the temple on top and in the debris in front of it. Later, more glyphs were found fallen in the debris. This panel of 80 glyphs has been installed in the Palenque Museum. The temple rises above a stepped base that has been partly restored, and inside the temple, on a step that enters the back sanctuary, painted stucco designs can be seen. From Structure XVIII the trail continues northeast to the front of the Temple of the Foliated Cross.

You now exit the Cross Group the way you entered and take a branch trail north along the east side of the Palace to the ball court. The court is cleared and has been partly restored. When looking down its playing alley, you get a view of the North Group. Five temples there share a common base that has an east-west axis. On the east (right) end, only the foundation of Temple I remains.

Fronts (south sides) of Temples IV, III, and II (from left to right) of the North Group, Palenque. Late Classic period.

A frontal representation of God K, Palenque. Late Classic period. Found at the right (east) side of the stairway to Temple II, at ground level.

Following that (toward the west) are Temples II, III, IV, and V.

A broad stairway leads up to Temple II, and to its right, at ground level, an interesting bas-relief stucco carving is protected by a thatch shelter. It depicts God K, who is often depicted at Palenque, but in this instance he is shown in a rare frontal view. Temples II and III are mostly intact, whereas parts of Temples IV and V have fallen. Stairways also approach these last two structures.

At the west end of this group and on a separate pyramidal base is the Temple of the Count. It has a broad stair on the east side, bordered by *alfardas*. It got its name from Count Jean Frédéric Waldeck, who reportedly lived there while studying Palenque in 1832. The temple is intact except for the upper part of its roof comb.

Structure X lies southwest of the Temple of the Count. Its southern stairway, made of large blocks, and the lower parts of piers of the south wall are all that remain today.

South of Structure X is the incredible complex of structures that form the Palace, which you have been circling around on

The Palace, view from the southeast, Palenque. Late Classic period.

other parts of the tour as given here. The Palace is a large complex of buildings rising on an artificial platform 300 feet (91.4 meters) long by 240 feet (73.2 meters) wide; it rises to a height of 30 feet (9.1 meters).

The Palace grew over time during the Classic period, and most of the construction seen today dates to the Late Classic, as do most of the other buildings at the site. A great deal of time could and should be devoted to the Palace, the best access to which is up the north or west side. If you climb the north stairway, look to the right partway up for a view of an exceptionally sensitive face in frontal view, probably a depiction of the sun god.

Something of interest can be found in all areas of the Palace. Stucco figures decorate the piers of most of the structures, and stucco decorations are found inside many of the rooms. Be sure to check the piers. Subterranean passages at the south end of the Palace are remains of the earliest construction, dating to late in the Early Classic period. Some of the individual structures have rem-

nants of decorations on the mansard roofs, and some buildings have remains of decorated roof combs. Far too many interesting spots are found in the Palace to be mentioned here, but the following highlights should not be missed.

On the east side of the East Court, large stone bas-relief figures flank a stairway. Opposite this, on the west stairway, a hieroglyphic inscription is carved on the treads and risers. The text records the birth and accession of Pacal, among other things. The *alfardas* flanking the stairway are carved with figures, and smaller figures are found in the wall of the platform that supports a building. In between these smaller figures are six panels, each carved with four glyphs. Decorations are also found at the base of the West Court, including panels of glyphs.

South of the West Court you will see Palenque's unique four-story tower--which visitors are no longer allowed to climb. To the east of the tower is Building (or House) E, a late Early Classic period construction and the only one at Palenque that never had

Glyph-carved steps on the west side of the East Court of the Palace, Palenque. Late Classic period.

a roof comb, according to Merle Greene Robertson in *The Sculpture of Palenque.* What it does have are remnants of painted wall decorations. On the exterior west facade, painted floral and quatrefoil motifs remain.

Recent History

Palenque was known in limited circles from the middle of the eighteenth century, and since the nineteenth century it has been one of the most visited and reported upon sites in all of Mayadom.

The relatives of Antonio de Solís, curate of the nearby town of Tumbala, explored the area in the mid-eighteenth century and reported their findings to the padre, who died before being able to visit the site himself. The stories, nevertheless, were repeated to the families involved. Some years later a boy told the story to Ramón Ordóñez, a friend who

later became a priest. When Ordóñez was working at his clerical duties in Ciudad Real (now San Cristóbal de las Casas) in 1773, he sent his brother to investigate the site. Ordóñez wrote a *memoria* about Palenque from the information his brother provided and sent a copy to Josef Estachería, president of the Royal Audiencia of Guatemala. (Both Ciudad Real and Palenque were part of Guatemala at that time.) Some years later, Estachería commissioned José Calderón to investigate.

Calderón, mayor of the town of Santo Domingo de Palenque—the town nearest to the ruins—reported to Estachería. Estachería wanted more information, and in 1785 he commissioned Antonio Bernasconi, the royal architect of Guatemala City, to investigate further.

Still dissatisfied, Estachería sent the two reports to Spain, where a royal historiographer,

Juan Bautista Muñoz, read them. He, too, wanted more information, so in 1786 Estachería commissioned new investigations. This time he sent Antonio del Río, a captain in the Spanish army, accompanied by Ricardo Almendáriz, an artist.

Del Río enlisted the help of Calderón, who provided laborers from the area, and the structures were cleared to some extent. Almendáriz drew some of the decorative panels, although his depictions of the glyphs seem crude today. Neither he nor del Río had much idea of what they were looking at, but del Río perhaps suspected that the glyphs were a form of writing. He took measurements, made some excavations, and removed parts of some bas-reliefs to be sent to Muñoz, who had given him a list of questions to be answered and a request for artifacts. Del Río returned to Guatemala and gave his report to Estachería in 1786 (some authorities say 1787). Estachería had a copy of the report made for his files, forwarding another copy, plus the drawings and artifacts, to Spain.

Somehow, a copy of this report was brought to England by a certain Dr. McQuy, who sold it to the London bookseller Henry Berthoud. Berthoud had the report translated and published in 1822, some 36 years after del Río had presented it to Estachería. It was the first detailed report on Palenque to reach print, although a short description of the ruins appeared in the book *History of Guatemala,* by Domingo Juarros, published in that country in 1808. In the interval between the issuance and publication of del Río's report, however, others visited Palenque.

In 1804, Charles IV of Spain ordered investigations of the aboriginal remains in New Spain, and Guillermo Dupaix—a retired captain of the dragoons—was selected to investigate. He had lived in Mexico for 20 years and had developed an intense interest in pre-Hispanic culture, studying it extensively. This and his above-average education made him well suited for the appointment. Dupaix investigated Palenque in 1807 and had with him the artist José Luis Castañeda. His report, like del Río's, was published only many years later. In this case, it was partially reproduced in England by Lord Kingsborough in 1831 and completely reproduced in Paris in 1834.

An account of Palenque by Juan Galindo—governor of the Petén in Guatemala—who had made a short visit to the site in 1831, was published later that year in England.

The colorful Count Waldeck became intrigued with pre-Hispanic remains when, as a freelance engraver, he prepared the drawings of the del Río expedition for the 1822 publication of that work. Ten years later he arrived at the site and remained for a little over a year. He explored the ruins and made numerous drawings of buildings and the living people of the area, which were published in Paris in 1866.

In 1840, two important pairs of visitors reached Palenque. The first to arrive were Patrick Walker, a politician from Belize, and his draftsman, John Herbert Caddy. Their expedition was conducted because of the jealousy aroused in Belize when it was learned that the Americans John Lloyd Stephens and Frederick Catherwood planned a trip to see the site. Stephens and Catherwood arrived at Palenque some four months after Walker and Caddy, but the publication in 1841 of their *Incidents of Travel in Central America, Chiapas, and Yucatán* overshadowed the work of their Belizean rivals.

The Frenchman Arthur Morelet visited Palenque in 1846 and 1871, and an English translation of his work was published in New York. Another Frenchman, Désiré Charnay, visited Palenque in 1858 and again some years later. He published his work in Paris in 1863 and 1885.

Some of the finest work published on Palenque, and still a standard reference, is that by the Englishman Alfred P. Maudslay. Maudslay was not only an explorer but also a superb photographer and a precise draftsman. He kept meticulous records, which made him well suited to his self-assigned tasks of writing about and illustrating the ruins he visited. The photographs and drawings provided in his monumental *Biologia Centrali Americana* (1889–1902) remain unsurpassed. In 1974 this five-volume set was reissued in facsimile form.

Other expeditions for various sponsors were undertaken during the following years. Of importance were those by Edward H. Thompson, who brought along the artist William Holmes, followed by those of Marshall Saville and Teobert Maler. Eduard Seler, Sylvanus G. Morley, Alfred Tozzer, and Herbert Spinden visited Palenque in the early twentieth century.

In 1923, the Mexican government sent Frans Blom to Palenque "to determine what could be done for the preservation of the ruined buildings." Blom collected new data and mapped the outlying groups of the site. While inspecting the Temple of the Inscriptions, he noticed holes in the floor slabs and commented, "I cannot imagine what these holes were intended for." It was these holes, noticed by Ruz Lhuillier 26 years later, that led to the discovery of the tomb below the temple. One wonders whether Blom would have investigated further had he the means to do so.

Other work carried out at Palenque was undertaken by Miguel Ángel Fernández and Ruz Lhuillier for INAH, and excavation and restoration continued into the 1970s.

Thanks to the efforts of a number of scholars, we now know a good deal about the rulers of Palenque—when they were born and acceded to the throne, and when they died. Prominent among those working on the early decipherment of Palenque's hieroglyphic texts, which provided this information, were Floyd G. Lounsbury, Linda Schele, and Peter Mathews. More recently, others have followed in their wake.

Since the 1960s, the indefatigable Merle Greene Robertson has studied and recorded Maya art, particularly that of Palenque. She has produced rubbings, drawings, photographs, and paintings of Palenque's stone and stucco carvings. A culmination of this work was published between 1983 and 1991 in four large volumes under the title *The Sculpture of Palenque*. This monumental work covers the sculpture in minute detail.

In the 1990s, the Group of the Cross Project began. This joint venture of INAH and the Pre-Columbian Art Research Institute is directed by Greene Robertson with Alfonso Morales as principal investigator. It is integrated into the Palenque Project, which functioned as the Special Palenque Project for a season, directed by the archaeologist Arnoldo González Cruz. The multidisciplinary project is staffed by an international group of archaeologists and other specialists. Many exciting discoveries have been made.

During the 1997–98 field season, a number of *incensarios* were discovered on the west and north sides of the base of the Temple of the Cross. The restoration of these vessels has been undertaken under the auspices of the Group of the Cross Project. Also under the project's auspices is the re-mapping of the entire site.

Other discoveries in 1998 and 1999 included a carved stucco panel in Structure XIX. It depicts a standing figure and originally was attached to a pier. Fragmented but restorable glyph blocks were also recovered. Later, archaeologists found a limestone throne with three seated figures portrayed on it, accompanied by a panel of 32 glyphs. On the right side of the throne was found another panel of more than 60 glyphs. This important find is "perhaps the most important Maya tablet to come along in years, probably decades," according to David Stuart, the project epigrapher.

The nearby Structure XX was also studied, and a spectacular tomb was found. Its walls are covered with murals, the first found in a chamber in Palenque. Eleven intact vessels and a multitude of jade were discovered inside.

Connections

1. Palenque (town) to Palenque (ruins): 5.0 miles [8.0 kilometers] by paved road (:10).

2. Villahermosa to Palenque (town): 87.2 miles [140.3 kilometers] by paved road (1:41).

3. San Cristóbal de las Casas to Palenque (town): 131.1 miles [211.0 kilometers] by paved road (4:01).

Getting There

1. From the Maya head at the entrance to Palenque (town), follow the road west to the site.

2. From Villahermosa, head east on Highway 186 to Highway 199, the cutoff for Palenque (marked with a sign), 70.3 miles [113.1 kilometers]. Turn right (south) onto Highway 199, proceed to Palenque (town), and follow the directions already given to the ruins.

3. From San Cristóbal de las Casas, head southeast on Highway 190 for 6.8 miles [10.9 kilometers] to Highway 199, the cutoff for Palenque (marked with a sign). Turn left (northeast) onto Highway 199, proceed to Palenque (town), and follow the directions already given.

Mini-buses make the trip from Palenque town to the ruins frequently during the day. In addition to the road connections, Palenque can be reached by scheduled regional airlines from several cities in Mexico, although not all flights are direct.

Palenque is open daily from 8:00 A.M. to 6:00 P.M. There are rest rooms, food, and drink at the entrance to the site, but carry a canteen or bottle of water when you tour the ruins. Since you should allow at least two full days to see the site, the nearby town is clearly the best place to stay.

★ ★ ★
MUSEUM OF THE ARCHAEOLOGICAL ZONE OF PALENQUE (PALENQUE MUSEUM)

The Palenque Museum, inaugurated in May 1993, is a tremendous improvement over the old site museum. It is really worth three and a half stars. At its entrance stands the only known carved stela from Palenque. It is unusual in that it represents a three-dimensional standing figure wearing an elaborate headdress.

Inside the museum is a wealth of material, well presented. The collection includes beautifully carved panels from various parts of Palenque, jade jewelry, and fine ceramic vessels. Most of the items date to the Late Classic period and were produced at Palenque, though some objects manufactured on the Gulf Coast but found at Palenque (*hachas* and a plain yoke) are also displayed.

Some of the outstanding exhibits include 80 stucco glyphs in mint condition that were originally found in the debris of Structure XVIII. Most of the individual glyphs are understood, but their proper order is unknown, so the full inscription cannot be read as yet. Unlike most other glyphs at Palenque, these were individually formed, then placed on a background.

A number of exquisite *incensarios,* in excellent condition, retain some of their original paint; red and blue seem to predominate. The so-called Tablet of the Orator and the Tablet of the Scribe are exhibited on either side of a reconstructed stairway. The quality of the carving on the tablets is superb, as is the carving on the Tablet of 96 Hieroglyphs.

In addition to the outstanding artifacts, a fine scale model of the Palace is displayed, along with maps, charts, and photographs. In all, the exhibits are truly educational as well as aesthetically pleasing.

A new addition to the collection is the exquisite, 12-foot-tall stucco panel found in Structure XIX. It had fallen and was found in many fragments, but after excavation it was restored and installed on the second floor of the museum. It portrays K'inich Ahkal Mo' Nahb' III, a Late Classic ruler of Palenque, as a richly dressed standing figure. He is accompanied by a panel of glyphs, and the monument retains a good deal of its original color. The restoration is beautifully done.

Nearby, and also a new addition, is a limestone bas-relief panel, about 11 feet tall.

NO TOCAR
NO FLASH

Eighty stucco glyphs from Structure XVIII, Palenque. Late Classic period. On display in the Palenque Museum.

It depicts the same ruler and was also found in Structure XIX.

The Palenque Museum is along the road (right side) that goes from the town to the parking area for the site. It is part of an easily spotted complex of buildings, 1.0 mile (1.6 kilometers) before you reach the site. There is a parking area for the complex just off the road.

The museum is open Tuesday through Sunday from 10:00 A.M. to 4:45 P.M. It is closed on Monday. *Note:* Due to a shortage of guards, sometimes the second floor of the museum is not open during normal hours. I recommend asking at the ticket window whether the second floor is open when you arrive. If it is, see it first. If the second floor

is closed, ask when it will open and see the first-floor displays in the meantime.

If you visit the site first, keep your ticket and you can enter the museum free of charge if you visit on the same day. Allow 45 minutes to see the collection. Labeling is good, and some items are labeled in both Spanish and English. Lighting is also fairly good, and photography without flash is permitted. If you are carrying a large camera bag or backpack, you must check it at the entrance to the museum. There are no rest rooms, food, or drink at the museum, but these are available elsewhere in the complex, which includes a snack stand, shop, and offices.

★ ★
MUSEUM OF THE CITY
(EMILIANO ZAPATA MUSEUM)

As you enter the Emiliano Zapata Museum in this town named for the early-twentieth-century Mexican revolutionary, the archaeological collection, with both Olmec and Maya remains, is in the room on the right. The room on the left houses the historical material and Emiliano Zapata memorabilia. The archaeological collection has a case with early Olmec-style figurine heads of humans. Another case has flat and roller stamps and an attractive black bowl with red incisions.

There are photo displays, maps showing the locations of sites, worked stone (including obsidian), figures of animals, and metates. Some molds and objects made from them are

Incensario base from the Palenque region. Late Classic period. On display in the Emiliano Zapata Museum.

exhibited, as are grinding stones, bark beaters, and spindle whorls. Along one wall of the museum are copies of four bas-reliefs, two Olmec and two Maya.

The Maya section has some polychrome and plain ceramics, some small eccentric flints, and small vases. Two *incensario* bases depicting faces are in excellent condition; both retain some remains of blue, green, and white paint, and both are believed to come from the Palenque region. Some minute, beautifully incised glyphs decorate a small stone.

An inscription of six glyphs, carved in low relief and well preserved, is found on a nearly square stone panel. For a time this panel was in the museum's warehouse, but happily it is now on display. The panel is not complete; the tops of the two top glyphs are missing. What remains of the panel was studied by Nikolai Grube, who in 1994 reported a date of A.D. 641 for the panel and identified the Toniná emblem glyph in the lower right corner. That and other information led him to believe that the panel came from the vicinity of Toniná. It is unknown how the panel became part of the Emiliano Zapata Museum collection.

The museum opened in December 1982 at the junction of the *malecón* (along the Usumacinta) and Calle Méndez Magaña. You can park nearby, but no longer in front of the museum, as that area has been raised to form a pedestrian mall along the *malecón*.

The museum is open Monday through Friday from 9:00 A.M. to 2:00 P.M. and from 6:00 P.M. to 8:00 P.M. On Saturday it is open from 9:00 A.M. to 2:00 P.M. It is closed on Sunday. Allow 20 minutes to see the collection. Photography, including the use of flash, is permitted. Lighting is fair, and some written information is provided next to some of the cases, but there is little specific labeling. There are no rest rooms, food, or drink at the museum, but there are restaurants nearby.

If you are without a vehicle, you could bus to Emiliano Zapata.

★ ★
POMONÁ
(poh-moh-NAH)

Derivation:
  Maya for "House of Copal."
Culture:
  Maya.
Location:
  Southeastern Tabasco.
Maps: 6 (p. 294) and 6C (p. 314)

The Site

Pomoná, with an area of 0.68 square miles (1.75 square kilometers), is composed of six groups of structures, though only Group I has been intensively studied and consolidated. It is also the only one open to visitors. There are 13 structures in Group I, of which 12 are arranged along the north, east, and west sides of a quadrangular plaza and 1 is found in the middle of the plaza. The whole area is well cleared, and it is easy to get around this engaging site.

Visitors enter the south end of the site, defined by a low stone wall. All of the structures are visible from there. On the north is the major pyramid, Structure 1, rising in seven stepped tiers with a stairway, bordered by *alfardas,* on the south, facing the plaza. A plain circular altar is found near the base of the stairway. Structures 9 through 13 (north to south) are basically low platforms aligned along the east side of the plaza, and Structure 8 is a small rectangular platform with stairways on all four sides, in the center of the plaza.

The most interesting part of the site is the group of adjacent buildings (Structures 3 through 7, from north to south) on the west side of the plaza, especially Structure 4. When the site was first consolidated and opened to the public, two two-part *alfardas* were in place bordering the stairway to the remains of the temple on top of Structure 4. The *alfardas* were carved in delicate bas-relief, were in pristine condition, and depicted representations of the sun or sun god. They have since been removed to the Pomoná Museum for protection, and copies have been installed in the original locations.

Structures 4, 5, and 6 have the lower remains of inner walls on top, and stairways lead to the upper buildings. A nice touch are signs at Pomoná describing the structures and showing drawings of them. A site plan is included, but it has been reversed from left to right (that is, east and west are reversed).

Preliminary analysis of the ceramics collected at Pomoná indicates that the site

Structures 7 through 3 (left to right), east side, Pomoná. Late or Terminal Classic period.

Carved *alfarda* next to the stairway to Structure 4, Pomoná. Late or Terminal Classic period. This monument has been moved to the Pomoná Museum.

was occupied from the Late Preclassic period until the Terminal Classic. When some of the other groups at the site are studied, more precision in the ceramic sequence is expected.

A number of inscriptions are known from Pomoná that include dates, Pomoná's emblem glyph, and the names of three of its rulers. In A.D. 795, Piedras Negras defeated Pomoná, and the beautiful Stela 12 was erected at the conquering city. Its style is different from that of other Piedras Negras monuments but similar to that used at Pomoná. It is thought that artists from Pomoná went as tribute to the victor and were responsible for the monument.

Recent History

The site of Pomoná is shown on a map by Teobert Maler dated 1900, which appeared in a publication of the Peabody Museum in 1901. Although Maler stayed in a village called Pomoná, he did not, in the accompanying text, mention visiting the site, which lies some distance away. The site was also shown on a 1940 Tulane map under the name Pamana.

Henrich Berlin mentioned Pomoná in a 1960 publication, as did César Lizardi Ramos in 1963. Three field seasons of excavation and consolidation were undertaken by INAH in 1986–88. This work was directed by Daniel Juárez Cossío and Roberto García Moll.

Connections

1. Emiliano Zapata to Pomoná: 24.2 miles [38.8 kilometers] by paved road (:29), then 1.8 miles [2.9 kilometers] by fair dirt road (:07).

2. Palenque to Emiliano Zapata (via Highway 186): 35.0 miles [56.3 kilometers] by paved road (:46).

Getting There

1. From Emiliano Zapata, take Highway 203 southeast and then south to the cutoff for Pomoná (marked with a sign) and turn left onto the dirt road. Along this road you will come to a fork (marked with a sign). Take the right branch to the museum and site.

2. From Palenque, go north on Highway 199 to Highway 186 and turn right. Go to highway 203 and turn right again. From there proceed to Emiliano Zapata and follow the directions already given.

Going from Palenque to Pomoná via the road to Libertad is a little shorter than going via Highway 186, but the road is sometimes poor, and it will take longer.

Pomoná is open daily from 10:00 A.M. to 4:00 P.M. Allow 45 minutes for a visit. There is no food or drink at the site, nor are there rest rooms.

If you are without your own vehicle, you could probably get a tour to Pomoná from Palenque or a taxi from Emiliano Zapata (which can be reached by bus).

★ ★ ★
POMONÁ MUSEUM

The delightful Pomoná Museum is just off the left side of the dirt road to the ruins and is reached shortly before the site itself. Opened in 1991, it is one of the new breed of site museums. The collection is housed in an attractive building especially designed for it, with good natural lighting.

Some major stone bas-relief monuments are displayed. There is an intact stela on which the main figure holds a manikin scepter; a panel of glyphs accompanies the scene. Some fragmented panels also bear glyphs, some of which are well preserved. The gem of the collection is part of a panel with a seated figure and part of a second. The numerous glyphs included are in almost pristine condition. This monument, called Panel 1 of Pomoná, dates to A.D. 771, and it displays the Pomoná emblem glyph on the far right, second down from the top.

Ceramics and worked stone, including obsidian and eccentric flints, are also exhibited. Among the ceramics, one bowl is especially attractive. It is painted in black and red on a buff-colored background, and it has a row of delicately painted black glyphs on the inside, just below the rim.

Signs in the museum give general information, but the artifacts are not individually labeled. Most of the items are Late Classic Maya, and most come from Pomoná, although there is an interesting Olmec piece from Ejido Rojo Gómez, a short distance southwest of Tenosique. It is an incised carving of a head on a roughly circular stone. What appears to be a rather recent Lacandón god pot is also displayed.

The Pomoná Museum is open daily from 10:00 A.M. to 5:00 P.M. Allow 40 minutes to view this interesting collection. Photography without flash is permitted. There is no food or drink at the museum, but there are rest rooms in a nearby building.

Panel 1 from Pomoná, A.D. 771. On display in the Pomoná Museum.

★ ★
DR. JOSÉ GÓMEZ PANACO MUSEUM
(BALANCÁN MUSEUM)
(bah-lahn-KAHN)

The Balancán Museum is a very good two-star enterprise. It is housed in a corner building facing the plaza in the town of Balancán. There are two floors in the museum; on the first floor are displayed some interesting though rather eroded stelae fragments. They came from Santa Elena, a site on the San Pedro Mártir River in eastern Tabasco, and were brought to the museum in 1985–86. Most of the fragments are entirely glyphic. A couple of fragments of circular altars, also bearing glyphs, can be seen nearby.

Also on view are the torso and legs of a kneeling stone figure with a tenon below. The prize of the collection is a Late Classic stela from the site of La Reforma (Morales), also in eastern Tabasco. Though fragmented, it has been repaired. On one side, a standing figure carrying a kind of staff dominates the scene; he grasps the hair of a kneeling captive, and behind him another kneeling captive can be seen. Two panels of glyphs accompany the scene, and the sides and back of the stela are all glyphic. A skylight has been placed above the stela, so it is easy to discern the design.

The second floor of the museum contains some Olmec remains, among them a nice celt. Other displays include a panel of Maya glyphs, a plain yoke, manos and metates, figurine heads, and other ceramics. There is little labeling upstairs and only a bit more downstairs.

The Balancán Museum is open daily from 9:00 A.M. to 8:00 P.M. Allow 30 minutes for a visit. Lighting is fairly good, and photography without flash is permitted. There are rest rooms at the museum but no food or drink. Restaurants can be found in town; try the Monte Carlo for a good shrimp cocktail. It is a few blocks from the museum, where you can get directions.

Stela from La Reforma (Morales) in eastern Tabasco. Late Classic period. On display in the Balancán Museum.

SECTION 7

• • • •
CHIAPAS

Fragment of Stela 7 at Yaxchilán. Late Classic period.

GENERAL INFORMATION FOR SECTION 7, CHIAPAS

Chiapas is Mexico's southernmost state and certainly one of its most varied. It has a narrow coastal plain (called the Soconusco) on the Pacific that is hot and humid. Northeast of that is the Sierra Madre of Chiapas, which reaches elevations of 8,045 feet (2,500 meters) and higher. Beyond that is the central depression of Chiapas (which is lower), followed by the Chiapas highlands, which reach as high as 9,654 feet (3,000 meters). In the highlands the temperature is cool to chilly (for instance, at San Cristóbal de las Casas). From the Chiapas highlands the mountains descend to foothills as they approach the northern part of Chiapas and the flat plains of Tabasco on the Gulf of Mexico.

The best stopovers in Chiapas are Palenque (also covered in Section 6), San Cristóbal de las Casas, Tuxtla Gutiérrez, and Tapachula. All four places offer hotels in various price ranges, travel agencies, and car rentals.

In addition, if you plan to visit Toniná, then Ocosingo is a possible stopover. The best bets there are the Hotel La Margarita, around the corner from the plaza (east side), and the Hotel Central, facing the north side of the plaza. The upstairs Restaurant Puebre's, connected with the former, serves good food, including an appetizer of Ocosingo's famous cheese. Both hotels are modest.

Comitán is a good stopover if you are going to Chinkultic. Try the rather nice Hotel Lagos de Montebello on Highway 190 on the north end of town (east side of the highway).

The points of reference for Section 7 are the following: (1) in Palenque, the *glorieta* with the large Maya head at the west entrance of the town, along Highway 199; (2) in Ocosingo, the junction of Highway 199 and the entrance into town that goes to the main plaza; (3) in San Cristóbal de las Casas, the junction of Highway 190 and the sign indicating the way to the Zona Centro (center of town); (4) in Tuxtla Gutiérrez, the junction of Highway 190 and the Libramiento Sur (south bypass) at the west edge of the city; (5) in Tapachula, the junction of Highway 200 and the entrance to the Hotel Loma Real on the northwest end of the city; and (6) in Comitán, the junction of Highway 190 and the westernmost sign for the Zona Centro.

Domestic airports can be found at Tuxtla Gutiérrez and Tapachula; each has connecting flights to the other and to Mexico City, and some flights connect to other points in Mexico as well. The airport at Palenque now handles some scheduled flights as well as charters, and the Ocosingo airstrip is available for charter flights.

Most of the major highways in Chiapas are fairly good, but there are fewer miles of four-lane roads than in some of the other sections. Some of the roads are mountainous, such as Highway 195, parts of Highways 199 and 190, and Highway 211. Highway 190 between San Cristóbal and Tuxtla Gutiérrez is not only mountainous but also heavily trafficked and rather poorly surfaced. Highway 211 has some rough spots on its north end, and its south end is narrow (owing to encroaching vegetation). Highway 200 is the longest stretch of four-lane highway in the state; part of it is a toll road. Drivers should be forewarned, however, that although it is mostly four lanes, there are short stretches of two lanes that you come upon without warning. Drive cautiously.

Besides the ruins and museums in Chiapas, other points of interest are the Misol Ha and Agua Azul waterfalls. Each is a short distance off Highway 199 south of Palenque. Swimming, picnicking, and camping are allowed at both places. The top of El Sumidero Canyon (a spectacular gorge through which the Grijalva River flows) can be reached by private vehicle or on tours from Tuxtla Gutiérrez, or you can get a boat tour from Chiapa de Corzo if you want to look up at the steep sides of the canyon from below.

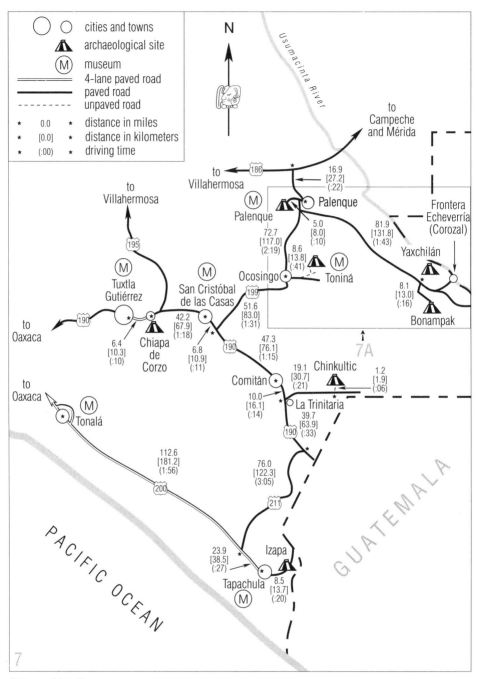

Chiapas (Map 7).

San Cristóbal de las Casas is a good place to shop. Its many shops, a daily crafts market around Santo Domingo church, and the Sna Jolobil (Tzotzil for "Weavers' House") weaving cooperative salesroom next to the church offer a wide array of handicrafts, especially textiles.

★ ★ ★ ★
YAXCHILÁN
(yash-chee-LAHN)

Derivation:
  Maya for "Green Stones," according to Teobert Maler. The site is named after a nearby arroyo.
Earlier Names:
  Usumacinta, Menché, and Menché Tinamit (used by Alfred P. Maudslay); Lorillard City (used by Désiré Charnay).
Culture:
  Maya.
Location:
  East-central Chiapas.
Maps: 7 (p. 338) and 7A (p. 340)

The Site

Although Yaxchilán is still not as easy to reach as the other four-star sites covered in this guide (or in the two previous parts of this trilogy), access has improved—and there is a great deal more to see. Hence its upgrade from three to four stars from my original 1982 book.

The site lies within a great omega-shaped bend in the Usumacinta River, along a stretch of the river where it forms the boundary between Mexico and Guatemala. Some structures range along the river bank, and others occupy an inland terrace and the hills beyond. The site is known for its exquisitely proportioned temples and magnificent carved monuments, which abound. It is perhaps one if the loveliest sites ever constructed by the ancient Mayas, and even now it has an air of romance that is unequaled.

Yaxchilán has changed dramatically over the years, and this includes the number of visitors that arrive. When we first visited the site in 1972 with Trudi (Gertrude) Duby Blom, our party of five and two boatmen was the only one there for a day and a half, except for the de la Cruz family, who lived at the site and were the caretakers. By 1981, the site was receiving 6,000 visitors a year. On our most recent trip, 200 people a day were arriving—more than a tenfold increase since 1981. But while Yaxchilán has perhaps lost a bit of its romance over the years due to this influx, the clearing of the vegetation, cleaning and reerection of the monuments, and consolidation of the structures make it even more worthwhile. A nice new feature is that the stelae and other monuments are protected mostly by translucent shelters that allow light through, so that the carvings can be better discerned and photographed.

You enter the site from the northwest on a trail that parallels the river, and you arrive first at the rear of Structure 19, the Labyrinth. On the way, you pass some stepped walls (on the right) and later some niches with benches. Then you enter Structure 19 proper from a nearby doorway. The rooms of the building are found on three levels, and there are interior stairways. You exit the structure at the front. The temple has four doorways on that side, three door-size niches in between the actual doorways, and the remains of a perforated roof comb. A couple of carved altars are found in front.

You now head southeast across the plaza, then follow a trail that climbs the terrace to Structure 30. This building has two parallel vaulted rooms and three doorways facing the plaza; a good deal of vaulting is intact. From

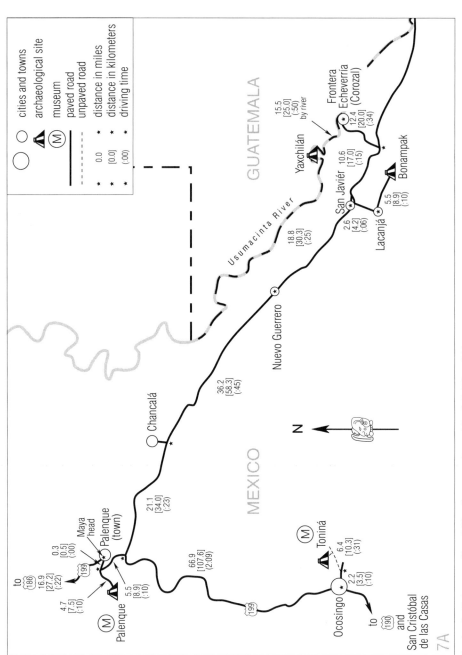

Routes to Palenque, Yaxchilán, Bonampak, and Toniná (Map 7A).

7A

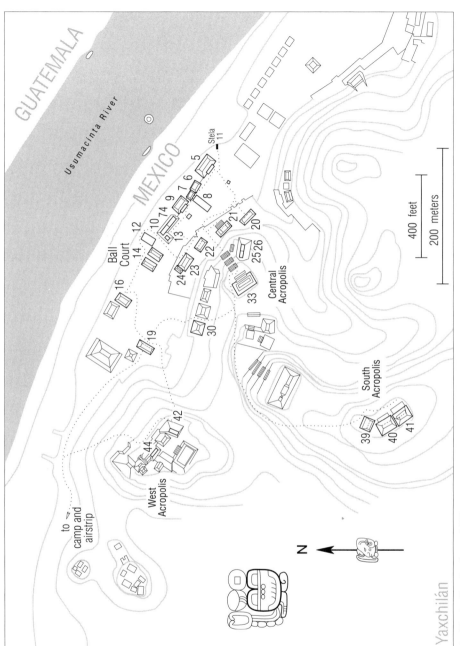

GUATEMALA

Usumacinta River

MEXICO

Stela 11

Ball
Court

West
Acropolis

to
camp and
airstrip

Central
Acropolis

South
Acropolis

N

Yaxchilán

Modified after Graham, 1977.

400 feet

200 meters

Front (east side) of Structure 19, Yaxchilán. Late Classic period.

the back of Structure 30, another trail climbs and then branches. The trail to the left goes to Structure 33, and the one to the right ascends to the South Acropolis, the highest part of Yaxchilán. The climb to the South Acropolis is rather tiring, but you are rewarded with the sight of three consolidated buildings (Structures 39, 40, and 41, from right to left) and associated carved stelae and altars. All three structures have three doorways entering a single chamber.

The doorways of Structure 39 are stepped, and its interior chamber is irregular. The building has remains of a perforated roof comb, and the upper facade (frieze) has projecting tenons that once supported long-gone stucco embellishments. Structure 40, in the middle of the group, also has remains of a roof comb and, on the inside, fragments of murals that once covered all the wall surfaces. Two carved stelae associated with the structure have been reerected—Stela 12 to the left and Stela 13 to the right as you face the building. Stela 11, which you will see later, once stood between the other two.

Structure 41 has not fared as well as the others in this group; much of its vaulting has fallen. The center doorway is stepped, the others are not, and buttresses have been placed against the front wall. A number of carved stelae were also associated with Structure 41, but they are not on view at the site today. Some eroded altars are found in and around the structures of the South Acropolis.

You now return downhill to the Central Acropolis and take the right branch trail to the rear of Structure 33, then walk around it to the front. This masterpiece in stone is truly one of the most beautiful buildings constructed by the ancient Mayas. Its lower walls are plain; above them is a sloped roof forming a frieze; and at the top is a mostly intact roof comb. Niches are found in the frieze and the roof comb, and the one in the latter houses the remains of a figure. Originally, stucco adornments covered the tenons in both areas. Three doorways enter Structure 33, and each is topped by a beautifully preserved lintel carved on the underside; these are Lintels 1, 2, and 3 (from left to right as you face the structure).

One of Yaxchilán's great rulers, Bird Jaguar IV, reigned from A.D. 752 to 772. We know more about him than any other Yaxchilán ruler, and he is depicted on all three lintels. On Lintel 1 he is accompanied by his wife, Lady Great Skull Zero; on Lintel 2, by his son and heir, Shield Jaguar II; and on

Front (northeast side) of Structure 40, Yaxchilán.

Front (northeast side) of Structure 33, Yaxchilán. Late Classic period. Note Stela 31 in right foreground.

Hieroglyphic Stairway 2, Step VIII, on Structure 33, Yaxchilán. Late Classic period.

Lintel 3, by an ally. Structure 33 was probably dedicated in 756. (Yaxchilán's monuments record dates from A.D. 454 to 808.)

There is a niche in the back wall of the structure, aligned with the center doorway; in it is found a headless statue of a human figure. The head lies nearby. The identity of the personage depicted is not certain, but it was probably Bird Jaguar IV.

In front of Structure 33, on the riser of the final step up to the doorways of the building, a row of 13 carved blocks was discovered in 1975. They form Hieroglyphic Stairway 2, Steps I through XIII (from left to right as you face the doorways). The middle three, Steps VI through VIII, are in nearly pristine condition. They portray Bird Jaguar IV and two earlier rulers dressed as ball players.

A short distance in front of the base of the platform of Structure 33 is an unusual monument, Stela 31. This is a stalactite, the bottom of which is incised with three figures and some glyphs; the monument rests in a pit. Unfortunately, no date survives on Stela 31, nor are the identities of the figures known.

From the front of Structure 33, a wide stairway once led down to plaza level, and today a rocky trail follows that path. The lower part of the stairway has been consoli-dated. In the eighth century, when Structure 33 was constructed, visitors approaching Yaxchilán by river would have had a view of the grand stairway crowned by the sublime structure at the top. What a majestic sight it must have been.

As you descend the stairway, you will pass Structures 25 and 26 (on the right). Structure 25 is closer to the stair and is better preserved than the adjacent Structure 26. No inscriptions are known from either structure, and neither has been excavated or consolidated. Both have stepped doorways, and Structure 25 has some intact vaults.

Still farther downhill you reach a terrace that supports Structure 21 (on the right). Lintels 15, 16, and 17 once spanned the three central doorways of the structure, but they were removed to the British Museum in 1882 and 1883. Those monuments are in pristine condition and have been widely published. The structure was excavated only in 1983, and two more major monuments were encountered. One is Stela 35, small but beautifully preserved, depicting Lady Eveningstar (Lady Ik Skull), Bird Jaguar IV's mother. The other consists of the considerable remains of life-size figures in stucco relief on the interior rear wall, behind the stela.

The vaults of Structure 21 had collapsed before 1882, filling the chambers with debris, and although the building has been excavated and consolidated, the roof has not been replaced. This is fortunate for photographers, because strongly directional light enters from the top, illuminating the stela and relief to best advantage.

On the lowest terrace, and in line with the grand stairway of Structure 33, you will find the reerected Stela 2, dating to A.D. 613. You now descend to the plaza level and walk to the southeast for a look at more carved monuments, arrayed in front of the terraces that support Structure 20. Stelae 7, 6, and 5 have all been reerected here. Though fragmented, Stela 7 has been reassembled, and the quality of the carving that remains is superb. The face of the kneeling figure (on the left as you face the monument) is sensitively portrayed. Stela 6 is mostly intact and depicts an early Late Classic ruler, Bird Jaguar III. Shield Jaguar II is the protagonist of the Late Classic Stela 5, only the upper part of which is displayed.

Now climb the terraces for a look at Structure 20, a three-room building in which carved Lintels 12, 13, and 14 originally topped the doorways (from left to right as you face the structure). Lintel 12 was taken to the Mexico City Museum after that part of the structure had already collapsed. Lintel 13 had fallen from its original position but was replaced when the building was consolidated, and Lintel 14 remains in place in the better-preserved part of the building. Both Lintels 13 and 14 are beautifully preserved. On the remaining frieze above the right doorway is a niche, and another is found on the side of the frieze. A small part of the roof comb remains. When Structure 20 was excavated, a step of many carved blocks was found in front. This was recorded and published by Ian Graham in 1982 and then re-covered for protection.

In the center of the plaza faced by Structure 20, Stela 3 (most of its fragments reassembled and reerected) rests on a platform. The carving on one side is well preserved. When the platform on which it stands was excavated, fragments of a previously unknown stela were uncovered. This has

Stela 35, depicting Lady Eveningstar, inside Structure 21, Yaxchilán. Late Classic period.

been designated Stela 33, and it rests on the ground near the platform.

To the northeast, near the riverbank and under a shelter, lies the beautiful Stela 11, originally found standing in front of Structure 40. In 1964, the stela was removed from its place, lowered to the river, and sent upstream to the lumber camp at Agua Azul. The intention was to fly it to Mexico City to be included in the displays at the then new Mexico City Museum. Other Yaxchilán monuments were moved there, but Stela 11 proved to be too heavy to fly out. Through the efforts

Front (northwest side) of Structure 20, Yaxchilán. Late Classic period.

of Gertrude Duby Blom, the monument was returned to Yaxchilán in 1965.

The side of the stela facing up portrays Bird Jaguar IV and his deceased father, Shield Jaguar I. The figures themselves and a large panel of glyphs at the base are beautifully preserved. Several dates are found on Stela 11, the earliest being A.D. 741. The top corner of the stela is broken off and is propped up beside the larger section. The side of the top showing two seated figures is actually part of the underside of the main section. The edges of the stela are carved with glyphs.

Head back to the plaza now and go a short distance to the northwest (right) to Hieroglyphic Stairway 1, which gives access to Structure 5. It is composed of six long steps that are carved on the risers; each step has numerous individual carved blocks. Unfortunately, many of the blocks are badly eroded and all are covered with moss.

Again to the northwest, you come to Structures 6 and 7. Structure 6 is well preserved and once had three doorways facing the plaza and another three that faced the river. The plaza doorways were blocked up in ancient times, and new entrances were cut into the side walls of the building. On the right side of the facade that faces the plaza, a large relief panel on the frieze depicts a head. Additional decorations are found on the other sides of the frieze as well. A double-wall perforated roof comb crowns the structure, which is believed to date to the Early Classic period. Structure 7 has lost most of its vaulting, but it, too, has doorways facing the plaza as well as the river.

Structure 8, a mound oriented perpendicular to the buildings just described, lies in front of Structure 7. It effectively divides the main plaza into two sections.

Structure 9 lies next to Structure 7, but it is simply a mound today. Stela 27, however, reerected in front of it, is worth a look. It dates to A.D. 514 and portrays an early ruler of Yaxchilán. Stela 1 is found on a platform behind you when you are looking at Stela 27. This impressive monument is carved on all four sides, and one of the broad sides is well preserved.

Continuing northwest, you reach a group of buildings resting on an L-shaped platform (Structures 13, 10, and 74, from left to right). Lintel 50 is found in the left-most doorway of Structure 13. Lintels 29, 30, and 31 of Structure 10 (from left to right) are all glyphic and form a continuous statement in which the birth and accession of Bird Jaguar IV are recorded.

Across the plaza from Structure 13 you will see Structures 22, 23, and 24 (from left to right), which rest on a terrace. All three buildings have some carved lintels in place, and all are worth a look. Afterward, recross the plaza and head toward the river, passing along the back of the terrace supporting Structure 13. This will get you to the small Structure 12.

Eight carved lintels are now known from this building, including Lintel 60, found in 1984 when the building was excavated and consolidated. Lintel 60 and some others are in their original positions. These interesting Early Classic monuments record nine generations of rulers, followed by the accession date and parentage statement of Ruler 10. It may be that Bird Jaguar IV (Ruler 16) had Structure 12 built specifically to house the ancient lintels that spoke of his ancestors.

Yaxchilán's ball court, Structure 14, lies just to the west of Structure 12. Five carved markers, three of them aligned on the playing alley and one each on the adjacent platforms, were found there. One has been removed and the others are mostly fragmented and eroded.

Structure 16 lies northwest of the ball court, and three of its carvings (Lintels 38, 39, and 40) have been restored to their original positions. These lintels are carved on their edges rather than on the undersides.

From there, return to Structure 19 and take the trail uphill to the southwest. This brings you to the West Acropolis, where Structures 42 and 44 can be seen. At least one carved lintel is in place in each structure. In addition, Structure 44 has carved steps, and stelae were originally associated with the building.

Recent History

In 1696, a Spanish expedition under Jacobo de Alçayaga discovered the remains of an unnamed city on the Usumacinta River. At one time it was thought to have been Yaxchilán; however, most modern scholars do not believe so.

Juan Galindo, a military man and governor of the Petén, prepared a paper describing the Usumacinta, and the Royal Geographical Society of London published it in 1833. In the paper he mentioned that "within an extensive cave on the left bank, are some extraordinary and magnificent ruins." It is thought that Galindo was reporting on a sighting by another person, and according to Ian Graham, because "this section of Galindo's report seems not to have been based on his own observations, one may perhaps speculate that the word *curva* (curve), in notes written by an informant, was misread by him as *cueva* (cave)." It is possible that Galindo was reporting Yaxchilán.

From the early nineteenth century onward, the existence of Yaxchilán was a rumor among settlers in the area. It was only in 1881, however, that Edwin Rockstroh, of the National College of Guatemala, visited the ruins and wrote a description of them. From Rockstroh, the Englishman Alfred P. Maudslay learned of the site, which he investigated scientifically the following year.

Oddly enough, Maudslay was one of two explorers who, it happened, visited the site at exactly the same time in 1882. The Frenchman Désiré Charnay arrived—to his dismay—shortly after the Englishman, but Maudslay graciously shared with Charnay the honor of exploring the site. Maudslay declared himself "an amateur," not interested in publishing (as he knew Charnay planned to do). They departed the best of friends. Eventually, in 1889–1902, Maudslay published an account of this and his other travels, but that was five years after Charnay's work appeared. Maudslay did, however, read a paper in London in 1882 that included his explorations at Yaxchilán (which he called

Usumacinta at that time) and other sites. It was published by the Royal Geographical Society in 1883.

Some years later, Teobert Maler conducted a thorough exploration of Yaxchilán during one short and two long visits, and his report and photographs were published in 1903 by the Peabody Museum of Harvard University. His work is still a fine source of information about the site.

Other scholars who studied Yaxchilán and its monuments in the early twentieth century were Alfred M. Tozzer, Sylvanus G. Morley, Linton Satterthwaite, and Herbert Spinden. Somewhat later, Tatiana Proskouriakoff conducted a thorough study of monuments at Piedras Negras, Yaxchilán, and Naranjo and concluded that many of the carved figures depicted rulers rather than deities or priests, as was formerly believed.

Ian Graham, during numerous short visits to the site from 1970 onward, recorded its inscriptions, which were published by the Peabody Museum of Harvard University in *Corpus of Maya Hieroglyphic Inscriptions,* starting in 1977.

Surprisingly, although Yaxchilán has been well known in the literature for its architecture and its carved monuments—more than 120 inscriptions have been found on lintels, stelae, and other monuments—the first excavations there began only in 1973, following the inception of the Yaxchilán Project by INAH in 1972. This work continued through 1986 under the direction of Roberto García Moll. During that time, 26 buildings were excavated and consolidated, the stelae were cleaned and reerected, and the low bush was cleared in the more important areas.

In 1992, the University of Texas Press published Carolyn E. Tate's *Yaxchilan: The Design of a Maya Ceremonial Center,* which covers the site in loving detail. It is highly recommended.

Connections

1. Palenque to Yaxchilán (by air): 78.1 miles [125.7 kilometers] (:41).

2. Palenque to Yaxchilán (by road and river): 104.9 miles [168.9 kilometers] by paved road (2:32), then 15.5 miles [25.0 kilometers] by launch (about :50).

Getting There

1. From Palenque, you fly directly to the grass airstrip near Yaxchilán's ceremonial center. It is also possible to fly in from San Cristóbal de las Casas, Comitán, or Tenosique.

2. From Palenque, head west 0.3 mile [0.5 kilometer] to the cutoff (marked for Ocosingo) and turn left. This is Highway 199. Follow it for 5.5 miles [8.9 kilometers] to a cutoff for Chancalá (marked with a sign). Turn left and follow the unnumbered highway for 86.7 miles [139.5 kilometers] to the road that is the cutoff for Frontera Echeverría (Corozal). Turn left and continue to Frontera Echeverría, 12.4 miles [20.0 kilometers]. *Note:* The driving time (:34) shown for this stretch on Map 7A was recorded when this was a dirt road. Since then the road has been surfaced, so you should be able to drive it faster.

You will pass an immigration post as you enter Frontera Echeverría. Be prepared to show your passport or other documentation. A hotel can be found a little past the post. Once you arrive at Frontera Echeverría, you will have to make arrangements for a launch to take you downstream to the site.

Yaxchilán is open daily from 8:00 A.M. to 5:00 P.M. Tours to Yaxchilán and/or Bonampak can be arranged through travel agencies in Palenque, and most trips allow two hours at Yaxchilán. Now that there is more to see at the site, that is really cutting it short for all but the most casual visit. If you fly in from Palenque (or elsewhere), tell your pilot or travel agent when you make arrangements that you want more time at the site (three hours minimum). There is a small extra charge for the additional waiting time. Be prepared to leave a deposit however you make arrangements. Since there are various possibilities for tours, you may want to discuss these with your travel agent. Often, four to six people are the minimum, but arrangements are flexible.

If you fly in, pack a lunch. Soft drinks are sold near the airstrip. There is a *champa* (thatch shelter) where you can eat lunch. Overnight stays in the *champa* are possible through some tour agencies, who will also provide food and camping equipment. When you tour Yaxchilán, carry a bottle or canteen of water. There are no rest rooms as such at Yaxchilán, but we saw a building under construction that will probably house some.

Boats dock near the airstrip, so by whichever means you arrive, this is where you start your tour. From there it is a 10-minute walk to Structure 19. Guides for the site can be found near the airstrip where you register.

★ ★ ★

BONAMPAK

(boh-nahm-PAHK)

Derivation:
   An attempt by Sylvanus G. Morley to convey "Painted Walls" in Maya.
Culture:
   Maya.
Location:
   East-central Chiapas.
Maps: 7 (p. 338) and 7A (p. 340)

The Site

Bonampak is a small but charming site best known for the spectacular murals in its main structure. In addition, it has three magnificent carved stelae and four carved lintels. The architectural remains are also interesting.

You enter the site at the north end of the Main Plaza on a trail that passes between Structures 15 (on the left) and 13 (on the right). A plain stela on a platform is found atop the center of Structure 15, and a short distance south, below the top of the structure, you can see the remains of a large three-dimensional figure protected by glass.

When you leave Structure 15, go south to the center of the plaza for a look at the plain Stela 4 and the larger and superbly carved Stela 1, which stands 16.7 feet (5.1 meters) tall and is sculpted on its south face. The monument is a portrait of Bonampak's last ruler, Chaan Muan II (Sky Screech Owl), who reigned from A.D. 776 to 795. The stela (dated 780) commemorates the first period ending after his accession. The stela was found fallen and fragmented but was repaired and reerected. On it, Chaan Muan II stands in a warriorlike pose, holding a spear and a shield. Below him is a panel depicting a Witz monster with a cleft at the top of its head. The head of the maize god faces upward in the cleft.

From Stela 1, you have a comprehensive view of the Acropolis to the south. As you climb the first level of its stairway, you come to Stela 2 on the left and Stela 3 on the right. Both monuments feature Chaan Muan II as the principal figure. Stela 2 records his accession in A.D. 776. He is shown with two women who are believed to be his mother and his wife. His mother (on the right) faces him, and his wife, Lady Rabbit (to the left), stands behind him. Both women were of the nobility of Yaxchilán. On Stela 3 (A.D. 785), the king is shown in elaborate attire with a captive kneeling at his feet.

Higher up the stairway, and resting on the next level, are three buildings, Structures 1, 2, and 3 from right to left. Structure 1, with three rooms, is the largest at Bonampak, and it is there that the murals are found. Structure 2 consists of the remains only of its lowest section, and it probably never supported a vaulted building. Structure 3 has three doorways.

The three rooms of Structure 1 are numbered from left to right (east to west), and each has a carved lintel spanning its doorway; the lintels are numbered the same way. This is the only multiroom building at Bonampak. A

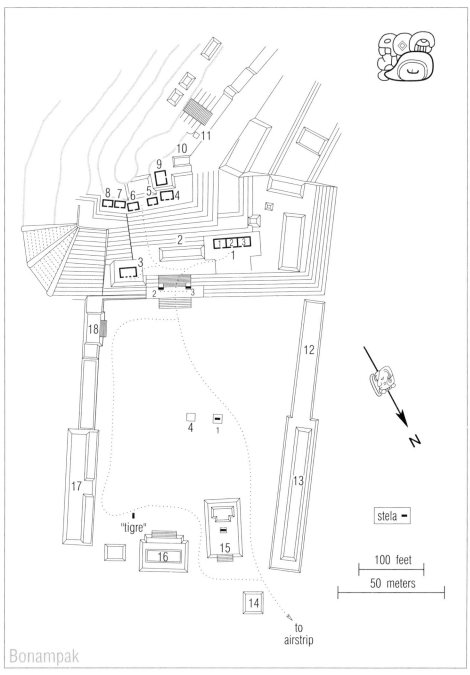

Bonampak

Modified after Ruppert, Thompson, and Proskouriakoff, 1955.

Overall view of the Acropolis, Bonampak. Structure 1, containing the murals, is on the right. Late Classic period.

large U-shaped bench takes up most of the floor space in each chamber, and there are no connections from one room to another. The entire expanse of the walls and vaults in all of the rooms is covered with paintings.

The scenes in Room 1 depict the presentation of Chaan Muan II's son and heir (whose mother's brother was Shield Jaguar II of Yaxchilán). The heir never acceded to the throne of Bonampak; the site was abandoned shortly after the murals (never quite finished) were painted. Near the figure of the son stands a row of richly garbed, wealthy nobles. Blue rectangles above the figures should have recorded their names, but the glyphs were never painted in. A ceremony with musicians and elaborately attired dancers makes up the lower section. The musicians are followed by figures in strange costumes.

In Room 2 are shown the scenes of a ferocious battle in which Chaan Muan II captures a prisoner for sacrifice. On the north wall, above the doorway, a row of tortured captives is seated. They are probably soon to be sacrificed.

On one of the end walls in Room 3, a group of noble ladies practices a blood sacrifice by piercing their tongues. A basket containing paper awaits the blood that will fall; the

Stela 2, Bonampak. A.D. 776.

Lintel of Room 1, Structure 1, Bonampak. Late Classic period.

paper will then be burned as an offering to the gods. Dancers in fantastic array accompany the scene.

When the murals were discovered, they were coated with a thick layer of calcium carbonate that had developed over many centuries by infiltration of rainwater, which leached the mineral out of the limestone building and deposited it on the walls. This somewhat obscured the murals, but it also formed a protective coating. The murals were cleaned of this deposit in the 1980s.

The three lintels of Structure 1 depict scenes of capture. On Lintel 1, Chaan Muan II is shown taking a captive in A.D. 787. On Lintel 2 (787), Shield Jaguar II is the captor, and on Lintel 3 (743), Knotted-eye Jaguar II, the father of Bonampak's last ruler, is the protagonist.

Chaan Muan II was Bonampak's ruler when Structure 1 and its murals were produced. The heir of Room 1 was presented in A.D. 790, the building was dedicated the following year, and in 792, the rites for Chaan Muan II's heir were ended.

There were many connections between Yaxchilán and Bonampak in addition to intermarriage. Sometimes the two cities were allies, sometimes enemies. Nobles from each place made reciprocal visits to the other. Early texts at Yaxchilán show that Bonampak was an important center in Early Classic times. Bonampak also had connections with the nearby Lacanhá, 6.3 miles [10.1 kilometers] away, whose people became vassals when Lacanhá was defeated by Bonampak and Yaxchilán.

The exterior of Structure 1 has niches in the upper facade above each doorway that hold remains of seated stucco figures. Between the center and west niches, a large striding stucco figure is found; he wears a decorated belt and there are some stucco decorations in front of him. On the west end of the building, another niche with a figure is encountered,

Lintel of Structure 6, Bonampak. Beginning of the Late Classic period.

with the remains of a stucco mask below. Some remnants of red and yellow paint are found on the lower section of the structure, on the west jamb of the east doorway and on the front wall.

Structure 3 is well proportioned with a two-part medial molding, the bottom part of which is beveled. Two rectangular columns form the three doorways to the single chamber. The structure rests atop a stepped base with a stairway on the north side. A plain stela is placed just to the west of the building. From the west side of Structure 3, a stairway leads to the upper levels of the Acropolis.

Structures 4 through 8, from right to left (west to east), form an irregular row on one level. The structures face north, and the vault of each is intact. Each has a single doorway except for Structure 4, which has two, formed by a column in the center. When first recorded, Structure 4 had a roof comb, but it mostly collapsed shortly thereafter. It is theorized that other buildings at the site may have had roof combs as well.

The most interesting building in this group is Structure 6, in the center of the row. Its doorway is spanned by the carved Lintel 4, picturing the bust of Chaan Muan I; it

dates to around A.D. 603. The ruler—for whom Chaan Muan II was probably named—is holding a ceremonial bar, and the carving is in excellent condition. Three short panels of glyphs accompany the scene.

Behind (south of) Structure 4 and on a higher level rests Structure 9, with a west-facing doorway and stair. A good part of its vault has fallen. You now return to the Main Plaza.

The structures on the east and west sides of the plaza are mostly low platforms with some stairways facing the plaza. A plain stela is found on the east side.

When we first visited Bonampak in 1972, two other carved monuments were on display. They were Sculptured Stones 1 and 2; they were found at the bases of Stelae 2 and 3, respectively. They were removed sometime later, and when I asked about them at the site in 1978, I was told that they were in storage. In 1997 they still were not on display. Tatiana Proskouriakoff believed that both stones were originally wall panels before being placed near the stelae.

Sculptured Stone 1, should you be fortunate enough to see it, has an incised design rather than being carved in low relief. It portrays a new ruler seated on a throne; he is being presented with a jester god headband by one of three dignitaries seated on a lower level. The carving is truly superb, with fluid lines that could have come only from the hand of a master artist. Proskouriakoff dated the carving stylistically to A.D. 692. The monument is in excellent condition except for a missing upper right corner.

Sculptured Stone 2 (A.D. 613 stylistically) is a very different monument. A figure is seated cross-legged in frontal view inside a moon glyph. It and the accompanying glyphs are moderately eroded.

Recent History

In February 1946, Charles Frey (actually Herman Karl Frey, also known as Carl Frey or Carlos Frey), an expatriate American who was living in Chiapas, and John Bourne, the 19-year-old heir to the Singer sewing machine fortune, who had an interest in archaeology, were taken to Bonampak by some Lacandón Indians, but they did not see Structure 1 or the murals.

In May of the same year, Giles G. Healey—a photographer-archaeologist working on a documentary film about the Lacandones, commissioned by the United Fruit Company—was also taken to the site by the Indians. While there, he saw and photographed the murals. Healey reported the find to Alfonso Caso of the National Museum in Mexico City and Alfred V. Kidder of the Carnegie Institution of Washington (CIW). Kidder sent Antonio Tejeda Fonseca, a CIW artist, to Bonampak with Healey to record the murals in the summer of 1946. The following year Tejeda was assisted in the copying work by Agustín Villagra Caleti, an artist working for INAH.

It seems to be uncertain whether the murals were painted in true fresco (where paint is applied to wet plaster before it hardens) or in fresco secco (where paint is applied to the dry plaster). Tejeda and Villagra believed that a true fresco technique was used, whereas Rutherford J. Gettens, chief of technical research at the Fogg Museum, Harvard University, believed an aqueous paint had been applied to dry plaster.

Healey's announcement of the discovery of the murals in 1947 was one of those spectacular events that archaeological dreams are made of. Although there are many remains of Maya sculptural art, most of their paintings have been lost to time and the elements—so the discovery of three entire rooms of paintings in a fair state of preservation was exciting. It ranks as one of the major discoveries in Maya archaeology.

A definitive report on the site was published by CIW; its authors were Karl Ruppert, J. Eric S. Thompson, and Proskouriakoff. A section on the pigments used was written by Gettens.

In the 1960s, INAH cleared the Acropolis, stabilized its structures, and placed a protective roof over Structure 1. Later, Stela 1 was repaired, and shelters were placed above all three carved stelae.

Bonampak, its murals, and its sculptures have been studied over the years by a host of scholars. In 1978, Peter Mathews began an epigraphic study of the stone monuments (published in 1980), and about the same time, Mary Ellen Miller did a detailed study of the murals (reported in her 1986 book, *The Murals of Bonampak,* though later she revised some of her conclusions). In 1984 the Mexican government undertook a three-year project of cleaning the paintings.

In 1996, the Bonampak Documentation Project began. Under the auspices of INAH and with funding from the National Geographic Society, the Getty Grant Program, and the Foundation for Ancient Religion and Mormon Studies, the project, directed by Miller (Yale University), has been conducted by Stephen Houston (Bringham Young University), Karl Taube (University of California, Riverside), and Beatriz de la Fuente (National Autonomous University of Mexico). This project is intended to thoroughly document Bonampak's murals. For details, see Miller's 1995 and 1997 publications as listed in the "Readings" section.

Connections

1. Palenque to Bonampak: 90.0 miles [144.8 kilometers] by paved road (1:59).

2. Palenque to Bonampak: 80 miles [128 kilometers] by air (:45).

Getting There

1. From Palenque, take the road that goes from the Maya head toward the ruins for 0.3 mile [0.5 kilometer] and then turn left onto the continuation of Highway 199. Follow the highway for 5.5 miles [8.9 kilometers] and turn left again onto the unnumbered road that goes toward Chancalá. Follow this road past the cutoff for Chancalá and through some villages, including Nuevo Guerrero, and go on to San Javier, 76.1 miles [122.5 kilometers]. At this junction there is a sign for Bonampak, where you turn right. Go 2.6 miles [4.2 kilometers] to the edge of Lacanjá (Lacanhá). Turn left and proceed to the parking area for the site.

2. From the airport at Palenque you fly directly to the airstrip at Bonampak, where your pilot will wait while you visit the ruins.

From the car parking area, it is a short walk to the airstrip, which you cross, and from there it is a bit farther to the site. Bonampak is open daily from 8:00 A.M. to 5:00 P.M. Allow 1.5 hours for a visit. There are no rest rooms, food, or drink at the site. Photography without flash is permitted.

Only three visitors at a time are allowed in each chamber of Structure 1—actually, any more than that would be a crowd, as you are not allowed to step up onto the benches. The murals and lintels of Structure 1 may now be photographed, without flash. At one time this was prohibited.

Light on Stelae 2 and 3 is best in the morning; it is better on Stela 1 in the afternoon. All three stelae are protected by shelters, but fortunately, they are translucent and allow enough light to reach the monuments to get good photographs.

Tours to Bonampak can be arranged through travel agencies in Palenque. If you wish to make your own arrangements to fly to Bonampak, check at the Palenque airport a day or two ahead and be prepared to leave a deposit. The airport is a short distance north of the town on Highway 199, on the east side of the highway.

★ ★ ★
TONINÁ
(toh-nee-NAH)

Derivation:
  Tzetzal Maya for "Stone House."
Culture:
  Maya.
Location:
  Central Chiapas.
Maps: 7 (p. 338) and 7A (p. 340)

The Site

Toniná has been greatly changed—and improved—since I first wrote about it in 1982, and that accounts for its upgrade from two to three stars. Its appearance is now truly outstanding, with terraces and buildings climbing the Acropolis to the top of a hill, 233 feet (71 meters) above ground level.

When you follow the trail from the parking area, you descend to a small stream and then climb to the site, which you enter from the east side near the south end. You come first to a partly consolidated ball court on a lower level; the ball court has circular markers. Slightly higher is a large open area called the Great Platform, upon which are several consolidated structures including a fair-size building (the Palace of Warfare) and five square altars along the north side.

Farther north is another ball court that lies at the foot of the Acropolis, but more interesting are four carved stone altars and other sculptures. The altars have glyphs around the

Monument T-20, one of the three-dimensional stelae characteristic of Toniná. Late Classic period.

circumference and in the center that are in various stages of preservation. The nearby sculptures include three-dimensional stelae portraying elaborately attired figures (now mostly headless). One unusual stela (originally from Rancho Pestac, 1 mile [1.6 kilometers] south), has outsize numerals in the Maya bar-and-dot system on one side, but it lacks the usual period ending glyphs.

A view to the north reveals a good part of the terraced hillside and the structures that form Toniná's Acropolis, much of which has been consolidated. It is an impressive scene indeed, and interesting remains are found throughout.

On the east side of the second level is the Palace of the Underworld, with three step-vaulted entrances facing south, though only two were visible at the time of our last visit. Also on the front wall you will see a cross-shaped window. At the very base of the structure's platform rests a circular stone with a single glyph in the center. On a higher level you will encounter residential structures and a stone and stucco monster mask.

Still higher you come to one of the most impressive buildings at Toniná, the Palace of the Frets. Its south facade is decorated with four absolutely enormous stepped frets. To the right (east) is a narrow 10-step stair that leads to a decorated stone and stucco throne. From the throne, an interior step-vaulted passage leads to an upper level where you will see the lower walls of rooms that were arranged around patios. In a nearby area, a long, narrow room has remains of a painted stucco decoration on the far narrow wall; the design represents feathered rattlesnakes and, below them, crossed bones.

On a level above this (on the east side) you get to the incredible stucco Mural of the Four Eras, many parts of which are in mint condition, although some top sections have fallen. It is read as a kind of four-page codex representing the myth of the four suns. It depicts heads of decapitated humans, death gods, celestial birds, and the mythical beings Hunapú and Xbalanqué of the famous Maya book known as the Popol Vuh. The mural is difficult to photograph in its entirety, owing to its protective roof and the placement of an altar in front of it, but you can get shots of some sections.

To the west, on the same level, is the Temple of the Water God, with a stone and stucco mask on its stairway. Nearby are the remains of a stucco panel that includes glyphs. A tomb with a stone sarcophagus is also found in this area.

On the next level (on the east side) is the Temple of Agriculture (or Temple of the Earth Monster). A large stucco figure of the earth monster is shown devouring a stone

Front (south side) of the Palace of the Underworld, Toniná. Late Classic period.

South side of the Palace of the Frets, Toniná. Late Classic period.

Detail of the Mural of the Four Eras, Toniná. Late Classic period.

solar sphere. Many details of the sculpture can still be studied.

The Temple of the Prisoners is found on the next level. The vaults of the rooms are mostly intact, and above them are remains of a perforated roof comb. The base of the structure has niches with inset stone and stucco sculptures of bound prisoners. At the top of the hill you will find the Temple of the Smoky Mirror, a tiered pyramidal structure with a stairway on the south side.

There are beautiful views of the lush valley below from various levels of Toniná's Acropolis.

The area around Toniná was occupied beginning about A.D. 200, but the city's heyday came basically during the Late Classic period. Among the numerous dated inscriptions recorded at Toniná, the earliest was A.D. 593. Dates continued to be inscribed until around 805, and then no known dated inscriptions appeared again until 901. The last known dated inscription of the Maya

Classic period at Toniná is 909, and it was recorded on the modest Monument 101.

Recent History

Toniná has been known in the literature for many years, sometimes as Ocosingo, the name of the nearby town. One of the earliest reports on the site was that of Guillermo Dupaix, who visited Toniná in 1807 on his way to investigate Palenque.

In 1832, Jean Frédéric Waldeck made a side trip to see Toniná while he was working at Palenque, and in 1840, John Lloyd Stephens and Frederick Catherwood visited the site. Stephens was aware of Dupaix's visit (published in 1834) and credited Dupaix with making the site known to the outside world. Stephens wrote an extensive description of the site, and Catherwood made a drawing of a stucco ornament—since destroyed—and a plan and elevation of one of the temples.

Stucco mask panel at the Temple of the Water God, Toniná. Late Classic period.

In 1870, E. G. Squier published a paper on a cache of jades from Toniná. The jades are now housed in the American Museum of Natural History and are known as the Squier Collection. A comparative study of this collection was undertaken by Elizabeth K. Easby, who published her findings in 1961.

Eduard Seler and his wife recorded the monuments at Toniná and published their data in 1900 and 1901. In 1926–27, Frans Blom and Oliver La Farge published the results of an exploratory expedition they made for Tulane University, which included a visit to Toniná.

In the 1970s, the French Mission for Archaeology and Ethnology in Mexico did extensive work at Toniná, directed by Pierre Bequelin and Claude Baudez. Additional work was undertaken by INAH in the 1980s and 1990s, under the direction of Juan Yadeun. His field crews made more spectacular discoveries, including the Mural of the Four Eras and an outstanding stela depicting Zotz

Choj (Tiger Bat), the most important of Toniná's rulers. A great deal of the consolidation at the site was also effected during this time, and work is continuing.

Connections

1. Ocosingo to Toniná: 2.2 miles [3.5 kilometers] by paved road (:10), then 6.4 miles [10.3 kilometers] by dirt road (:31).

2. San Cristóbal de las Casas to Ocosingo: 58.4 miles [94.0 kilometers] by paved road (1:42).

3. Palenque to Ocosingo: 72.7 miles [117.0 kilometers] by paved road (2:19).

Getting There

1. From Ocosingo (Highway 199 junction), head west to the plaza of the town and turn right at the far end. You will then pass the

front of the church. Continue on this paved road as it curves around. You then come to a marked junction on the left for the dirt road that takes you to the site. Go 5.5 miles [8.9 kilometers] on this road, then turn left again and go on the parking area for Toniná.

2. From San Cristóbal de las Casas, head southwest on Highway 199 to the junction with Highway 190. Turn left and proceed to Ocosingo, where you turn right. Then follow the directions already given.

3. From Palenque, head south on Highway 199 to Ocosingo and turn left. Then follow the directions already given.

The dirt road to Toniná was being improved at the time of our last visit, so perhaps the driving time will eventually be lessened.

Toniná is open daily from 9:00 A.M. to 4:00 P.M. Allow 2.5 hours for a visit. There are rest rooms near the ticket booth, and cold drinks are sold there, but no food is available.

At one time there was a small museum at Toniná, but it was closed the last time we visited the site. At least some of the stone monuments once exhibited there are now in the Tuxtla Gutiérrez Museum, including a panel depicting K'inich K'an Hoy Chitam II (formerly called Kan Xul II), a lord of Palenque. Later we heard that the Toniná Museum had reopened. Surely it would be worth a visit.

The recommended way to reach Toniná is in your own vehicle, but you could bus from San Cristóbal de las Casas or Palenque to Ocosingo and then taxi to the site. The problem is that it would be difficult to get a taxi back to town, and having the driver wait for you might be expensive. If you have a group of people, of course, it would be more reasonable. Negotiate the price of the trip with the driver, including the anticipated wait, before you leave Ocosingo.

You could also arrange for a tour through travel agencies in Palenque and San Cristóbal de las Casas.

★ ★
NA BOLOM MUSEUM

Na Bolom, in the town of San Cristóbal de las Casas, is a beautiful structure built originally as a seminary in 1898. It was the home of the late Frans and Gertrude Duby Blom. Frans Blom was an archaeologist, and Gertrude Duby Blom was a conservationist, social activist, and exceptional photographer. Na Bolom is located at Avenida Vicente Guerrero 33, on the northeast edge of San Cristóbal.

Na Bolom is still maintained as a center for the study of Mexican archaeology and anthropology, as it was when the Bloms were alive. It houses an extensive reference library that is open to the public Monday through Friday from 9:00 A.M. to 2:00 P.M. and on Saturday from 10:00 A.M. to 2:00 P.M.

The Na Bolom Museum is composed of several rooms in the house, devoted to different subjects. The Moxviquil Room houses the archaeological specimens; its name refers to a Late Classic Maya site located on a hilltop near San Cristóbal. The collection from Moxviquil includes molded figurines, ceramics, and stone artifacts. Burial urns, calcified skulls, and ceremonial objects are also displayed, as are maps and photographs of Frans Blom's 1952–53 excavations at the site.

The Lacandón Room contains ethnographic objects related to that group and collected by the Bloms in the 1940s. It is well worth a visit.

The chapel, renovated in 1982, displays sculptures and paintings dating from the sixteenth to the nineteenth centuries, along with a number of iron crosses collected by Frans Blom.

In addition to these three rooms, others that were living quarters for the Bloms and contain personal effects can be visited.

Tours of Na Bolom, including these rooms and the lovely central patio, are conducted daily at 11:00 A.M. in Spanish and at 4:30 P.M. in Spanish and English. Guests enjoy coffee and cake as part of the tour.

Na Bolom also has a guest house and restaurant that can be used by visiting researchers and travelers, but please note that this is not a hotel.

★ ★

CHIAPA DE CORZO

(chee-AH-pah deh KOHR-soh)

Derivation:
Chiapa is Nahuatl for "Sage (Plant) Place." Corzo is the name of a historic person.
Culture:
Isthmian (see text).
Location:
West-central Chiapas.
Map: 7 (p. 338)

The Site

Two areas of Chiapa de Corzo are now open to visitors, and both are worth a look—hence my upgrading it from one to two stars. One area is right on Highway 190 at its east junc-tion with the bypass that goes around the north side of the modern town of Chiapa de Corzo. There you will see Mound 32, a single-tier platform with sloping sides. It has a stair facing southeast, bordered by wide double *alfardas*. A protective metal door marks the entrance to Tomb 206. Some years ago, the caretaker would open the door for visitors and you could see the remains of human bones and offerings of ceramic bowls and pots. It now seems that the door to the tomb is kept closed; it appeared to be welded shut.

Beyond the tomb are the low remains of the walls of three rooms. At the back of Mound 32, its builders added a rectangular projection and two stairways; nearby you can see a couple of low rectangular platforms. Mound 32 had several different construction stages dating from around 550 B.C. to A.D. 1.

Southeast side of Mound 32, Chiapa de Corzo. Late Preclassic period.

The second area of interest is a few blocks away. There, Mounds 1 and 5 have been excavated and consolidated. Mound 1 borders the south end of a long plaza now planted with corn. The building has one tier and a stairway, bordered by alfardas, on the north side, facing the plaza. At the base of the structure is a low platform, and above this is a vertical wall topped by a sloping overhang. On top of this tier, the remains of low walls can be seen, as can walls and stairways of the earlier construction stages. Mound 1 was erected and added to from the Middle Preclassic period through Early Classic times.

Mound 5 faces west and has a stairway, bordered by double *alfardas,* on that side. The structure lies on the east side of the plaza, near Mound 1. Mound 5 apparently served as a platform for habitations, and it, too, went through several building stages, the most extensive of them from around 125 B.C. to A.D. 250. Though not very large, Mound 5 was a rather sophisticated building for its time.

Chiapa de Corzo had no fewer that 18 successive occupations, and remains of more than 250 structures have been recorded there, including platforms, pyramids, and palaces. The site was occupied almost continuously from around 1500 B.C. to the time of the Spanish conquest; it is still occupied today. The lowest point in the site's history was around A.D. 950.

During its long history, Chiapa de Corzo had contacts with various parts of Mesoamerica, including La Venta, the Pacific Coast of Chiapas and Guatemala, the Maya lowlands, and Monte Albán. Later connections were with Kaminaljuyú, southern Veracruz, Oaxaca, El Salvador, Campeche, Yucatán, and the Petén of Guatemala.

A tremendous number of ceramic vessels were excavated at Chiapa de Corzo, enabling archaeologists to create a detailed chronological sequence for the site. Many other interesting artifacts were made of stone, bone, and shell. A fragment of Stela 2 bears a bar-and-dot date that has been reconstructed by Michael D. Coe as 36 B.C., the earliest known Long Count date in Mesoamerica. Two delicately and intricately carved human femurs were another important find. Both items are displayed in the Tuxtla Gutiérrez Museum, and I cover them in the text under that heading. A pair of carved shell ear pendants dating to the Late Preclassic period is unusual; the design on each portrays a feathered serpent, the earliest known depiction of this deity found at Chiapa de Corzo.

The northeastern part of Chiapas, with the important sites of Yaxchilán, Bonampak, and Palenque, is logically considered an extension of the lowland Maya area, but the southwestern part of the state, where Chiapa de Corzo lies, poses something of a problem. According to Gareth W. Lowe and J. Alden Mason, who worked in the area, it "has not lent itself so well to inclusion in any of the usual Mesoamerican culture areas, though it has in part been broadly labeled as belonging to the highland Maya territory." They refer to Chiapa de Corzo as being part of an "Isthmian culture."

Recent History

In 1869, C. H. Berendt produced a map of Chiapa de Corzo and noted the presence of three pyramids on a hill. His map was copied from an original drawn by or for D. Julian Grajales in 1868. Another early visitor to the site, Karl Sapper, left an account of Chiapa de Corzo in 1895.

The first excavation at the site was made in 1941 by Jorge A. Vivó, a geographer. He turned over the material he collected to Heinrich Berlin, who in 1955 conducted investigations for Brigham Young University's New World Archaeological Foundation at Chiapa de Corzo. Berlin was the first director of the project and was followed in that position from 1956 to 1959 by Gareth W. Lowe. A great deal of information was collected by numerous scholars working on the project. In 1960, Frederick Peterson consolidated Mounds 1 and 5.

The construction of a bypass around the town in 1972 damaged Mound 32, and INAH stepped in to conduct salvage work. An earthquake hit Chiapa de Corzo in 1975 and damaged Mounds 1 and 5, which were then closed to the public for some time before they were repaired. They have since reopened.

Connections

1. Tuxtla Gutiérrez to Chiapa de Corzo (Mound 32): 6.4 miles [10.3 kilometers] by paved road (:10).

2. San Cristóbal de las Casas to Chiapa de Corzo (Mound 32): 42.2 miles [67.9 kilometers] by paved road (1:18).

Getting There

1. From Tuxtla Gutiérrez, head east on Highway 190 and take the bypass around the north side of Chiapa de Corzo. When you arrive at the junction and rejoin Highway 190 on the east end of town, you will be at Mound 32.

2. From San Cristóbal de las Casas, head west to Chiapa de Corzo on Highway 190, and stop at the junction with the bypass (at Mound 32).

Mound 32 is not fenced off and can be visited at any time. From there, take Highway 190 west (not the bypass) and go a long block to Calle La Libertad (they intersect at an oblique angle). Turn left on La Libertad, go two blocks, and turn left again onto Calle Miguel Hidalgo. Proceed ahead for about three blocks, the last one of which is dirt, to the house and gate that are the entrance to that part of the site. The gate is on the right, and you can park along the street nearby. Ask permission at the house to walk through the property alongside the cornfield (*milpa*). There is a small charge, and generally a couple of children will accompany you; you may want to give them a small tip. From the gate you can see Mound 1 a short distance away.

Although some printed material indicates that Chiapa de Corzo is open Tuesday through Sunday from 9:00 A.M. to 4:00 P.M., I imagine the second area is open more or less on demand during daylight hours. There are not many visitors. Allow 15 minutes to see Mound 32 and 30 minutes for Mounds 1 and 5.

No food, drink, or rest rooms are available at either part of the site, but there are restaurants near Mound 32, on the Zócalo in town, and near the river where the boats dock. A charming colonial period fountain is found on the Zócalo. You will pass it if you drive through the town rather than taking the bypass.

Chiapa de Corzo can be reached by bus from both of the connections given.

★ ★ ★ ★

REGIONAL MUSEUM OF CHIAPAS (*TUXTLA GUTIÉRREZ MUSEUM*)

The Tuxtla Gutiérrez Museum is nicely arranged and is designed so that visitors circulate in a counterclockwise direction. As you enter, you see the Late Classic Lintel 33 from Yaxchilán; it is in excellent condition. After that, the displays start with the early phases of pre-Columbian history and include a migration chart, mastodon bones, and diagrams. The prehistory of Chiapas is shown, as are displays of early hunters and the tools they used.

The earliest ceramic phase from the Pacific Coast of Chiapas (near the Guatemala border) is called Barra and dates from 1900 to 1700 B.C. Examples of it and the following Ocós pottery phase (1500 to 1200 B.C.) are displayed in well-lighted cases. Early figurines (1700 to 900 B.C.) are included. Agricultural products and examples of early corncobs are shown.

After that you proceed through the Preclassic, Classic, and Postclassic sections and another area devoted to the Mayas in Chiapas. The state of Chiapas is very rich archaeologically, and this is well demonstrated by the various exhibits of sculpture, ceramics,

Stela 1 from Chinkultic, Late Classic period. On display in the Tuxtla Gutiérrez Museum.

jewelry, and worked stone. In addition, maps and diagrams with extensive information add to the educational value of the collection.

Some of the highlights are as follows. In the Preclassic section there are an Olmec-style figurine, two delicately carved human femurs depicting variations of dragon masks, and fragments of Stelae 2 and 3, all from Chiapa de Corzo. The Olmec-style figurine dates between 1000 and 200 B.C., whereas the femurs (which may have been imported) and stelae fragments are Late Preclassic. Interesting boulder sculptures from the vicinity of Arriaga and Tonalá form a separate display.

A painted copy of an Olmec-style bas-relief is also displayed in this section. The original carving was found on a rock face at Xoc, in east-central Chiapas. The figure was 7 feet (2.1 meters) tall and was photographed in 1968. By 1972, the entire face of the stone had been chipped away by looters.

The Classic period section exhibits stone monuments from different parts of Chiapas and a reproduction of one of the murals from Bonampak. One wall holds a diagram showing Teotihuacán's presence in various parts of Mesoamerica.

Some fine stone monuments are exhibited in the Mayas of Chiapas section, including a circular stone bas-relief from Tenam Rosario representing ball players. One item, though not the most exciting visually, is quite unusual; it is a stone carved with a three-dimensional depiction of an I-shaped ball court from the area of El Mirador (Chiapas).

Polychrome and other pottery from Largatero, an elaborate ceremonial urn from Comitán, another from around Ocosingo, and an *incensario* from around Palenque make up some of the more interesting ceramic displays in the Classic period section. Carved stone monuments include Stelae 1 and 11 from Chinkultic, an all-glyphic stela from Petalcingo, the beautifully carved fragment called Miscellaneous Stone 1 from Yaxchilán, a circular ball court marker from Toniná, and Monument 122, a panel from the same site depicting K'inich K'an Hoy Chitam II (formerly called Kan Xul II), lord of Palenque, as a captive. This lord, the king of Palenque at the time of his capture in A.D. 711, was the second son of the great Pacal and younger brother of K'inich Kan B'alam II (formerly called Chan Bahlum II), both previous rulers of Palenque.

Monument 122 is different in style from earlier carvings at Toniná, and it has been speculated that perhaps a sculptor from Palenque, taken in tribute, carved the monument.

Ceramics, copper bells, alabaster pieces, wood artifacts, and two small gold items are displayed in the Postclassic section.

Several rather large three-dimensional and bas-relief stone sculptures are exhibited outside the museum on two levels. They are unlabeled, but the bas-relief on the lower level, depicting the lower part of a standing figure, comes from Padre Piedra in west-central

Chiapas. It is in Olmec style and probably dates to the Middle Preclassic period.

The Tuxtla Gutiérrez Museum, inaugurated on September 4, 1984, lies a little northeast of downtown Tuxtla Gutiérrez. It is on Calle 5ª (Fifth) Norte Oriente. The museum is part of a complex of buildings that also houses a theater (near which you can park) and an orchid display. From the theater, follow a broad stepped walkway to the right until you reach the museum (on the right). It is open Tuesday through Sunday from 9:00 A.M. to 4:00 P.M. but is closed on Monday. Allow one hour for a visit. Labeling in the museum is generally good, as is the lighting. The glass cases are unusually clean. Photography without flash is permitted; large camera bags or backpacks must be checked at the entrance. There are rest rooms near the museum on a lower level and restaurants nearby.

★ ★
CHINKULTIC
(cheen-kool-TEEK)

Derivation:
Tojolabal (a language spoken in highland Chiapas) for "Small Woods."
Culture:
Maya.
Location:
East-central Chiapas.
Map: 7 (p. 338)

The Site

A relatively large site, Chinkultic is composed of about 200 large and small mounds in six main groups. Of these, parts of four (Groups A, B, C, and D) have been cleared and partly consolidated. Eleven carved stone stelae are known from Chinkultic, and the site, especially Group A, is magnificently situated on lakes, a river, and a cenote.

You drive into the site from the south, stopping at the entrance to sign a registration book. From there, continue straight ahead to the parking area (on the left). The approach on foot to Groups D and B is via a trail that goes over an ancient *sacbé*; these groups lie to the right of it, and Group A is reached by a path that ascends the big bluff on which it is situated.

You come first to Group D, where the feature of interest is the lower section of an unconsolidated pyramid. One corner of the base has been well cleared and is made of very large and neatly squared building stones. Trees still grow on the top of the pyramid.

Next you come to Group B, composed of several buildings. Three long structures border three sides of a sunken plaza with a small, rectangular, stepped platform in its center. On the plaza's fourth side is a row of three unconsolidated mounds. From the first long building you reach (Structure 8), a broad stairway leads down to plaza level. The structure and a good part of the stairway have been consolidated.

Continue along the trail, cross a small river on a sturdy footbridge, and follow the trail as it climbs to Group A. The trail is steep, and it will take about 30 minutes to go from the bridge to the top. Several buildings make up Group A; the largest and most imposing is Structure 1 (El Mirador), a stepped pyramid with a stairway, bordered by *alfardas,* facing southeast. A two-room temple originally topped the structure, and evidence indicates that it had a beam and lime-concrete flat roof. Only a little of the temple remains.

A connecting small platform lies at the base of the stairway, facing three other square platforms in front. Stela 9 was found broken off at its base between the center platform

Front (southeast side) of Structure 1 (El Mirador), Group A, Chinkultic. Late Classic period.

and the one abutting Structure 1; it had originally stood in a stone-lined pit in the same location. As you face Structure 1, the sizable Structure 2 lies to the right. From this top level of the site, there are beautiful views of Cenote Agua Azul below to the northeast.

When Chinkultic was constructed, a huge stairway connected this upper section of Group A with a lower plaza and additional structures. If the vegetation has been cut back recently, you will be able to see these lower buildings from the top of the hill.

You now return the way you came and go back to the entrance gate for the site. There you will see a sign for a trail (on the right) that leads a short distance to Group C—noted for its large, enclosed, l-shaped ball court, which has been partly restored. A number of carved stelae were found associated with the ball court; clearly the structure was one of the most important at Chinkultic. A stairway from the outside leads to the top of one side of the ball court, and from there you can climb down to the court proper. The carved monuments are found under thatch shelters.

Chinkultic was occupied from around 50 B.C. until A.D. 350, after which it apparently went uninhabited until A.D. 700. From 700 to 900, the site reached its peak, and most of the architecture and sculpture seen

at Chinkultic date to this time. The site continued in operation until around 1250. It is believed that the early inhabitants and the later ones were totally separate groups of people.

Although a beautifully preserved ball court marker dated A.D. 591 (now in the Mexico City Museum) is often listed as coming from Chinkultic, it actually came from Colonia La Esperanza, 14.9 miles [24.0 kilometers] to the west. This monument was carved during Chinkultic's hiatus.

Recent History

Chinkultic was first reported in 1901 by Eduard Seler, the German archaeologist, who had visited the site with his wife in 1895. At that time he discovered two carved stelae. A sketch map of the site was made by Frans Blom and Oliver La Farge after their 1925 visit for Tulane University. They illustrated and described six additional carved stelae in their 1926 book *Tribes and Temples*. In 1928, Blom returned to the site, resurveyed it, and found three more stelae. A brief survey of Chinkultic was published by Rafael Orellana Tapia in 1954, and a more comprehensive one was undertaken the following year by Edwin M. Shook, whose work was published by the New World Archaeological Foundation in 1956.

In 1966 and again in 1968, the Milwaukee Public Museum undertook brief reconnaissance surveys of the Comitán area and Chinkultic in particular. The latter survey was primarily concerned with studying the possibility of exploring Cenote Agua Azul. Both trips were reported by Stephan F. de Borhegyi in 1970, in a Middle American Research Institute publication by Tulane University.

Between 1968 and 1970, and again in 1976, under the auspices of INAH, Cenote Agua Azul and other areas of Chinkultic were investigated. The level of the cenote was lowered by pumps, and excavations were made into the sides. When the lower level of Group A was studied, fragments of stone carvings in Izapan style were found. The ball court in Group C was excavated and partly consolidated. Scholars involved in the work were Gareth W. Lowe, Pierre Agrinier, and Eduardo Martínez Espinosa of the New World Archaeological Foundation, Borhegyi of the Milwaukee Public Museum, and Roberto Gallegos and Carlos Navarrete of INAH.

Connections

1. Comitán to Chinkultic: 29.1 miles [46.8 kilometers] by paved road (:35), then 1.2 miles [1.9 kilometers] by dirt road (:06).

2. San Cristóbal de las Casas to Comitán: 54.1 miles [87.0 kilometers] by paved road (1:26).

Getting There

1. From Comitán, head southeast on Highway 190 to the junction with the unnumbered road that goes toward Chinkultic (marked with a sign) and turn left. Continue until you come to the marked junction with the dirt road (on the left) that goes to the site; this road is just after a small *comedor* (restaurant) facing the paved road. Follow the dirt road to the entrance gate and stop to sign the registration book. Proceed a bit farther to the parking area (on the left).

2. From San Cristóbal de las Casas, head southeast to Comitán on Highway 190.

Chinkultic is open daily from 10:00 A.M. to 6:00 P.M. Allow 2.5 hours for a visit. There are no rest rooms at the site. No food is available, but you could get something to eat at the *comedor,* and vendors sell soft drinks from coolers.

Although buses run along Highway 190, few travel the road that goes toward Chinkultic. You could try to get a travel agency in San Cristóbal to arrange a trip to the site if you are without your own vehicle.

IZAPA
(ee-SAH-pah)

Derivation:
   Possibly Nahua for "Place of Cold Water."
Culture:
   Izapan.
Location:
   Far southeastern Chiapas.
Map: 7 (p. 338)

The Site

Izapa, a very large and important site, covers 1.4 square miles (3.6 square kilometers). It was occupied from around 1500 B.C. to A.D. 1200. The eight groups of structures known are arranged around plazas, and three of these (Groups A, B, and F) are open to visitors. Groups A and B are near each other and both lie south of Highway 200; Group F is on the north side of the highway and is visible from it.

Stela 11 in Group B, Izapa, Late Preclassic period.

When you arrive at Group A, you enter a plaza at its northeast corner. Four large and mostly overgrown mounds face the plaza, and in front of three of them (the north, east, and south mounds) are 10 carved stone monuments; plain stones are found in front of the west mound. Unfortunately, the monuments are difficult to photograph because of the low relief of the carvings and the protective thatch shelters above them. Just circle around the edge of the plaza for a look; you can actually discern the designs better than you can photograph them.

When you drive to Group B, you enter on the west side of a platform that supports the large Mound 30a and other, smaller structures. A plaza lies to the right (south) and is bordered by three other large mounds on the east, south, and west sides, respectively. A reconstruction drawing of the extensively excavated Mound 30a shows it to be a six-tiered pyramid with a stairway on the south side, facing the plaza. Carved monuments in Group B are found on the platform in front

of Mound 30a, just to the south on a slightly lower level, and in front of the mound on the west side of the plaza. One of the best preserved is Stela 11, in front of this mound, near the north end. In the central part of the plaza, three stone pillars topped by stone spheres are also found.

One of the most interesting monuments in Group B is outside the area just described; it is Miscellaneous Monument 2, found to the northeast of Mound 30a. When you are facing this mound, head to the right (east) a short distance, then follow a trail to the left (north) along the east side of the mound. The trail goes through an unlocked gate, and a bit farther on you come to the monument, a three-dimensional carving of a faceless human within the jaws of a mythical monster, perhaps a serpent or jaguar. This is the earliest carving known at Izapa, dating to around 300 B.C.

No architecture has been consolidated in Group A or B.

Group F at Izapa has consolidated stepped platforms with stairways bordered by *alfardas,* and a ball court. All are faced with boulders, and it is believed that all of Izapa's structures originally were coated with a clay plaster. The largest building in the group is Mound 125a, a pyramid that once rose in six tiers and had a stairway on the south side. It was excavated but not consolidated and appears as a grass-covered mound today.

Several carved monuments are found in various parts of this group. The thatch shelters that protect them are easy to spot as you walk around. Near the entrance to Group F are two eroded frog heads (Altars 53 and 54) and a plain stela; nearby, the bas-relief Stela 22 is displayed. This monument was discovered during highway construction and was later stolen and recarved, certain details being added.

Three carved monuments are associated with the ball court, one at each of the east and west ends (Stela 60 and Throne 2, respectively) and a fragment (Stela 67) embedded in the north wall. Stela 67, the lower part of a monument, depicts a figure wearing a mask. His arms are outstretched, and he holds an unidentified but doubtlessly ceremonial object in each hand. He is seated in a boat above a stream in which ring-tail fish swim. This

Three stone pillars and spheres in the plaza of Group B, Izapa. Late Preclassic period.

monument was probably carved between about A.D. 1 and 250. Throne 2 is a tablelike legged throne with an animal head projection. To the right (north) of the throne is a tall stone column with the remains of a kneeling figure on top; this is called Miscellaneous Monument 4 and may date to the Classic period.

To the south of the throne you see a large basin with a plaited band around its rim (Miscellaneous Monument 24) and a head (Miscellaneous Monument 3), possibly representing a serpent. A hollow running through the head forms a trough through which it is believed water once ran. Perhaps the monument originally served a function in a spring or stream.

It is worthy of note that the carved monuments in Group F are earlier sculptures that were reused and reset later in Izapa's history when Group F developed.

At its beginning, around 1500 B.C., Izapa was one of a number of small agricultural villages that developed along the Pacific Coast. It is believed that the inhabitants were Mixe-Zoque. Between about 1200 and 850 B.C., Izapa is thought to have experienced

Miscellaneous Monument 2 in Group B, Izapa. Dates to around 300 B.C.

Stela 67 in the north wall of the ball court in Group F, Izapa. Late Preclassic period.

part of a widespread Early Olmec occupation, and Olmec-like figurine heads were produced there. It has been proposed that the Olmecs spoke Mixe-Zoquean. Around 850 to 650, there was a foreign intrusion from the east, possibly Maya. From 650 to 450, the community expanded at Izapa, but only a little construction from that period has been found. Between 450 and 300, the earliest known jade offering was made at the site, and associated ceramic vessels indicate an alignment with Guatemala or El Salvador.

Izapa reached its peak during the Late Preclassic period with massive constructions. Between 300 and 50 B.C. it arrived at the apex of its growth cycle, and all of the groups except Group F apparently reached their present size. Almost all of Izapa's carved monuments were probably produced during this time. Afterward, very little construction took place in central Izapa, and the focus shifted to Group F, although some ritual activity seems to have taken place in the central area in Group B.

From A.D. 100 to 250, Group F underwent accelerated growth. Teotihuacán's influence became manifest around 500 to 600, when locally produced ceramics in Teoti-

huacán style were manufactured; all of them were recovered from Group F.

A great deal of construction took place in Group F during the Early Classic period, and that area continued to be occupied during the Late Classic. By Early Postclassic times, evidence suggests either that Izapa was lightly populated or that someone from elsewhere was reusing the ruined ceremonial plazas. Although offerings were still being deposited—as they had been throughout Izapa's history—those of the Early Postclassic were intrusive into existing structures.

Apparently Izapa was abandoned at the end of this period, as no evidence of a Late Postclassic occupation has been found. Throughout its long history, while Izapa received influences from various parts of Mesoamerica—from central Mexico to El Salvador—it remained basically Mixe-Zoque.

Recent History

Oddly, in view of its considerable size, Izapa was unknown to archaeologists until the late 1930s, even though it was well known locally. Apparently Karl Ruppert of the Carnegie Institution of Washington was the first archaeologist to visit Izapa, in 1938. The following year, Alfred V. Kidder also inspected the site.

Matthew W. Stirling learned of the site in 1941 while he was leading a National Geographic Society–Smithsonian Institution expedition and working at sites on the coast of Veracruz. Miguel Covarrubias, who was visiting Stirling at the time, had seen photographs of some of the monuments at Izapa and told Stirling that the sculptures reminded him somewhat of those at La Venta. Stirling resolved to visit Izapa and made a trip there with his wife, Marion, and National Geographic photographer Richard H. Stewart. They spent a week at the site and located 30 stelae and altars. Stirling felt that his group had been "well repaid for our efforts."

He mentioned Izapa briefly in an article published in *National Geographic* in September 1941, but he published a more detailed report on the site in 1943 in a Smithsonian Institution publication.

In the early 1950s, Rafael Orellana Tapia reported with text and photographs on his visit to Izapa.

The New World Archaeological Foundation began a five-year program of investigation in 1961, and its work resulted in a number of detailed published reports. This was the most thorough work carried out at the site, and it involved many scholars, including Gareth W. Lowe, V. Garth Norman, Suzanna M. Ekholm, Thomas A. Lee, Jr., and Eduardo Martínez Espinosa. For the best illustrations of Izapa's carved monuments, see Norman's 1973 publication, *Izapa Sculpture.*

Connection

Tapachula to Izapa (Group F): 8.5 miles [13.7 kilometers] by paved road (:20), but see the details that follow.

Getting There

When you leave Tapachula to visit Izapa, you have a couple of choices. If you opt to visit Group F first, then the connection listed will give you the details. This is also the information shown on Map 7. If, however, you decide to stop first at Groups A and B (the closest to Tapachula), head west and then northwest from Tapachula on Highway 200 to the cutoff (marked with a sign) for Groups A and B, 8.1 miles [13.0 kilometers]. Turn right onto a dirt road and follow it to Group A, 0.6 mile [1.0 kilometer] (:07). (Along the way you will pass a marked cutoff to the left for Group B, which you could visit before or after Group A. The directions used here take you to Group A first.)

After visiting Group A, return the way you came for 0.1 mile [0.2 kilometer] and turn right; go another 0.1 mile [0.2 kilometer] (:05) to Group B. After seeing that group, return to the junction just mentioned, turn right, and go back to Highway 200. Turn right at the highway and go 0.4 mile [0.6 kilometer] (:02) to the entrance for Group F (on the left).

The dirt road from the highway to Groups A and B is poor, and it traverses boulder-strewn hills (actually mounds). When it is wet you will need four-wheel drive. If the road seems too bad to drive, you could walk in; if you do, wear boots and carry a canteen of water.

Groups A and B are supposed to be open Tuesday through Sunday from 9:00 A.M. to 5:00 P.M. and closed on Monday. We arrived on a Monday, however, and no one questioned our entering. This part of Izapa gets fewer visitors than Group F, which is open daily from 6:00 A.M. to 6:00 P.M. Small entry fees are collected at both Groups A and F.

Allow 30 minutes at Group A and 45 minutes each at Groups B and F. In other words, allow two hours for the whole site plus a little for the driving time between the groups. There are no rest rooms at any of the groups, and no food is available, but you may be able to get soft drinks.

From Tapachula you could taxi to Group F and at least to the cutoff for Groups A and B, but there might be a problem getting a taxi back. Or check with travel agencies in Tapachula; they may be able to arrange a tour to Izapa.

Note: Some of Izapa's carvings are in the Regional Museum of the Soconusco in Tapachula, on the west side of Parque Hidalgo. We attempted to visit it at 10:00 A.M. on a Tuesday morning, when it was supposed to be open, but owing to a staff meeting, it wasn't. Maybe you will have better luck.

★ ★
TONALÁ PLAZA, PARK, AND MUSEUM

Three areas in Tonalá have sculptured remains, and all are worth visiting. The most impressive is Stela 3 from Los Horcones, a Chiapas Pacific Coast site that lies about 20 miles [32 kilometers] southeast of Tonalá. This outstanding Classic period monument is displayed in the Tonalá plaza on Highway 200—in town this is Avenida Hidalgo. The stela is carved in a native granite, stands 15.4 feet (4.7 meters) tall, and is erected on a platform. The front and one side of the carving are in pristine condition, whereas the back and the other side have suffered some damage. The standing figure on the principal side represents Tlaloc in frontal view. There is a Teotihuacán year-sign in his headdress (and elsewhere on the monument), and he wears a symbol for turquoise at his waist. This symbol is repeated several times on all sides of the stela.

Ask anyone standing around the plaza to direct you or take you to a nearby park

Stela 3 from Los Horcones, on display in the Tonalá plaza. Classic period.

where three more carved monuments are on display. The park is a couple of blocks away. Stela 4 from Los Horcones is lying on the ground; it depicts a seated jaguar sculpted around the block. Unfortunately, the front of the monument rests on the ground, but the jaguar's haunches can be discerned. Design elements carved on the stela are related to Teotihuacán motifs, and the stela dates to the Classic period. Nearby, a simple carving is said to represent a monkey, and a rectangular stone has remains of a framelike design and numerous circular pits.

A couple of blocks east of Tonalá's plaza, on the south side of Avenida Hidalgo, is the third area of interest. A collection of carved stones is piled together under a shelter in a yard that is part of a complex including a school and a municipal library. The shelter itself serves as the Tonalá Museum.

Nothing in the museum is labeled, but two of the sculptures, Monuments 1 and 2, come from Tzutzuculi, a site at the southeastern edge of Tonalá. Oddly, the site was unknown until 1958, when it was recorded in a coastal survey by Carlos Navarette for the New World Archaeological Foundation. Tzutzuculi was occupied from around 1100 to 300 B.C., and 11 carved stones are known from the site. Monument 1 is a bas-relief carving of a frontal face in clearly Olmec style; Monument 2, also a bas-relief, depicts what may represent a stylized serpent's head in profile, although it looks like meandering lines on first view. Monuments 1 and 2 both date to between 650 and 450 B.C., and both were part of the facade of a structure where they were set up flanking a stone stairway.

The stela in the plaza and the monuments in the park are, of course, always on view. I am unsure of the schedule for the museum. Allow 45 minutes to see all three displays, including the travel time between them. Restaurants can be found near the plaza and on Avenida Hidalgo in Tonalá. There are hotels in town as well.

GLOSSARY

ahau (*ahaw*): A Maya word for "lord" and the name of the last day in the Maya 20-day month. Its glyphic form represents a stylized face.

alfarda: In architecture, a raised, sloping side section that borders a stairway; a balustrade.

Atlantes (also *Atlantean figures*): Statues of men used as supporting columns for roofs and altars. Prevalent at Tula.

avenida: Avenue.

bar-and-dot numerals: A system of enumeration in which a bar represents five and a dot represents one. Used by the ancient Mayas and some other Mesoamerican peoples.

boulevar: Boulevard.

calle: Street.

calzada: Causeway, road.

chacmool: A statue of a figure in a recumbent pose, holding a receptacle on its abdomen. Found at Tula, Chichén Itzá, and other sites in Mexico, at Quiriguá, Guatemala, at Casa Blanca, El Salvador, and farther south in Central America.

Cocijo: The Zapotec rain god.

codex (plural *codices*): Painted books of pre-Columbian or, in some cases, post-Columbian date. They are made of deerskin or bark paper and are folded like a screen.

consolidated, consolidation: In architecture, refers to a structure that has been stabilized and repaired to prevent further deterioration, without being fully restored.

corbeled vault: The prevalent type of roofing used in Classic Maya structures. The vault is built up from the tops of vertical walls, and each layer of stone or brick juts past the one below it. When the sides of the vault approach each other closely enough, a capstone is added to bridge the remaining gap.

danzantes (Spanish for "dancers"): Life-size figures carved on stone slabs found at Monte Albán and thought to resemble dancers due to their fluid poses.

They depict not dancers, however, but sacrificed captives.

eccentric flints: Knapped flint (and sometimes obsidian) worked into various unusual shapes, sometimes into human profiles. They are found in offertory caches in the Maya lowlands and may have been attached to wooden staffs for use on ceremonial occasions.

Ehécatl: The wind god of central Mexico; an aspect of Quetzalcóatl.

emblem glyph: A glyph (generally in three parts) whose main sign refers either to a dynastic name or to a place name.

glorieta: Traffic circle.

glyphs (also *hieroglyphs*): The form of ancient Maya writing, which includes both pictographic and ideographic elements; some glyphs have phonetic value.

Goodman-Martínez-Thompson correlation (also *GMT correlation*): A correlation between the Maya and Christian calendars proposed by Goodman, Martínez, and Thompson. This correlation equates the Maya Long Count date of 11.16.0.0.0 with A.D. 1539. This correlation is generally, though not universally, accepted.

hacha (Spanish for "ax"): A thin stone object in the shape of an ax, often carved. Associated with the ritual ball game. Prevalent in the culture of Classic Veracruz and also found in areas influenced or occupied by people of this culture.

hieroglyphs: *See* glyphs.

Huasteca: An area of Mexico occupied by the Huastecs, a group linguistically related to the Mayas. It includes portions of several Mexican states: southern Tamaulipas, northern Veracruz, and small parts of San Luis Potosí, Querétaro, Hidalgo, and Puebla.

Huehuetéotl (also *Xiuhtecuhtli*): The old fire god, a deity of central Mexico.

Huitzilopochtli: The Aztec god of war.

INAH: Instituto Nacional de Anthropología e Historia (National Institute of Anthropology and History), the Mexican government agency that is responsible for the care of ancient remains. It also sponsors excavations and publishes scholarly reports.

incensario: An incense burner, censer. These are generally made of fired clay and are often elaborately decorated.

Izapan style: A style of carving produced at Izapa, Mexico, in the Late Preclassic period. Some traits are U elements, long-nosed gods, baroque qualities, and narrative scenes. Monuments in this style are also found at sites along the Pacific slope of Guatemala, in the highlands and the Petén of Guatemala, and elsewhere.

lienzo: Native Mesoamerican manuscript.

Long Count date (also *Initial Series*): A method of recording dates in the Maya calendar. It represents the total number of days that have elapsed from a mythical starting point, calculated at 3114 B.C. according to the GMT correlation (see *Goodman-Martínez-Thompson correlation*).

mano: *See* metate.

merlon: In architecture, a decorative element that juts above the roof line of a structure. One merlon is separated from the next by an empty space.

Mesoamerica: The areas of Mexico and Central America in which high civilizations arose in pre-Columbian times. The region includes parts of western and eastern Mexico; all of central and southern Mexico and the Yucatán Peninsula; all of Belize, Guatemala, and El Salvador; western Honduras; and parts of the Pacific Coast areas of Nicaragua and Costa Rica.

metate: A trough-shaped stone used for grinding foodstuffs, generally corn (maize), and accompanied by a cylindrical handstone (mano).

Mexican yearsign (also *Teotihuacán yearsign, Mixtec yearsign,* and *imbricated trapeziform*): A motif of overlapping geometrical elements, probably originating in Mexico, that is associated with warriors. Its shape is similar to that of a sign that marks year dates in the Aztec codices.

Mixteca-Puebla style (painting): A Postclassic painting style that was a synthesis of the styles of Teotihuacán, Xochicalco, and Veracruz. It was used on polychrome pottery and in codices.

Nahua: A group of people who spoke a Uto-Aztecan language; also the language itself.

Nahuatl: The language of the ancient Aztecs.

New Fire ceremony: A ceremony that marked the end of one and the beginning of another 52-year time cycle in Aztec culture. It celebrated the avoidance of the end of the world.

obsidian: A naturally occurring volcanic glass used to make cutting tools and projectile points. An important trade item throughout Mesoamerica.

palma: Stone ritual object, often carved. Associated with *hachas* and yokes in the sacred ball game.

pectoral: An ornament worn on the chest.

periférico: Periferal road, bypass.

quechquémitl: A triangular overblouse worn by women since ancient times in Mexico.

Quetzalcóatl: The feathered serpent, the major deity of central Mexico. He brought knowledge of agriculture, arts, and science.

roof comb: In architecture, a stone superstructure built on the roof of a structure to give additional height and grandeur. In ancient Mesoamerican architecture, the combs were sometimes perforated and were generally decorated.

sacbé: (plural in Maya, *sacbeob*): Literally, "white road." An ancient Maya road or causeway made of rough stone blocks topped with crushed stone and then plastered.

stela (plural, stelae): A freestanding monolithic stone monument, either plain or carved on one or more sides. Especially prevalent in the Maya area; often accompanied by a drum-shaped altar.

stepped fret: A design composed of a squared spiral and a step element. It is derived from the stylized head of the "sky serpent" and is therefore a symbol of

Quetzalcóatl. Found throughout Mesoamerica but especially prevalent at Mitla and other sites in Oaxaca.

talud-tablero: In architecture, a sloping lower section, or *talus* (*talud*), topped by a vertical, rectangular, recessed panel (*tablero*).

Tarascans: The most important ethnic group of western Mexico from the tenth century to the Spanish conquest. Noted as craftsmen in copperwork, feather mosaics, and fine painted pottery.

Tlahuica: One of the seven groups that migrated to the Valley of Mexico from the legendary Chicomoztoc in A.D. 1168. They settled in what is now Mexico's state of Morelos.

Tlaloc: The rain god of central Mexico. He also has an aspect as a war or warrior god.

tope: Speed bump. Ubiquitous in and on the outskirts of Mexican towns. The purpose is to slow traffic going through populated areas. They are sometimes, but not always, marked with a warning sign. Drivers should slow to a crawl when they see a *tope* or a sign warning of one.

Triple Alliance: An alliance of Tenochtitlán, Texcoco, and Tlacopan from the reign of Moctezuma I (A.D. 1440 to 1468) until the Spanish conquest.

tzompantli: A skull rack where heads of sacrificial victims were placed. Also, a platform with depictions of carved skulls on its sides. Postclassic period.

Witz monster: A zoomorphic creature that is a symbol of a living mountain. The creature is shown with eyelids and *cauac* signs (clusters of discs or circles arranged in a triangle).

Xipe Totec: The god of spring of central Mexico. He is generally depicted wearing the skin of a flayed victim.

Xiuhcóatl: The fire serpent, a deity of central Mexico.

yácata: A pyramid-like mound unique to the Tarascans.

yoke: Yoke-shaped stones, sometimes elaborately carved. Related to the ritual ball game. Prevalent in the culture of Classic Veracruz but also found in other areas influenced or occupied by people of this culture.

Zócalo: The main plaza in Mexico City and, by extension, the main plaza in some other cities in the republic.

zopilote: Buzzard.

SELECTED READINGS

Acosta Laguna, Agustín, Michael D. Coe, Felipe Solís, and Beatriz de la Fuente
1992   *Museum of Anthropology of Xalapa.* Jalapa: Government of the State of Veracruz.
Adams, Richard E. W.
1977   *Prehistoric Mesoamerica.* Boston: Little, Brown. Rev. ed., Norman: University of
        Oklahoma Press, 1991.
Andrews, George F.
1989   *Comalcalco, Tabasco, Mexico: Maya Art and Architecture.* 2d ed. Culver City,
        Calif.: Labyrinthos.
Bernal, Ignacio
1958   *Monte Albán, Mitla: Official Guide.* Mexico, D.F.: INAH.
1969   *The Olmec World.* Berkeley: University of California Press.
1985   *Official Guide: Teotihuacan.* Mexico, D.F.: INAH-Salvat.
Blom, Frans, and Oliver La Farge
1926   *Tribes and Temples.* New Orleans: Tulane University.
Bricker, Victoria Reifler, and Jeremy A. Sabloff, eds.
1981   *Supplement to the Handbook of Middle American Indians,* vol. 1. Austin: Univer-
        sity of Texas Press.
Brueggemann, Juergen K., Sara Ladrón de Guevara, and Juan Sánchez Bonilla
1992   *Tajín.* Mexico City: El Equilibrista, and Madrid: Turner Libros.
Charnay, Désiré
1887   *The Ancient Cities of the New World.* New York: Harper and Brothers. Reprint,
        New York: AMS Press, 1973.
Coe, Michael D.
1984   *Mexico.* 3d ed. New York: Thames and Hudson.
1988   *The Maya.* 4th ed. London: Thames and Hudson.
Coe, Michael D., and Richard A. Diehl
1980   *In the Land of the Olmec.* 2 vols. Austin: University of Texas Press.
Cyphers Guillén, Ann
1994   Three New Olmec Sculptures from Southern Veracruz. *Mexicon,* vol. 16, no. 2.
        Berlin.
Díaz del Castillo, Bernal
1957   *The Discovery and Conquest of Mexico.* Translated by A. P. Maudslay, edited by
        Gínero García. New York: Farrar, Straus and Giroux. Sixth printing, 1972.
Flannery, Kent V., and Joyce Marcus, eds.
1983   *The Cloud People.* New York: Academic Press.
García Payón, José
1976   *El Tajín: Official Guide.* Mexico, D.F.: Instituto Nacional de Anthropología e
        Historia.
Gaxiola González, Margarita
1984   *Huamelulpan: Un centro urbano de la Mixteca Alta.* Colección Científica:
        Arqueología, Centro Regional Oaxaca INAH, Mexico, D.F.
Graham, Ian
1977   *Corpus of Maya Hieroglyphic Inscriptions,* vol. 3, part 1. Cambridge, Mass.:
        Peabody Museum, Harvard University.
1982   *Corpus of Maya Hieroglyphic Inscriptions,* vol. 3, part 3. Cambridge, Mass.:
        Peabody Museum, Harvard University.
Greene Robertson, Merle
1983–1991 *The Sculpture of Palenque.* 4 vols. Princeton, N.J.: Princeton University Press.

Grove, David C.
1984   *Chalcatzingo: Excavations on the Olmec Frontier.* London: Thames and Hudson.
Grube, Nicolai
1994   A Hieroglyphic Panel in the Emiliano Zapata Museum, Tabasco. *Mexicon,* vol. 16, no. 1. Berlin.
Heyden, Doris, and Paul Gendrop
1975   *Pre-Columbian Architecture of Mesoamerica.* New York: Harry N. Abrams.
Kelly, Joyce
1982   *The Complete Visitor's Guide to Mesoamerican Ruins.* Norman: University of Oklahoma Press.
Lombardo de Ruíz, Sonia, Diana López de Molina, Daniel Molina Feal, Carolyn Baus de Czitrom, and Oscar J. Polaco
1986   *Cacaxtla: El lugar donde muere la lluvia en la tierra.* Mexico, D.F.: Instituto Nacional de Antropología e Historia.
Lowe, Gareth W.
1962   *Mound 5 and Minor Excavations, Chiapa de Corzo, Chiapas, Mexico.* Papers of the New World Archaeological Foundation, no. 12. Provo, Utah.
Lowe, Gareth W., and Pierre Agrinier
1960   *Mound 1, Chiapa de Corzo, Chiapas, Mexico.* Papers of the New World Archaeological Foundation, no. 8. Provo, Utah.
Maler, Teobert
1901–1903 Researches in the Central Portion of the Usumasintla [Usumacinta] Valley. *Memoirs of the Peabody Museum,* vol. 2, no. 1. Cambridge, Mass.: Harvard University.
Marcus, Joyce, and Kent V. Flannery
1996   *Zapotec Civilization.* New York: Thames and Hudson.
Marquina, Ignacio
1951   *Arquitectura prehispánica.* Memorias del Instituto Nacional de Anthropología e Historia, no. 1. Mexico, D.F. Revised 1964.
Martínez Vargas, Enrique
1993   Transcendental hallazgo en Zultepec. *Arqueología Mexicana,* vol. 1, no. 4. Mexico, D.F.
Mathews, Peter
1980   Notes on the Dynastic Sequence of Bonampak, Part 1. In *Third Palenque Roundtable,* 1978, vol. 5, part 2. Edited by Merle Greene Robertson. Austin: University of Texas Press.
Maudslay, Alfred P.
1889–1902 *Archaeology.* Biologia Centrali Americana, 5 vols. London. Facsimile ed., New York: Milpatron Publishing, 1974.
Mayer, Karl H.
1984   *Maya Monuments: Sculptures of Unknown Provenance in Middle America.* Berlin: Verlag von Flemming.
1995   *Maya Monuments: Sculptures of Unknown Provenance, Supplement 4.* Graz: Academic Publishers.
Miller, Mary Ellen
1986   *The Murals of Bonampak.* Princeton, N.J.: Princeton University Press.
1995   Maya Masterpieces Revealed at Bonampak. *National Geographic,* vol. 187, no. 2. Washington, D.C.
1997   Imaging Maya Art. *Archaeology,* vol. 50, no. 3. New York.
Morley, Sylvanus G.
1946   *The Ancient Maya.* 2d ed., revised by George Brainerd, 1956. 5th ed., revised by Robert J. Sharer, 1994. Stanford, Calif.: Stanford University Press.

Norman, V. Garth
    1973   *Izapa Sculpture, Part 1: Album.* Papers of the New World Archaeological Foundation, no. 30. Provo, Utah.

Pasztory, Ester
    1997   *Teotihuacan: An Experiment in Living.* Norman: University of Oklahoma Press.

Porter Weaver, Muriel
    1972   *The Aztecs, Mayas, and Their Predecessors.* New York. 3d ed., San Diego, Calif.: Academic Press, 1993.

Proskouriakoff, Tatiana
    1946   *An Album of Maya Architecture.* Washington, D.C.: Carnegie Institution of Washington. Reprint, Norman: University of Oklahoma Press, 1963.

Quirarte, Jacinto
    1973   *Izapan-Style Art: A Study of Its Form and Meaning.* Washington, D.C.: Dumbarton Oaks.

Ruppert, Karl, J. Eric S. Thompson, and Tatiana Proskouriakoff
    1955   *Bonampak, Chiapas, Mexico.* Washington, D.C.: Carnegie Institution of Washington, Publication 602.

Ruz Lhuillier, Alberto
    1960   *Palenque: Official Guide.* Mexico, D.F.: INAH.

Schele, Linda, and David A. Freidel
    1990   *A Forest of Kings: The Untold Story of the Ancient Maya.* New York: William Morrow.

Schele, Linda, and Peter Mathews
    1998   *The Code of Kings.* New York: Scribner.

Spranz, Bodo
    1966   *Las pirámides de Totimehuacan: Excavaciones 1964–65.* Instituto Poblano de Anthropología e Historia, pub. 1. Puebla, Mexico.

Spores, Ronald
    1967   *The Mixtec Kings and Their People.* Norman: University of Oklahoma Press.
    1984   *The Mixtecs in Ancient and Colonial Times.* Norman: University of Oklahoma Press.

Stephens, John Lloyd
    1841   *Incidents of Travel in Central America, Chiapas, and Yucatan.* 2 vols. London. New York, 1854. Reprint, New York: Dover Publications, 1969.

Tate, Carolyn E.
    1992   *Yaxchilan: The Design of a Maya Ceremonial Center.* Austin: University of Texas Press.

Wauchope, Robert, ed.
    1965–1971 *Handbook of Middle American Indians,* vols. 2, 3, 10, 11. Austin: University of Texas Press.

Wilkerson, S. Jeffery K.
    1987   *El Tajín: A Guide for Visitors.* Jalapa: S. Jeffery K. Wilkerson.

Winter, Marcus
    1996   *Cerro de las Minas: Arqueología de la Mixteca Baja.* Oaxaca City: Casa de Cultura de Huajuapan de León.

INDEX